French Bed & Breakfast

French Châteaux & Hotels

Spain

British Bed & Breakfast

Alastair
Sawday's

Special Places to Stay

Eighth edition
Copyright © 2014
Alastair Sawday Publishing Co. Ltd
Published in 2014
ISBN-13: 978-1-906136-65-9

Alastair Sawday Publishing Co. Ltd,
Merchant's House, Wapping Road,
Bristol BS1 4RW, UK
Tel: +44 (0)117 204 7810
Email: info@sawdays.co.uk
Web: www.sawdays.co.uk

The Globe Pequot Press,
P. O. Box 480, Guilford,
Connecticut 06437, USA
Tel: +1 203 458 4500
Email: info@globepequot.com
Web: www.globepequot.com

Series Editor Alastair Sawday
Editors Zoe Winterbotham,
Nicole Franchini
Editorial Assistance Camilla Pease-Watkin,
Lianka Varga, Stephanie Clement,
Jennie Coulson
Picture Editors Alec Studerus,
Ben Mounsey
Production Coordinators
Lianka Varga, Sarah Frost-Mellor
Writing Jo Boissevain, Nicola Crosse,
Monica Guy, Annie Shillito, Matthew Hilton-
Dennis, Sarah Bolton, Florence Fortnam,
Zoe Winterbotham
Inspections Jill Greetham, Lois Ferguson,
Janine Raedts, Heidi Flores, Katrina
Power, Pamela Romano, Jennifer Telfeyan,
Caroline Feetam, Abbi Greetham, Ellen
Lloyd, Christine Georgeff, Angelica Grizi,
Nicole Franchini, Zoe Winterbotham
And thanks to those people who did an
inspection or two.

Thank you to Florence Fortnam for all of
her hard work on the series and thanks to
Camilla Pease-Watkin for her invaluable
support.

Marketing & PR 0117 204 7810

*We have made every effort to ensure the accuracy
of the information in this book at the time
of going to press. However, we cannot accept
any responsibility for any loss, injury or
inconvenience resulting from the use of
information contained therein.*

Production: Pagebypage Co. Ltd
Maps: Maidenhead Cartographic Services
Printing: Butler, Tanner & Dennis, Frome
UK distribution: The Travel Alliance, Bath
Diane@popoutmaps.com

Cover photo credits.
Front 1. Vento di Rose B&B, entry 330 2. Agriturismo Alla Madonna del Piatto, entry 277
    3. Fattoria Viticcio Agriturismo, entry 184
Back: 1. Fattoria Barbialla Nuova, entry 177 2. Pieve di Caminino Historic Resort, entry 250
    3. Dimora Bolsone, entry 43

Alastair Sawday's

Special Places to Stay

Italy

4   Contents

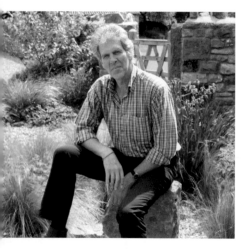

It is easy to forget how many countries Italy really is. She was a patchwork of states and statelets until 1861, so her survival as a whole is a gentle miracle. Travelling from tip to toe, I recently learned quite how energisingly her regions differ, and how rich is the whole fabric of the country.

I was there to meet our inspirational Italian owners. (One has since written to let us know that she lets her house free to artists, out of pure sympathy for their economic plight and love for their work.) In Turin I stayed in a handsome apartment high up over a grand colonnaded street. Then to La Spezia to meet Ilaria, who is slowly re-igniting a tiny mountain village, and on to Umbria and Tuscany. We gathered 25 owners together and were bowled over by their support for our stand against conformity and corporate tourism. In Verona we met the same support and even, too, in Venice. It is a tough, cynical city, with centuries of wheeler-dealing, and we

expected to be told we were too small to matter. But no — they love what we do. We gathered in a beautiful house with that rarest of Venetian assets — a garden.

Puglia, too, revealed deep support for our campaign for individuality. We met organic olive and wine producers, and saw towns and cities of ravishing beauty. Naples is another story — chaotic and grand, anarchic and gorgeous.

Our owners are embracing the Slow Food movement's new campaign: Buono, Pulito e Giusto. The Italian passion for food has to be experienced! It comes from their history of independence and different 'gastronomies'. Such is the length of Italy that landscapes, soils and climates vary from one end to the other. My high gastronomic point was a six-course organic dinner at the Masseria Il Frantoio, in Puglia, where every dish came with a different olive oil, much of the food was foraged and wines were home-grown.

Italians are reacting to the economic and political pantomime by reinventing themselves. While the government decides who is in the driver's seat, Italians are taking matters into their own hands, and there are now many spontaneous grass-roots associations concerned with ecological issues, schools, civil education, consumer rights, etc. This is all good news for the independence of spirit that we relish and support.

Alastair Sawday

Photo: Tom Germain

How do we choose our Special Places?

It's simple. There are no rules, no boxes to tick. We choose places that we like and are fiercely subjective in our choices. We also recognise that one person's idea of special is not necessarily someone else's so there is a huge variety of places, and prices, in the book. Those who are familiar with our Special Places series know that we look for comfort, originality, authenticity, and reject the insincere, the anonymous and the banal. The way guests are treated comes as high on our list as the setting, the architecture, the atmosphere and the food.

We have selected the widest range of places, and prices, for you to choose from – castles, villas, city apartments, farmhouses, country inns, even a monastery or two. It might be breakfast under the frescoed ceiling of a Renaissance villa that is special, or a large and boisterous dinner in a farmhouse kitchen, or a life-enhancing view. We have not necessarily chosen the most opulent places to stay, but the the most interesting and satisfying. But because Italy has, to quote Lord Byron, 'the fatal gift of beauty' it is easy to forget that it hasn't all been built with aesthetics in mind. Don't be put off when you discover that there are swathes of industrial plant (yes, even in Tuscany). These things can't be airbrushed out, but acknowledge that they exist and they won't spoil your fun.

Inspections

We visit every place in the guide to get a feel for how both house and owner tick.

We don't take a clipboard and we don't have a list of what is acceptable and what is not. Instead, we chat for an hour or so with the owner or manager and look round. It's all very informal, but it gives us an excellent idea of who would enjoy staying there. If the visit happens to be the last of the day, we sometimes stay the night. Once in the book, properties are re-inspected every few years, so that we can keep things fresh and accurate.

Feedback

In between inspections we rely on feedback from our army of readers, as well as from staff members who are encouraged to visit properties across the series. This feedback is invaluable to us and we always follow up on comments.

So do tell us whether your stay has been a joy or not, if the atmosphere was great or stuffy, the owners and staff cheery or bored. The accuracy of the book depends on what you, and our inspectors, tell us. A lot of the new entries in each edition are recommended by our readers, so keep telling us about new places you've discovered too. Send them in to info@sawdays.co.uk.

However, please do not tell us if your starter was cold, or the bedside light broken. Tell the owner, immediately, and get them to do something about it. Most owners, or staff, are more than happy to correct problems and will bend over backwards to help. Far better than bottling it up and then writing to us a week later!

Membership

Owners pay to appear in this guide. Their membership fee goes towards the costs of inspecting, publishing, marketing, and maintaining our websites and producing an all-colour book. We only include places that we find special for one reason or another, so it is not possible for anyone to buy their way onto these pages. Nor is it possible for the owner to write their own description. We will say if the bedrooms are small, or if a main road is near. We do our best to avoid misleading people.

Disclaimer

We make no claims to pure objectivity in choosing these places. They are here simply because we like them. Our opinions and tastes are ours alone and this book is a statement of them; we hope you will share them. We have done our utmost to get our facts right but apologise unreservedly for any mistakes that may have crept in. The latest information we have about each place can be found on our website, www.sawdays.co.uk.

You should know that we don't check such things as fire alarms, swimming pool security or any other regulation with which owners of properties receiving paying guests should comply. This is the responsibility of the owners.

Using this book
Finding the right place for you

All these places are special in one way or another. All have been visited and then written about honestly so that you can take what you want and leave the rest. Those of you who swear by Sawday's books trust our write-ups precisely because we don't have a blanket standard; we include places simply because we like them. But we all have different priorities, so do read the descriptions carefully and pick out the places where you will be comfortable. If something is particularly important to you then check when you book: a simple question or two can avoid misunderstandings.

Maps

Each property is flagged with its entry number on the maps at the front. These maps are a great starting point for planning your trip, but please don't use them as anything other than a general guide – use a decent road map for real navigation. Most places will send you detailed instructions once you have booked your

stay. Self-catering places are marked in blue on the maps; others are marked in red.

Symbols

Below each entry you will see some symbols, which are explained at the very back of the book. They are based on the information given to us by the owners. However, things do change: bikes may be under repair or a new pool may have been put in. Please use the symbols as a guide rather than an absolute statement of fact and double-check anything that is important to you – owners occasionally bend their own rules, so it's worth asking if you may take your child or dog even if they don't have the symbol.

Wheelchair access – The ♿ symbol shows those places that are keen to accept wheelchair users into their hotels and have made provision for them. However, this does not mean that wheelchair users will always be met with a perfect landscape, nor does it indicate that they have been officially assessed for such a status. You may encounter ramps, a shallow

step, gravelled paths, alternative routes into some rooms, a bathroom (not a wet room), perhaps even a lift. In short, there may be the odd hindrance and we urge you to call and make sure you will get what you need.

Limited mobility – The limited mobility symbol 🚶 shows those places where at least one bedroom and bathroom is accessible without using stairs. The symbol is designed to satisfy those who walk slowly, with difficulty, or with the aid of a stick. A wheelchair may be able to navigate some areas, but these places are not fully wheelchair friendly. If you use a chair for longer distances, but are not too bad over shorter distances, you'll probably be OK; again, please ring and ask. There may be a step or two, a bath or a shower with a tray in a cubicle, a good distance between the car park and your room, slippery flagstones or a tight turn.

Children – The 🧒 symbol shows places which are happy to accept children of all ages. This does not mean that they will

Photo: Casa Bellavista, entry 202

necessarily have cots, high chairs, etc. If an owner welcomes children but only those above a certain age, we have put these details at the end of their write-up. These houses do not have the child symbol, but even these folk may accept your younger child at quiet times. If you want to get out and about in the evenings, check when you book whether there are any babysitting services. Even very small places can sometimes organise this for you.

Pets – Our  symbol shows places which are happy to accept pets. It means they can sleep in the bedroom with you, but not on the bed. It's really important to get this one right before you arrive, as many places make you keep dogs in the car. Check carefully: Spot's emotional wellbeing may depend on it.

Owners' pets – The ⚗ symbol is given when the owners have their own pet on the premises. It may not be a cat! But it is there to warn you that you may be greeted by a dog, serenaded by a parrot, or indeed sat upon by a cat.

Practical Matters
Types of places

Each entry is simply labelled (B&B, hotel, self-catering) to guide you, but the write-ups reveal several descriptive terms. This list serves as a rough guide to what you might expect to find.

Agriturismo: farm or estate with B&B rooms or apartments

Albergo: Italian word for an inn, more personal than a hotel

Azienda agrituristica: literally 'agricultural business'

Casa (Ca' in Venetian dialect): house

Cascina: farmhouse

Castello: castle

Corte: courtyard

Country house: a new concept in Italian hospitality, usually family-run and akin to a villa

Dimora: dwelling

Fattoria: farm

Locanda: means 'inn', but sometimes used to describe a restaurant only

Masseria: Apulian farmhouse or country house

Podere: farm or smallholding

Palazzo: literally a 'palace' but more usually a mansion

Relais: an imported French term meaning 'inn'

Residenza: an apartment or house with rooms for guests

Tenuta: farm holding, or 'tenancy'

Trullo: traditional Apulian stone house

Villa: country residence

Photo: Villa Giulia, entry 317

Rooms

Bedrooms — We tell you about the range of accommodation in singles, doubles, twins, family rooms and suites, as well as apartments and whole houses. A 'family' room is a loose term because, in Italy, triples and quadruples often sleep more than the heading suggests; extra beds can often be added for children, usually with a charge, so check when booking.

When an entry includes more than one place type, e.g. B&B & Self-catering, assume that the accommodation with a per week price is self-catering, unless otherwise specified.

Bathrooms — Assume that bathrooms are en suite unless we say otherwise. Italian bathrooms often have a shower only.

Meals

Eating in Italy is one of life's great pleasures. There is plenty of variety, and each region has its own specialities and surprises. Many owners use organic, local or home-grown ingredients, and more often that not will have produced some part of your meal themselves.

Vegetarians — Although fresh, seasonal vegetables are readily available in Italy, most Italian dishes contain meat and some Italians still find the concept of vegetarianism quite bizarre. Our owners who offer a good range of vegetarian options have a special symbol — but don't be surprised if those without it struggle to understand a meal without meat.

Breakfast — What constitutes breakfast varies hugely from place to place. Many hotels don't offer it at all, especially in towns, where it is normal to walk to the nearest bar for your first espresso. (Prices double or triple as soon as you sit down, so if you want to save money, join the locals at the bar.) If you are confronted with a vacuum-packed breakfast it's because B&Bs are only allowed to serve fresh ingredients if they meet certain strict regulations. On farms, however, you are likely to find homemade jams and cakes as well as home-produced cheeses and fruit.

Dinner — Hotels are other places with restaurants usually offer the widest à la carte choice. Smaller places may offer a set dinner (at a set time) and you will need to book in advance. Many of our owners are

Photo: Tenuta Le Sorgive – Le Volpi Agriturismo, entry 45

breakfast included. For self-catering the price is per week. Where we have given a price for dinner and/or lunch included in the stay, it may be per person (p.p.). Meal prices are always given per person; we try to give you an approximate price and say if wine is included. Prices quoted are given to us for 2014 but be aware they may change; treat them as a guideline rather than as infallible. We try to list any extra hidden costs – e.g. linen, towels, heating – but always check on booking.

Tassa di soggiorno is a small tourist tax that local councils can levy on all paying visitors; it is rarely included in the quoted price and you may find your bill increased by €0.50-€2 per person per day to cover this.

Booking and cancellation

Hotels will usually ask you for a credit card number at the time of booking, for confirmation. Remember to let smaller places know if you are likely to be arriving late, and if you want dinner. Some of the major cities get very full (and often double in price) around the time of trade fairs (e.g. fashion fairs in Milan, the Biennale in Venice). And book well ahead if you plan to visit Italy during school holidays.

Some cancellation policies are more stringent than others. It is also worth noting that some owners will take the money directly from your credit/debit card without contacting you to discuss it. So ask them to explain their cancellation policy clearly before booking so you

excellent cooks so, if you fancy an evening sitting two steps from your bedroom on your host's terrace overlooking the Tuscan hills or Umbrian valleys, be sure to ask your hosts – on booking or arrival – if they are able to share their culinary skills and serve up a sumptuous dinner on site. Sometimes you will eat with the family; sometimes you will be eating in a separate dining room, served by a member of the family. Small farms and inns often offer dinners which are excellent value and delicious, so keep an open mind. Nonetheless, be aware that laws in some regions of Italy do not allow B&Bs to serve dinner to their guests.

Prices and minimum stays

The prices we quote are the prices per night per room unless otherwise stated,

Photo: Hotel Cavallino d'Oro, entry 49

understand exactly where you stand; it may well avoid a nasty surprise. And consider taking out travel insurance (with a cancellation clause) if you're concerned.

Arrivals and departures

Housekeeping is usually done by 2pm, and your room will usually be available by mid-afternoon. Normally you will have to wave goodbye to it between 10am and 11am. Sometimes one can pay to linger. Some smaller places may be closed between 3pm and 6pm, so do try and agree an arrival time in advance or you may find nobody there.

Payment

The most commonly accepted credit cards are Visa, Eurocard, MasterCard and Amex.

Many places in this book don't take plastic because of high bank charges. Check the symbol at the bottom of each entry before you arrive, in case you are a long way from a cash dispenser!

Tipping

In bars you are given your change on a small saucer, and it is usual to leave a couple of small coins there. A cover charge on restaurant meals is standard. A small tip (*mancia*) in family-run establishments is also welcome, so leave one if you wish.

Closed

When given in months this means for the whole of the month stated. So, 'Closed: November–March' means closed from 1 November to 31 March.

Photo: Trullo Bellissimo, entry 396

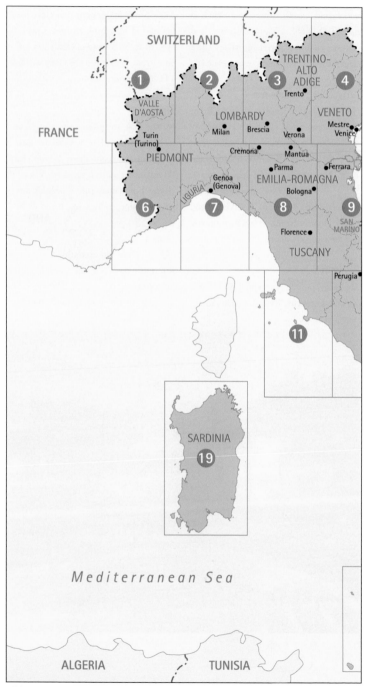

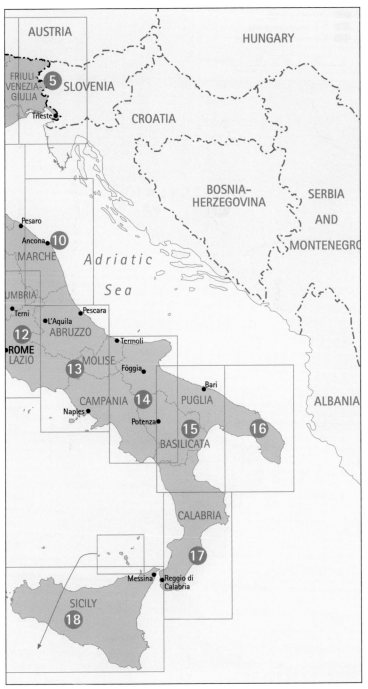

©Maidenhead Cartographic, 2014

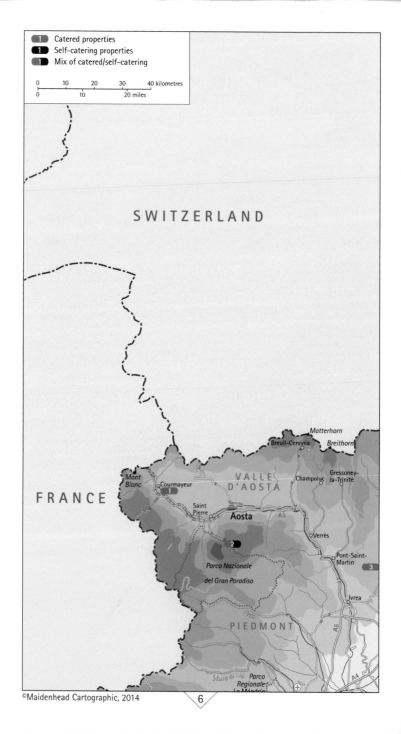

Catered properties
Self-catering properties
Mix of catered/self-catering

0   10   20   30   40 kilometres
0   10   20 miles

SWITZERLAND

Matterhorn
Breuil-Cervinia   Breithorn

Mont
Blanc   Courmayeur   VALLE   Champoluc   Gressoney-
         D'AOSTA   la-Trinité

FRANCE
         Saint
         Pierre
                 Aosta   A5

                              Verrès

                                   Pont-Saint-
                                   Martin   3

         Parco Nazionale
         del Gran Paradiso   Ivrea

                 PIEDMONT   A5

         Stura di Iuù   Parco
                 Regionale   A4
                 La Mandria

Map 2   17

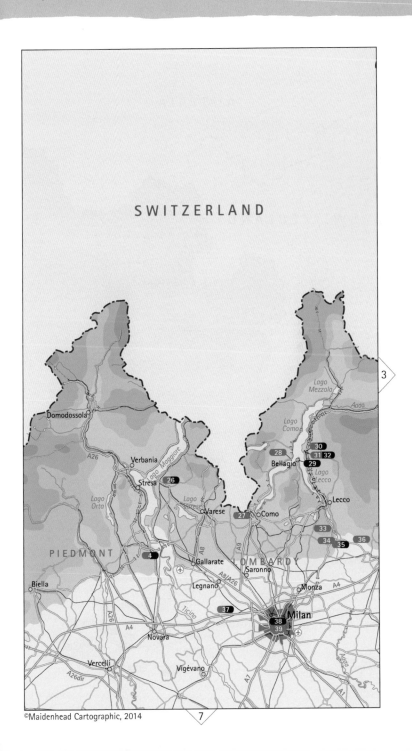

SWITZERLAND

Domodossola

Verbania

Stresa 26

Lago Orta

Lago Maggiore

Lago Varese

Varese 27 Como

Lago Mezzola

Lago Como

Bellagio 28 30 31 32 29 Lago Lecco

Lecco

Adda

3

33

34 35 36

PIEDMONT 4

Gallarate LOMBARDY Saronno

Biella

Legnano

Monza A4

Novara Ticino 37 38 39 Milan

Vercelli

Vigévano

A26dir

©Maidenhead Cartographic, 2014   7

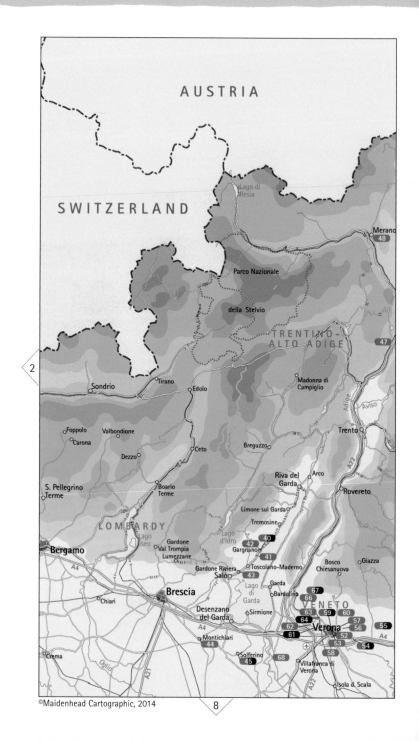

Map 4 19

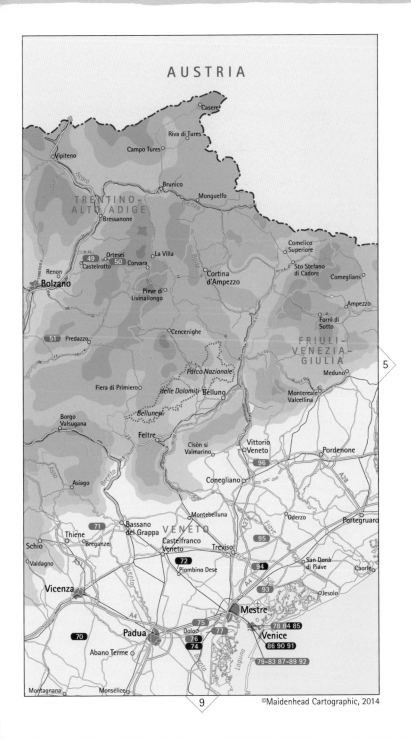

AUSTRIA

Casere

Riva di Tures

Campo Tures

Vipiteno

Brunico

Monguelfo

TRENTINO–
ALTO ADIGE

Bressanone

Comelico
Superiore

Ortesei   La Villa

49   Castelrotto
50   Corvara

Sto Stefano
di Cadore

Comeglians

Renon

Bolzano

Cortina
d'Ampezzo

Ampezzo

Pieve di
Livinallongo

Forni di
Sotto

Cencenighe

FRIULI–
VENEZIA
GIULIA

51   Predazzo

Meduno

5

Parco Nazionale
Fiera di Primiero   delle Dolomiti   Belluno

Montereale
Valcellina

Bellunesi

Borgo
Valsugana

Feltre

Cisòn si
Valmarino

Vittorio
Veneto

Pordenone

96

Asiago

Conegliano

Montebelluna

Oderzo

Portegruaro

71   Bassano
del Grappa

VENETO

Thiene   Breganze

Schio

Castelfranco
Veneto

Treviso

95

Valdagno

72

Piombino Dese

94

San Donà
di Piave

Caorle

Vicenza

93

Jesolo

Mestre

75   Dolo

78 84 85

Padua

77

Venice

70

76
74

86 90 91

Abano Terme

79–83 87–89 92

Montagnana

Monsélice

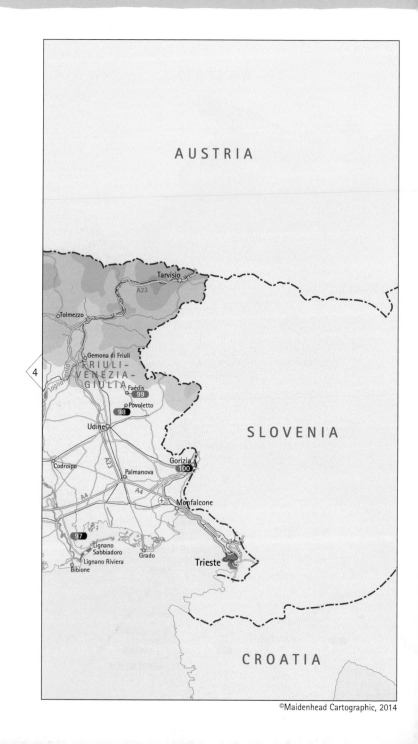

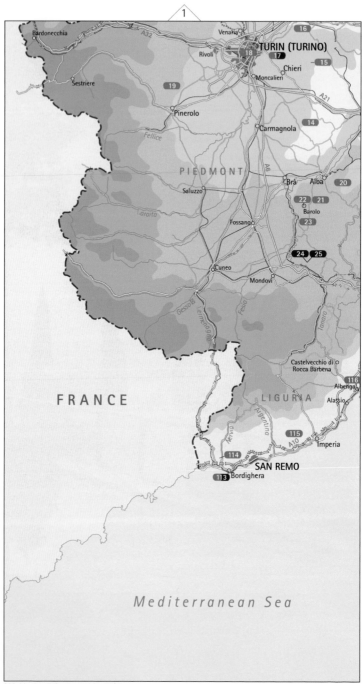

Map 7   23

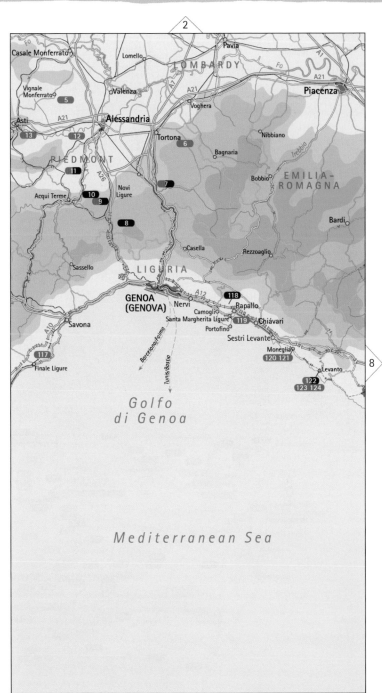

©Maidenhead Cartographic, 2014

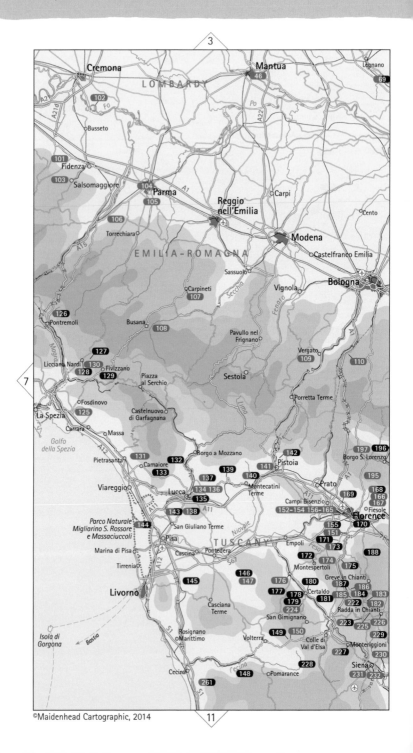

Map 9   25

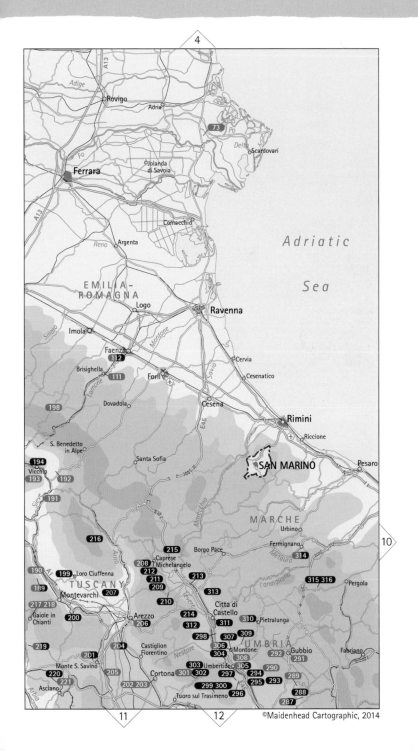

4

Adige
Rovigo
Adria
73
Po
Po
Delta
Scardovari
Ferrara
Jolanda
di Savoia

Comacchio

Adriatic

EMILIA-
ROMAGNA
Reno
Argenta

Logo
Sea
Ravenna
Silaro
Imola
Montone
Faenza
112
Cervia
Brisighella
111
Forlì
Cesenatico
Lamone
Dovadola
Savio
Cesena
198
Rimini
E45
Riccione
S. Benedetto
in Alpe
194
Santa Sofia
SAN MARINO
Pesaro
Vicchio
193
192
MARCHE
191
Urbino
10
Steve
Montecchio
216
Fermignano
215
Borgo Pace
Metauro
314
190
Caprese
199 Loro Ciuffenna
208
Michelangelo
213
Candigliana
A1
212
315 316
Pergola
189
211
Montevarchi
209
Tevere
313
217 218
207
210
Città di
Gaiole in
200
Arezzo
214
Castello
310 Pietralunga
Chianti
206
312
311
219
298
307 309
204
Castiglion
306
308
UMBRIA
201
Fiorentino
Nestore
304 Montone
292 Gubbio
Fabriano
Monte S. Savino
205
303 Umbertide
305
290
291
220
299 300
301 302
297
294
289
221
Cortona
295 293
Asciano
Albia
202 203
Tuoro sul Trasimeno
296
288
287

11   12   ©Maidenhead Cartographic, 2014

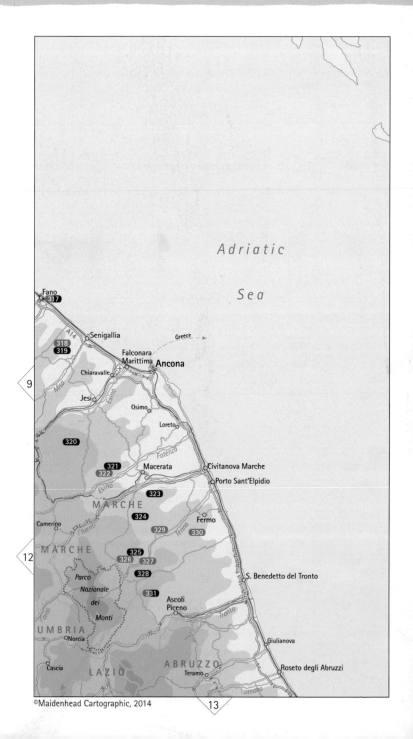

Adriatic

Sea

Fano
317
A14
318
319
Senigallia
Falconara
Marittima   **Ancona**
Chiaravalle
Greece
9
Jesi
Osimo
Loreto
Fotenzo
320
321
322
Macerata
Esino
Civitanova Marche
Porto Sant'Elpidio
323
MARCHE
324
Camerino
Chienti
329
Fermo
Tenna
330
12
MARCHE
325
326 327
328
Parco
Nazionale
dei
Monti
331
Ascoli
Piceno
Tronto
S. Benedetto del Tronto
UMBRIA
Norcia
Giulianova
Cascia
LAZIO
ABRUZZO
Teramo
Roseto degli Abruzzi
Tomano

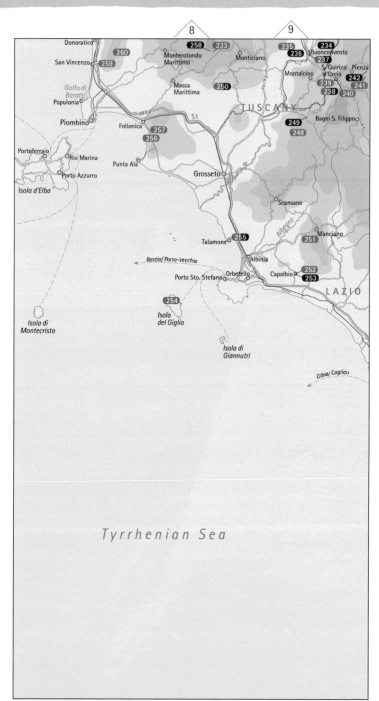

8   9

Donoratico
260
San Vincenzo
259
258   233
Monterotondo
Marittimo
Monticiano
235
236
234
Buonconvento
237
S. Quirico   Pienza
d'Orcia
242
Montalcino
239   241
238   240

Golfo di
Baratti
Populonia
Massa
Marittima
250
TUSCANY

Piombino
Follonica
257
256
S1
249
248
Bagni S. Filippo

Portoferraio
Rio Marina
Porto Azzurro
Punta Ala
Grosseto

Isola d'Elba
Scansano

Talamone
255
Manciano
251

Bastia/ Porto-Vecchia
Albinia
Porto Sto. Stefano
Orbetello
Capalbio
252
253
LAZIO

254

Isola di
Montecristo
Isola
del Giglio

Isola di
Giannutri

Olbia/ Cagliari

Tyrrhenian Sea

Map 12   29

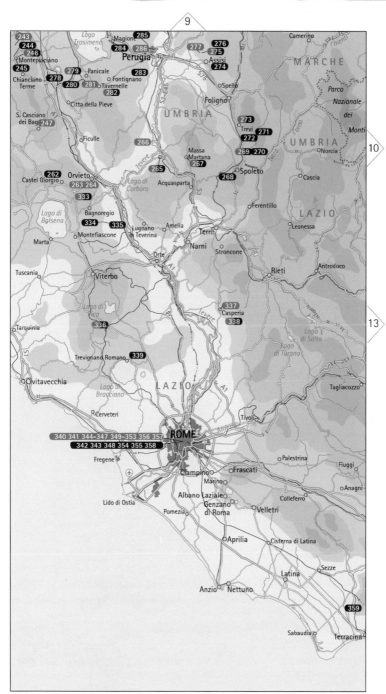

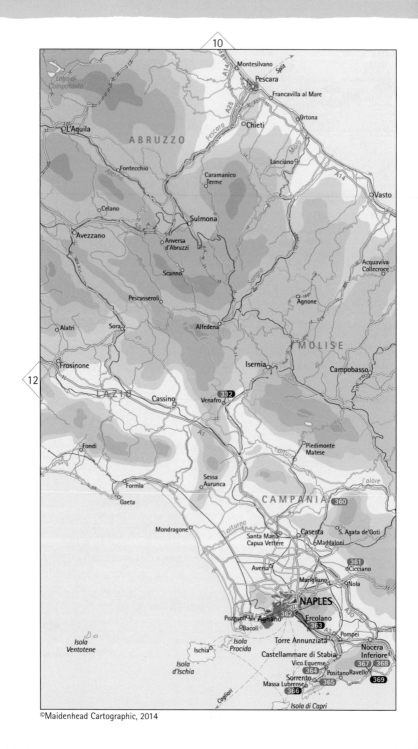

Map 14 31

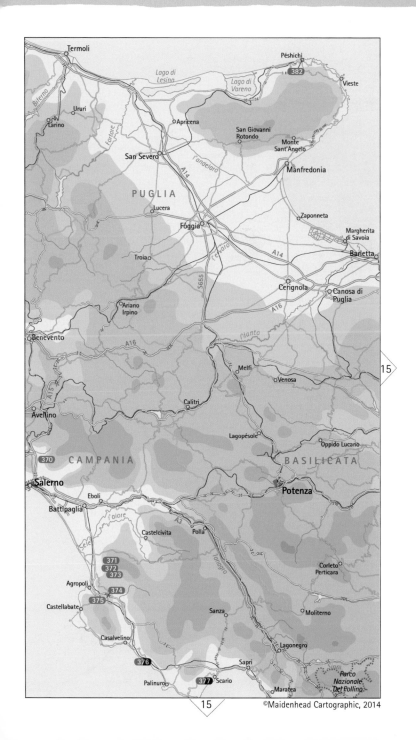

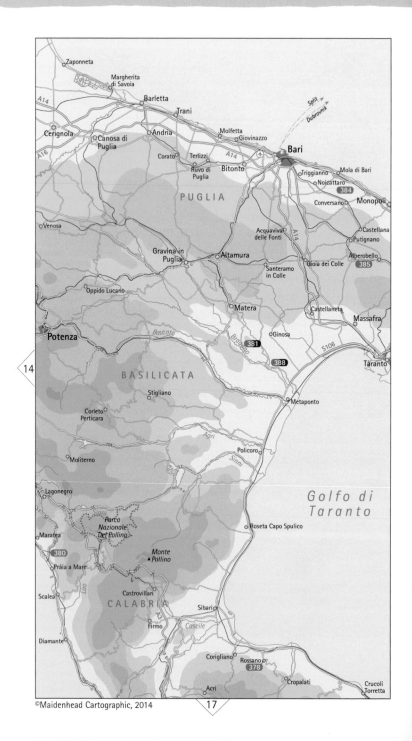

Map 16 33

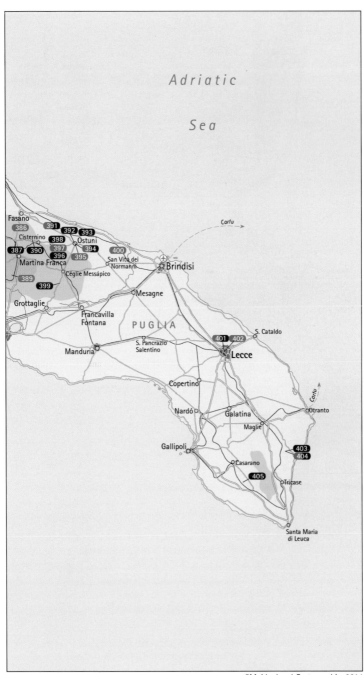

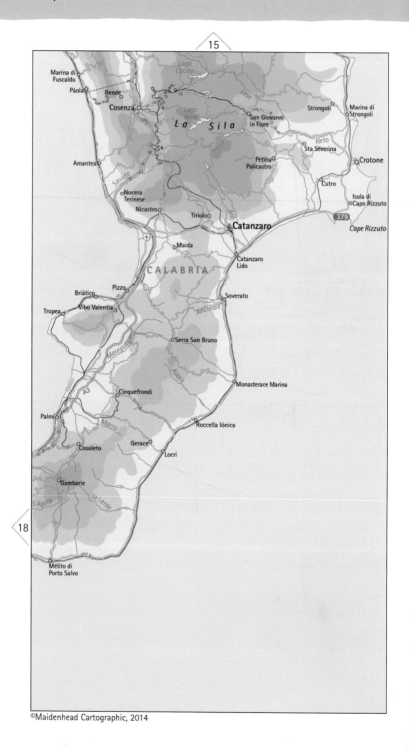

Map 18   35

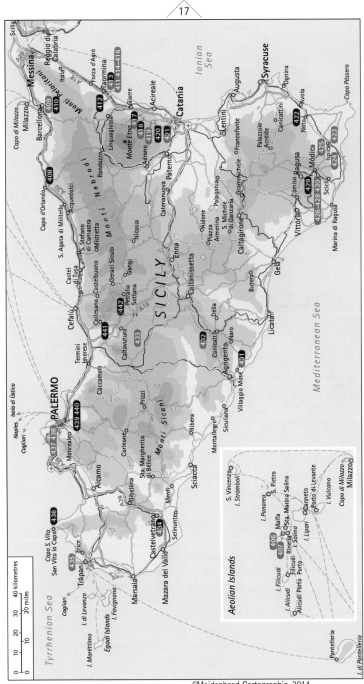

©Maidenhead Cartographic, 2014

Aosta Valley and Piedmont

Auberge de la Maison

What a setting! You're in the old part of the village of Val Ferret, three kilometres from Courmayeur, in sight of Mont Blanc, surrounded by gentle terraces, gardens, meadows and majestic views. The Auberge has a quietly elegant and exclusive feel yet is not in the least intimidating, thanks to the cheerful, efficient staff. Bedrooms are uncluttered, stylish and comfortable with mellow colours. Many have a third bed disguised as a sofa; nearly all have balconies and the views range from good to superb. A Tuscan influence is detectable in the décor; the owner is passionate about the region. Her impressive collection of images of the Valle d'Aosta, from old promotional posters to oil paintings, makes a fascinating display, while a reassembled wooden mountain house is a most unusual feature of the reception and sitting area. There's a wellness centre, too, with a sauna and hydromassage. Come in any season: to fish for trout or play a round of golf, or to ski (right to the ski lift) or don crampons for a winter ascent.

Rooms	14 doubles; 4 suites for 2; 13 triples; 2 family rooms for 4: €140–€310. Dinner, B&B €195–€340 p.p.
Meals	Dinner €38. Wine €12.
Closed	Rarely.

Alessandra Garin
Auberge de la Maison,
Via Passerin d'Entrèves 16/A, Fraz.
Entrèves, 11013 Courmayeur

Tel	+39 0165 869811
Email	info@aubergemaison.it
Web	www.aubergemaison.it

Hotel Bellevue

Climb the narrow valley from Aosta, wind around the river, traverse the valley, and enter the cobbled streets of Cogne. Built two years after the consecration of the Gran Paradiso National Park, this marvellous 1920s hotel, in the family for four generations, has the best views in town. It appears deceptively small; in fact, a tunnel connects it to a second building, the spa rolls under the green fields, and there are three chalet suites across the road. There's lots to love: a Persian-rugged lounge with a Benedictine monks' fireplace and a piano that is played before dinner; relics and artefacts in every nook and cranny; a bar with a mural dominating the ceiling; two restaurants (gourmet gnocchi with lobster or hearty fondue?) and a brasserie in town; a super playroom; and, from every window, glorious views. And... a wonderful new woody spa, its upper half (pool, loungers, sauna) open to all ages, its lower half hiding a citrus sauna, a hammam and a magical pool. Bedrooms are equally original: grandfather clocks, fires in the grate, glowing timber ceilings and marble baths that hold two.

Rooms	28 doubles: €180-€330. 7 suites for 2: €350-€400. 3 chalets for 2: €260-€330. Singles €160-€250.
Meals	Hotel has 2 restaurants on site & 1 in town.
Closed	October/November.

Jeantet – Roullet Family
Hotel Bellevue,
Rue Grand Paradis 22,
11012 Cogne

Tel	+39 0165 74825
Email	info@hotelbellevue.it
Web	www.hotelbellevue.it

Villa Tavallini

Wind your way up, up the curvy drive, past broad banks of rhododendrons, splendid in late spring, to an airy 1900s villa built as a summer retreat. Step inside to find rugs on wooden floors, colourfully painted walls and fine framed photographs from trips around the world; welcome to a charming home. It is wonderful for kids, super hospitable and, refreshingly, does not ooze perfection. Gaetano and his elderly mother greet you with charming English and show you to three bedrooms: in a separate wing, with bright-tiled, near-retro bathrooms (two with box showers, one with a tub) and family furniture professionally restored by Gaetano. The sitting room is cosy with filled bookshelves and big sofas, the old-fashioned furnace is lit in winter, and the kitchen for breakfast is homely and inviting. Best of all is outdoors: manicured lawns, five acres of forest to explore, shrubs for kids to get lost in. All feels fresh and lofty. Gaetano is proud of the natural beauty of his territory and eager to take guests on hikes of the mountains and hills. And for winter? Skiing is a 30-minute drive.

Rooms	2 doubles; 1 double with separate bathroom: €80. Singles €60.
Meals	Restaurants in Biella, 6km.
Closed	Never.

Gaetano Versaldo
Villa Tavallini,
13814 Pollone

Mobile	+39 393 0162580
Email	info@villatavallini.it
Web	www.villatavallini.it

Cascina Motto

Flowers everywhere: spilling from the balcony, filling the patio, clasping the walls of the cottage... wisteria, vines, azaleas, roses. It's an immaculate garden, with lawns, spreading trees, boules pitch and a discreet summer pool. Roberta's lovely, too, so warm and friendly; you are made at once to feel part of the family. They came here years ago – she and David, their daughters, Roberta's parents Sergio and Lilla, three dogs. They clearly love the house, which they've restored and filled with paintings and beautiful things. In a quiet street, in a quiet village, this is a happy and restful place to stay. The twin room, named after Roberta's grandmother, has windows facing two ways – over the garden and towards Monte Rosa – plus whitewashed walls, blue cotton rugs, blue-painted iron beds, books, a comfy sofa, a big bathroom. The cottage, its bedroom in the hayloft, is bright, airy, charmingly romantic, with country furniture, a well-equipped kitchenette, a balcony; it's completely independent of the main house. Breakfast is a feast, and the lakes of Orta and Maggiore are a 20-minute drive. *Minimum stay two nights.*

Rooms	1 twin: €75.
	1 cottage for 2-4: €85-€150.
Meals	Restaurants 800m.
Closed	December-February.

Roberta Plevani
Cascina Motto,
Via Marzabotto 7, 28010 Divignano
Mobile   +39 340 7625711
Email   cascinamotto@gmail.com
Web   www.cascinamotto.com

Cascina Alberta Agriturismo

Cascina Alberta is an attractive hilltop farmhouse deep inside a famous wine-producing area. Marked by two stately cypress trees, the house is two kilometres from the town and has sensational panoramic views of the vineyards and hills. The business is run on agriturismo lines by smiling, capable, real-farmer Raffaella, who lives just across the courtyard with her town-planner husband, their son and two boisterous dogs. Tiled guest bedrooms are country-pretty: an old marble-topped table here, a rustic wardrobe there, beds painted duck-egg blue, walls in soft pastel and many pieces beautifully painted by Raffaella. Both the bedrooms and the frescoed dining room lie across the yard from your hosts' house; if you choose to eat in, you dine at your own table on well-priced local dishes with wines from the estate; some of them are pretty special, having been aged in wooden barrels. Raffaella speaks excellent English and is happy to help guests get the most out of this enchanting area. It may be off the beaten track but it's only an hour's drive to the coast.

Rooms	4 twin/doubles: €64–€75.
	1 triple: €80–€90.
Meals	Dinner with wine, €16–€22.
Closed	20 December to February; August.

Raffaella de Cristofaro
Cascina Alberta Agriturismo,
Loc. Ca' Prano 14,
15049 Vignale Monferrato

Tel	+39 0142 933313
Email	cascinalberta@netcomp.it
Web	www.cascinalberta.net

Agriturismo Terensano

Sitting above the gorgeous Curone Valley, surrounded by vineyards and hazelnut groves, the cascina is reached by a beautifully wooded drive through 12 hectares of working estate... then a stroll across a courtyard hung with vines and flower boxes. The setting is utterly gorgeous. Valentina and Luigi usher you into their home, where invitingly simple bedrooms are scattered about, some in the old stables (on the ground floor), others upstairs in the main house, all traditional and homely with their high-beamed ceilings, terracotta floors, large wooden wardrobes and cheery yellow and purple walls. More authenticity in the dining room with its sweet wooden tables and fireplace – an intimate setting for a Valentina creation inspired by her own organic produce and wine before withdrawing with a digestif to the billiard room. Spend the following day relaxing by the pool after a typically sweet and savoury breakfast on the patio; unless adventure calls you into irresistible countryside, or to one of the great cities within reach. Lovely for a few days' escape. *Minimum stay two nights in high season.*

Rooms	1 double with kitchen (breakfast not included); 4 doubles: €90. 1 triple: €130. 1 apartment for 2 (breakfast included when kitchen not used): €90. Singles €60. Extra bed/sofabed available €20 per person per night.
Meals	Dinner €25-€27. Wine €8-€12.
Closed	Never.

Luigi Capsoni
Agriturismo Terensano,
Cascina Terenzano, 15059 Monleale

Tel	+39 0131 806741
Mobile	+39 335 5433944
Email	info@terensano.it
Web	www.terensano.it

La Traversina Agriturismo

Come for the roses, the irises, the hostas! You'll find over 230 different varieties of plant here – they are Rosanna's passion. With drowsy shutters, buzzing bees and walls festooned in roses, the house and outbuildings appear to be in a permanent state of siesta. As do the seven cats, basking on warm window sills and shady terraces. There's a touch of *The Secret Garden* about the half-hidden doors, enticing steps and riotous plants, and the air is fragrant with lavender, oregano and roses, many from France. The house and farm, on a wooded hillside, have been in Rosanna's family for nearly 300 years; she gave up a career as an architect to create a paradise 40 minutes from Genoa. Homely, imaginatively decorated, bedrooms have handsome furniture, books, pictures; bathrooms come with baskets of goodies. Everyone eats together at a long table in the conservatory or outside, where lights glow in the trees at night. Rosanna, Domenico and young Vijaya are the most delightful hosts and the home-grown food is a revelation: agriturismo at its best. *Children over 12 welcome.*

Rooms	2 doubles: €95-€105.
	3 apartments for 2: €115-€130.
	Dinner, B&B €70-€80 per person.
Meals	Dinner €25-€35, by arrangement.
	Wine €8. Restaurant 7km.
Closed	Rarely.

Rosanna & Domenico Varese Puppo
La Traversina Agriturismo,
Cascina La Traversina 109,
15060 Stazzano

Tel	+39 0143 61377
Email	latraversina@latraversina.com
Web	www.latraversina.com

Castello di Tagliolo

The low beams and the warm walls entice you in, demand you unpack and make this captivating place your home. The castle, part of a medieval borgo, has been in the family since 1498; from the windy cobblestone paths to the 900-year-old church the place oozes history. And it's a very peaceful, very safe place for young families to stay, with child-friendly gardens below. The apartments, neither huge nor hugely luxurious, have heaps of charm. Thick walls are painted the family's trademark ochre and terracotta, sweet flowery duvets cover down comforters, wardrobes are antique, Grandpa's sketches are lovingly framed, showers are spacious. You can use the communal oven in the garden, or rustle up a meal in your own decent-sized kitchen in the corner; expect antique marble sinks with cute curtains hiding cupboard space below, cheery oil cloths covering tables and copper pots adorning walls. A Swedish housekeeper shows you the ropes and settles you in. This is arguably Italy's best wine region so book up wine tastings at the family's cantina or head to Asti for a nice glass of bubbly.

Rooms	1 apartment for 3; 2 apartments for 4; 1 apartment for 5; 1 apartment for 6: €700–€1,220 per week.
Meals	Self-catering.
Closed	November to mid–April.

Luca Pinelli Gentile
Castello di Tagliolo,
Via Castello 1, 15070 Tagliolo Monferrato

Tel	+39 0143 89195
Mobile	+39 335 261336
Email	castelloditagliolo@libero.it
Web	www.tagliolo.se

Castello di Rocca Grimalda

Wander off Piedmont's tourist trail up into the clouds to a grand castle fringing a charming village. It's an imposing sight with its manicured gardens and 13th-century tower, but the family give you the warmest of Italian welcomes. Highlights are a beautiful domed and stuccoed chapel swirling with frescoes and trompe l'oeil paintings, and a courtyard with a solar clock where summer concerts and exhibitions are held – among deeper, darker rooms and secrets. The sisters serve Italian coffee and breakfast pastries in a giant ballroom of soaring ceilings and chequered floor – a favourite wedding spot – and have created bright bedroom suites among the thick stone walls and beams. One has a kitchenette, but self-caterers take an apartment – sweet, ancient, up winding castle stairs. From the elegant garden and scented herb patch, views swoop over village and valleys. Seek out hiking, biking, golf, Acqui Terme's hot springs, the Castle or Wine Route, or Genoa and the Ligurian coast, under an hour away. There are restaurants and shops beyond the castle gates; rich history and the family's warm generosity within.

Rooms	1 suite for 2;
	1 suite for 3 (with kitchenette):
	€100–€120.
	2 apartments for 4: €800–€1,000
	per week.
Meals	Restaurants within walking distance.
Closed	December–February.

Anna Giulia de Rege Sola
Castello di Rocca Grimalda,
Piazza Borgatta 2,
15078 Rocca Grimalda

Mobile	+39 334 3387659
Email	info@castelloroccagrimalda.it
Web	www.castelloroccagrimalda.it

Casa degli Orsi

You are sandwiched between vineyards, hot springs and the Ligurian coast. 'Romeo' and 'Juliet' – once simple stone cottages in a lovely Piedmontese hilltop village – exemplify excellent restoration and Peter and Carolyn's love of antiques and art. Crunch over gravel and enter Romeo's chunky walls. The kitchen is a delicious blend of vintage limed wood with state-of-the-art appliances; chop and chat at a central island, dine at an antique table. Or eat under a shady portico in the private courtyard, with a side dish of green valley views (if the sun's hot, there's an outdoor solar shower). In the large tiled living room, cushions pile high on leather sofabeds and artworks dance on limewashed walls. Juliet's hotspots are a four-poster; an antique tiled breakfast room with sunny balcony; two private roof terraces and massage showers. Elegant bedrooms hold antique wardrobes; Romeo's double has a shower and tub. The local trattoria can deliver meals and Alba (famous for truffles) and Genoa are close.

Rooms	Romeo for 4-6; Juliet for 6 let to same party only: €900–€1,000. Both houses together: €1,900. Romeo + 1 room in Juliet: €1,300. Romeo + 2 rooms in Juliet: €1,600. All prices per week.
Meals	Self-catering.
Closed	Never.

Peter & Carolyn Bear
Casa degli Orsi,
Via XX Settembre 3,
15010 Orsara Bormida

Tel	+33 (0)4 70 67 58 34
Email	p.bear@wanadoo.fr
Web	www.bear-holidays.com

La Granica

When Karen, with Mark, went in search of her Italian roots, their adventure ended in an 18th-century grain barn in a secluded dell surrounded by rolling vineyards. Enter the beautifully renovated *granica* through a foyer of limestone floors, a wet bar and exposed brick walls: to the left is the library with deep leather sofas and chocolate and lime colours; to the right is the dining room, sleekly minimalist with polished marble floors and Lithuanian oak chairs. Here, fresh buffet-breakfasts of yogurts, fruit, croissants and pastries are served. Beneath a high cathedral ceiling, the four bedrooms are luxuriously furnished with lashings of silk, velvet chenille armchairs (or chaise longue), splashes of raspberry tones, Egyptian cotton sheets. In the more traditional rooms are mahogany sleigh beds and resplendent bohemian chandeliers. The self-catering terrace house holds a diminutive sitting room, a fully equipped kitchen and double and twin bedrooms in house style – the former with a 'Jacobean' four-poster. Trees and lawns neatly frame the discreet swimming pool. *Minimum stay two nights in B&B, three nights in cottage.*

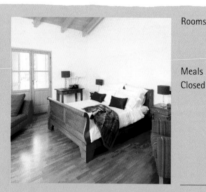

Rooms	4 doubles: €155–€170.
	1 cottage for 2-4: €210.
	20% discount for stays of 7 nights or more.
Meals	Snacks €5–€10. Restaurant 3km.
Closed	October–May.

Karen Langley
La Granica,
Cascina Mulino Vecchio 5, Regione
Mulino Vecchio, 14044 Fontanile

Tel	+39 0141 739105
Email	info@lagranicahotel.com
Web	www.lagranica.com

Casa Isabella

Computer programmer and whizz-at-cocktails Alessandro, and architect/designer Monica, alive with happiness and creativity, gave up lives in Turin for this dream: to renovate a village farmhouse in lovely Piedmont with glorious vineyard views. Casa Isabella is heaven. Doors and tiles have been reclaimed and walls painted in classic hues (ochre, slate blue, a dash of claret); elegant 1920s furnishings mix with unusual paintings and contemporary quirkery; lights have been inserted into stone stairs, bathrooms have exquisite hand-made mirrors, and coloured candles illuminate grandmother's cutlery. Bedrooms are huge and two have balconies. Monica's food is delicious, the breads and pastas homemade, the menus regional, the wines local; a sample of salami or a snack of crudités from the kitchen garden are yours whenever you like. Heavenly breakfasts are served, when you want them, in the dining room or in the shade of a tree; in winter, logs smoulder. Books by the score, boules in the garden, a charmingly natural pool for swimmers, and a bustling market town 15 minutes down the road.

Rooms	2 doubles; 2 twins: €100–€140.
Meals	Dinner €36. Wine from €9.
Closed	Rarely.

Monica Molari & Alessandro
Barattieri
Casa Isabella,
Via La Pietra 5, 14049 Vaglio Serra

Tel	+39 0141 732201
Email	info@casa-isabella.com
Web	www.casa-isabella.com

Entry 12   Map 7

Bramaluna

Welcome to a little-known corner of Italy. Up in the forested hills on the edge of a small village outside Asti, this neat, chic conversion of an 18th-century cascina is quite a surprise. The renovation is a beautifully romantic gesture from architect Maurizio, who saw just how much his wife Mara loved her father's old home. Maurizio's artistic eye is everywhere, and much of the original charm has been preserved: exposed brick and wooden beams blend with both minimalist and whimsical touches, such as the huge oversized flowers that line the steel staircase. Bedrooms are a similar mix of bare wood and bold colours, with no compromise on the amount of natural light they receive, nor indeed on the quality of the linen. The dining room sits at the heart of this modern country retreat, the setting for a deliciously sweet and savoury breakfast – unless you prefer your pastries on the terrace overlooking a sylvan scene. After a wonderful day's walking, dinner, cooked by Mara, is the best way to sample Piedmontese produce – and to enjoy the very personal style of these attentive hosts.

Rooms	1 double: €90.
	2 suites for 3-4: €90-€120.
Meals	Dinner with wine, €25-€35.
	Restaurant within walking distance.
Closed	Rarely.

Maurizio Lazzarini
Bramaluna,
14100 Asti
Mobile   +39 335 7464211
Email   relax@bramaluna.it
Web   www.bramaluna.it

Cascina Papa Mora Agriturismo

Authentic agriturismo in northern Italy. Adriana and Maria Teresa run grandmother's old house, speak fluent English and make you truly welcome. The farm produces wine, vegetables and fruit; the pantry overflows with oil, jam, chutney and wine. (This is one of the main regions for Barbera, Dolcetto, Bracchetto, Spumante.) We can't say that the farmhouse has been lovingly restored – more razed to the ground and rebuilt, then bedecked with simple stencils of flowers. Bedrooms, some hiding in the roof area, have no-nonsense 1930s furniture and light floral spreads. There's a little sitting room for guests with a wood-burning stove and, outside, a garden with roses, lavender and herbs sloping down to the pool and stables. The sisters also run a restaurant here and are passionate about their organic credentials. Dinner is a feast of gnocchi and tagliatelle, pepperoni cream puffs, anchovies in almond sauce, all delicious, and fun. Don't leave without sampling some homemade organic ice cream. Breakfast on the veranda where the blossom is pretty, the hills surround you, the bread comes fresh from the wood oven.

Rooms	4 twin/doubles: €70. 1 triple: €85. 2 quadruples: €95. Singles €40. Dinner, B&B €60 per person.
Meals	Lunch/dinner with wine, €25–€30.
Closed	December–February.

Adriana & Maria Teresa Bucco
Cascina Papa Mora Agriturismo,
Via Ferrere 16, 14010 Cellarengo

Tel	+39 0141 935126
Email	papamora@tin.it
Web	www.cascinapapamora.it

Entry 14   Map 6

Viavai

Alberto and Francesca inherited a big country house in hilltop Casalborgone, exploited the family's talent, taste and respect for Viavai's origins, renovated and then moved in. Now three generations live here, cheerfully spread across the big first floor. The second and third floors, reached via a small lift and a beautiful stone stair, are devoted to six uncluttered guest rooms, four with lush valley views. At ground level is a huge courtyard with a pool to one side and a courtyard garden dotted with wicker chairs. The stylishness spreads into the bedrooms, all harmonious colours, perfect wooden floors and striking textiles – linen, silk, organza, hessian. Bathrooms have plaster and brick walls, eco soaps and fluffy colour-matched towels. Up here too is the dining room for (delicious) breakfasts. And then there's Francesca, full of life and ideas, keen to introduce you to the highlights (cultural, oenological, gastronomic) of this undiscovered region. There are eco walks from the village, personal shoppers (just ask!) and special prices at the little restaurant down the hill. A treat for all seasons.

Rooms	3 doubles; 2 suites for 2; 1 family room for 4: €80–€105.
Meals	Restaurant 5-minute walk.
Closed	Rarely.

Francesca Guerra Vai
Viavai,
Via Valfrè 7, 10020 Casalborgone
Mobile +39 393 0678511
Email info@viavai.to.it
Web www.viavai.to.it

Castello di San Sebastiano Po

You arrive at the top of a tiny medieval town. An ancient red-washed door buzzes you in – to a courtyard of centuries-old trees, chirruping birds and warm, gentle Luca, whose family has lived here for 25 years. Eleven bedrooms are divided between the 'noble' (early 1800s) part of the estate and the farmhouse that goes back to medieval times. Each room is steeped in character: thick stone walls, cool tiled floors, huge chunky beams. There are old wooden sleigh beds and wrought-iron day beds, pretty patches of worn paint and humble bathrooms with box showers, and a suite with a wonderful claw foot tub; it oozes charm. Views – into a courtyard with glorious trees or over the valley below – do not disappoint; breakfasts are enjoyed at cheery check-clothed tables. It's a special place for weddings but also for families, with so much outdoor space to roam... old oaks give glorious shade, there are magnolias, palms and a greenhouse that dates from the 1700s. A delightful family runs this place, and are totally hands-on. Come for nature, authenticity, a relaxed feel... and log fires ablaze in winter.

Rooms	9 doubles; 1 suite for 6; 1 suite for 2-4: €110 for 2. Singles €75.
Meals	Dinner €25. Wine €8. Restaurants 2km.
Closed	Rarely.

Luca Garrone
Castello di San Sebastiano Po,
Via Novarina 9,
10020 San Sebastiano da Po

Tel	+39 0119 191177
Email	info@castellosansebastiano.it
Web	www.castellosansebastiano.it

Entry 16 Map 6

Casa Ale Bed & Breakfast

Alessandra's home in the Turin hills is as warm and inviting as she: a perfect antidote to impersonal city hotels. The old country villa sits in lush gardens in which birds and wildlife run free – a few kilometres from Turin city centre. It's a lovely Italian home, pale yellow with racing green shutters, flanked by pond, palms and potted plants. You breakfast in the kitchen or garden gazebo, and sleep tight in bedrooms of pale blue or blush, with sweet curtains, tea kettles and tidy shower rooms. You can self-cater in the apartment with its cheery orange kitchen and antique table, or dine on *fritto misto* and *bagna cauda* in the local trattorias – Alessandra will point out those with authentic Piedmontese cuisine. Follow the riverside boardwalk into the city for museums, shops, cafés and festivals – the Salone del Gusto (Slow Food Fair) is a favourite. Or leap into the hills for some of Italy's best wines and walking country. Not luxurious but spacious, quiet and immensely welcoming... a place where the hostess's grace and generosity shine through. *Minimum stay two nights.*

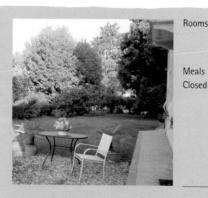

Rooms	1 twin/double: €85–€90.
	1 triple: €120
	1 apartment for 2: €90. Extra beds available in apartment.
Meals	Restaurant 1.5km.
Closed	Rarely.

Alessandra Oddone
Strada comunale di Mongreno 341,
10132 Turin
Tel   +39 0118 990808
Mobile   +39 333 4376220
Email   info@casaale.it
Web   www.casaale.it

Alla Buona Stella

Turin: grandiose home to baroque architecture and art, irresistible cafés, divine chocolatiers, prestigious opera house… and capital of the aperitivo. Here, in a respectable residential street in the heart of the old town, is Roberta's B&B. Take the lift of this very elegant building to a wide landing on the fourth floor and there is Roberta to greet you, with her lovely big smile and infectious laugh. There's an elegant oval dining table for breakfast, a cluster of shiny blue matching sofa and chairs, a little computer corner and a comforting, comfortable décor. Then there are the guest quarters on the floor above, high under the eaves, reached by a wooden open-tread stair. Expect three big, friendly, generous, traditional rooms, all polished antiques, gleaming floors, patterned rugs and easy chairs. The suite has its own little terrace, looking right down to the courtyard below, and the bathrooms are excellent, with showers and baths, bottles of shampoo, coloured towels. Roberta is super-organised, loves the city, loves her B&B, knows all there is to know. You could not be in better hands.

Rooms	1 twin/double; 1 suite for 2-3; 1 triple: €100-€110.
Meals	Restaurants nearby.
Closed	Rarely.

Roberta Simonetti
Alla Buona Stella,
Via del Carmine 10,
10122 Turin

Tel	+39 0111 9710823
Email	info@allabuonastella.it
Web	www.allabuonastella.it

Il Furtin

In the hills above the village of Cantalupa, up the road from its sister hotel, is an old stone building with stunning views across the valley; all feels truly peaceful and remote. The moment you enter you know this is a special restoration, employing materials reclaimed from the old farmhouse, roof beams from the chestnut woods and wool for insulation. The work has been carried out by the best local artisans; the uncluttered interiors are a beautiful example of Italian rustic-chic. Off the grassy garden is a big stone-walled living room with white Ikea sofas either side of a central fireplace, and sparkling spot-lit floors. There's a kitchen for large groups to use, and bedrooms – just six – that glow with rustic charm; expect big beds and gorgeous terracotta-tiled bathrooms. Breakfast is at La Locanda, the sister hotel down the road, served in a little room off the bar. You can dine in the restaurant where regional, creative dishes are smilingly served, and use the spa (booking required). The sun-dappled gardens, the outdoor pool and the hotel bikes (you're in fabulous hiking and biking country) come free.

Rooms	6 doubles: €80–€95. Singles €65-70. Extra bed/sofabed €20.
Meals	Restaurant 1km.
Closed	January.

Luca Ferrero
Il Furtin,
Via Rocca,
10060 Cantalupa
Tel   +39 0121 354610
Email information@maisonvertehotel.com
Web   www.ilfurtin.com

Ada Nada Agriturismo

A passion for fine wine infuses this Piedmontese vineyard, whose nine hectares are tended by the fourth generation of the Nadas. You can taste the estate's best bottles – Barbaresco, Moscato – at any time. And you can sample other local treats, like farinata crêpes and Langhe valley cheeses, in the rustic breakfast room or under the garden arbour, gazing over endless vines to the Alps. Behind the colourful plants and wooden doors of the 1700s cascina are country-pretty bedrooms with big windows that swap light for views. Warm and inviting, they have sponge-painted walls in soft, winey colours, antique beds and wardrobes, oil paintings. The master bedroom has sofas by the fire and a balcony for stargazing. Easy-going Anna Lisa and Elvio welcome guests warmly and serve dinner on advance booking; generous with their time and space, they offer winery tours and use of a small pool up by the family home. Come in autumn for the grape harvest and Alba's white truffles; come any time for peace, countryside and some of Italy's best wine and food.

Rooms	9 doubles; 1 twin: €65. 1 suite for 2; 3 suites for 2 (kitchen available for longer self-catering stays): €85. Singles €55. Extra bed €15.
Meals	Dinner on request. Breakfast €8. Restaurants 5km.
Closed	Never.

Anna Lisa Nada
Ada Nada Agriturismo,
Azienda Vitivinicola e Agriturismo, Via
Ausario 12, Località Rombone, 12050 Treiso

Tel	+39 0173 638127
Email	info@adanada.it
Web	www.adanada.it

Hotel Castello di Sinio

Sitting atop the tiny village of Sinio surrounded by rolling hillsides, hazelnut plantations and a multitude of vineyards, this 12th-century castello belonged to the noble Carretto family for some 600 years. On the village side, the stone façade appears impregnable, but move to the courtyard and a different mood prevails: lush green lawn, colourful flower beds, cascades of geraniums falling from windows boxes... a delicious little swimming pool has been tucked to one side. American Denise has done a tremendous job of restoration, at the same time becoming an ardent exponent of the region's wines, gastronomic delights and traditions. Denise is also the chef, personally creating the memorable meals which can be taken in the upstairs dining room. Good-sized bedrooms have terracotta floors, many with exposed stonework, beams and individual examples of beautiful vaulted stonework and fine Barocco furniture. Bathrooms are equipped with shower cabins and handy magnifying mirrors. Stunning. *Minimum stay two nights.*

Rooms	16 doubles: €150–€325.
Meals	Breakfast €8.
	Dinner, 4 courses, €45 (Wed–Sun).
	Wine from €15.
Closed	8 January to February.

Denise Pardini
Hotel Castello di Sinio,
Vicolo del Castello 1,
12050 Sinio

Tel	+39 0173 263889
Email	denise@hotelcastellodisinio.com
Web	www.hotelcastellodisinio.com

Il Gioco dell'Oca Agriturismo

People love Raffaella: her home is full of tokens of appreciation sent by guests. She spent much of her childhood here – the farm was her grandparents'. She is happy to be back, looks after her guests beautifully, feeds them well, and has tampered with the pretty, 18th-century farmhouse as little as possible. The well-worn, welcoming kitchen, much as it must have been 50 years ago, is for you to use as and when you like – the warm hub of a sociable house. Next door is a breakfast room set with little tables, but if it's fine you'll prefer to breakfast under the portico in the garden, which is big enough for everyone to find their own secluded corner. The bedrooms are simple and cosy, with family furniture and wooden beds, one with a hob, sink and fridge – a bonus if you have little ones. Bathrooms are bright and new. The farm, up in the hills near Barolo – a wonderful area for cheeses and wines – produces wine, fruit and hazelnuts. A pity the road is so close but you'll forgive that for the pleasure of staying at such a relaxed, welcoming and thoroughly Italian agriturismo.

Rooms	6 twin/doubles: €65–€75. 1 triple: €75–€85.
Meals	Restaurant 500m.
Closed	January.

Raffaella Pittatore
Il Gioco dell'Oca Agriturismo,
Via Alba 83,
12060 Barolo,

Tel	+39 0173 56206
Email	info@gioco-delloca.it
Web	www.gioco-delloca.it

Relais Divino

Ah, the heavenly trio of good food, good wine and seclusion: that's the secret of Relais Divino. Thread through Piedmont's rolling landscapes, up a rural drive to a working estate and you're greeted by the all-pervasive perfume of vines. The holiday bodes well... Definitely opt for dinner: it's a four-course extravaganza here, of meat-stuffed pastas, savoury tarts and mouthwatering morsels paired with the estate's wines. Ugo and Petra's local specialities are irresistibly more-ish, and the brick arches, candlelight and crisp linen create a magical atmosphere from which to glide up to bed. Great care has been taken over the colourful king-size bedrooms and the mezzanine family rooms — the level of comfort is consistent but the individual styling means you can try a different room each visit. Breakfast at leisure under the portico or indoors, savour your espresso as you survey hazelnut groves, grazing horses, and gardens that are a child's delight. After a swim, if you fancy a jacuzzi or a Turkish bath, just ask Ugo and he'll prepare it for you, with a smile. Italy at its best.

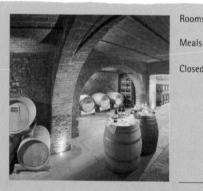

Rooms	3 doubles: €120–€150.
	3 family rooms for 3–5: €150–€200.
Meals	Lunch €20. Dinner €35.
	Wine €10–€25.
Closed	January–February.

Petra Stechert
Relais Divino,
Loc. San Sebastiano 68,
12065 Monforte d'Alba

Tel	+39 0173 789269
Email	info@relaisdivino.it
Web	www.relaisdivino.it

Cascina Adami – Il Nido

A short drive down a country lane, the 17th-century farmhouse is set into its hill with superb views over a gentle landscape patchworked with wheat fields and vineyards, leading the eye to snowy peaks beyond. This is the best wine-producing area of Italy, and opposite the lane is a dairy where you can stock up on the sheep's cheese – soft, mild, delicious Murazzano. Discreetly distant from the main house, down a steep unpaved track – watch your wheels! – is a four-square, two-storey stone structure, once a goats' shed. Il Nido (the nest) is a delicious bolthole for two. Owner Paolo is a master at putting salvaged finds to unusual use with charming results, so expect pale new stone floors and chunky old rafters, a delicate wooden fretwork door, a stylish steel table and chairs, a charming kitchen tucked under a chunky white stone stair, a bedroom with a big cream bed and small blue shutters, driftwood and pebbles prettifying quiet corners. Outside is smart wooden furniture from which to gaze on the views and a huge linen parasol. Contemporary rusticity, ancient peace.

Rooms	1 cottage for 2 (1 double; 1 shower room): €750 per week. €350 per weekend. Additional cleaning charge.
Meals	Self-catering.
Closed	October–April.

Paolo & Flavia Adami
Cascina Adami – Il Nido,
Fraz. Mellea 53, 12060 Murazzano

Tel	+39 0118 178135
Mobile	+39 347 9721761
Email	flavia.adami@yahoo.it
Web	www.cascinaadami.it

Cascina Adami

Easy to laze the day away here, taking in the views: an exquisite panorama unfurls before you, and there's a hillside for children to run wild on. The owners live in Turin, and giving life to old structures is their passion. Inside the long L-shaped building are stunning brick floors and characterful rafters, limewashed stone walls and rustic niches, curtains made from saris and antique French tables. Most apartments sleep two, some have a sofabed downstairs for a child, others interconnect. And there are interesting Japanese touches, including a wooden bathtub in Zafferano. We loved the pure white walls, the modern art, the chunky stone arches, the fabrics from travels abroad, and the doors that throw open to a narrow shared lawn and four private terraces. Views reach to the hills and distant mountains, and there is a delicious little pool flanked by rosemary and lavender, tucked away to the side. Cook a simple meal in your modern kitchen (hob, fridge, microwave), make friends around the barbecue, eat out in Murazzano, famous for its cheese.

Rooms	1 apartment for 4; 3 apartments for 2: €700-€1,100 per week. Rates exclude charge for final clean.
Meals	Restaurants 2km.
Closed	October-April.

Paolo & Flavia Adami
Cascina Adami,
Frazione Cornati 9, 12060 Murazzano
Tel   +39 0118 178135
Mobile   +39 347 9721761
Email   flavia.adami@yahoo.it
Web   www.cascinaadami.it

Lombardy and Trentino–Alto Adige

Polidora

Are you in a Fitzgerald novel, a guest at some expat's ridiculously lush estate? From the vast botanical garden on the shores of Lake Maggiore, where islands hover on the glistening water and the Alps stand protectively in the distance, you will feel at total peace with the world. The changing light mischievously catches rare species of plant, flower and tree in moods you would not think possible, in supernatural shades. What luck that GianLuca decided to convert the stables in the grounds of his elegant 1900s villa into a spacious and stylish B&B. Now the WWF-protected acres of rare plants and trees, which he still tends and adds to so passionately, are yours to explore; with lonely benches, pebble beaches and shady patches inviting you to unwind, we defy you to read a book without being distracted by the beauty – or to not swim in the cool waters of the lake the moment you see their enticing ripples. While GianLuca is away, his staff are on hand for breakfasts and conversation. Lunch in the nearby village of Cerro or picnic in the grounds; it's so big you can stay here all day and not see another soul.

Rooms	2 doubles; 1 suite for 2: €150.
	Sofabeds available in suite.
	Whole house €3,000 per week.
Meals	Restaurants 1-3km.
Closed	Rarely.

GianLuca Sarto
Polidora,
Via Pirinoli 4,
21014 Cerro di Laveno Mombello

Mobile	+39 349 7826474
Email	info@polidora.com
Web	www.polidora.com

Cascina Rodiani

Slow down as you spiral up from Lake Como to a 400-year-old cascina floating in Spina Verde's bucolic hills. Be inspired by soaring Alpine views and by Samuel's stylish eco-friendly restoration. The smell of fresh pine wafts through stone-walled bedrooms with huge beams, fireplaces, oriental rugs and bold red splashes. You lay your sleepy head on organic pillows, scribble postcards on reclaimed tables, fling open shutters to mountain views. Nature keeps the old farm estate beautiful with wild flowers, birds, bees and other creatures who buzz, tweet, flutter and scurry around the chestnuts, fruit trees and olives. Stroll through them to a hidden thousand-year-old sanctuary. Breakfast – perhaps homemade pancakes, organic eggs, garden berries – is a treat under the portico or in the vaulted *Sala da Pranzo*, where logs crackle in a new fireplace. Above this, an Open Space offers a blank, bean-bagged canvas for creative gatherings. Pop to the village restaurant for dinner or roll through the hills to Switzerland. Samuel and Mimma's enthusiasm for this special spot will warm your spirit, and the scenery will thrill your heart.

Rooms	3 twin/doubles: €120.
	1 suite for 4: €180.
	Singles €80.
	Extra bed/sofabed available €30.
	Cot available.
Meals	Aperitif on request. Restaurants 3km.
Closed	15 December to 15 March.

Samuel Crisigiovanni
Cascina Rodiani,
Via Ronco 251, 22020 Drezzo

Tel	+39 0315 22052
Mobile	+39 340 3413325
Email	info@colledrezzo.com
Web	www.colledrezzo.com

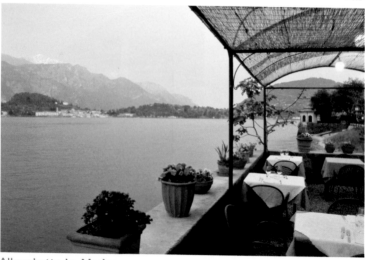

Alberghetto La Marianna

On the banks of Lake Como, a very charming family-run hotel, housed in a villa simply modernised and redecorated with a nicely laid-back feel. Bedrooms are humble, functional, with cheery shower rooms and (mostly) lakeside views. Some have balconies, one has its own little terrace. A road runs between you and the busy lake, so if you're a light sleeper, it may be worth giving up those shimmering views for a room at the back — at least in summer. No need to tip-toe round the owners: Paola is a delight, very generous and treats guests as friends. Breakfasts include homemade bread, cakes, savoury offerings and jams, husband Ty prepares a different menu of wholesome food every day, while Paola is a "mistress of desserts". You can eat inside and admire the ever-changing local art work lining the walls or outside where you can embrace the lake views on the terrace that juts onto the water. You won't be short of advice here on things to do: visits to gardens and villas, boat tours to Isola Comacina, day trips to St Moritz and the Engadine. The ferries are a step away.

Rooms	7 doubles: €85-€95.
	1 single: €60-€65.
Meals	Dinner with wine, €30.
Closed	Mid-November to mid-March
	(open 26 December to 6 January).

Paola Cioccarelli
Via Regina 57,
22011 Cadenabbia di Griante
Tel   +39 0344 43095
Mobile   +39 333 9812649
Email   inn@la-marianna.com
Web   www.la-marianna.com

Il Poggio di Bellagio

A spectacular setting, on a hillside, with the lake glistening below and a footpath leading down to Bellagio – you'll understand why some people go no further. There's a feeling of natural abundance in the grounds here: green, green lawns, flowers, an old olive grove. Plenty of space to sit and ponder with a glass of prosecco and those captivating views, from the private pool and the house too. Francesca and Odilla's grandparents might not recognise their spruced-up farmhouse; you can rent the whole place in summer and you'll have use of the old cantina – perfect for cookery classes – and cellar. There's a good flow to the straightforward design of the apartments, each room complementing the next: terracotta floors, wrought-iron beds with white bedspreads, large wardrobes, wooden furniture, new sofas, practical, no frills small kitchens and bathrooms. All are similar though the *trilocale* has a good-sized terrace for dining out under the stars. Take day trips from the village – by boat, of course – to other lakeside gems. Very restful and appealing. *Bookings Saturday to Saturday.*

Rooms	3 apartments for 2; 1 apartment for 4: €920–€2,010. Whole house available June-Sept, €4,980–€8,490. Prices per week.
Meals	Restaurant 5-minute drive.
Closed	November-March. Apartments available only Sept-Nov & March-June.

Francesca Pelloli
Il Poggio di Bellagio,
Via Suira 38,
22021 Bellagio

Mobile	+39 335 7118943
Email	info@ilpoggiodibellagio.it
Web	www.ilpoggiodibellagio.it

Albergo Milano

You wander down the cobbled streets of Varenna and, suddenly, there it is: the grand lake. The life of the village bustles below, as colourwashed houses cluster round the church on a rocky promontory perched above Lake Como. The setting is enchanting. Smack on the lakeside is Albergo Milano, pretty, traditional and disarmingly small. Owners Bettina and Egidio are engaging people, delighted to be running their own small hotel. Everywhere is freshly and stylishly furnished, bedroom floors are covered in colourful old tiles, traditional furniture makes a striking contrast with sleek modern bathrooms and each has a balcony or terrace with a lake view. The dining room's big new windows open onto a wonderful wide terrace where you eat out on fine days, the lake stirring beside you. The food is divine gourmet-Italian, the wine list irresistible. A step away, in the old part of town, is a charming sister dwelling housing apartments with kitchenettes and living rooms. Bettina is a mine of information about this area and there's a regular train service into Bergamo and Milan. It's a gem. *Private parking available, on request at extra charge.*

Rooms	12 doubles: €130–€190.
	1 triple: €130–€225.
	3 apartments for 2-5: €130–€330.
Meals	Dinner €38. Wine from €18.
Closed	November–March.
	Apartments open all year.

Bettina & Egidio Mallone
Albergo Milano,
Via XX Settembre 35,
23829 Varenna
Tel +39 0341 830298
Email hotelmilano@varenna.net
Web www.varenna.net

Castello di Vezio

Vezio is, in essence, a small friendly holiday village, draped around a medieval castle with panoramic views stretching over Lake Como and the mountains. Several lovely houses and cottages share a tennis court, a huge games room with table football, swimming pool, large lawn and heaps of outdoor space, so you won't be bumping into other people much. The children may play football or rounders while you nod off in the shade of one of numerous trees, or sunbathe in peace beside your own private pool; you can also look over the 12th-century castle. Large or small parties will be happy here: kitchens are state of the art with Villeroy & Boch china, pretty bedrooms have fresh painted walls, crisp linens, heavy curtains and 18th-century floral furnishings, bathrooms are spotless and functional. Stock up in the delicatessens of Perledo, walk to restaurants (one lies at the foot of the castle) or hop in the car to beautiful Varenna. Tons of space to explore and play makes this place a dream for families. Vezio itself is a sweet hamlet of church bells and cobblestones with a steep rocky path to Varenna below.

Rooms	2 houses for 4; 1 house for 6; 1 house for 7; 1 house for 8: €1,100–€3,000 per week.
Meals	Restaurants nearby.
Closed	Never.

Maria Manuela Greppi
Castello di Vezio,
Via del Castellano, 23828 Varenna

Tel	+39 0258 190940
Mobile	+39 335 1802302
Email	vezio@robilant.it
Web	www.agriturismocastellodivezio.it

Castello di Vezio

A small, but perfectly formed and friendly holiday village, draped around a medieval castle with panoramic views stretching over Lake Como and the mountains. And if you can't be bothered to look after yourselves then you can go for a B&B option in any one of six lovely houses and cottages. All share a tennis court, a huge games room with table football, swimming pool, large lawn and heaps of outdoor space, so you won't be bumping into other people much. The children may play football or rounders while you nod off in the shade of one of numerous trees, or sunbathe in peace beside your own private pool; you can also look over the 12th-century castle. Large or small parties will be happy here: breakfast is left for you — toast, jam, tea and coffee, or if you want the full buffet then it's all on offer at the main house for an extra sum. Sleep well in pretty bedrooms with fresh painted walls, crisp linens, heavy curtains and 18th-century floral furnishings; bathrooms are spotless and functional. You can walk to restaurants (one lies at the foot of the castle) or hop in the car to beautiful Varenna. *Per person prices available.*

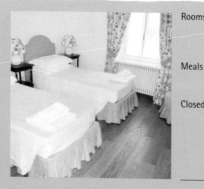

Rooms	3 houses for 4; 1 house for 6; 1 house for 7; 1 house for 8: €240-€560. Reduced rates for weekly stays.
Meals	Breakfast €15 (some items left in apartments free of charge). Restaurants nearby.
Closed	Never.

Maria Manuela Greppi
Castello di Vezio,
Via del Castellano, 23828 Varenna

Tel	+39 0258 190940
Mobile	+39 335 1802302
Email	vezio@robilant.it
Web	www.agriturismocastellodivezio.it

Villa Menta

Minutes from Lake Lecco, an hour from Milan, is a warm, colourful B&B – welcome to a 40-year-old house up in the hills. Behind the electric gates lies peacefulness, lushness and beauty. The house is surrounded by three acres of terraces and rolling lawns, a little wood for mushrooms, a huge pool below, fruit trees, vegetables, flowers, butterflies and bees, and your hostess's playful, whimsical sculptures. Licia and Andrea, an adorable pair (she an artist and architect, he a garden designer) have recently moved into her parents' former home. Inside has a welcoming retro feel – a lovely L-shaped sofa here, old-fashioned carpeting there, floor-to-ceiling books and Licia's father's paintings lining the walls. Bedrooms may not be cutting-edge but include designer pieces; sunny and inviting, they overlook the gorgeous grounds. In summer, breakfast is brought to the patio tucked away by the lily pond, pure *Alice in Wonderland*. A feast of homemade cakes and crostata, juices and jams, it is served on whimsical china of Licia's own production. At night, more magic, as you sit outside and watch the sun slide down. *Minimum stay two nights, four nights in high season.*

Rooms	2 doubles; 1 twin: €100–€120. Singles €90.
Meals	Guest kitchen. Restaurants 5km.
Closed	Rarely.

Licia Martelli
Villa Menta, Via del Zero 5, Località
Trescano, 23848 Oggiono

Tel	+39 0341 576168
Mobile	+39 347 5892359
Email	info@villamenta.it
Web	www.villamenta.it

Il Torchio

Marcella's happy personality fills the house with joy. She and Franco are artists – she an animator, he a painter; if you love the bohemian life you will love it here. Franco also has an antiquarian bookshop in Milan, which explains the shelves in the sitting room. Their home began life in 1600 as the stables of the noble Calchi family; you enter through a fine stone archway into a courtyard. Franco's paintings enliven the walls and every corner is adorned with stained-glass, prints and curios that Marcella has found on her flea market forays. Bedrooms are endearingly old-fashioned – no frills but good, comfortable beds. The big private suite, entered via French windows, has green views down to Calco, a great big bed, family photos on the walls, and a cabinet filled with children's old toys. The bathrooms are basic but have lovely hand-painted tiles. The whole family is a delight – including the cats – and Marcella's cooking is superb, with many delights from the garden. Active types can canoe in summer and ski in winter (just a one-hour drive); or visit Verona, Lake Como, and the stunning shops of Milan. *Free WiFi.*

Rooms	3 doubles: €60.
	1 triple: €80.
	Singles €35. Children 6-12 years €15.
	Free for children under 6.
Meals	Restaurant 2km.
Closed	Rarely.

Marcella Pisacane
Il Torchio, Via Ghislanzoni,
Loc. Vescogna, 23885 Calco

Tel	+39 0395 08724
Mobile	+39 348 8124929
Email	il_torchio@hotmail.com
Web	iltorchio.wordpress.com

Villa La Vescogna

A courtyard heavy with the scent of jasmine leads to a pair of mile-high, gleaming doors: welcome to this opulent, 17th-century palazzo. It is home to the Fasoli family, wonderfully easy-going and kind. Signore is a particularly passionate ambassador for this (surprisingly) unsung area, a font of knowledge on historic villas, day trips to Como and Lecco, and shopping in Milan. Use the gracious, ground-floor rooms if you wish… but you're most likely to be lured by the captivating, tiered, Italianate garden where formal hedging, urns and romantic pathways lead inexorably to a sublime pool – large enough to do a few laps (and there's a pool house with a tiny kitchen if you fancy a lazy day in). Bedrooms, on the same floor as your hosts, are of the romantic variety with a touch of whimsy – "Laura Ashley meets Alice in Wonderland" says our inspector – while the double with the en suite has a vaulted ceiling bright with frescoed cherubs. Breakfast on locally cured meats, home-baked breads and jams in the cheery blue and white kitchen, or on the atmospheric patio shaded by ancient trees. *Minimum stay two nights.*

Rooms	1 house for 6: €1,500–€3,000 per week. B&B on request (min. 2 nights) €130. Extra double available on request.
Meals	Restaurant 2km.
Closed	November–Easter.

Lorenza Bozzoli Fasoli
Villa La Vescogna,
Loc. Vescogna 2,
23885 Calco

Mobile	+39 339 8927777
Email	bozzoli@tiscali.it
Web	www.lavescogna.com

Agriturismo Casa Clelia

The agriturismo has been sculpted out of the 11th-century convent, using the principles of eco-bio architecture. Cows peer from sheds as you arrive, chickens, geese and sheep bustle – this is a working farm. The main house stands against wooded hills; beyond are convent, outhouses, orchards and barns. Anna is a darling, so welcoming and kindly informal you feel at home the minute you arrive. There is a talented local cook and one of the treats is the taster menu, your chance to sample numerous delicacies all at once. The good size bedrooms are uncluttered and original, all wood, stone and bold colours; bathrooms are modern, lighting subtle. Heat comes from a wood-burner supplemented by solar panels; cork and coconut ensure the sound-proofing of walls. Children are most welcome, free to run wild in the gardens, orchards and eight hectares of woods. Hard to imagine a more wonderful place for families... or for a get-away-from-it-all weekend. There's horse riding nearby, too, and Bergamo, mid-way between Lake Como and Lake Iseo, is a cultural treat.

Rooms	6 doubles; 1 family room for 2-4; 2 triples: €100-€125.
Meals	Lunch/dinner with wine, €20-€35, except Mondays.
Closed	Never.

Ferruccio Masseretti
Agriturismo Casa Clelia,
Via Corna 1/3,
24039 Sotto il Monte Giovanni XXIII
Tel   +39 0357 99133
Email   info@casaclelia.com
Web   www.casaclelia.com

San Giacomo Horses & Agriturismo

A delightful surprise – one minute you're navigating Milan's industrial hinterland, the next you're in Roccolo National Park, sweeping down a tree-lined drive past paddocks of horses. This is a working stud farm, with a stable block next to the peachy villa. Here lie four stylish, spacious bedrooms, reached via their own entrances directly from the garden; the fifth, with a gorgeous white-painted four-poster bed and a terrace up a flight of stairs, sits under the eaves of the family home. There are a couple of apartments tucked away in the house, too. Each elegant sunlit double room is named after a horse – 'Bagheera', 'Dorothy', 'Elastic Girl'; antique furniture and pale linen abound, and sleek modern bathrooms have super walk-in showers. The bright chandeliered breakfast room (also the reception area) has windows on three sides so your organic buffet breakfast is accompanied by views of pomegranate trees and happy horses. Isabella and Patrizia run the whole place with a calm and efficiency tailored to the needs of their clientele – businessmen and women visiting Milan. *Pets by arrangement.*

Rooms	1 double; 4 twin/doubles: €95-€150. Singles €85-€110.
Meals	Restaurant 1km.
Closed	Christmas & New Year.

Isabella Castelli
San Giacomo Horses & Agriturismo,
Cascina San Giacomo, 20010 Arluno

Tel	+39 0290 377123
Mobile	+39 339 7381988
Email	posta@sangiacomohorses.it
Web	www.sangiacomohorses.it

Casa Broggi

This is an elegant part of town. The florist below is like an art gallery, Sotheby's is around the corner and chic shoppers get their fix on the shopping streets nearby. No need to worry about noise though as this first-floor apartment in a historic Liberty style building is in a leafy residential area. Pass a beautifully maintained communal courtyard, then up to the first floor and… space! High ceilings and period details abound, and furnishings are a mix of antiques, art and 'homely Italian', to a backdrop of cheery yellow. Bedrooms have queen-size beds and first-rate linen while a sparkling green mosaic bathroom has – a rarity for Italy – fluffy towels. The cute kitchen (with hob but without oven) is great for the basics. Jane moved from Scotland 20 years ago and lives in a separate wing with her Italian husband and daughter. Immensely kind and helpful, she's particularly sensitive to people travelling en famille and provides everything from strollers to high chairs. A wonderful peaceful place to return to after a day's exploring magnificent Milan. *Minimum stay two nights.*

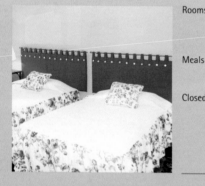

Rooms	1 apartment for 4: €600–€800 per week. Rates depend on number of guests. €40 cleaning, €15 daily apartment cleaning.
Meals	Continental breakfast hamper €6.50 per person. Restaurants within walking distance.
Closed	Rarely.

Jane Wilson
Casa Broggi,
Via Broggi 17,
20129 Milan

Mobile	+39 346 7498565
Email	info@casabroggi.com
Web	www.casabroggi.com

Antica Locanda dei Mercanti

Entering the great courtyard of this 18th-century building in the heart of Milan, you wouldn't imagine the lightness and charm of the small, discreet boutique hotel on the second floor. Heavy glass doors slide open to a simple reception where chic Italians and visitors mingle; young staff whisk you off to rooms whose individuality and style promise more country-house comfort than spartan modernity. The place is run by real people with passion. From the smallest room with its elegant Milanese fabrics and wicker chair with cherry striped and piped cushions to the largest, airy room with its muslin-hung four-poster, terrace, olive tree and scented climbers, each space surprises. Fine linen, deep mattresses, dramatic murals, fresh posies, stacks of magazines, small, gleaming shower rooms – and air conditioning: each room bears the distinctive hallmark of the energetic owner. In the new grey-floored, aubergine-sofa'd communal space, too, for basic breakfast beneath glistening chandeliers. Cool simplicity, and La Scala a heartbeat away. *Pets by arrangement.*

Rooms	15 doubles (4 with terrace): €195–€315. Suites €245–€295.
Meals	Light lunch & dinner in room on request. Restaurants nearby.
Closed	Never.

Alessandro Basta
Antica Locanda dei Mercanti,
Via San Tomaso 6,
20121 Milan

Tel	+39 0280 54080
Email	locanda@locanda.it
Web	www.locanda.it

Entry 39 Map 2

Villa Muslone

Muslone is a walkers' paradise. Lake Garda is bordered by olive groves, lemon trees and vines; climb higher for alpine pastures; gaze beyond to snow-capped mountains. The climate is as clement as that of the Bay of Naples. Your house, half way up a rocky hill, belongs to the young Campanardis and you couldn't wish for a kinder pair. They live in the basement, you live upstairs, sharing your space with the other guests. Emma and Mirko speak a little English, and German, and give you maps for walks and timetables for ferries for the outstandingly beautiful Italian Lakes. Breakfast's organic eggs, ricotta, olive oil and tomatoes are their own. Step into a sitting/dining room with lovely high rafters, magazines, candles and a super new kitchen to the side; each guest has a shelf in the fridge. Off here lie the bedrooms, very comfortable and pristine, one with a wonderful lake view, another opening to the garden. Bathrooms are squeaky clean, with stacks of coloured towels; upstairs are two rooms for cards, cushions and CDs. For sociable self-caterers, this is a treat. *Minimum stay two nights. Children over 12 welcome.*

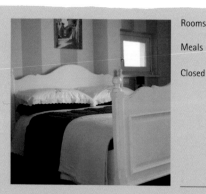

Rooms	3 doubles (sharing sitting room & kitchen): €110–€130.
Meals	Guest kitchen. Restaurant/pizzeria 1km.
Closed	November–Easter.

Emma Campanardi
Villa Muslone,
Via Muslone 64/A, 25084 Gargnano

Tel	+39 0365 72648
Mobile	+39 334 8165513
Email	info@villamuslone.it
Web	www.villamuslone.it

Hotel du Lac

The hotel oozes old-style charm. A 1900s townhouse in a quieter, less touristy part of the lake, it's in the same street as the villa where DH Lawrence eulogised about the "milky lake" of Garda. The oxblood façade, with white relief and green shutters, is as striking as the view from the patio that overhangs the water; you can swim from here. Valerio's grandparents had a piano shop in Milan and lived here until 1959; much of their furniture remains. The family could not be more helpful. Roomy bedrooms are wonderfully old-fashioned with big beds and wardrobes, 1930s lights and polished terrazzo floors; beds are deeply comfortable and dressed in crisp cotton. Six rooms look onto the lake and have small balconies or terraces. The dining room, around a central courtyard with a palm tree that reaches the clouds, looks directly onto the water. You can also dine upstairs on the open terrace, where metal tables and chairs are shaded by an arbour of kiwi, a magical spot at night, the water lapping below, the lights twinkling in the distance. There's even a small music room with a piano to play – guests sometimes do. *Out of season call +39 036 571269.*

Rooms	12 doubles: €90–€160. Singles €67–€120.	
Meals	Menu à la carte, from €30. Wine from €13.	
Closed	1st week of November & week before Easter.	

Valerio Arosio
Hotel du Lac,
Via Colletta 21,
25084 Villa di Gargnano

Tel	+39 0365 71107
Email	info@hotel-dulac.it
Web	www.hotel-dulac.it

Entry 41   Map 3

Hotel Gardenia al Lago

Jasmine-scented gardens and green lawns reach to Lake Garda's edge: lounge here, drinking in the views, and drop down the ladder to the sparkling water, said to be the purest in Italy. There's also a small beach 100 yards away. The hotel stands, a feast of colour and design, against the steep, wooded foothills of Mount Baldo. It was bought by the Arosio family as a summer home in 1925. They were piano-makers from Lodi – note the original piano in the music room – and in the 1950s turned the house into a guesthouse. Today it is a small, restful, civilised hotel with a gentle 1920s charm. The entire family, parents and sons, are delightful. Some bedrooms have been renovated – frescoes were uncovered in the process – and are beautiful, with distinctive Empire antiques, exquisite floor tiles, muslin billowing at French windows and superior Edwardian-style bathrooms. Many have balconies or terraces. Others, more functional, less charming – and cheaper – await regeneration. In summer you eat under the trees, by candlelight, surrounded by lemon and olive trees – they produce wonderful olive oil. *Out of season call +39 036 571269.*

Rooms	25 doubles: €88–€230. Singles €66–€172.
Meals	Menu à la carte, from €30. Wine from €12.50.
Closed	10 October & week before Easter.

Giorgio & Andrea Arosio
Hotel Gardenia al Lago,
Via Colletta 53,
25084 Villa di Gargnano
Tel   +39 0365 71195
Email   info@hotel-gardenia.it
Web   www.hotel-gardenia.it

Dimora Bolsone

Film-like, the lake glitters between the cypress trees – an expanse of blue far below. Gaze in wonder as gentle, cultured, charming Raffaele – and spaniels Rocky and Glenda – invite you to the terrace with a jug of freshly squeezed orange juice. Economist, lecturer, sailor, antique collector, big game hunter and green aficionado, Raffaele is the lifeblood of this property, meets and greets you and gives you free run of these 46 acres, a glorious mix of of protected parkland and terraced gardens. The 15th-century house reposes gracefully among jasmine-strewn loggias and lemon trees; step in to a cool, ordered calm. Big, dark, immaculate bedrooms have light polished floors, soft washed walls, family portraits, delicious linen. All are different – gilt cornices and flirty rococo in one, sober masculinity and a 15th-century bed in another. Start the day feasting on almond cookies, local cheeses, cold meats, fresh fruits; tour Verona, or the lake. Return to a delicious soak in the jacuzzi, surrounded by breathtaking views. An essay in perfection, a feast for the senses. *Minimum stay two nights. Children over 12 welcome.*

Rooms	5 doubles: €200.
	Singles €170.
Meals	Restaurants 1km.
Closed	30 November to 28 February.

Raffaele Bonaspetti
Dimora Bolsone,
Via Panoramica 23,
25083 Gardone Riviera

Tel	+39 0365 21022
Email	info@dimorabolsone.it
Web	www.dimorabolsone.it

Villa San Pietro Bed & Breakfast

A splendid 17th-century home run by Anna, warm, vivacious and multilingual, and Jacques, French and charming. This is a family affair and long-term friendships may be formed. It's a rather grand name for a house that is one of a terrace, but once inside you realise why we have included it. Anna's interiors are are immaculate, with oak beams, ancient brick floors, family antiques and floral fabrics; not a speck of dust! Guests have their own sitting room with a frescoed ceiling, the bedrooms are delightful and original frescoes were discovered in the *sala da pranzo* during the restoration. Another exceptional thing about San Pietro is its large garden and terrace. There is also a pretty ground-floor loggia for meals: Anna's dinners are regional and, we are told, delicious. Clearly they pour their hearts into the operation and their enthusiasm is contagious. You are in a peaceful street near the town centre, off the beaten path yet perfectly sited for forays into Garda, Brescia, Verona and Venice. Lake Garda is only ten kilometres away. Rustically special. *Minimum stay two nights.*

Rooms	5 doubles: €85–€110.
	Extra bed/sofabed €25–€30.
Meals	Dinner with wine, 4 courses, €30.
	Restaurants 50m.
Closed	Rarely.

Jacques & Anna Ducroz
Villa San Pietro Bed & Breakfast,
Via San Pietro 25, 25018 Montichiari

Tel	+39 0309 61232
Mobile	+39 334 7814481
Email	villasanpietro@hotmail.com
Web	www.abedandbreakfastinitaly.com

Tenuta Le Sorgive – Le Volpi Agriturismo

One cannot deny the beauty of Lake Garda, but it's a relief to escape to the unpopulated land of Lombardy. This 19th-century cascina has been in the Serenelli family for two generations; siblings Vittorio and Anna are justly proud of their 28-hectare working family farm. Everything is organic, solar panels provide electricity and a wood-chip burner the heating. Le Sorgive, crowned with a pierced dovecote, houses the rooms, flanked by carriage house and stables. Big guest rooms, with wooden rafters, are a mix of old and new. Some have attractive, metalwork beds, some a balcony, two have a mezzanine with beds for the children, all are crisp and clean. This is a great place for families to visit as there's so much to do: horse riding and mountain biking from the farm, go-karting and archery nearby, watersports, including scuba diving courses, at Garda. There is also a large gym and a well-maintained pool. Anna runs Le Volpi, the cascina, where you can sample gnocchi, Mantovan sausages and mouthwatering fruit tarts – great value. *Minimum stay three nights in high season; one week in apartments.*

Rooms	8 doubles/triples/quadruples: €85–€105. 2 apartments for 4: €580–€950 per week.
Meals	Breakfast €5 for self-caterers. Dinner with wine, €15–€28. Closed January & Mon/Tues evening. Restaurant nearby.
Closed	Never.

Vittorio Serenelli
Tenuta Le Sorgive –
Le Volpi Agriturismo,
Via Piridello 6, 46040 Solferino

Tel	+39 0376 854252
Email	info@lesorgive.it
Web	www.lesorgive.it

Palazzo Arrivabene

The history of this huge palazzo – built by Mantua's ruling family in 1480 – hits you the moment you see the magnificent Ludovico Dorigny fresco on the cupola of the main hall. There are more grand frescoes and the Arrivabene coat of arms over the door, but, despite its grandness, Claudio and Luciana bring a warmth and friendliness to every stay here. Each of the rooms, all en suite, all on the second floor (reached by stairs only), reflects a particular passion of a particular family member. 'Camera 800' houses a beloved aunt's paintings and prints alongside thick Persian rugs and gilt mirrors. The vast mezzanine 'Mansarda' glows with rich rust-coloured carpeting, batik prints and appliqué patchwork gathered over the years. And the towering walls and windows of 'Camera degli sposi' give plenty of light and space for Claudio's prized collection of golf diplomas, his father's university degrees and a trove of family antiques. Breakfast is served in two large *salones* that double as lounges for the rest of the day – a huge feast consisting of brioches, fresh fruit and the traditional *sbrisolona*. *Small pets welcome by prior arrangement.*

Rooms	1 double; 1 double; 1 twin/double: €120-€150. Singles €100-€120. Extra beds/sofabeds & cots available. Dinner, B&B €60-€75 per person.
Meals	Restaurants nearby.
Closed	Christmas & August.

Claudio & Luciana Bini
Palazzo Arrivabene,
Via F.lli Bandiera 20, 46100 Mantua

Tel	+39 0376 328685
Mobile	+39 335 6561254
Email	info@palazzoarrivabene.net
Web	www.palazzoarrivabene.net

Schwarz Adler Turm Hotel

All around are the soaring, craggy Dolomites – and if you feel overawed, you'll be soothed on arrival. Manfred and Sonja – calm, elegant, intelligent – will be delighted to see you, and eager to do all they can to please. Though the building is young, it is a faithful reproduction of a 16th-century manor and blends in beautifully with the pretty village of Cortaccia (known as 'Kurtasch' by the locals). Light roomy bedrooms, alpine-cosy with lots of pine and warmly carpeted, have blissful views to vineyards, orchards and mountains; each has a loggia, a balcony or access to the garden. This was Austria (the area turned Italian in 1919) and the hotel's cuisine, served in the family restaurant opposite – a fascinating example of German Renaissance architecture – reflects this; it's a tour de force of Italian and South Tyrolean dishes, and comes with a well-stocked bar: the perfect place to gather after a day's hiking. Take a trip to Bolzano or Merano, go on a wine tour, rent bikes, play golf – there are three courses nearby. Return to sauna, steam room and lovely pool.

Rooms	24 doubles: €150-€195. Dinner, B&B €80-€115 p.p.
Meals	Lunch/dinner €42. Restaurant in village.
Closed	2 weeks in February; 22-27 December.

Famiglia Pomella
Schwarz Adler Turm Hotel,
Kirchgasse 2,
39040 Cortaccia (Kurtatsch)

Tel	+39 0471 880600
Email	info@turmhotel.it
Web	www.turmhotel.it

Maratscher Kultur Hotel

When she's not reeling off restaurant tips, vivacious owner Doris Moser is fixing epic breakfasts of homemade jams and chutneys, organic eggs, cured hams, fine cheeses, posh tea blends from Florence's La Via del Tè... Collector as well as epicure, Frau Moser has spruced up this former farmhouse (her childhood home) with gorgeous photos, handmade lampshades and works by local painters; statues dot the gardens, lines from Goethe and Rilke adorn the walls. Bedrooms are dreamy, soothing, with wooden floors, soft pastel walls, Japanese lamps and built-in floor lighting. Each has unique touches reflecting its theme: tulle drapes embroidered with German poetry in 'Vellau', ghostly tree silhouettes on the door in 'Silberbaum' (silver tree). All rooms bar one have French windows opening onto balconies, from where you can follow the contours of the valley past orchards, vineyards and castles to the feet of peaks that soar 3,000 metres. It's 2km to the centre of Merano, celebrated for its spas – though you may find the alpine air and Doris's hospitality to be all the therapy you need.

Rooms	8 twin/doubles: €118-€170.
Meals	Restaurants 1km.
Closed	Rarely.

Doris Moser
Plars di Mezzo 30,
39022 Lagundo Presso Merano

Tel	+39 0473 448469
Mobile	+39 335 422942
Email	info@maratscher.com
Web	www.maratscher.com

Hotel Cavallino d'Oro

In a postcard-pretty Tyrolean village, the 'Little Gold Horse' has been welcoming travellers for 700 years. The market runs every Friday in summer, the local farmers set up their stalls at the foot of the 18th-century bell tower. This was Austria not so very long ago: the local customs are still alive, and regular concerts take place at the inn over dinner. Inside, all is as charming and pretty as can be, and bedrooms mostly delightful (note a few rooms have roof windows only). Some look onto the medieval square, the best have balconies with incredible views. There's a fascinating mix of antique country beds – some hand-decorated, some four-poster, some both. Room 9 has the original ceiling. Dine in the sparkling dining room, breakfast in the rustic *stübe*, a wood-panelled room with checked tablecloths and geraniums at the window. Susanna and Stefan are as friendly as they are efficient and the service throughout is wonderful. Take the free shuttle to the cable car up to the stunning Alpe di Siusi; swim, hike or bike in summer, sleigh ride and ski in winter, steam in the spa all year round. *Pets by arrangement.*

Rooms	7 doubles; 2 twins; 4 triples: €125–€185. 3 suites for 2: €145–€230. 4 singles: €75–€95. Extra bed/sofabed €35–€65.
Meals	Lunch €18. Dinner €25. Wine from €14.
Closed	November.

Susanna & Stefan Urthaler
Hotel Cavallino d'Oro,
Piazza Kraus 1,
39040 Castelrotto

Tel	+39 0471 706337
Email	cavallino@cavallino.it
Web	www.cavallino.it

Hotel Grones

Drama from the mountains, deep peace from the lush plateaux — you have the best of everything here. Valley views climb to craggy peaks from every bedroom window and stars and silence wrap you up at night. The Grones family converted their B&B into an immaculate hotel in 2008 and the combination of Austrian efficiency and Italian bubbliness is unbeatable: personalised menus pop up at dinner, your waitress can guide you through the wine list, and if you think five courses a night will beat you — it won't: every plate is light, fresh and totally irresistible. Take a digestif at the bar with other guests and you'll be swapping tips on where to find the most powdery snow or magnificent view. Bedrooms are capacious, light and quiet; new bathrooms gleam. Walk downhill for five minutes and you're in the centre of Ortisei, a sweet town famous for its wood carving, with shops for souvenirs and ski gear, and bars and cafés for excellent local wines and cream cakes. Above: a magical landscape, superb for skiing, cycling and hiking. Our inspector only heard one English voice on a whole week's trip — and was enchanted.

Rooms	25 doubles: €94-€230.
	Dinner, B&B €88-€230 p.p.
Meals	Wine from €15.
Closed	May & November.

Nadia Grones-Feichter
Hotel Grones,
Via Stufan 110, Val Gardena,
39046 Ortisei

Tel	+39 0471 797040
Email	hotel@grones.info
Web	www.hotelgrones.com

14 Suiten Hotel Berghofer

At the end of the meandering track: birdsong and fir trees, cowbells and meadows, the scent of larch and pine. The tranquillity continues: there are shelves of books and magazines beside the fire, pale modern furniture, an abundance of flowers, a cuckoo clock to tick away the hours. Bedrooms, named after the peaks you can see from large windows, have glazed doors to private balconies, and breathtaking Dolomites views. Rugs are scattered, pale pine floors and light walls are offset with painted wardrobes and stencilled borders. Some rooms have an extra store room, a few can be linked – ideal for a family; all have a separate sitting area and a spacious bathroom. Dine in the charming 1450 pine-cossetted stübe; the wood was purchased from a local farmer and painstakingly moved, up the hill. The restaurant is warmed by a wonderful 18th-century stove; the food is regional and stylish. Hike among the alpine flowers in summer, return to a massage or hay-sauna, catch the sunset over the mountain. The small ski resort Jochgrimm (Passo Oclini) has seven kilometres of piste and is recommended for families. *Smoking area available.*

Rooms	14 suites for 2-4: €300-€390.
	1 chalet for 2-4: €360-€390.
	Prices are for dinner, B&B for 2.
Meals	Dinner, B&B only. Wine from €20.
	Restaurant 500m.
Closed	October to end of May.

The Manager
14 Suiten Hotel Berghofer,
South Tyrol, Redagno di Sopra 54,
39040 Aldino-Redagno

Tel	+39 0471 887150
Email	info@berghofer.it
Web	www.berghofer.it

Veneto and Friuli-Venezia Giulia

Relais Ristori

In a peaceful sidestreet lies a dramatically renovated house whose bedrooms are named after literary and mythological lovers: 'Romeo and Juliet', 'Tristan and Isolde', 'Apollo and Daphne'. Step inside and all is spotless and new, with polished wooden floors and discreet air con and every wish and whim catered for: a garage, a lift, fridges in painted cabinets, a shared kitchen for a bedtime cocoa. Colours range from palest pink to canary yellow, there's a contemporary sofa in white leather, a gilt-edged rococo chair, an opulent mirror, and bathrooms are rustic-stylish, one with a jacuzzi. The big split-level rooms (with mezzanine beds under the eaves) cut the biggest dash. Plan your day over a leisurely breakfast at little tables in the breakfast room or in the courtyard (lovely in the evening). Come and go as you please in this beautiful city – and remember the code for the entrance and jot down Valentina's number just in case! Teatro Ristori on the doorstep is a must – reopened after 30 years for concerts and dance. On romantic beds between crisp white sheets you'll maybe dream of star-cross'd lovers... *Minimum stay two nights in high season. Pets by arrangement.*

Rooms	4 doubles: €135–€220.
	2 family rooms for 2 (1 double on mezzanine, 1 sofabed): €175–€225.
Meals	Restaurants nearby.
Closed	Never.

Valentina Bedogni
Relais Ristori,
Vicoletto Circolo 1, 37122 Verona

Mobile	+39 329 8376544
Email	info@relaisristori.it
Web	www.relaisristori.it

B&B Domus Nova

Stroll down the Via Mazzini, nod at Gucci and Bulgari. People-watch on the Piazza delle Erbe, where the crowds throng until 2am. Soak up grand opera beneath a starry summer sky at the Roman amphitheatre. And return to the warmth and classicism of the Domus Nova, in the car-free heart of Verona; it is wonderfully quiet. This is a grand family house that has been restored to its former splendour. Giovanni grew up here, three relatives are architects and his wife's sister is an interior designer – no wonder it's perfect. The look is luxy hotel, the feel is B&B and the views are fabulous: onto the large and lovely Piazza dei Signori and its historic tower. Bedrooms, on the third and top floors, are spacious yet cosy, immaculate yet friendly... natural pigments on walls, rich fabrics, painted beams, fine antiques, and one with a balcony so you can be Juliet for a day. The salon is equally inviting, with its comfortable leather armchairs and elegant breakfast tables, classical music and antique books. You'll imagine yourself in another century staying here. *Minimum stay two nights in doubles, three nights in suite.*

Rooms	1 double; 2 twin/doubles: €150–€230. 1 suite for 2 (with kitchenette): €250–€280. Extra bed €60.
Meals	Restaurants nearby.
Closed	Epiphany–February.

Anna & Giovanni Roberti
B&B Domus Nova,
Piazza dei Signori 18,
37121 Verona

Mobile	+39 380 7071931
Email	info@domusnovaverona.com
Web	www.domusnovaverona.com

Agriturismo Musella Relais & Winery

There's a canoe at your disposal, to ply the small river that runs through. And bikes for the roads, towels for the plunge pool and pastries for breakfast each day. Such is the generosity of the Pasqua di Bisceglie family, two of whom live within the walls of Musella; the rest live on the estate. Sweep through electric gates, park under the pergola and there's Paulo to greet you, with impeccable English and an irresistible smile. This 16th-century estate, built around a vast courtyard of grass, is a modern winery and superb B&B; and there are four apartments should you wish to do your own thing. Expect chunky rafters and country antiques, wrought-iron beds and crisp cotton sheets, harmonious colours and art on the walls. Some rooms are on the upper floors, others have their own outdoor space; others have open fires. Bathrooms are fabulous, and spacious. You may replenish your fridges from the small shop a walk away, make friends in the guest sitting room (books, open fire), savour the olive oils and the Valpolicella, fish on the river – bring your rod. Special place, special people. *Minimum stay two nights.*

Rooms	9 doubles: €145–€165.
	1 single: €100.
	1 triple: €175.
	1 apartment for 2; 3 apartments for 4:
	€225–€295.
Meals	Breakfast for self-caterers included.
	Restaurant nearby.
Closed	15 December to 1 February.

Famiglia Pasqua di Bisceglie
Via Ferrazzette 2,
San Martino Buon Albergo, 37036 Verona

Tel	+39 0459 73385
Mobile	+39 335 7294627
Email	paulo@musella.it
Web	www.musella.it

La Rosa e Il Leone

Everything about La Rosa e Il Leone, from the ancient Roman columns in the flower-filled garden to the Juliet-style balcony of the marble-floored master bedroom, breathes feeling and romance. Named after Valeria's Veronese father and Milanese mother – the Rose of Lombardy, the Lion of the Veneto – the villa is an ode to their love both for each other and for the arts. The walls sing with framed musical scores and programmes from nights at La Scala (Milan) and L'Arena (Verona), while adjoining first-floor sitting rooms celebrate the juxtaposition of the masculine (hard lines, dark colours, stacks of leather-bound books) and the feminine (curves, pastel colours, a passion for music and dance). The soft hand-woven sheets on antique-framed beds were part of Valeria's mother's dowry, the furniture part of her parents' lifetime collection. Stroll under leafy pergolas; listen to the history humming in the ancient cypresses; breakfast, deliciously, outside and admire an extraordinary replica of the Louvre's Winged Victory. Like her house, Valeria is a gold-mine of high culture. A must for anyone visiting Verona. *Minimum stay two nights.*

Rooms	2 doubles: €145.
	1 single: €85.
	Whole house, €2,050 per week.
Meals	Restaurants nearby.
Closed	Mid-October to mid-April.

Valeria Poli
La Rosa e Il Leone, Via Trieste 56,
Colognola ai Colli, 37030 Verona

Tel	+39 0457 650123
Mobile	+39 342 1084622
Email	vvpoli@libero.it
Web	www.larosaeilleone.it

Agriturismo Delo

The silence – except for the voices of vineyard workers drifting up to your window – is supreme. You would expect no less from the majestic plateau setting of this country estate surrounded by hills and mountains. Down in the valley below is Delo di Mizzole, taking its name from the Greek 'delos' meaning luminous… an entirely apt description for the 14th-century farmhouse that's been in Mariantonia's family since 1894 and is caressed by the sun all day long. The ninth-century tower is romantically derelict but that doesn't deter fabulous views of terraced olive groves and open woodland – enjoyed from the picture window in the old hay barn suite, and from the finely furnished breakfast room over handmade sweet things and savouries… views too from the bedrooms on both levels, which offer a mix of family heirlooms and mod cons. Ettore and Mariantonia are warm and hard-working; she loves dancing tango and cooking, and is happy to offer classes in either. Otherwise, go for a walk or a swim before dropping down for the high cultural delights of Verona, just five miles away.

Rooms	7 twin/doubles; 1 twin: €135–€170. 1 suite for 2-4 (1 twin/double, 1 sofabed & kitchenette): €200–€250. Extra bed €30. Singles €100–€140.
Meals	Dinner on request for groups. Restaurants nearby.
Closed	Rarely.

Ettore Mozzanega
Agriturismo Delo, Via del Torresin,
Novaglie, 37141 Verona

Tel	+39 0454 858380
Mobile	+39 333 4753688
Email	info@agriturismodelo.it
Web	www.agriturismodelo.it

Casa Rossa

Rumour has it that a temple dedicated to Venus lies in the grounds of this rust-red Verona house — something to consider over abundant homemade breakfasts on the lawn. Selva Borquez, a true polyglot, welcomes you with fresh-baked cakes and a lovely smile. You arrive down a majestic cypress-lined drive — such a surprise! — and there is the farmhouse (beyond is a villa); join hares and squirrels for peaceful bimbles in generous grounds. The atmospheric breakfast room is cosy beneath its low chunky beams, while a Persian rug perches on the mezzanine beside a sofa with computer, maps, DVDs and toys. Delightful colour-coordinated bedrooms have superb garden views: catch glimpses from the tubs and showers of big bathrooms. The blue room has a generous bed and heirlooms on the walls; the red, decorative iron bedsteads and a well-loved bureau; the yellow, a romantic canopied bed and amazing sunsets. Feast at the friendly local trattoria, marvel at nearby Santa Maria's 300AD pantheon, lose yourself amid swaying trees and half-remembered lines from Romeo and Juliet. *Small pets welcome.*

Rooms	1 double; 1 double with sofabed; 1 twin/double: €100–€110. Singles €70–€90. Extra bed €10 for children under 13; €20 for adults. Free cot available.
Meals	Guest kitchenette. Restaurant 5-minute walk.
Closed	Rarely.

Selva Borquez
Casa Rossa, Via Vendri 39,
Quinto di Valpantena, 37142 Verona

Tel	+39 045 551905
Mobile	+39 347 0569750
Email	reservation@casarossa.biz
Web	www.casarossa.biz

Delser Manor House Hotel

The views from this chic hilltop hotel are amazing, sailing over vineyards to the city of Verona. This ancient flat-topped Sicilian-like building, rescued from disrepair by designer-owner Alberto, is now (a decade on) a minimalist, museum-like hotel. Vaulted brick ceilings, Roman columns and stone arches have been reclaimed and revived in one man's homage to stone – daringly unusual for Italy! Alberto's church-like lobby and breakfast area are an archaeologist's dream. As for the bedrooms, they're a unique blend of modern luxury, natural materials and a handsome scattering of 16th-century furniture. Be spoiled by pure linen sheets and un-rugged oak floors, subtle behind-brick lighting and rainforest showers. Bio wines and olive oil are produced on the estate; breakfasts are feasts served on designer white china: tuck into local cheeses, hams, jams, fruits, cakes and breads. And then there's Verona, just minutes below, with all the romance of cobbled alleyways, Juliet's balcony, and opera beneath starry skies in a Roman arena illuminated by hand-held candles. Sensational.

Rooms	3 doubles; 6 twin/doubles: €160–€260.
Meals	Dinner on request. Restaurants in Verona, 3-minute drive.
Closed	Rarely.

Alberto Delser
Delser Manor House Hotel,
Strada dei Monti 14/B, 37124 Verona

Tel	+39 0458 011098
Mobile	+39 339 8153601
Email	info@delserverona.com
Web	www.delserverona.com

Ca' del Rocolo

Such an undemanding, delightful place to be and such an enthusiastic young family to be with. Maurizio ran a restaurant in Verona, Ilaria was a journalist and has three cookbooks to her name; they gave it all up for a country life for their children. Their 1800s farmhouse is on the side of a hill overlooking forested hills and the vast Lessinia National Park. Over a decade has passed since their move; Maurizio did much of the renovation himself and the result is authentic and attractive. Simple cotton rugs cover stripped bedroom floors, rough plaster walls are whitewashed, rooms are big and airy, with solid country furniture and excellent beds and bathrooms. There's also a shared kitchen. Breakfasts are at the long farmhouse table or out on the terrace, making the most of the views: delicious food, seasonal cakes, home-grown fruits, happy conversation. Dinner, mostly vegetarian, is an occasional affair. This is a seven-hectare, all-organic farm, with olives and fruit trees, hens, horses and beehives; there are nature trails galore, and always something going on.

Rooms	2 doubles: €63–€75; €600–€800 per wk.
	1 suite for 2 (with kitchenette): €90–€120; €410–€450 per week.
Meals	Light meals €16. Wine €6–€8. Restaurant 4km.
Closed	Rarely.

Ilaria & Maurizio Corazza
Ca' del Rocolo,
Via Gaspari 3, Loc. Quinto,
37142 Verona

Tel	+39 0458 700879
Email	info@cadelrocolo.com
Web	www.cadelrocolo.com

Agriturismo alle Torricelle

The renovation of this old convent — where Fiorella's husband was born and raised — has removed most of its crumbling history but filled every corner with its proprietor's personality. The kitchen and Fiorella's constant activity in it fill the place (and, most importantly the breakfast table) with food. Having sent the men out to work gathering and tending ingredients in the grounds, she sets herself to cooking... everything from baked quince jelly to breads, cakes, pastries and three types of biscuit. When she isn't cooking, Fiorella is seeking out and hoarding antiques and handmade flea market finds for decorating the ground-floor, the first-floor and the two (big) attic rooms. Views are either to the olive groves at the back or of the houses and hills at the front, with central Verona drawing the eye. Torricelle is agriturismo as it should be, with the charming clutter and hubbub of a working environment, strutting geese and a joyous host; it's a wonderfully warm-hearted and relaxing place. Visitors bustle in for a chat or for lunch, and the sleepy city of Verona is just down the hill.

Rooms	3 doubles (shared bathroom): €70–€90. 1 suite for 3: €90–€120. 5 triples (shared bathroom): €80–€105. 1 quadruple (shared bathroom): €120–€140. Singles from €50 to €70.
Meals	Dinner €20–€50. Restaurants 5-minute drive.
Closed	Never.

Fiorella dal Negro
Agriturismo alle Torricelle,
Via Bonuzzo S.Anna 4/A,
37128 Verona

Tel   +39 0458 300230
Email info@agriturismotorricelle.com
Web   www.agriturismotorricelle.com

Entry 60   Map 3

Casa Colonica

Live la dolce vita in these splendid apartments, one on top of the other in a renovated farmhouse in the grounds of a 16th-century villa. Each flat is bright and airy, with 85 square metres to stretch out in and fine views; they reach across the villa's parkland and to the Lessinia mountains. Décor is pure charm – stone tiled floors, chunky beamed ceilings, rich rugs and curtains, pretty flower prints, a child's wardrobe in the shape of a lighthouse… Modern furnishings – iron bedsteads in the twin rooms, wooden beds in the doubles – mingle with rustic antiques, and there's no TV: tune out of the 21st century! Shaded by the tiled roof, the terrace is a great spot to sip prosecco or burrow into a book. Rustle up breakfast in your well-equipped kitchens or join the B&B guests around the oval table in the villa for a lavish spread featuring local goodies; you can also use the garden's big fenced pool. The owners are sisters; charming Chiarastella lives in the grounds with her family, and can organise everything, from a box of Lego for the kids to a private flight over Verona. Wonderful.

Rooms	2 apartments for 4: €1,000–€1,400 per week.
Meals	Breakfast €15. Light meals and supper on request. Restaurants 1km.
Closed	Never.

Ludovica Sagramoso Sacchetti
Casa Colonica,
Via Giovanni Battista Dalla Riva 3,
37139 Verona
Mobile   +39 333 7236582 / +39 345 3010330
Email   ludovicasagramoso@olona11.com
Web   www.villasagramososacchetti.it

Relais Villa Sagramoso Sacchetti

Nothing quite prepares you for the splendour of this 16th-century Venetian villa, gazing over the Valpolicella valley to the mountains of Lessinia; from bedrooms to gardens to pool it exudes atmosphere and style. The 40-year-long restoration by the Sagramoso Sacchetti family has been a labour of love and is a source of pride; sisters Chiarastella and Ludovica take huge pleasure in sharing its bounty. Enter the lofty hallway, marvel at the frescoed drawing room, climb the stone stair to luxurious suites. Who would not love the elegant wallpapers and the perfect counterpanes, the chunky chestnut beams and the sweeping terracotta, the huge flowers and the family antiques? Bathrooms are bliss. The day starts at the big oval table overseen by the ancestors; fruits are from the orchard, butter from the farmer up the road, special diets are no problem. Outside the gate is the bus to Verona, the cycle path too (five miles); there's a stunning new cable car to Monte Baldo, wine lovers can follow the Strada del Vino Valpolicella, foodies can swoon over the Veneto risottos. *Children over nine welcome.*

Rooms	4 doubles: €160–€180.
	2 suites for 3-4: €220–€280.
Meals	Restaurants 500m.
Closed	10 November to 31 March.

Chiarastella & Ludovica
Sagramoso Sacchetti
Via Giovanni Battista Dalla Riva 5/1,
Loc. Corno, 37139 Verona
Mobile +39 333 7236582 / +39 345 3010330
Email info@villasagramososacchetti.it
Web www.villasagramososacchetti.it

Bagolina B&B

Once run as a tobacconist's by her grandfather, this 18th-century house in the Veronese suburb of Parona is now in Elena's deftly modern hands. Living on site with her family close by, she has overseen the transformation while grandfather enjoys wine tasting in the cellar next to his old *Sali & Tabacchi* sign. Everything is new, right down to the window frames. Beginning at the top, the three bedrooms are delightfully presented with wooden floors and pale beams providing the framework for gentler touches such as heather pink and cream walls, gauzy curtains and pretty rose-prints above the beds. The best overlooks the inner courtyard with its garden sofa and rust-coloured chairs; the river Adige can just be glimpsed from another. In the sitting room downstairs a large bookcase is crammed with books about the Veneto and cookery, while a new white wood-burning stove keeps things cosy. Elena prides herself on her breakfasts, her fruit salads in particular, enjoyed in the bright kitchen or the courtyard. This is the time to ask her about day trips, or booking opera at the Arena.

Rooms	2 doubles: €80–€150.
	1 single: €70–€130.
	Singles €90.
Meals	Restaurants nearby.
Closed	Rarely.

Elena Marastoni
Bagolina B&B,
Via Valpolicella 10,
37124 Verona
Mobile   +39 340 5225747
Email   info@bagolina.it
Web   www.bagolina.it

Bagolina Apartments

Grandfather has taken the *Sali & Tabacchi* sign down to the cellar, where you can join him for wine tasting and stories; he once ran this 18th-century townhouse as a tobacconist's. That was before everything fell into Elena's deftly modern hands. Now she has created two brand new self-catering apartments beneath her own home where she does B&B. You enter a well-equipped kitchenette framed around a simple white wooden table and chairs, before moving towards, on one side, the bedroom with its green wrought-iron bedstead and purple cover; on the other side is the pretty blue-tiled shower. There's a food shop right outside and a trattoria minutes away – perfect. But it's almost as easy jumping on the bus to Verona and the welcoming Elena is as happy arranging opera tickets for the Arena as she is organising trips to Lake Garda and Monte Baldo; cookery lessons too. Relax at the end of the day in Elena's living room, shared with the other guests and packed with books on the Veneto – or in the pretty courtyard with a glass of something special from the welcome basket. Two romantic apartments on the edge of Verona, for couples.

Rooms	2 apartments for 2: €75–€95; €420–€540 per week.
Meals	Restaurants nearby.
Closed	Rarely.

Elena Marastoni
Bagolina Apartments,
Via Valpolicella 10,
37124 Verona
Mobile   +39 340 5225747
Email   info@bagolina.it
Web   www.bagolina.it

Barca Innamad

Hop aboard Venice's one and only gonda-lodge. With personal space being hard to come by in this frenetic city Barca Innamad is a mini haven. Moored beside Venice's spectacular Basilica di San Marco, this buoyant B&B is both a cosy bolt-hole and the perfect means of seeing the sinking city. You'll be oared by how spacious this little boat is, sleeping up to three (top to tail). Bathrooms aren't in short supply — just spare a thought for your neighbours! Bedding has been made using the finest sails in Veneto and wood prevails in this exquisitely carved vessel. Leaks are rare. This floating treasure was dreamed up by your host, Signor Dola, a champion boatwright and self-proclaimed Maestro of the accordion. He will be happy to serenade you come low or high tide. Breakfast in bed on the catch of the day, dropped in by the local gulls. Row your way down meandering canals, stop off for lunch at Venice's lesser-known locandas, reachable only by water. Perfect for adventurous couples and those wanting to rock the boat. Don't forget to pack your sea legs!

Rooms	1 double: €5.
Meals	Fresh seafood, whether requested or not.
Closed	Never.

Signor Gon Dola
Barca Innamad,
Via Aqua 6, 54321

Tel	+39 0000 000000
Email	gon@barcainnamad.it
Web	www.barcainnamad.com

Antico Casale Bergamini

You're in Valpolicella country, just beyond Verona, where clusters of houses alternate with tilled terraces glowing with vines. Here lies the Bergaminis' enormous 17th-century farmhouse with a dapper outdoor pool. Set around a large garden, outbuildings that date to the 17th-century have been transformed into light, bright, immaculate guest suites with classic furnishings and dashing colours. Take your pick from first-floor rooms (one with steps to its own little garden) endowed with elegant bedsteads, gleaming tiled floors, two sets of curtains (and handy mini fridges) and second-floor suites with bedrooms under the eaves and hidden mini kitchens. All have super bathrooms and showers with shower benches, and there's a very lovely bedroom on the ground floor. In the breakfast room, big and beamy, gentle young Silvia spoils you with lavish breakfasts and pies bursting with home-grown fruit... don't miss the garden's plums, the plumpest you'll ever see! Tempting to stay but there's Verona to discover, vineyards galore (the family is soon to get their own label), Lake Garda close by and restaurants a short drive.

Rooms	2 doubles; 4 twin/doubles: €120–€150. 2 suites for 3; 1 suite for 4: €160–€220. Singles €95–€120.
Meals	Restaurants in Valpolicella, a 5-minute drive.
Closed	Rarely.

Silvia Bergamini
Antico Casale Bergamini, Via Stazione
Vecchia 764, 37015 Gargagnago

Tel	+39 0456 831546
Mobile	+39 392 8787404
Email	info@anticocasalebergamini.com
Web	www.anticocasalebergamini.com

Pianaura Suites, The Towers in the Vineyards

In the hills above Verona, surrounded by olive groves and vines, a slice of Veneto heaven. Two fat mellow towers linked by an underground tunnel stand side by side: one, Mara and Filippo's home; the other, 17th-century with an exquisite renovation, the B&B. On its ground floor is the breakfast/living room, above are two suites on two floors. There's a spa house alongside (yoga, Balinese massage, sunken jacuzzi) and a bottle of wine from Mara, whose welcome is as warm as can be. Heating/cooling is geothermal, solar panels are hidden, the metal and iroko stairway is a work of art and the views are to die for. Inside are modern resin floors, wooden ceilings painted white, and walls in ivory and dove grey – a minimalist and immaculate backdrop to an inspirational mélange of vintage and designer pieces. No wardrobes but ingenious rails, no curtains but shutters, no paintings but treasures from oriental travels, and a kitchenette for the top floor. Breakfasts are different every day, perhaps homemade cake or cherries from the trees. Wonderful – and you get your very own rustic pergola, too. *Children over 13 welcome.*

Rooms	2 suites for 2: €140–€180.
	Extra bed €30 for adults.
	Singles €30 discount.
	€910–€1,050 p.w. for self-caterers.
Meals	Restaurants 1.5km.
Closed	Rarely.

Mara Pasqualicchio
Pianaura Suites, The Towers in the
Vineyards, via Pianaura 7,
37020 Marano di Valpolicella

Mobile	+39 329 4944884
Email	pianaura@libero.it
Web	www.pianaura.it

La Finestra sul Fiume

An easy drive from Verona, close to Borghetto, is a 14th-century mill in bird-chirped grounds. Here live Pietro, Mattea and little Diletta, plus cats and three resident geese – welcome to the loveliest family. The guest bedrooms are in two outbuildings – rustic, ivy-strewn and charmingly revived. One is super private, with its bedroom up a spiral stair. White walls are rough plastered, colours are blue, brown, cream and grey, bathrooms are contemporary and views are breathtaking – over park, river, 14th-century bridge and hilltop castello. Breakfast on a rainy day in a big canvas gazebo; on a fine one, by the water under the willows. Pietro and Mattea go out of their way to give each guest the breakfast of their dreams… find yourself feasting on pastries, fruits, hams and cheeses lovingly and locally sourced. Swim in the natural pool, watch the swans drift by, nod off in the hammock, or check out one of the golf courses – Pietro is a golf instructor! Then stroll into the village – watery, exquisite – for a delicious tortellini or a perfect gelato. *Children and pets welcome by arrangement.*

Rooms	3 doubles: €140–€170.
Meals	Restaurants in Borghetto, a 15-minute walk.
Closed	December-February.

Pietro & Mattea Gandini
La Finestra sul Fiume, Vicolo Corte
Sega 2, 37067 Valeggio sul Mincio

Tel	+39 0457 950556
Mobile	+39 340 933 8194
Email	info@lafinestrasulfiume.it
Web	www.lafinestrasulfiume.it

Agriturismo Tenuta La Pila

Raimonda and Alberto will soon have you chatting over a welcome drink; he speaks a clutch of languages, she's bubbly, both are committed to the green way of life. Each B&B room is named after a fruit and smartly decorated: find cream walls, exposed brick, crisp linen, fluffy towels, and antique furniture to add a homely touch. Two of the apartments are in a separate building once used for drying tobacco; they have immensely high beams and are decorated in a similar style. You get a table, chairs and sofabed in the large central living area, and a neat corner kitchen; cheerful bedrooms have flower prints and checked bedspreads; two further apartments have oak floors and country antiques. Breakfast is a spread of home produce: kiwi jam, eggs, fruit, bread, yogurt. The farm is surrounded by fertile fields, trees and kiwi vines meandering across the plains, with the beautiful towns of Rovigo and Chioggia close by. Return to a peaceful patio-garden, a dip in the pool, and skittles and boules beside the huge magnolia. A happy place. *Minimum stay two nights.*

Rooms	2 twin/doubles; 3 triples: €65–€80. Singles €45–€55. 2 apartments for 2–4; 2 apartments for 4–5: €678–€905 per week.
Meals	Breakfast €5 for self-caterers. Dinner €20. Wine €5–€10. Restaurants 2km.
Closed	Rarely.

Raimonda & Alberto Sartori
Agriturismo Tenuta La Pila,
Via Pila 42, Loc. Spinimbecco,
37049 Villa Bartolomea

Tel	+39 0442 659289
Email	post@tenutalapila.it
Web	www.tenutalapila.com

Il Castello

A narrow road winds up to the *castello* at the foot of the Berici hills – a special getaway. Also known as the Villa Godi-Marinoni – it was built by Count Godi in the 15th century – its massive hewn walls enclose a compound of terraced vines, orchard, Italian garden and views that stretch all the way to Padua. You enter via an arched entrance, ancient cobbles beneath your feet. The villa itself is still lived in by the courteous owners, Signora Marinoni and her son, who run this vast estate together. Olive oil is produced, and there's a wine cellar in the bowels of the castle – ask if you can buy a bottle. The apartments, bright and clean (note, one with its kitchen on the far side of the courtyard), are in an outbuilding with gothic details in the plastered façade; all are simply, pleasantly furnished with family antiques and modern pieces. Hidden below the castle walls is the garden with fish pond; in spring, hundreds of lemon trees are wheeled out to stand on grand pedestals. The climate is mild and the hillside a mass of olive groves; recline on the lawns, stroll down to the village for supper. *Minimum stay three nights. Price per person on request.*

Rooms	1 apartment for 2; 2 apartments for 3; 1 apartment for 5: €476–€1,190 per wk. Extra bed/sofabed €29 per night. Discount for stays over 7 nights.
Meals	Self-catering.
Closed	Never.

Elda Marinoni
Il Castello,
Via Castello 6,
36021 Barbarano Vicentino

Tel	+39 0444 886055
Email	info@castellomarinoni.com
Web	www.castellomarinoni.com

Due Mori

On a pretty street plumb in the heart of medieval Marostica lies an 18th-century townhouse. Step through the glass doors and it's bright and inviting: modern design abounds, wood and stone blend with glass and steel. Choose from 12 blissfully quiet, sleek bedrooms, four on each floor and all en suite: think white walls, dark linseed-oiled floors, cherry-wood headboards, perhaps a sofa. Bathrooms have soft lighting and sleek taps. The 'Castle' rooms with beams and tile ceilings are the most luxurious – and you glimpse the upper castle through the windows. 'King' bedrooms are brilliant for families, 'Queen' are for those on a budget. Out on the small patio, feast on a breakfast of Asiago cheese, fruit and pastries. The lovely young family who run Due Mori live nearby; Monica is a tourist guide and knows her stuff. Explore the two castles, lively square and untouristy shops – you might even witness the giant chess game enacted with human chess pieces! And taste Marostica's legendary cherries before you leave.

Rooms	11 twin/doubles: €94–€179.
	1 single: €64–€84.
Meals	Restaurant 50m.
Closed	Rarely.

Monica Facchini
Due Mori,
Corso Mazzini 73,
36063 Marostica

Tel	+39 0424 471777
Email	info@duemori.it
Web	www.duemori.it

Ca' Marcello

Mythical statues, manicured lawns, potted lemon trees, Italian fountain: the grounds are rich in wonderful plants and the woods consist of century-old trees. Such is the setting for this Palladian-style villa with its warm, elegant, slightly faded cream façade, and your wing comes with its own private garden. Venice owes her history of great naval battles in part to the long line of captains in the Marcello family: this represents their legacy. So take a private tour of the main house and its fresco-filled ballroom; peer in awe at the ancestral portraits on the walls. Despite its history and significance Ca'Marcello is still a family home, and the atmosphere is relaxed and inviting: kind, softly spoken Jacopo grew up here and will ensure a luxurious stay. Expect beeswax-polished stairs and lovely low-ceiling'd rooms spread over two floors, in perfect condition yet virtually untouched since the 18th-century; a well-equipped kitchen (though a chef can be arranged if that's what you'd prefer; a stylish salon and your own exquisite pool. Guiding art tours are on request. *Minimum stay seven nights in high season.*

Rooms	1 apartment for 8: €2,800–€4,200 per wk.
Meals	Breakfast €12, lunch/dinner €35.
	Children's menu €20.
	Restaurants 2km.
Closed	Never.

Jacopo Marcello
Ca' Marcello,
Via del Marcello 13,
35017 Levada di Piombino Dese

Tel	+39 0499 350340
Email	info@camarcello.it
Web	www.camarcello.it

Agriturismo La Presa

The agriturismo is Lucia's baby, she looks after both farm (crops and cattle) and guests wonderfully, having done B&B for five years now. So bowl along the flatlands of the Po delta, pass the chicken factory, sweep up the poplar-lined drive – Lucia has planted hundreds – into a peaceful, jasmine-scented farmstead, resuscitated after carpet insect-bombing and now humming with frogs, bees and birds. Bats and swallows are back, too, and Lucia's nature trail is brilliant. Brick paths link the main house (two bedrooms) to the rest in a converted farm building. Inside, all feels clean, simple, spacious and cool. Shower rooms are new, floors are warm with rugs, walls are light green and the 'single' beds in the annexe are more like small doubles. The beamed dining room is most inviting, meat roasts (and pizzas) are done in Lucia's new wood-fired pizza oven. Breakfasts promise homemade tarts and the chestnut table seats 16. Friend Alberto knows the delta deeply – let him take you up the river for oysters. Or bicycle out into the flat reclaimed countryside. *Minimum stay two nights.*

Rooms	2 doubles (sharing bath): €85. 1 suite for 2; 4 mezzanine suites for 4–6 in annexe: €85–€145. Cot available in suite.
Meals	Dinner with wine, €30. Restaurant 6km.
Closed	6–31 January.

Lucia La Presa
Agriturismo La Presa, Via Cornera 12,
Taglio di Po, 45019 Rovigo

Tel	+39 0426 661594
Mobile	+39 338 8683431
Email	info@lapresa.it
Web	www.lapresa.it

Villa Tron Carrara Mioni

You're in a central spot – perfect for exploring the delightful towns of the Veneto region. Gabriella and Sandro are a considerate, charming couple who give you three lovely apartments in the rural annexe of their 19th-century villa surrounded by acres of elegant gardens and woodland. Whichever apartment you choose you'll find the original style and atmosphere of an old Venetian house with wooden and terracotta tiled floors, beamed ceilings and doors leading to the portico and gardens. Antique furniture is from the owners' collection and is offset with some more modern pieces for a fresh, lively style. 'Altana' (the biggest) has a small private sitting space under the linden trees with a table, chairs and chaise longue; 'Mezà' and 'Portico' (both for two) can use the *barchessa* garden with their own table, chairs and benches for dining. Kitchens are slick with mod cons and American coffee machines, air-conditioning keeps you comfortable on the hottest days and views soar across the historical garden with its old trees – wander round the serene lake, feed the ducks, discover the shy grey heron. *Minimum stay two nights B&B, four nights self-catering.*

Rooms	2 apartments for 2; 1 apartment for 4: €490–€1,260 per week. Ask about B&B prices.
Meals	Restaurants 200m.
Closed	Rarely.

Alessandro & Gabriella Mioni
Villa Tron Carrara Mioni,
Via Ca' Tron 23,
30031 Dolo

Tel	+39 0414 10177
Email	villatron@libero.it
Web	www.villatron.it

Entry 74 Map 4

Hotel Villa Alberti

Pluck fruit from the orchard, wash it in the fountain, pick a quiet spot in the walled garden. This 17th-century villa, once the summer residence of Venetian nobility, has been restored by the delightful Malerbas to combine grand features with a warm and unstuffy mood. Beautiful shutters and floors, Murano lights and chandeliers, decorative ironwork lamps and balconies... all has been reclaimed and revived. And it is no wonder Gianni is proud of his garden, its box-lined paths, statues and century-old trees, its exceptional roses, its carpets of wild flowers; it develops as it matures. The reception hall – a sweep of dark polished wood, rich rugs and deep sofas – leads to three floors of bedrooms furnished in a simple but refined style: wooden or stone floors, silky bedspreads, a few antiques; ask for one overlooking the garden rather than the road. The rooms in the *barchessa* are more rustic and somewhat blander. Feast on delicious risottos on the terrace in the summer; you could get used to the aristocratic life! A direct bus runs quickly to Venice from Dolo, or you can go by boat; here you are peacefully out of town.

Rooms	20 doubles: €90–€130.
Meals	Dinner €25. Wine €15. Restaurant 300m.
Closed	Rarely.

Famiglia Malerba
Hotel Villa Alberti,
Via E. Tito 90, 30031 Dolo
Tel   +39 0414 266512
Email   info@villalberti.it
Web   www.villalberti.it

Ca' Priuli

Midway between Venice and Padua: what a spot for a big old village villa overlooking the Brenta river. The plain red-wash exterior is dwarfed by the houses behind but inside is another story; welcome to a light, bright, minimalist restoration, a modernist's delight. White walls and clean lines heighten the beauty of chunky beams and Venetian terrazzo floors, creating an atmosphere of light, serenity and space. There's a suite with a kitchenette in the barn and four bedrooms on the first floor, private and peaceful behind double wooden doors. Your architect-designer hostess, delightful Mirva, lives above. Fabulous beds have thick pale bedspreads, bathrooms are marble-clad, shuttered windows flutter in white voile. Go for a room that faces the pretty river if you can. There's no garden but a *salone* with suave leather sofas, a bar for a drink on the house, and a quiet room for books: all you need to know on villas to visit (some Palladian) and birdwatching, boating and fishing on the Brenta. Breakfasts are long and leisurely, shops and restaurants are walking distance. Great value.

Rooms	4 doubles, 1 suite for 4 (2 doubles): €60–€130.
Meals	Restaurants nearby.
Closed	Rarely

Mirva Bertan
Ca' Priuli,
Ettore Tito 72, 30031 Dolo

Tel	+39 0414 266895
Mobile	+39 329 2297454
Email	info@capriuli.it
Web	www.capriuli.it

Entry 76   Map 4

Villa Colloredo

Handsomely ranged around a courtyard, these 18th-century Venetian buildings – all peachy stone and olive shutters – hold a cool surprise. Bold paintings, modern sculptures and colourful collages dot their interiors: part of the collection of the Meneghelli family. Architecturally, these former stables and grain stores, next to the family villa, fuse modern styling with original features. Beamed ceilings and wooden or tiled floors contrast with streamlined kitchens, simple rustic furniture and artwork on white walls. Spaces have been imaginatively used – a shower, perhaps, in a glass-topped cube – to maximise the open feel. Upper floors have lovely low windows, with views to fields, orchards or courtyard. Two of the larger apartments can be joined together – great for families. The outdoor cloisters are a tranquil place to sit and read, or set out lunch; behind the villa are wonderful natural gardens to explore. Drop in on Padua, look forward to the restaurants of Dolo, cool off in the Dolomites, or catch the water bus (from Fusina) to Venice. Family-run with a welcoming feel – plus two friendly dogs and a cat. *Minimum stay two nights.*

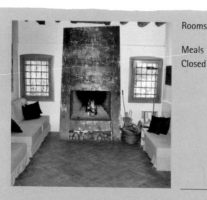

Rooms	1 double: €60-€80.
	4 apartments for 4: €80-€110.
Meals	Restaurant 500m.
Closed	7 January to 4 February;
	17 February to 26 March;
	3 November to 20 December.

Sara Frison
Villa Colloredo,
Brusaura 24,
30030 Sambruson di Dolo

Mobile	+39 348 2102337
Email	info@villacolloredo.com
Web	www.villacolloredo.com

Entry 77   Map 4

Locanda al Leon

Such friendly people and such a perfect spot: three minutes walk from everything that matters (the Basilica end of St Mark's Square, the airport bus and the vaporetto stops). This small, unpretentious, family-run hotel, its characterful old entrance down a tiny alley, is an excellent choice if you're visiting Venice on a tightish budget but want to be at the centre of it all. It's been modestly modernised. Clean, carpeted bedrooms (the biggest on the corner of the building, looking onto the Campo San Filippo e Giacomo and the Calle degli Albanesi) have Venetian-style bedheads with scrolled edges and floral motifs; there are matching striped counterpanes and curtains, modern Murano chandeliers and neat shower rooms. The apartment, a five-minute walk from the hotel, is ideal for families. Breakfast is taken at a handful of tables on the big, first-floor landing (no lift) buffet-style: breads and croissants, yogurts and fruit juice – what you'd expect for the price. And there's no shortage of advice – one or two members of the delightful dall'Agnola family are always around. *Minimum stay two nights at weekends.*

Rooms	8 doubles: €80-€210.
	2 singles: €60-€130.
	1 triple: €100-€250.
	1 apartment for 4: €100-€300.
	Singles €60-€130.
Meals	Restaurants nearby.
Closed	Rarely.

Marcella & Giuliano dall'Agnola
Locanda al Leon,
Campo Santi Filippo e Giacamo 4270,
Castello, 30122 Venice

Tel	+39 0412 770393
Email	leon@hotelalleon.com
Web	www.hotelalleon.com

Al Teatro

For four generations, Eleanora's family have watched the gondolas and singing gondoliers glide by this bright palazzo opposite the Teatro La Fenice. No one really knows the age of the house, but it's surely 15th century judging by the frescoes, marble stairs, stucco and floors *alla Veneziana*. Old world luxury meets new in three canal-facing bedrooms: colourful fabric on antique chairs, headboards and even walls matches old walnut – a seriously Italian indulgence – and one room opts for the red velvety cube-style armchairs that would have graced a patrician's posterior. The Green Room might just be the prettiest, and a glimpse through ephemeral curtains sees white cushions playfully fastened to an iron bedstead... all beneath a chandelier and eventually sliding onto terrazzo floors of a state-of-the-art bathroom. That's what works here: it's smart and chic, but has the intimacy and pedigree of something smaller, grander. As well as managing three children, Eleanora greets each guest personally; over breakfast in the dining room is a good time to question this bona fide Venetian. *Singles prices on request.*

Rooms	3 twin/doubles: €90–€200. Extra beds available.
Meals	Wine €20–€25. Restaurants nearby.
Closed	Rarely.

Eleonora Agostini
Al Teatro, San Marco 2554,
Fondamenta de la Fenice,
30124 Venice

Tel	+39 0415 204271
Email	bbalteatro@alice.it
Web	www.bedandbreakfastalteatro.com

Bloom & Settimo Cielo Guest House

In the heart of Venice, yet not overwhelmed by tourists, is a perfectly restored house and *residenza*. You check in round the corner, then delightful reception escorts you to your room. No lift, so be prepared to carry bags to the second (Settimo Cielo) and third (Bloom) floors; on the fourth is the sitting room – books, guide books, your own prosecco in the fridge. From here, step out to the roof top terrace, a privileged spot with a panoramic view, magically lit at night. Back down to the six bedrooms – what fun the owners had in their creation! Spacious and filled with light, named after colours not numbers, they are a beguiling mix of funky and grand. Bows in navy, lilac, cerise attach themselves to doors behind which a heady mix of Venetian baroque and modern minimalism lies; romantic too, though 'Cream' takes the biscuit. Expect raw silk and floating organza, button-back leather and pale painted beams, gilt mirrors and glass-fronted fridges, fine antiques and bathrooms small but exquisite. Buffet breakfasts are elegant and the Chiesa San Vidal is three minutes away – a peerless setting for Vivaldi. *Minimum stay two nights, three nights in high season.*

Rooms	4 doubles: €118-€309.
	2 triples: €158-€329.
Meals	Restaurants nearby.
Closed	Never.

Alessandra Vazzoler & Paolo Battistetti
Bloom & Settimo Cielo Guest House,
Campiello Santo Stefano, San Marco
3470, 30124 Venice

Mobile	+39 340 1498872
Email	info@bloom-venice.com
Web	www.bloom-venice.com

Corte Vecchia

Aesthetics sweep the board at this rust-red Venetian palazzo, where sober retro meets modern and tradition meets design; it's a classic, colourful space. Ascend white marble steps to meet your lovely, heart-on-sleeves hosts, Antonella and Mauro (both architects); follow their tips to avoid tourist traps. Space is at a premium on this man-made isle so breakfast's hot croissants and Venetian biscuits arrive on a trolley. Enjoy it in your room or in the lofty hall, the *piano nobile* of the house, an arched space with vast, sunlight-streamed windows, vintage velvet chairs and books jostling to be thumbed. In the sea-green room, mozzie nets drape iron bedsteads and ornate antique dressers stand sentry. Summery gauze billows at windows... enjoy Rio Terra San Vio views or your room's contemporary artworks. The four-poster Corte bedroom overlooks the courtyard; bright-red accent walls are set off by citric Sixties' armchairs and a sparkling Murano glass chandelier. Vibrant mosaic bathrooms are state-of-the-art. With just three B&B rooms, you'll soon feel at ease with your lovely bright hosts. *Minimum stay two nights.*

Rooms	1 twin/double; 1 twin/double with separate shower: €90–€130. Singles: €65–€100. Extra bed/sofabed available €15–€20 per person per night.
Meals	Restaurants 10-minute walk.
Closed	Rarely.

Antonella Maione
Corte Vecchia,
Dorsoduro 462, Rio Terà San Vio,
30123 Venice

Tel +39 0418 221233
Email info@cortevecchia.net
Web www.cortevecchia.net

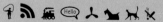

Pensione La Calcina

Catch the sea breezes of early evening from the terrace butting out over the water as you watch the beautiful people stroll the Zattere. Or gaze across the lagoon to the Rendentore. Ruskin stayed here in 1876, and for many people this corner of town, facing the Giudecca and with old Venice just behind you, is the best. The hotel has been discretely modernised by its charming owners; comfortable bedrooms have air con, antiques and parquet floors. Those at the front, with views, are dearer; the best are the corner rooms, with windows on two sides. A small top terrace can be booked for romantic evenings and you can breakfast, lunch or dinner at the delightful floating restaurant, open to all – delicious dishes are available all day and the fruit juices and milkshakes are scrummy. Pause for a moment and remember Ruskin's words on the city he loved: "a ghost upon the sands of the sea, so weak, so quiet, so bereft of all but her loveliness, that we might well doubt, as we watched her faint reflection on the mirage of the lagoon, which was the City and which the shadow." The vaporetto is a step away.

Rooms	20 doubles: €110–€350.
	7 singles: €90–€150.
Meals	Lunch/dinner with glass of wine, €30–€60.
	Restaurant closed Mondays.
Closed	Never.

Tognon Corrado
Pensione La Calcina,
Ruskin's House, Dorsoduro 780,
Zattere, 30123 Venice

Tel	+39 0415 206466
Email	info@lacalcina.com
Web	www.lacalcina.com

Fujiyama Bed & Breakfast

Jasmine, wisteria, shady trees – hard to believe this pool of oriental tranquillity is minutes from the hurly-burly of Venice's streets and the grandeur of the Rialto and St Mark's Square. Even more unusual – for this city – is to step through an oriental tea room to reach your bedroom. The four bedrooms are on the upper two floors of this tall, narrow, 18th-century townhouse and continue the gentle Japanese theme. The owners lived in Japan for years, and their love of the Far East is evident throughout. With views over the garden or the lovely Venetian rooftops, the rooms exude a light, airy and ordered calm with their polished dark wood floors, white walls, Japanese prints and simple oriental furnishings. Shower rooms are small but neat and spotless. Breakfast on the terrace in summer or in the tea room in winter. A charming and warm host, full of stories and happy to chat, Elena will recommend good local restaurants – especially those specialising in fish. Retreat here after a busy day exploring this magical city and sip a cup of jasmine tea on the shady terrace.

Rooms	4 doubles: €70–€160.
Meals	Restaurants next door.
Closed	Never.

Elena Piaggi
Fujiyama Bed & Breakfast,
Calle Lunga San Barnaba 2727A,
Dorsoduro, 30123 Venice

Tel	+39 0417 241042
Email	info@bedandbreakfast-fujiyama.it
Web	www.bedandbreakfast-fujiyama.it

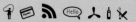

Palazzo Tiepolo

Old-fashioned grandeur at its best, and the approach down the narrow alley gives nothing away. This 16th-century beauty has been in the Tiepolo family forever and friendly Lelia oversees the ongoing restoration. 'Tiepolo', the ground-floor studio, has been cleverly thought out. A beautifully equipped and stocked kitchen tucks behind cupboard doors, the shower room is in a corner, the gem of a dining area overlooks the life of the Grand Canal, and you fall asleep to the lapping waters: such a privileged position. 'Valier', the more spacious apartment across the garden, is beautifully peaceful; enjoy a glass of wine in your own courtyard and listen to the chirruping birds. Cream and pale terracotta walls bedecked with prints and gilt mirrors set off rich rugs and Venetian furniture in the living room, the walk-in shower and kitchen are in opposite corners and wide wooden stairs lead to the mezzanine's bed, encased in embroidered linen. For grand old style, go B&B and take the antique-filled suite in the house. Breakfast is formally served on bone china and the history of the Tiepolos surrounds you. *Minimum three nights in apartments.*

Rooms	1 suite for 2: €150–€250 per night.
	2 apartments for 2: €850–€1,050 per wk.
Meals	Restaurants nearby.
Closed	Never.

Lelia Passi
Palazzo Tiepolo,
Calle Centani, San Polo 2774,
30125 Venice

Tel	+39 0415 227989
Email	leliapassi@gmail.com
Web	www.cortetiepolo.com

B&B Corte 1321

Go down a narrow alleyway, through a large and lovely courtyard, high walls towering above, and enter a 15th-century palazzo. The apartment is on the ground floor, the B&B on the first. Inside, catch your breath at the calm, eclectic décor of oriental rugs, silk curtains, fresh flowers and influences from Bali and Morocco. Amelia is a Californian artist and her paintings hang on every wall. She, her baby and her mother Deborah live nearby; it's her likeable assistants Maria and Suhbash, both with good English, who minister impeccably to your needs. Most guests are English speaking and bedrooms have been designed to meet American expectations: the best linen, mattresses and showers; hand-crafted beds; WiFi. One room looks onto the canal, the other two onto the courtyard. In the apartment downstairs the style is uncluttered, the whitewashed walls making the most of the light. Breakfast is a pretty basket of brioche and bread in the courtyard. The little vaporetto is five minutes away – no bridges! – the local shop is across the square and the Rialto, markets and Accademia are nearby. *Pets by arrangement.*

Rooms	1 family room for 2-3; 2 family rooms for 2-4; 1 apartment for 4: €125-€220 per night.
Meals	Restaurants nearby.
Closed	Rarely.

Amelia Bonvini
B&B Corte 1321,
San Polo 1321,
30125 Venice

Tel	+39 0415 224923
Email	info@corte1321.com
Web	www.corte1321.com

Casa San Boldo – Grimani, Loredan & Manin

Your own tennis court – in Venice! Borrow a racket, or watch others from the jasmine-covered bandstand in the garden. Francesca's parents live on the ground floor and share both court and garden. These well-restored apartments are elegant yet cosy, with family antiques, fresh flowers, smart sofas and Persian rugs on parquet floors. There are intriguing quirks too: an original window and its glass preserved as a piece of art, a 1756 dowry chest from Alto Adige. And you're never far from a window with bustling canal views. 'Loredan', the smaller apartment on the first floor, has a sweet twin/double tucked away beneath the rafters, and a larger double room downstairs with modern paintings by a local artist. The little kitchen is beautifully equipped, the dining room has high ceilings and a Venetian marble floor. 'Grimani' has a bedroom on the ground floor with garden views and another up; the super new 'Manin' is also on the ground floor. Multi-lingual Francesca who lives nearby is kind, friendly and runs cookery courses that include buying the produce from the Rialto market, just around the corner.

Rooms	1 apartment for 2; 2 apartments for 4: €900-€1,950 per week. Breakfast €8.
Meals	Self-catering.
Closed	Never.

Francesca Pasti
Casa San Boldo,
San Polo 2281,
30125 Venice

Tel   +39 0421 66171
Email   info@adriabella.com
Web   www.adriabella.com

Entry 86   Map 4

Oltre Il Giardino

A corner of paradise in off-beat San Polo – take a water taxi to the door! What a joy to find, behind the iron gates, a dreamy courtyard garden scented with jasmine and lavender. To breakfast under the pergola – April to October – is a treat. This enchanting cream stone villa once belonged to Alma Mahler, the composer's widow; now it is the home of Signora Zambelli Arduini and her son Lorenzo, and is run by the sweetest staff. Gaze from your bedroom window onto a magnolia, an olive and a pomegranate tree – wonderfully restorative after a day discovering Venice. Each room is elegant, spacious and filled with light, each has its own charm; three have sitting rooms and the ground-floor suite its own lovely piece of garden terrace. Colours range from vibrant turquoise to dark chocolate to pale ivory, there are family antiques and art on the walls and lovely mosaic'd bathrooms with Bulgari products. Deep green sofas in the lounge, the international papers on the table: all feels calm, inviting, intimate. The Rialto is a 15-minute walk; artisan shops and eateries outside the door.

Rooms	2 doubles: €150–€250.
	4 suites for 2: €200–€500.
Meals	Restaurant 200m.
Closed	Mid–January to mid–February.

Lorenzo Muner
Oltre Il Giardino,
San Polo 2542,
30125 Venice

Tel	+39 0412 750015
Email	info@oltreilgiardino-venezia.com
Web	www.oltreilgiardino-venezia.com

Cima Rosa

In magical Venice, take a water taxi to a 15th-century palazzo that overlooks the Grand Canal and oozes all the elegance a stylista could wish for. Owners Brittany and Danielle, architects and interior designers both, have poured energy and love into this project and have an eye for the sublime. Deeply satisfying bedrooms have dark chocolate tones and cool turquoises, perfectly set off by polished marble tiles and original parquet, exposed beams and well-chosen antiques. One has a bath tub to disappear into, another a renovated wash basin from the 1700s(!)... all have inspirational views across the canal where the palazzos are lit up at night. To complete the indulgence you can have breakfast brought to your room, though in fine weather you might prefer to linger over coffee on the vine-tinged private courtyard. The rest of the day is yours. Seasoned curios-seeker Brittany is happy to point you in the direction of all the best antique shops and museums; the ubiquitous gondola calls those seeking something more traditional. It's romantic, hugely welcoming, and you can live like the *donne nobile* before you.

Rooms	1 suite for 2; 1 suite for 2-3 (1 double, 1 sofabed); 1 suite for 2-4 (1 double, 2 single sofabeds): €195-€375. Singles 10% discount.
Meals	Restaurants nearby.
Closed	Rarely.

Brittany Hymore
Cima Rosa,
Santa Croce 1958,
30135 Venice

Mobile	+39 346 1468666
Email	info@cimarosavenezia.com
Web	www.cimarosavenezia.com

Red Carpet Rooms

When in Venice, stay where the Venetians stay – in buzzing Santa Croce. Steps from the bars and restaurants of Campo San Giacomo dell'Orio, a 15-minute vaporetto ride from the train station, this ground-floor studio is cosy, convenient and cleverly designed by local architects Antonella and Mauro. The 'red carpet' is actually a deep red resin floor, matched by red walls, red tiles, red chairs, red lamps and bright colours everywhere from rugs to bed linen. Whitewashed walls and beams make the room feel larger and lighter, and there's air conditioning for Venice's hot summer months. Clever use of space gives a roomy feel, with metal storage boxes for bedside tables and a handmade wardrobe that slides across to separate the bedroom area from the living room and sofabed. You can shop in Rialto market and come home to cook in the neat, tidy kitchenette, which has a three-hob burner, microwave and everything stored neatly on shelves or under the sink. Your super-friendly hosts will give you the scoop on local restaurants, galleries, churches and more – you will soon love the city as much as they do.

Rooms	1 apartment for 2: €600–€800 per wk. Sofabed available.
Meals	Restaurants nearby.
Closed	Rarely.

Antonella Maione
Red Carpet Rooms,
Santa Croce,
30135 Venice
Tel   +39 0418 221233
Email   info@cortevecchia.net

Blu Mood

A five-minute walk from the railway station on the way to Piazza San Marco, this bright, funky apartment is incredibly convenient for exploring the city by foot, gondola or vaporetto. It lies off a quiet lane between the shopping street of Rio Terà de la Maddalena and the Renaissance palace of Vendramin Calergi, home to a centuries-old casino and the Wagner Museum. Freshly renovated by local architects Antonella and Mauro, the apartment feels spacious and welcoming with big windows and shutters, a deep blue resin floor and splashes of red among the white walls, beams and furniture. You can cuddle up on a plump red sofa, cook a plate of pasta in the zany red kitchenette (hobs, toaster, coffee maker, microwave) and eat on red dining chairs around a modern white table. Two peaceful bedrooms, each with a comfy double bed and colourful linen, share a spotless shower room and storage space. Your young, friendly hosts are passionate about Venice, art, design and good food. So pick up some tips on local restaurants and attractions – from Cannaregio's fruit and veg markets to the Jewish Ghetto – and step out to explore.

Rooms	1 apartment for 4: €650–€900 per wk.
Meals	Self-catering.
Closed	Rarely.

Antonella Maione
Blu Mood,
Cannaregio,
30121 Venice

Tel   +39 0418 221233
Email   info@cortevecchia.net

Ca' Masena

Tuck yourself away a stone's throw from Venice's lively Zattere promenade. Richard and Suzette's quest for a Venetian bolthole led them down a narrow lane in vibrant Dorsoduro to Ca' Masena, to the ground-floor apartment of a beautifully restored mill house. Perfect for couples, small groups, families with children of all ages (as long as they're well-behaved!), this place has spacious light-filled rooms filled with antique lights, long silk curtains and Richard's wonderful oil paintings. Exposed beams in the master bedroom reveal the structure's centuries-old origins, complimented by a fresh modern twist; adults can sleep on a comfy sofabed in the good-sized living room. You're at the centre of the Arts of the *città dell'amore* with countless galleries and museums on your doorstep, not least the Guggenheim. Take a stroll to La Salute where the Grand Canal meets the Bacino di San Marco; the views across the lagoon are incredible. Want to stay in? Cookery books, DVDs, CDs, an iPod dock are at your disposal, and surround sound. Or take an aperitivo to the delightful walled courtyard.

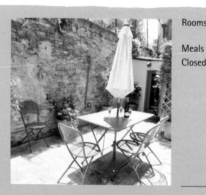

Rooms	1 apartment for 3: £865–£1,250 per wk. Sofabed & cot available.
Meals	Restaurants nearby.
Closed	Rarely.

Suzette Colson
Ca' Masena,
Calle della Masena 1476B,
30123 Venice
Mobile   +44 (0)7930 964798
Email   suzette_colson@hotmail.com
Web   www.camasena.com

Dune Agriturismo Relais

Why stay in Venice, when half an hour away (by boat or train) lies this estate, deeply rural and a stroll to a private beach space at Eraclea Mare? The family farm (mostly beef) is going strong but it's daughter Francesca who runs the show. And what a splendid show it is: an airy reception bright with art by cousin Lorenzo; a huge garden with barbecue and big swimming pool; an inexpensive restaurant whose young chef cooks with passion (ask about the half-board option); and a little shop selling home-grown produce you can cook yourself. The apartments are fabulously well-equipped: simple stylish bedrooms dressed in earthy tones, luxurious bathrooms, dreamy kitchens. You can tell the family care about the environment and love seasonal, organically grown food – some of the produce comes from the fields outside. Local staff give a great performance, smile spontaneously and do their utmost to make you feel part of the family, even when they're packed out in summer. A poster in reception sums it all up: "Good company, good wine, good welcome: good people." *Minimum stay three nights in apartments, flexible out of season.*

Rooms	5 doubles; 2 suites for 2; 2 family rooms for 4; 2 singles; 4 triples: €90–€190. 3 apartments for 2; 4 apartments for 4; 4 apartments for 4–6: €70–€160 for 2; €100–€200 for 4.
Meals	Breakfast €8 for self-caterers. Dinner €20–€30. Closed mid-October to mid-April. Restaurant 100m.
Closed	Rarely.

Francesca Pasti
Dune Agriturismo Relais,
Via S. Croce 6, Eraclea Mare,
30020 Venice

Tel	+39 0421 66171
Email	info@adriabella.com
Web	www.adriabella.com/en/dune

Relais Ca' Maffio

The delightful young Levi Morenos welcome you to their huge villa in the Sile nature reserve; they live at one end, their parents at the other and the guests in between. They're a family with a history: in 1939 they bought Jesurum, legendary producers of Venetian lace; some historic examples are on display here. The guest bedrooms are on the first floor, classically elegant, harmoniously colour-themed, immaculately furnished. Imagine the best of new (gleaming wooden floors, luxurious fabrics) and a touch of the old (an antique bibelot, a gilt-framed botanical print) and bathrooms that are top of the range. The villa's round-arched façade is striking, its vast open 'veranda' furnished with sofas, tables and an open stone fireplace; breakfast out here in summer and let Nicolò help you plan your day. The house is perfectly placed for birdwatching rambles and bike rides along the river Sile, as well as for cultural forays into Treviso and Venice (drive to Quarto d'Altino, then take the train). Or ask Nicolò to ferry you on his little boat down the river – it flows by at the end of the garden.

Rooms	3 doubles: €95–€135.
	1 suite for 2-4: €180.
Meals	Restaurant 1km; choice 8km.
Closed	Occasionally.

Nicolò Levi Morenos
Relais Ca' Maffio,
Via Principe 70, 31056 Roncade
Tel   +39 0422 780774
Email   info@camaffio.com
Web   www.camaffio.com

Castello di Roncade Agriturismo

An imposing entrance and a 16th-century villa do not mean impossible prices. Be welcomed by a glass of cool prosecco on arrival, in a garden resplendent with statues, roses, magnolias and century-old trees. Baron Vincenzo and wife Ilaria, their son Claudio and little dog Pimms are wonderful hosts, and their core business is wine. Ask for a tour of the winery and you may be tempted to take a case home – we loved the Villa Giustinian Rosso della Casa, and the pinot grigio. They've been making wine for centuries, and produce whites, reds and a sparkling rosé (including raboso – a grape unique to the Veneto). For B&B guests the have a vast and stately double room furnished with antiques – a mix of mod cons and creaking wooden floors; for self-caterers, a cluster of simpler apartments beyond, some perfect for families. They seldom do dinner here but there are restaurants close by, and you're always welcome to throw a rug on the lawn for a picnic. You are 30 minutes from Venice by train (from Quarto d'Altino, the next village); even closer to Treviso – for frescoes, cloisters and canals.

Rooms	1 double: €85-€110. 2 apartments for 2; 3 apartments for 4: €70-€100.
Meals	Occasional dinner €50. Restaurants 500m.
Closed	Rarely.

Vincenzo Ciani Bassetti
Castello di Roncade Agriturismo,
Via Roma 141, 30156 Roncade

Tel	+39 0422 708736
Email	info@castellodironcade.com
Web	www.castellodironcade.com

Locanda RosaRosae

Nothing prepares you for the charm and creaky charisma of this rose-smothered flour mill, lost down narrow lanes by the Meolo river. Rescued from ruin and imaginatively restored, reclaimed wooden floors, beams and brickwork abound with an undressed exuberance: gentle hosts Silvio and Elisabetta have flair! High ceilinged common rooms are decked out simply with antique finds from France and Morocco and quirky touches: exposed mill machinery, a festoon of crystal baubles, antique wall sconces with candles, suspended books, a stylish woolly mattress-cum-sofa. The restaurant's four dining alcoves are enchanting. Rooms have pretty wooden or metal bedsteads with antique bed linen, linen curtains, ceramic lamp holders with matching switches. Wooden columns make for bedside tables and each has a pièce de résistance: perhaps a stylish Vuitton trunk, an antique metal bath tub, a clad mannequin. Stencilling flounces polished cement bathrooms. Try their own wine, relax in the lovely long riverside garden, drift off to the creak of the mill wheel. Or borrow bikes for the day. A boost for the soul.

Rooms	4 doubles: €130.
Meals	Dinner €55 (Friday–Sunday; closed August). Restaurant 5-minute walk.
Closed	Rarely.

Elisabetta Pagnossin
Locanda RosaRosae, Via Molino 1,
31030 S. Bartolomeo di Breda di Piave

Tel	+39 0422 686626
Mobile	+39 333 320857 / +39 335 8136706
Email	locandarosarosae@gmail.com
Web	www.locandarosarosae.it

Giardino di Mezzavilla

In a town with a history — it was the site of the Italian victory over the Austro-Hungarian forces: the end of the First World War — is a house of bohemian beauty owned by the nicest people. The pretty 17th-century courtyard is still intact, as are the haylofts, the wine cellar and the greenhouse, all enveloped by acres of garden, theirs and their neighbours' — and a beloved old tree that fell in a storm has miraculously survived and grown into a natural parasol. The character continues inside, up to two big guest rooms with sober planked floors, colourwashed walls, old-fashioned radiators and the odd antique; no safes or gadgets, just good books, natural soaps, super-comfortable beds. Janine (who speaks five languages) will lend you maps for free council bicycles — yes, really; her breakfasts, organic feasts of homemade everything, set you up beautifully. Or you could jump in the car and visit the Dolomites or the sea. Return to Aga-cooked dinners that are pure pleasure — fruit and veg from the garden, local meats, Angelo's well-chosen wines. All this and fresh mountain air at night… you'll sleep like a baby.

Rooms	2 family rooms for 3; 1 family room for 4: €60–€110. 1 single: €25–€30. Dinner, B&B €30 p.p. Extra bed/sofabed €10.
Meals	Dinner with wine, €20. Vegans catered for. Restaurant 300m.
Closed	Rarely.

Janine Raedts & Angelo Vettorello
Giardino di Mezzavilla, Via Mezzavilla 26,
31029 Vittorio Veneto

Tel	+39 0438 912585
Mobile	+39 320 0525289
Email	giardinomezzavilla@gmail.com
Web	www.giardinomezzavilla.it

Tenuta Regina Agriturismo

Views stretch to Croatia on a clear day. Great for a sociable family holiday: an hour to Treviso, Trieste (beloved of James Joyce) and Udine, a 12x6m pool with snazzy loungers and a big garden with volleyball. Table tennis, bikes and a children's playground too; the owners, who have children themselves, are proud of their restoration. Now grandfather's farmhouse and grain store are manicured outside and in, and there's a distinct small-resort feel, but the lovely old ceiling rafters remain. The most homely apartment is the largest, on the western end of the farmhouse: two storeys of wooden floors and gleaming doors, pristine white kitchen, four immaculately dressed beds, a sprinkling of family pieces. Perhaps even a bunch of fresh roses – Giorgio's passion. The other apartments, some in front of the pool, some just over the road, feel more functional. Comfortable and open-plan, two on the ground floor, they come with spotless showers, dishwashers and safes, and top-quality linen. A relaxed and untouristy spot for families who love to make new friends. *Apartments also available for B&B.*

Rooms	3 suites for 2: €80-€120. 3 apartments for 2-4; 1 apartment for 4-5: €400-€1,360 per week.
Meals	Restaurants 1.5km.
Closed	Rarely.

Giorgio Pasti
Tenuta Regina Agriturismo,
Casali Tenuta Regina 8,
33056 Palazzolo dello Stella
Tel   +39 0431 587971
Email   tenutaregina@adriabella.com
Web   www.adriabella.com/tenutaregina

Agriturismo La Faula

An exuberant experience on a modern, working farm where rural laissez-faire and modern commerce happily mingle. La Faula has been in Luca's family for years; he and Paul, young and dynamic, abandoned the city to find themselves working harder than ever. Yet they put as much thought and energy into their guests as into the wine business and farm. The house stands in gentle countryside at the base of the Julian Alps – a big, comfortable home, and each bedroom delightful. Furniture is old, bathrooms new. There is a bistro-style restaurant where wonderful home-reared produce is served (free-range veal, beef, chicken, just-picked vegetables and fruits); on summer nights there may be a barbecue. An enormous old pergola provides dappled shade during the day; sit and dream awhile with a glass of estate wine or aquavit. Or wander round the vineyard and *cantina*, watch the wine-making in progress, practice your skills with a golf club on the residents' driving range, cool off in the river, visit the beaches of the Adriatic. Perfect for families. *Minimum stay two nights.*

Rooms	11 twin/doubles: €80.
	1 apartment for 2; 1 apartment for 4: €700-€840 per week.
	Extra beds available in some doubles & apartments.
	Discounts for children & long stays.
Meals	Lunch/dinner €19. Wine €10.
	Restaurant 500m.
Closed	30 September to 1 March.

	Paul Mackay & Luca Colautti
	Agriturismo La Faula,
	Via Faula 5,
	Ravosa di Povoletto,
	33040 Udine
Mobile	+39 334 3996734
Web	www.faula.com

Casa del Grivò Agriturismo

This is the house that Toni built – or, rather, lovingly revived from ruin. The smallholding sits in a hamlet on the edge of a plain; behind, wonderful, high-wooded hills extend to the Slovenian border, sometimes crossed to gather wild berries. Your lovely hosts have a wonderful family. Simplicity, rusticity and a 'green' approach are the keynotes here; so you'll sample traditional wool-and-vegetable-fibre-filled mattresses. Beds are comfy and blanketed, some with wonderful quilts. You will adore all the open spaces, the animals and the little pool that's been created by diverting a stream. Relax with a book on a bedroom balcony, or in a distant corner of the garden. Maps are laid out at breakfast, and there are heaps of books on the region; the walking is wonderful, there's a castle to visit and a river to picnic by. Paola cooks fine dinners using old recipes and their own organic produce. There's a lovely open fire for cooking, and you dine by candlelight, sometimes to the gentle accompaniment of country songs: Paola was once a singer. *Minimum stay two nights, five nights in high season.*

Rooms	1 double; 2 family rooms for 4 (sharing bathroom); 1 family room for 4 (separate private bathroom): €70. Dinner, B&B €60 p.p.
Meals	Picnic by arrangement. Dinner from €25. Wine from €10.
Closed	Mid-November to Easter.

Toni & Paola Costalunga
Casa del Grivò Agriturismo,
Borgo Canal del Ferro 19,
33040 Faédis

Tel	+39 0432 728638
Email	info@casadelgrivo.com
Web	www.casadelgrivo.com

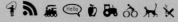

Palazzo Lantieri

In Gorizia, through an archway off a beautiful piazza, you pull up into a courtyard of luscious lawns and elegant palms. This 14th-century palazzo may have grand proportions, but the immediate feel is of an affectionately tended home. The amiable Contessa guides you past chandeliers and fresh flowers, broad stone staircases and miles of herringbone parquet to two light-filled bedrooms, each intended to delight. Wooden floors creak charmingly, sunlight floods in through soft white curtains, and bathrooms ooze indulgent luxury: just bliss. 'La dolce vita' surrounds you here, with vineyards and good restaurants to visit, country walks to build up your appetite and operas and Roman history to quench cultural thirst. Do explore the palazzo's Persian-style garden and ask the Contessa for a guided tour of the hand-drawn frescoes, the modern art and the memorabilia. Napoleon, Schiller and Casanova stayed here, and wrote about it; but as you rest in the garden listening to birdsong, you will think yourself the only one to have discovered this Italian jewel.

Rooms	1 double: €140.
	1 suite for 2: €150.
	1 apartment for 4;
	1 apartment for 2: €160-€220.
Meals	Restaurant within walking distance.
Closed	Rarely.

Carolina di Levetzow Lantieri
Palazzo Lantieri,
Piazza Sant'Antonio 6, 34170 Gorizia

Tel	+39 0481 533284
Mobile	+39 340 5590155
Email	contatto@palazzo-lantieri.com
Web	www.palazzo-lantieri.com

Emilia Romagna

Villa Bellaria

Off the track, but not isolated, tucked under a softly green hillside, this cream-painted *casa di collina*, with its wide hammock'd veranda and well-established garden, has been a retreat from summer heat since 1900. Having moved here with her husband 20 years ago, Marina, warm and kind, herself a keen traveller, decided to throw open her doors – and share her enthusiasm for this under-sung area, all medieval villages, castles and thermal cures. A much-loved, ornately carved mirror, made by her cabinet maker father at his renowned atelier in Milan, graces one wall. Immaculate bedrooms in old-fashioned style are a friendly mix of wrought-iron bedsteads, delicately embroidered blinds, tile floors and contemporary art. After breakfast al fresco – perhaps a delectable homemade tart – head off through leafy lanes to the walled hill town Castell'Arquato, or Piacenza and Parma. After a hard day exploring or being sporty, consider the area's gastronomic treats: nothing sums up Emilia-Romagna so well as its food. A comfortable, cute, civilised home to return to – and great value.

Rooms	4 doubles: €65–€70.
	Singles €55–€60.
Meals	Restaurant 300m.
Closed	Rarely.

Marina Cazzaniga Calderoni
Villa Bellaria,
Via dei Gasperini Loc. Fellegara 380,
29010 Cortina di Alseno

Tel	+39 0523 947537
Email	info@villabellariabb.it
Web	www.villabellariabb.it

Antica Corte Pallavicina Relais

As you turn down the estate's driveway, ancient breeds of cattle and horse pause their grazing, and geese and hens scuttle out of your way. You have arrived at the home of one of Italy's most cherished salami producers, the Spigarolis, who opened their relais with the intention of winning tourists over to the gastronomy of the region. Elegant bedrooms nod to the past in their traditional guise, but have an exquisitely modern edge thanks to round zinc basins, medusa-like lamps with bulbs cascading to the floor, and delicious poplar-wood decked showers. Days can be spent in the kitchen with inspiring Massimo teaching how to chop and stir, or out exploring the area on one of the estate's bikes. But you cannot leave without visiting the castle's famed cellars, where thousands of Culatello di Zibello salamis and Parmigiano Reggiano cheeses are left to age. Savour both delights at either of the family's two restaurants here. Then finish your day with an aromatic bath in your suite's tub, next to the glowing fire. Look forward to fresh brioches at breakfast beneath frescoed ceilings.

Rooms	4 doubles: €140–€250.
	2 suites for 2: €160–€280.
Meals	Dinner €50–€75. Restaurant nearby.
Closed	Rarely.

Massimo Spigaroli
Antica Corte Pallavicina Relais,
Strada del Palazzo Due Torri 3,
43010 Polesine Parmense

Tel	+39 0524 936539
Email	relais@acpallavicina.com
Web	www.acpallavicina.com/relais

Antica Torre Agriturismo

The farm dogs ambling across the pristine gravel paths in the lee of the 14th-century tower and enormous colonnaded barn, covered in vines, exude a peaceful contentment – which belies the energy that the family pour into this enterprise. From sweeping flagstones at dawn to the final flourish of a delicious bottle at dinner, this family is devoted to agriturismo. Don't expect to stumble across farm machinery or be set upon by winsome lambs: Antica Torre, with its many buildings, has the air of a model farm. The big rooms in the *casa rustica*, with their ancient polished brick and tile floors, have strange and wondrous rustic furniture, and curly metal bedheads inject a light-hearted air. Otherwise, expect simple bathrooms, immaculate housekeeping and an honest rurality. With its huge fireplace and long tables covered in red gingham, the barn, where generous breakfasts are served, has a distinctly alpine air. In the evening, deep in the ancient Cistercian cellar, to the strains of plain chant and Verdi, feast with guests on Vanda's astonishingly good cooking.

Rooms	8 twin/doubles: €100–€110. Dinner, B&B €75 p.p.
Meals	Dinner €25. Wine €5–€12.
Closed	December–February.

Francesco Pavesi
Antica Torre Agriturismo,
Case Bussandri 197, Loc. Cangelasio,
43039 Salsomaggiore Terme

Tel	+39 0524 575425
Email	info@anticatorre.it
Web	www.anticatorre.it

Al Battistero d'Oro

This grand two-storey yellow palazzo lies off a tranquil square in a traffic-free zone, tucked behind the Duomo. You enter via a double *portone*, then take a lift from the cobbled courtyard to the first floor, and enter Patrizia's home. In the dining room, awash with light from tall windows, are family antiques and a big oriental rug, serene pictures, a long table at which breakfast can be served, and a cosy fire for winter stays. Your hostess, accommodating and delightful, lives here with her teenage family and gives guests two elegant bedrooms: a very private double, 'Duchessa', down a steepish but well-lit stair (also reachable from the entrance floor), and a twin/double 'Reina', close to the dining room with an as-private feel. Beds are handsome, mattresses are inviting, pillows plump, lighting is excellent, and discreet, and mini safes, fridges, WiFi, satellite TV, fluffy towels and beautiful toiletries are de rigueur. And then there's history-rich Parma, with its wine bars, delis, trattorias and passion for gastronomy, and the Teatro Regio, one of the three great homes of Italian opera.

Rooms	1 double; 1 double with extra bed available: €90–€130. Singles €80–€90. Extra bed/sofabed €20. Cot on request.
Meals	Restaurants nearby.
Closed	August.

Patrizia Valenti
Al Battistero d'Oro,
Strada Sant'Anna 22,
43121 Parma

Mobile	+39 338 4904697
Email	contatti@albattisterodoro.it
Web	www.albattisterodoro.it

Villino di Porporano

It may be surrounded by smart houses, but this impressive B&B stands out in the village of Porporano. A converted stone stable, it oozes Italianness, sitting behind wrought-iron gates in an enclosed (but overlooked) park of trees, roses and lawn – great for picnics. The neat villa attached is where welcoming owner Elena lives with four children and two dogs. She keeps everything in apple-pie order, and can also (as befits Emilia-Romagna) arrange cooking courses. The four compact double rooms are a delight. Expensive linens and embroidered drapes, all whites and creams, soften exposed stone and wooden floors; inviting bathrooms have cotta tiles, and fluffy towels, slippers, nice smellies. 'Le Rose' comes with flowery touches and an antique bath in the bedroom. Lots of high windows (note the building's hayloft heritage) flood the place with light, including the spacious living room where buffet breakfast is served: homemade cakes, local hams and cheeses. Dinner's available on request, there's an excellent restaurant 500m away, and the gastronomy of Parma is a ten-minute drive. *Minimum stay two nights from March to October.*

Rooms	4 twin/doubles: €130–€190.
	1 suite for 3: €220.
	Singles €120–€180. Rates exclude
	taxes, €0.50 per person per day.
Meals	Dinner on request. Restaurants 500m.
Closed	Rarely.

Elena Maria Ciotti
Villino di Porporano,
Strada Bodrio 26, 43123 Parma

Tel	+39 0521 642268
Mobile	+39 349 4126037
Email	info@villinodiporporano.com
Web	www.villinodiporporano.com

Il Richiamo del Bosco

Detach yourself from the outside world and unwind in this blissful contemporary eco build in the middle of the Boschi di Carrega national park. Carla and Stefano live here with their daughter Sofia, and have created a chic, light-filled space that complements its natural surroundings, thanks to talented designer Alessandro Mora. His cleverly handcrafted furniture, which uses reclaimed wood and stone, is found throughout. Bedrooms are bright and unfussy, with solar-powered underfloor heating for cooler nights and fantastic views over the forest. An open-plan kitchen, dining room and lounge provide a beautiful, convivial space; cook if you wish, independently or in a cooking class, then sink into comfy sofas. Sit at the long wooden table for tasty local pastries, marmalades, yogurt and cheeses at breakfast. Alternatively, start the day lounging in a hammock on the covered patio. Want to explore? Friendly Tatiana helps out and is happy to suggest walking routes through the park – spot the deer and wild boar peeking out at you through the trees. Parma is less than half an hour by car. Wonderful for all ages.

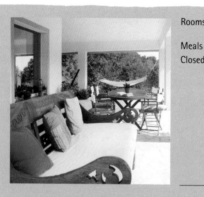

Rooms	1 double; 2 doubles each with separate bathroom: €80-€100.
Meals	Restaurants 2km.
Closed	Rarely.

Carla Soffritti
Il Richiamo del Bosco, Via Capanna 18,
Boschi di Carrega, 43038 Sala Baganza

Tel	+39 0521 336376
Mobile	+ 39 335 8388895
Email	info@ilrichiamodelbosco.it
Web	www.ilrichiamodelbosco.it

B&B Valferrara

On an ancient road between Canossa and Carpineti, this 17th-century travellers' lodge sits in the silent hamlet of Valferrara. Weary merchants would rest their heads in peace – and absorb the calm and protection of the forested hills and distant castle of Carpineti. Ruined when Giuliano and Cosetta discovered it in 1994, the *casa di scale* ('tiered house'), complete with flat-roofed Emilian tower – where a clutch of apartments are almost ready – has been completely and masterfully restored with local materials, and parquet flooring fashioned from recycled beams of oak. Cosetta restores local antique furniture and the house is full of it; crisp cotton envelops large, beautifully framed beds and an eye-catching walnut writing desk stands elegantly near one of her several finely polished wardrobes. Expect a warm welcome and a delicious breakfast under the cool portico, in the walled garden or the dining room: a fabulous conversion of the old stables. Fresh parmesan can be sampled locally and smiling Cosetta, also a great cook, provides dinner on request.

Rooms	1 double; 2 doubles, sharing bath: €76–€90.
Meals	Restaurants 1km.
Closed	Rarely.

Cosetta Mordacci & Giuliano Beghi
B&B Valferrara,
Via Valferrara 3, Pantano,
42033 Carpineti
Mobile   +39 340 1561417
Email   info@bb-valferrara.it
Web   www.bb-valferrara.it

La Stella

The long, twisting road to La Stella dances from Modena into the Apennines and this secluded farmhouse set in deepest nature. The reward: magnificent views of Monte Cusna, an enthusiastic welcome, a nightime carpet of stars. No wonder Belgians Peter and Christine fell for this rural spot by the Tuscan-Emilian National Park, with hiking, biking, a river beach on the Secchia, skiing in winter, stunning mountains all year round. You will fall for it too – if you value tranquillity – and for the house with its chunky stone walls, fire-warmed sitting room, antique piano and breakfast room with chandelier. The bedroom, just as charming, has dainty pillows, a reading corner, a sofabed for a child – and views. Outside, a delicious bite-sized plot of birds, trees, flowers: a taste of what lies beyond. In summer, breakfast out here on cured meats and Christine's scrumptious pastries. La Stella may be off the beaten path but it is well-positioned between several wonderful cities. For those who love nature: an adventure to arrive, a pleasure to stay… and there's a restaurant a ten-minute drive away.

Rooms	1 twin/double: €95.
Meals	Restaurant 10-minute drive.
Closed	Rarely.

Christine Tiebout
La Stella,
Via San Venerio 9,
42030 Carù di Villa Minozzo

Tel	+39 348 6354836
Email	info@bb-lastella.it
Web	www.bb-lastella.it

La Piana dei Castagni Agriturismo

Write, paint, read or potter: here, deep in the woods, there's nothing to distract you. This is a secret little Hansel and Gretel house with a vegetable patch, demure shutters and lace-trimmed curtains. It stands isolated among chestnut and cherry trees, reached via a long, wriggling track; below are bucolic meadows, falling to a farm or two, and a further distant descent along the yawning valley. An old stone farmhouse converted and adapted for B&B, La Piana is a modest place to stay. The bedrooms, named after local berries, are a good size and painted in clear pastel colours; tiny pictures hang above beds, little windows in thick walls look out over the glorious valley. The shower rooms – one of them a restyled chicken shed! – are simply tiled. Valeria lives ten minutes away at La Civetta. She is gentle, kind, spoiling; even the breakfast *torte di noci* are homemade. She will also help organise everything, from trekking to truffle hunting. An ideal spot for those who love the simple pleasures of life: good walks by day, good food by night. *Minimum stay two nights.*

Rooms	2 doubles: €72–€95.
	1 single: €40.
	2 triples: €80–€100.
Meals	Dinner €19–€21. Wine €8–€20.
	Restaurant 3km.
Closed	November–March.

Valeria Vitali
La Piana dei Castagni Agriturismo,
Via Lusignano 11,
40040 Rocca di Roffeno

Tel	+39 0519 12985
Email	info@pianadeicastagni.it
Web	www.pianadeicastagni.it

Lodole Country House

An exceedingly well-renovated 17th-century stone cottage with views over breathtaking Apennine countryside; it's a treat to arrive. Flowers brighten windows, wooden shutters are hung and varnished, terracotta planters march up to the front door, and a paved path curves up to a swimming pool from which you can exclaim at the view. Bedrooms — Sun, Sky, Stars — reflect their names, and are wonderfully romantic; 'Moon' has semicircular end tables and a skylight in its bathroom; 'Dawn', pale pink, faces east; 'Sunset', pale orange, faces west. All have low lighting, wooden boards, exposed beams, soothing hues. Well-chosen pieces add interest: polished armoires, antique vanities, free-standing antique washbasins and fine wrought-iron beds, some canopied in soft cotton. The living room has a fireplace, big white sofas, a window to the hills, and a raised area beyond for delicious, lovingly sourced breakfasts served at separate tables by Alice. Numerous local trattoria provide discounted meals to guests and the Molino del Pero golf course lies handily next door.

Rooms	5 doubles; 1 triple: €90.
Meals	Restaurants nearby.
Closed	Rarely.

Alice Frontini
Lodole Country House,
Loc. Lodole 325, 40036 Monzuno

Tel	+39 0516 771189
Email	info@lodole.com
Web	www.lodole.com

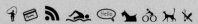

Relais Varnello

In young gardens just above the pretty town of Brisighella – you'll need the car, it's quite a hike – the brick buildings stand sparkling and tickety-boo. Nicely furnished rooms have views across the valley or the garden; the suites are in a separate building with a sauna. The setting among the *calanchi* (chalk hills) is stunning and the farm produces Sangiovese DOC wine and olive oil, which you can buy along with Faenza pottery showing the family crest. Giovanni has been producing oil and wine all his life and you won't leave here without a bottle or two – it's delicious. If you speak a little Italian, pick his brains, he has a vast knowledge of Italian grapes (over 1,000 varieties) and will happily tell tales of some of the best wines going. Spend your days lounging by the pool (he's also very proud of his fully plumbed poolhouse): there are wide views over the Padana and to the Adriatic, and just a stroll away, a private wild park, Giovanni's pride and joy: a lovely place for a picnic and a book. Higher up the hill is the Pacro Carnè, with Club Alpino Italiano (CAI) walking trails. *Minimum stay two nights.*

Rooms	4 twin/doubles: €130.
	2 suites for 2: €180.
Meals	Restaurant 300m.
Closed	January to 15 March.

Vincenzo Liverzani
Relais Varnello,
Via Rontana 34, 48013 Brisighella
Tel   +39 0546 85493
Email   info@varnello.it
Web   www.varnello.it

Azienda Vitivinicola e Agrituristica Trerè

Braided vines, with their companion grasses, stretch as far as the eye can see... in the middle of this flat green patchwork stands a compact group of rosy buildings and a clump of tall trees to one side. The entertainingly angular farmhouse is surrounded by barns and stables, modernised as apartments and a conference room. This is very much a wine-growing estate – around the house are certificates and awards, a shop and a little rose-and-gold wine museum – but there's a family feel with the owners' children, a tribe of peacocks and an easy atmosphere. The bedrooms in the house have the light and pretty elegance of beamed ceilings, pastel walls, lovely old family furniture and books, and memorable touches such as the deep lace trim of a white sheet folded over a jade bedcover. The apartments (with kitchenettes) are attractive but more functional in feel. Each has French windows opening onto a private patio and a mezzanine with an extra bed tucked under a skylight – always fun for kids. Eat in a stall in the unspoilt former cowshed, now the restaurant, open for four days a week (there are other restaurants nearby).

Rooms	6 doubles; 1 twin; 1 triple: €68–€78. 2 suites for 2; 1 suite for 4 (1 single, 1 triple, 1 sofa bed; 1 bathroom): €120–€180. 2 apartments for 5; 2 apartments for 3: €80–€150. Extra bed €20.
Meals	Breakfast €6.50. Dinner €30 (except Jan/Feb & Mon-Wed). Wine €7–€22. Restaurants 5km.
Closed	Rarely.

Morena Trerè & Massimiliano Fabbri
Azienda Vitivinicola e Agrituristica Trerè
Via Casale 19, 48018 Faenza
Tel   +39 0546 47034
Email   trere@trere.com
Web   www.trere.com

Liguria

Villa Elisa

The climate is kind: visit at any time of the year. The hotel was created in the 1920s when Bordighera, a pretty town with sloping tree-lined roads and pastel houses, became a winter retreat. The owner's father-in-law ran it for years, was a painter and had artists to stay – bedroom walls are still hung with the works they left. Some still come, following in the steps of Monet. This is a friendly place for walkers and families: Rita and husband Maurizio take groups off into the Maritime Alps in their minibus, then guide them back on three-hour treks. They also have a playroom for children, and organise special activities for summer. The restaurant is traditional and charming, the bedrooms are old-fashioned and double-glazed. Bathrooms are white-tiled with floral friezes and heated towel rails; the larger rooms have terraces with views to the hills. Best are the gardens: the courtyard bright with bougainvillea and oranges, the pool area lushly planted. Set off for the pebbled beach, a ten-minute dash down the hill; return to fresh fish on the menu served by attentive and delightful staff. *Half or full-board option for week-long stays.*

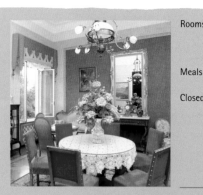

Rooms	30 doubles: €120-€180.
	1 suite for 2: €200-€250.
	3 singles: €80-€110.
	1 apartment for 4-6: €220-€300.
Meals	Lunch/dinner from €40.
	Wine €16-€50.
Closed	5 November to 22 December.

Rita Oggero
Villa Elisa,
Via Romana 70, 18012 Bordighera
Tel   +39 0184 261313
Email   info@villaelisa.com
Web   www.villaelisa.com

Casa Villatalla Guest House

Revel in the peace – and the views: they sweep across the wooded valley to the blue-grey mountains beyond. Roger (British) and Marina (Italian-Swiss) had the delightful Casa Villatalla built in traditional style, ochre-stuccoed and green-shuttered. They are wonderfully welcoming hosts – and the cheerful, eclectic décor of the house reflects their warm personalities and love of travel. Through the brick archway, a Swiss armoire presides over a dining room furnished with rustic wooden tables on which seasonal breakfasts and dinners (do book) are served. Upstairs: charming modern bedrooms, some leading to balconies and those views. All are different: in 'Quercia', a bedstead woven from banana tree fronds, in 'Corbezzolo', rose tones and a flowery patchwork quilt. Marina, a keen horticulturist, nurtures her garden full of roses, and there's a swimming pool terrace which is crowned by a fine oak tree, beautifully illuminated at night. Together they organise occasional painting, yoga and cookery courses: another reason to stay. *Minimum stay two nights July / August.*

Rooms	1 double; 4 twin/doubles: €80-€95. Discounts for long stays. Extra bed/sofabed €25.
Meals	Dinner, 3 courses with wine, €30. Restaurant 5km.
Closed	Never.

Roger & Marina Hollinshead
Casa Villatalla Guest House,
Loc. Villatalla, 18035 Dolceacqua

Tel	+39 0184 206379
Email	info@villatalla.com
Web	www.villatalla.com

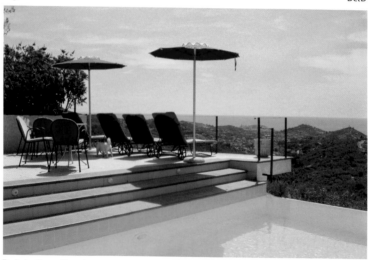

Relais San Damian

Wind your way up through endless olive groves to this organic working estate. Through the gate... to find child-free seclusion and spa-like calm. Manicured lawns give way to a fine terrace, and breathtaking bougainvillea-framed views over village-studded hills to the glinting sea (even better appreciated from the stunning infinity pool). Rooms, all with their own private outdoor space, are savvy and sophisticated yet simple: open brickwork, marble basins, cream iron beds and sofas, bare wooden floors, beautiful country antiques. Relaxation is what San Damian is about. Bring a book or browse the library, slip into the pool, feel time go slow-mo to the serenade of the cicadas. Local osteria dining tips are readily provided by serene hosts Pamela and Roberto; breakfast – an abundant buffet of homemade breads and cakes, fresh fruit, cheeses and cured meats served under portico'd arches – should under no circumstances be slept through. Should you stray from the garden and grounds, the surrounding hills promise superb hiking – and the lavish Ligurian coast is the shortest drive.

Rooms	10 doubles: €140–€170.
Meals	Restaurant 4km.
Closed	December–February.

Pamela Kranz Gardini
Relais San Damian,
Azienda Agricola Strada Vasia 47,
18100 Imperia

Tel	+39 0183 280309
Email	info@san-damian.com
Web	www.san-damian.com

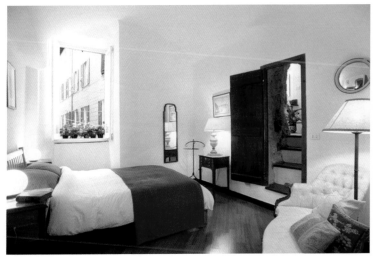

Torre Cepollini

You'll feel part of the buzz in the heart of history-filled Albenga with its famous medieval towers. Yours is the tallest one, 12th century with a slight lean. Through the door and up the black-and-white tiled steps it feels grand and homely all at the same time, with a beautiful living room, elegant marble fireplace, antique tiled floor, gold-framed mirror. The three bedrooms are off this room and have sturdy, simple beds, stone walls, high vaulted ceilings, antiques and mirrors. Two of the bathrooms are spotless and fine, but the third, off the tower room, is stunning; not one for giants, it's on three levels culminating in a gorgeous tub. This is a small, family-run operation with plenty of flexibility; friendly English owner Michael lives nearby, gives you keys, and pops in to make delicious breakfast (he can also arrange a private cook for dinner). The kitchen is charming with its antique marble sink, crystal, china and bright red scales – a great place to linger over breakfast (locally grown fruits, home-baked breads). The beach is a ten-minute walk, you can hike, taste wines, have a boat ride. Lovely. *Pets by arrangement.*

Rooms	2 doubles; 1 twin: €90–€110. Singles from €65 to €85. Extra bed/sofabed €20.
Meals	Dinner available on request. Restaurants nearby.
Closed	Rarely.

Michael Hewlett
Torre Cepollini,
Via Medaglie 25,
17031 Albenga
Mobile   +39 346 0586804
Email   albenga@torrecepollini.it
Web   www.torrecepollini.it

Ca' de Tobia

In the little fishing village of Noli – a big surprise! Behind the potted box trees is a friendly B&B with a boutique feel. Enter a communal space, sharp, chic, white, a reflection of the dazzling seaside beyond. Traditional furniture (a wooden hutch full of antique plates) is juxtaposed with funky modern (a ceramic collage) and whimsical touches ('plastic' dishes that turn out to be glass). A big restoration has taken place to lick this former warehouse into shape and Andrea does it all – reception, breakfast, laundry. He loves both house and guests so lap up the luxury. There are currently three bedrooms but more will follow; ceilings are high and windows generous (though views are unmemorable), thick curtains flow, down pillows are heaped high, bursts of colour come from pleasing art and bathrooms are hugely spoiling. Best of all are the breakfasts, served on the terrace in summer: prosciutto and melon, buffalo mozzarella, fresh smoothies, homemade cakes; some of it finds its way into picnic baskets if you set off on the bikes. There's hiking in the hills and delicious villages to be discovered. *Minimum two nights in high season.*

Rooms	3 doubles: €170–€250.
Meals	Picnics available. Restaurants nearby.
Closed	September.

Andrea Tobia
Ca' de Tobia,
17026 Noli Savona

Tel	+39 0197 485845
Mobile	+39 346 9923318
Email	info@cadetobia.it
Web	www.cadetobia.it

Sognando Villa Edera

At the top of the winding road from Rapallo is a family agriturismo noted for its spectacular views: they swoop from your deckchair down to the coast. These 1.5 hectares of olive groves and orchards were planted by Sara's grandfather, there are well-behaved dogs, cats, a donkey and a pony, and Rosanna's delightful tiered gardens. Below the gardens are five simple, sunny and spotless guest apartments recently created from the farmworkers' houses (two on the the ground floor and three above.) Some have bunks and beds in the living room, each has its own piece of garden or terrace. You may choose to set off for the day – for the beaches of Portofino, or the peaceful palmed promenade, two harbours and little castle of Rapallo – but you can happily spend all day here too, high up among the birdsong and the roses, the deckchairs and the terraces, the pool and the heavenly views. The beach is three kilometres away, the restaurants are down the hill, the Cinque Terre is 40 minutes by car and the buses run three times a day. *Minimim stay three nights; five July-August. Air con extra charge.*

Rooms	1 apartment for 2; 3 apartments for 4; 1 apartment for 5: €700–€1,330 per wk.
Meals	Self-catering.
Closed	Rarely.

Sara Piaggio
Sognando Villa Edera,
Salita San Giovanni 3,
16035 Rapallo

Mobile +39 338 5211381
Email   info@sognandovillaedera.com
Web   www.sognandovillaedera.com

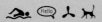

Villa Gnocchi Agriturismo

Once you've negotiated the steep and windy access drive, you are rewarded with sensational views over Santa Margherita. Roberto, a Ligurian farmer, trained at Pisa University and inherited the house from his grandfather in a dilapidated state; he's made a few changes! He is a wonderful host and loves this place, deep in the country but within sight of the sea... enjoy breakfast or a glass of wine from the terrace and gaze down the coast. Each bedroom is colourful, spotless, different: white, ochre or saffron; all are simply furnished and decorated with dried flowers. Bright bedcovers dress grandfather's beds, muslin curtains flutter at windows, old framed prints hang on the walls and many shower rooms are tiny. Apart from the hoot of the train and the faint hum of the traffic below, the only sound to break the peace is birdsong. Forget the hire car: Santa Margherita – a 15-minute walk downhill, a bumpy bus or taxi up – is a charming little town, with beach, fishing boats, shops, bars and restaurants. Paths lead to most of the villages and buses from the gate. *Strict check-in / out times (before 13.30 or between 16.30-19.45).*

Rooms	5 doubles; 2 twins; 2 family rooms for 4: €90-€110.
Meals	Restaurant 500m.
Closed	Mid-October to mid-April.

Roberto Gnocchi
Villa Gnocchi Agriturismo,
Via San Lorenzo 29, San Lorenzo della
Costa, 16038 Santa Margherita Ligure
Tel   +39 0185 283431
Email   roberto.gnocchi@tin.it
Web   www.villagnocchi.it

Abbadia San Giorgio

Sublimely romantic and peaceful, this 15th-century monastery recalls the life of St Francis in frescoes and sculptures beneath vaulted ceilings. You can almost hear the sandalled Franciscans padding round the cloister garden. Dipping into a delicious spread for breakfast, served by candlelight in the refectory, you breathe more monastic air. Nothing monkish about the bedrooms: Orietta and Francesca, a mother and daughter team, have searched Italy for antique furniture and sensual fabrics to make them both sumptuous and individual. Many of the beds are wrought-irons; one's a four-poster and floors are of original octagonal terracotta tiles. The large and ethereal honeymoon suite is swathed and festooned with gauze and ivory furnishings. Elsewhere, tones range from lavish red to green, apricot and gold, all opulently matched. Neat marble bathrooms sport spa shower cabins with pretty olive-oil-based toiletries. An amorous evening might begin with wine tasting in the cellar, then stepping out for dinner. A haven of peace in the centre of beautiful Moneglia. *Minimum stay three nights.*

Rooms	3 doubles; 1 twin/double: €195–€290. 2 suites for 4: €320–€350. Single €175–€310. Extra bed/sofabed €50.
Meals	Restaurants 100m.
Closed	Christmas & New Year.

Orietta Schiaffino
Abbadia San Giorgio,
Piazzale San Giorgio,
16030 Moneglia

Tel	+39 0185 491119
Email	info@abbadiasangiorgio.com
Web	www.abbadiasangiorgio.com

Entry 120   Map 7

Hotel Villa Edera

The villa is perched above the beautiful town of Moneglia and is a beautifully run, family owned hotel. The hosts make any stay a joy; Orietta and Francesca pour themselves into their business. Orietta is a mine of information about Ligurian art and history, sings in the local choir and loves meeting people who share her interest in music. Rooms are light and airy if a little retro, but there are plans to update the décor. Chef Adriano will prepare Ligurian dishes, some vegetarian, with the freshest organic produce, and does fabulous breakfasts; sister Edy is a cake-making genius. Orietta is a keen walker who may take guests out for real hikes – though you can always catch a boat to Portofino and explore the Cinque Terre by sea. You are fairly close to the railway here (a significant part of the landscape, threading the Cinque Terre villages together) but you'd never know, and now there's a lift up to the hotel from the street – handy! Lots of treats to come back to: a fitness room, sauna, a lovely pool. The beach is a ten-minute walk. *Pets by arrangement.*

Rooms	4 doubles; 20 twin/doubles: €110–€200. 1 family room for 4: €160–€190. 2 singles: €85–€135. 1 triple (extra bed available): €165–€200.
Meals	Lunch/dinner €28–€35. Wine €12.
Closed	Christmas & New Year.

Orietta Schiaffino
Hotel Villa Edera,
Via Venino 12, 16030 Moneglia
Tel   +39 0185 491119
Email   info@abbadiasangiorgio.com
Web   www.villaedera.com

Agriturismo Villanova

Villanova is where Barone Giancarlo Massola's ancestors spent their summers in the 18th century, and has barely changed. It's a mile from Levanto yet modern life feels far behind as you wind your way up the hills through olive groves, then down an unremarkable street... to an unexpected gem. Behind its gates the red and cream villa – with private chapel – stands in a small sunny clearing. Giancarlo, quiet, charming, much-travelled, loves meeting new folk; his golden retriever will welcome you too. Guest bedrooms are in the main house and in two small stone farmhouses behind; all have an elegant, country-house feel and rooms are large, airy, terracotta tiled. Furniture is of wood and wrought iron, beautiful fabrics are yellow and blue. As for the apartments, they have private entrances and terraces with pretty views. Two apartments are separate, a third is in the farmhouse. Giancarlo grows organic apricots, figs and vegetables and makes his own wine and olive oil; breakfasts are delicious. This is a great place to bring children: swings and table tennis in the garden, space to run around in, the coast nearby.

Rooms	3 doubles: €100-€130. 6 suites for 2-3 (with sofabed): €120-€180. 2 apartments for 2 (sofabed available); 1 apartment for 6; 1 apartment for 5: €600-€1,500 per week. Extra bed €20.
Meals	Restaurants 1.5km.
Closed	January.

Giancarlo Massola
Agriturismo Villanova,
Loc. Villanova, 19015 Levanto

Tel	+39 0187 802517
Email	info@agriturismovillanova.it
Web	www.agriturismovillanova.it

La Sosta di Ottone III

Legend has it that Otto III stayed here on his way to his coronation in Rome in 996, creating La Sosta, a 'stopover' of some magnificence. Now a listed building, the house's unadorned stone façade stands proudly over the hamlet of Chiesanuova, scanning a vista from all rooms of olive groves, village and vineyard-clad hills, before dropping down to Levanto and the sea. The terrace is a superb breakfast and dinner setting, perfect too at sunset with a glass of chilled vermentino. At night, the glow from a host of illuminated bell towers is enchanting. Angela has taken great care to gather the best local slate, marble and wood in the renovation of dining and sitting rooms. Bedrooms, named after Otto and his family members, come in an elegant range of neutrals and corals. There are parquet floors, antique pieces, indoor shutters and iron beds graced by fine bedspreads… take time to pamper yourself in stylish marble and slate bathrooms. Aficionados of all things Ligurian, Angela and Fabio can be depended on for local information, the freshest ingredients and one of the best wine cellars around. Superb. *Minimum stay two nights.*

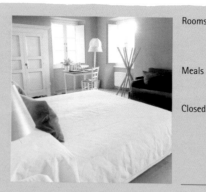

Rooms	1 double: €200. 1 suite for 4; 2 family rooms for 2-4: €200-€280. Extra bed/sofabed €40.
Meals	Breakfast €15; €7.50 for children under 12. Dinner €35-€65. Restaurant 5km.
Closed	Beginning of October to end of April.

Fabio Graziani
La Sosta di Ottone III,
Loc. Chiesanuova 39, 19015 Levanto
Tel   +39 0187 814502
Email   lasostadiottone@hotmail.com
Web   www.lasosta.com

L'Antico Borgo

Oozing tranquillity, it could be a setting for a film, so private is it with its gorgeous views over green hills and down to the sea. Once you reach tiny Dosso, leave the car and walk intrepidly down the short steep path to the B&B. You are surrounded by olive groves and pocket vineyards, yet Levanto is only four kilometres away. A pretty pebbled square and a stone arch form the entrance to this 1700s *casa padronale*, fully restored with the soft-ochre façade and dark green shutters so typical of Liguria. The panoramic terrace is a fine place for breakfast or an aperitif and Cecilia is happy for guests to have their own picnics here. Relax in the sitting room with a book from the small library, breakfast at round tables in the rustic taverna. Bright and generous bedrooms, two with sea views, have timber beams; all are comfortably furnished with wrought-iron beds and warmed by gentle shades of yellow. Modern bathrooms use solar-heated water. Siblings Cecilia and Carlo, a local surfing hero, are shy but natural hoteliers and are both supporters of the Slow Food movement so they know the best places for dinner. *Children under three free.*

Rooms	1 double; 1 twin/double: €85-€120. 2 family rooms for 4: €160-€180. 3 triples: €120-€150.
Meals	Restaurant 1km.
Closed	Rarely.

Cecilia Pilotti
L'Antico Borgo,
Loc. Dosso, 19015 Levanto

Tel	+39 0187 802681
Email	antico_borgo@hotmail.com
Web	www.anticoborgo.net

Entry 124 Map 7

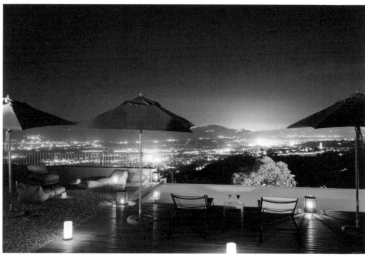

Casa Colleverde

You arrive at the top of the hillside – having braved a few hairpins on the way – to a stunning modern structure with views down to the sea; you can see Corsica on a fine day. The many-window'd 1970s house has had a brilliant restoration: polished concrete floors, glass-walled staircases, flowing curtains and cool artistic touches that nod to the Renaissance greats. Simon and Carmelo know how to spoil and welcome you with open arms; and adorable Sam the Norfolk terrier shares their spirit. Put your feet up wherever you choose: on the sleek lounger by the pool, the leather sofa by the fire, or indeed in the bath: each suite offers an oversize tub as well as a walk-in shower. Suites are huge, beds are topped with fat pillows and high quality linens, sofas are plush, rugs are textured, there are iPod docks, TVs and WiFi. Breakfast is wherever you want it and lasts until 11am: homemade breads and jams, figs from the garden. Dinner could be risotto with wild fennel or barbecue'd meats and focaccia made with their own olive oil. Birds sing, cicadas hum… you'll never want to leave! *Minimum stay two nights. Children over 12 welcome. Extra beds available.*

Rooms	3 suites for 2: €140–€240. Extra bed €50.
Meals	Meals available on request. Lunch from €8, dinner from €15. Restaurants 5km.
Closed	November–March.

Simon Carey
Casa Colleverde, Via Marciano 48,
Loc. Sarticola, 19033 Castelnuovo Magra

Tel	+39 0187 670023
Mobile	+39 333 8221992
Email	info@casacolleverde.com
Web	www.casacolleverde.com

Tuscany

Podere Conti

Set in an organically certified, 200-acre olive estate beneath the magnificent Apennine mountains, this 17th-century hamlet, procured by Corrado and English Cornelia, recently renovated whilst raising a family, is agriturismo perfection. Follow a winding five-kilometre drive through chestnut, hazelnut and oak forest (ensuring utter seclusion), be greeted by charming Cornelia, decant into rooms beautifully designed with Arabian (not Tuscan) flair; both spent time in Abu Dhabi. Find exquisite rugs on cotto floors, raw beams, antique screen bedheads, richly textured cushions, delicious cotton bedding, little chandeliers, creaky trunks, glass bedside lights, and breezy bathrooms with free-standing tubs and monogrammed towels... all feels uncluttered and balanced. La Tavolata, their restaurant, serves delicious estate-produced meals (game in season) against sensational valley sunsets. There's loads to do both on the estate and off – this is heaven for free-range kids. And, with secluded nooks, poolside daybeds and hammocks in secluded crannies, it's pretty nice for adults too. Oh, and a haunted ruin! *Pets by arrangement.*

Rooms	6 doubles: €95-€140.
	3 suites for 4: €150-€200.
	1 apartment for 5; 2 apartments for 4: €190-€300.
	Singles €80-€120.
	Extra bed/sofabed €35 per person per night.
Meals	Breakfast €10.
	Lunch/dinner with wine €25.
	Book in advance.
Closed	Rarely.

Cornelia Conti
Podere Conti,
Via Dobbina Macerie 3,
51023 Filattiera
Mobile   +39 348 2681830
Email   info@podereconti.com
Web   www.podereconti.com

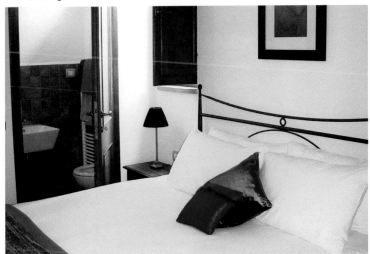

Casa Gisella

In the chestnut-mantled Lunigiana mountains, Bastia village is quaint, cobbled, labyrinth'd with lanes and dominated by an ancient, surely unassailable fort. Sitting on the breakfast terrace at Casa Gisella, distracted by gaspworthy views, you feel on top of the world. In the dream holiday home of Irish owners Ronnie and Alison the bedrooms are cosy, comfortable and classy all at the same time and show exceptional attention to detail; nothing too flash, just carefully considered and harmonious: a clean use of space and the odd contemporary painting; big wrought-iron beds covered with beautiful cream fabrics, textured throws and lots of cushions; power showers, snazzy lighting and WiFi. Thick, exposed medieval walls and beams make rooms snug and the big sitting room has a fire for winter. The very modern kitchen is charming and there are guest discounts to be had at local restaurants. The place is a walkers' paradise – you could veer off in any direction for hours – and, being close to both sea and snow, is family-fabulous all year round.

Rooms	1 house for 6: £550–£890 per week.
Meals	Self-catering.
Closed	Never.

Ronnie & Alison Johnston
Casa Gisella, Via Bastia 20, Bastia,
54016 Licciana Nardi

Tel	Please enquire by email.
Mobile	+44 (0)7967 188017
Email	info@casagisella.com
Web	www.casagisella.com

Dimora Olimpia

When they arrived it was a ruin; a decade on, Olimpia and Gaetano's 16th-century farmhouse is an exquisitely restored home for them and their little girl. For the full force of its charm, approach by the cobbled back street where chickens potter. There are long views of fields, woods and rumpled hills from elegant terrace and pool. Passionate lovers of old things, your hosts are also fluent guides to the region. Gorgeousness abounds: bare beams and exposed brickwork have been lovingly preserved, there are old wall hangings, fine, early country furniture and, in the snug bedrooms, original shutters at tiny windows. The small apartment is simple and charming, peaceful and cool, the beds aligned with the Earth's magnetic field to ensure perfect sleep. The shower room is first-class, the kitchen tiny, the pillow cases lined with lace. You will dine well in nearby restaurants and self-caterers are most welcome to join B&B guests round the antique Indian table. Outside, you have a verdant, unspoilt and unsung part of Tuscany to explore — country roads, tiny villages, good walks, fine wines. *Minimum stay two nights.*

Rooms	1 double; 1 suite for 4: €80. 1 apartment for 2-3: €380-€450 per week.
Meals	Breakfast €5. Restaurants 4km.
Closed	Never.

Olimpia De Caro & Gaetano Azzolina
Dimora Olimpia,
Via Molesana,
54017 Licciana Nardi

Tel	+39 0187 471580
Email	info@dimoraolimpia.it
Web	www.dimoraolimpia.it

The Watermill at Posara

Enjoy secluded millstream gardens in little Posara, with the wonderful Rosario cascading below. This was a working mill until the 80s and downstairs nothing has changed: the flagged floors, the beams, the ancient passageways to different sections. Bill, Lois, their daughters and their dogs have moved from a castle in Scotland; and if they're not here to greet you, charming Kerstin will. Apartments have lovely views and an eclectic combination of furniture old and new, from a faux leopard skin-clad chaise longue to flowery shower curtains. Beds are new, fabrics are in natural colours, shower rooms are spotless and there are some marvellous old floor tiles. In summer, cool off in the plunge pool and cross the bridge to the 'bamboozery', a vast thicket of giant bamboo, a joy for hide-and-seekers. The little town of Fivizzano is a 20-minute walk and treks and horse tracks abound, but most people come for the spring and autumn courses, a vibrant programme of workshops in painting and writing. There's a kiwi garden near the courtyard, picnics at millstone tables, and a lovely sociable barbecue.

Rooms	1 apartment for 2;
	2 apartments for 4: £350-£795 per wk.
Meals	Self-catering.
Closed	Rarely.

	Bill Breckon
	Via del Mulino 12-20, Loc. Posara,
	54013 Fivizzano
Tel	+44 (0)20 7193 6246
Mobile	+39 366 4882587
Email	info@watermill.net
Web	www.watermill.net

Entry 129 Map 8

La Luna di Quarazzana

The entrance, across rough-mown grass – engagingly scruffy – softens you for the impact of the courtyard: the very essence of special. Ilaria, whose commitment to doing things sensitively is catching, laid the paving stones herself and the dappled sun falls on a table set for lunch. On one side is a ruined barn, doors patched and mended. Her entrance doors are handsome, solid – paint peeling. Inside at every turn there are engaging and surprising touches of authenticity and art. Rooms are simple, pretty, delightful – all with the hand of Ilaria whose personality is also stamped on the verdant garden. The village is half-ruined, an engaging hotch-potch of old buildings at the top of a rough road high in these beautiful hills, chestnut forests all around. Ilaria, gentle, smiling and endlessly generous, is bringing new life to Quarazzana and new vitality to the concept of 'special'. She will be entirely there for you, and you may not want to stray beyond the house. But do, for the coast is not far and the walks are beautiful.

Rooms	2 doubles: €65-€85. 1 family suite for 3; 1 family room for 4 (2 doubles): €85-€120. Singles €65.
Meals	Dinner available on request.
Closed	Rarely.

Ilaria Bacherini
La Luna di Quarazzana, Nardi 16,
Quarazzana, 54013 Fivizzano

Tel +39 0585 949181
Mobile +39 331 3111202
Email lalunadiquarazzana@gmail.com
Web www.quarazzana.it

Lemons Guest House

An aesthetic treat – Erica and Massimo's restoration of this 18th-century village house beneath the Apuan Alps is a triumph. They've created a setting of huge charm and calm with all the personal touches of a cherished, artistic home. You'll see Erica's sculptures among the many other treasures here – ancient and modern: a 10th-century portrait in the dining room, St Francis in the hallway, Sicilian bathroom tiles. Sculptors can use the studio then take a break in the beautifully intimate garden, perhaps on the canopied day bed. On warm days lingering breakfasts – with plenty of good homemade things – can be outdoors too, in the shade of the pergola. Beamed bedrooms are all differently lovely, comfortable and elegant, some with masterfully restored frescoes, one with a roll top bath. Every piece – some reflecting Erica's life in Turkey – fits perfectly. There's an inviting book-filled, first-floor sitting room; a sauna and a jacuzzi. Hill-walk from the back door, cycle to the artists' village of Pietrasanta. Sandy beaches are a 15-minute drive, Pisa is 30. The trick is not to book too short a stay! *Whole house available on request.*

Rooms	4 doubles; 1 twin/double: €120–€160.
Meals	Occasional dinner with wine, €35.
	Restaurants nearby.
Closed	Rarely.

Erica Cavalli
Lemons Guest House,
Via del Pizzetto 1,
55045 Pietrasanta
Tel   +39 0584 772402
Email   info@lemonsguesthouse.com
Web   www.lemonsguesthouse.com

Entry 131   Map 8

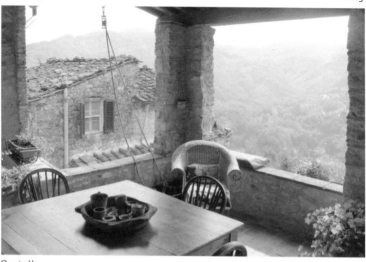

Castello

If you seek adventure and seclusion in deepest Tuscany, read on – for this authentic hillside hamlet, unchanged for centuries, holds a certain thrill. It clings precariously to terraced olives and vines just north of Lucca, a jumble of stone farm workers' houses, not all inhabited. Up 45 low steps is No. 13, a cool, rustic cocoon of chunky stone, terracotta and chestnut, whose wonderful terrace gazes south and west over the multi-coloured Serchio valley. Laze out here on wicker chairs, reading in the sun, chatting over an espresso, enjoying meals prepared with the owner's complimentary home-produced olive oil. The rustic kitchen flows through an original arch into a large, whitewashed sitting room with local furniture and a wood-burner for autumn nights. The simple bedrooms share a big tiled bathroom – and that stunning view. It's a 20-minute walk down a steep, ancient mule path to Valdottavo village, or set off in the car down the hairpin bends. An intriguing place of seclusion and inspiration, where you may hole up to pen a novel or spend happy days roaming the Garfagnana and Apuan Alps.

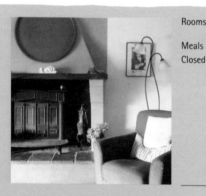

Rooms	1 house for 4: £590 per week.
	Sofabed available.
Meals	Restaurants 3km.
Closed	December–March.

Mike Wilson
Castello, 55067 Valdottavo

Tel	+44 (0)20 8965 4494 /
	+39 0583 835820
Mobile	+44 (0)7968 286019
Email	to-mike@hotmail.co.uk
Web	www.tuscanycastello.com

Rosignoli

A warm friendly farmhouse: unadulterated Tuscany. With coolly tiled cotto floors, whitewashed beamed ceilings and a dusky pink wood-burner in the master bedroom, it's a peaceful year-round retreat. This colourful ivy and rose-clad building comes surrounded by olive groves, as any Tuscan estate worth its salt should be; aspiring artists should come easel-armed to capture the symmetry and wildness of the trees and the grounds. Relax in the shady pergola, debating where garden ends and green countryside begins. Birds, trees and flowers abound, views are expansive, nothing offends eye or ear. Inside, pictures dot colourwashed walls and the cosy kitchen has table, chairs and a fireplace for twilight gatherings. One twin bedroom has ornate pink and green beds and a characterful sloping ceiling, sunlight warms large antique wardrobes, ceilings have fans and bathrooms are functional. Intelligent Emanuela will ensure your stay is comfortable. Near heavenly Lucca, you're close to both city and sea. What a spot to while away the summer. *Minimum stay three nights.*

Rooms	1 house for 8: €1,000–€1,200 per wk.
Meals	Restaurants 3km.
Closed	Rarely.

Emanuela Cenami Spada
Rosignoli,
Via Orbicciano, 55041 Orbicciano

Tel	+39 0584 956013
Mobile	+39 348 6044110
Email	spada@versilia.toscana.it
Web	www.sweetuscany.blogspot.it

Entry 133 Map 8

Albergo San Martino

What a position: in a secluded corner of Lucca, a minute from bars, restaurants and ramparts. There's a fresh-faced enthusiasm about the little San Martino now that the young Morottis have taken over; smiling faces behind reception and breakfasts that shine. Expect cheese and salami platters, baskets of different breads, homemade cakes, yogurts and fresh fruits every day – enjoyed in the courtyard in summer. No architectural flourishes, no rushes to the head – just a simple, comfortable, family-run hotel in one of Italy's loveliest towns. Gone are the fitted carpets, new are the wooden floors. The traditionally furnished, uncluttered bedrooms have creamy silk-like curtains and soft coloured walls, cute shuttered windows and interesting paintings, refurbished bathrooms, the odd fresco. Two new suites in the adjoining building have hydromassage baths and showers and Room 108 gets its own terrace, but all of them will please you. The Duomo is a stroll, there's a concert in San Giovanni every night, and bike rental – for Lucca's cycle-friendly walls – is nearby.

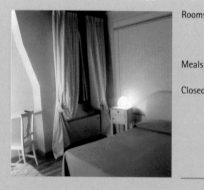

Rooms	9 doubles (some rooms interconnect): €80–€110.
	2 suites for 2: €130–€170.
	Private car park €15.
Meals	Breakfast €10.
	Special price for guests at osteria, 500m.
Closed	Rarely.

Andrea Morotti
Albergo San Martino,
Via della Dogana 9,
55100 Lucca

Tel	+39 0583 469181
Email	info@albergosanmartino.it
Web	www.albergosanmartino.it

Palazzo Orsucci

You're in Lucca, unrivalled spot for a romantic escape and this 16th-century *palazzo signorile* was once one of the most important buildings in the city. A wide stone staircase takes you to the second floor and a big beautiful living room suffused with light and views from two huge windows; you can even see the oak tree-topped Guinigi Tower! Ceilings are double height and beamed, doorways are high, sofas are capacious and cardinal red. Off one end is the bathroom, deep-blue tiled and stocked with immaculate towels; off the other is the peaceful bedroom, spacious and inviting, with an elegant chaise longue and exquisite frescoes on every inch of the walls and ceiling. As for the kitchen, its a joy to work in and has all you need, right down to two types of coffee maker. No surprise that these owners also run a superb hilltop B&B: Sawday's La Palazzetta del Vescovo in Umbria. Gaze on Tuscan hills as you stroll along the great Roman walls, sip a fruit cocktail on the Piazza San Martino, make a beeline for the churches, and don't miss San Michele, Italy's loveliest. *Minimum stay four nights.* .

Rooms	1 apartment for 2: £590–£750 per week.
	Price per night available on request.
Meals	Restaurants nearby.
Closed	Never.

	Paola Maria & Stefano Zocchi
	Palazzo Orsucci,
	Via Guinigi 16,
	55100 Lucca
Tel	+39 0758 745183
Email	info@lapalazzettadelvescovo.it
Web	www.palazzorsucci.com

Albergo Villa Marta

The travel book-strewn table in reception, crafted from an Indonesian bed, sets the mood: elegant, not stuffy. The villa-hotel is the creation of the young Martinellis who personally welcome you and attend to your every whim… a Tuscan Christmas? A wine and chocolate tour? All can be arranged. With two flights of steps leading to an entrance on either side, the elegant, loftily positioned 19th-century villa stands in sweeping lawns enfolded by the Monti Pisani, from whose verdant hills you can spot Pisa's leaning tower. The whole feel is intimate yet there's masses of space, and a terrace for spring and summer wafted by magnolias, jasmine and pines. Bedrooms ooze subtlety and comfort: fabrics with flowers and stripes, peach and grey walls, modern art. Bed linen is delicious, walk-in showers luxurious, views bucolic. Return after a day in Lucca (catch the bus) to cocktails in the garden and a dip in the pool. The chef gives an international twist to her delicious Tuscan dishes, and in winter you breakfast by an open fire, on breads and brioche straight from the oven. Gorgeous.

Rooms	8 twin/doubles; 7 twin/doubles (annexe): €79-€450. Singles €69-€450.
Meals	Menu à la carte, €25-€50. Wine €20-€80. Gluten-free options available.
Closed	January.

Andrea Martinelli
Albergo Villa Marta,
Via del Ponte Guasperini 873,
San Lorenzo a Vaccoli, 55100 Lucca
Tel   +39 0583 370101
Email   info@albergovillamarta.it
Web   www.albergovillamarta.it

Fattoria Mansi Bernardini

Extra virgin olive oil is pressed from the groves that clothe this ancient estate in rural Lucca, and a cluster of vines produce DOC wine. It doesn't get much more Mediterranean than this: a hamlet of farmhouses immersed in gardens, all stone walls and steps, climbing vines and nodding roses. It's a bucolic scene that could come straight from an easel – indeed, you may meet an artist or two, sketching in the shade of the big magnolia, finding inspiration in the hills around. Generations of the Bernardini family have lived and loved this place; we were equally enamoured. There's B&B in the cottages of Il Borghetto – you skip across to the greenhouse for breakfast – and self-catering in the big 'villas' (one the old farm manager's house, another the hayloft). All have been beautifully renovated in a palette of Tuscan colours. Original stonework, cotto floors and beams are softly illuminated, kitchens are fitted, each house has its pool and garden and there's maid service most days. The owner lives in the main villa; Monica runs the office. A taste of Italy you thought no longer existed: elegance, comfort and peace.

Rooms	9 doubles; 3 twins: €130–€160 per night. 2 suites for 2-4: €180–€200 per night. 2 houses for 10; 1 house for 12; 1 house for 14: €1,000–€6,000 per wk.
Meals	Dinner €35, by arrangement. Wine €10. Restaurant 5km.
Closed	Rarely.

Marcello Salom
Fattoria Mansi Bernardini,
55018 Lucca
Tel   +39 0583 921721
Email   info@fattoriamansibernardini.it
Web   www.fattoriamansibernardini.com

Villa Michaela

A lifetime's treat. Writers, celebrities and a First Lady have all stayed here, in the opulent Tuscan villa with its *House & Garden* interiors. You can even make it your own: indulge family and friends and get married in its chapel. It's beautiful throughout the seasons here. Come for a few days, join a Slow Food house party, sample local wines, listen to opera. An interior designer has worked his magic on every room, mingling fine English furniture with classic Italian style, while Puccini, Verdi and Dante lend their names to the grander bedrooms, awash with frescoed ceilings, lavish fabrics, king-size beds and double sinks. Also: a family kitchen, a formal dining room, a library and a multimedia room, tennis and an outdoor pool. Dine al fresco, on divine Tuscan cuisine, and let your gaze drift over the floodlit gardens, heady with gardenias, to the 50 acres of pine forests and olive groves beyond. You are bathed in tranquillity yet it's a five-minute walk to the delightful village of Vorno, and unspoilt Lucca is a ten-minute drive. *Whole villa & wedding chapel on request.*

Rooms	15 suites for 2: €180–€220. Singles from €40 to €70. Dinner, B&B €135–€165 p.p. Extra bed/sofabed €50–€65.
Meals	Lunch/dinner by arrangement. Restaurant within walking distance. Other restaurants few minutes' drive.
Closed	Never.

Vanessa Rhode
Villa Michaela,
Via di Valle 8, 55060 Vorno

Tel	+44 (0)1428 683815/+39 058 3971112
Mobile	+39 345 1743733/+44 (0)7768 645500
Email	villamichaelatuscany@yahoo.co.uk
Web	www.villamichaela.com

Fattoria di Pietrabuona

Drink in gulpfuls of mountain fresh air in the foothills of the *Svizzera Pesciatina* – Tuscany's 'Little Switzerland'. Home to a beguiling brood of ancient breed Cinta Senese pigs, this huge estate immersed in greenery is presided over by an unlikely pig farmer, elegant, bubbly Signora. The farm buildings have been cleverly divided into apartments that fit together like a puzzle; we like the three oldest best, near the main villa, each very private. The rest – near the pool – are quite a drive up winding roads, precipitous in parts: not for the faint-hearted nor heavily-laden hire cars! All have gardens, barbecues and outside seating. The exteriors are full of character, the interiors are simple, and some of the newer have steep stairs. Help with the harvests, bring a Tuscan cookbook: the kitchens, with old sinks but with new everything else, beg to be used, and there's a lovely shop next to the office selling their own delicious vin santo and Cinta Senese sauce. The views are stunning – particularly from the pool – and the villages are worth a good wander. *Minimum stay two nights.*

Rooms	4 apartments for 2; 4 apartments for 4; 4 apartments for 6; 1 apartment for 8: €400–€1,525 per week.
Meals	Self-catering.
Closed	Never.

Maristella Galeotti Flori
Fattoria di Pietrabuona,
Via per Medicina 2, Pietrabuona,
51017 Pescia

Tel	+39 0572 408115
Email	info@pietrabuona.com
Web	www.pietrabuona.com

Entry 139 Map 8

Antica Casa "Le Rondini"

Imagine a room above an archway in an ancient hilltop village, within ancient castle walls. You lean from the window and watch the swallows dart to and fro; there are *rondini* inside too, captured in a 200-year-old fresco. The way through the arch – the via del Vento ('where the wind blows') – and the front door to this captivating house await just the other side. Step into a lovely room, a study in white – fresh lilies and snowy walls and sofas – dotted with family antiques and paintings. Fulvia and Carlo are warm, interesting hosts who have lovingly restored the house to its original splendour. The delightfully different bedrooms have wrought-iron bedheads, big mirrors and some original stencilling. Several, like the 'Swallow Room', have pale frescoes. All have good views. The little apartment, too, is simple, charming, peaceful. Just across the cobbled street is a walled garden with lemon trees – an idyllic place for breakfast on sunny mornings. A short walk brings you to the square where village ladies sit playing cards, children scamper and the church bell rings every hour, on the hour.

Rooms	5 doubles: €75–€130.
	1 apartment for 2-4: €65.
Meals	Breakfast €5 for self-caterers.
	Restaurant 200m.
Closed	Rarely.

Fulvia Musso
Antica Casa "Le Rondini",
Via M. Pierucci 21,
51011 Colle di Buggiano

Tel	+39 0572 33313
Email	info@anticacasa.it
Web	www.anticacasa.it

Tenuta di Pieve a Celle

Fiorenza welcomes you with coffee and homemade cake, Julie – the retriever – escorts you round the garden, and there are freshly-laid eggs for breakfast. This is pure, genuine hospitality. Off a country road and down a cypress-lined drive, the shuttered, ochre-coloured *colonica* sits amid the family farm's olive groves and vineyards. The Saccentis (three generations) live next door but this house feels very much like home. Bedrooms (one downstairs) are furnished with well-loved antiques, rugs on tiled floors and handsome wrought-iron or upholstered beds. Cesare, Fiorenza's husband, designed the fabrics – pretty country motifs – and his collection of African art is dotted around the rooms. Books, flowers, soft lighting give a warm and restful feel. There's an elegant but cosy sitting room, with fireplace, where you eat breakfast if it's too chilly on the patio, and dinner – delicious – is by request. Sometimes the Saccentis join you: a real family affair. Laze by the pool with views to distant hills, walk in the woods, borrow bikes or visit nearby Lucca.

Rooms	5 twin/doubles: €140–€160.
Meals	Dinner €30, by arrangement.
	Wine €10–€25. Restaurant 200m.
Closed	Rarely.

Cesare & Fiorenza Saccenti
Tenuta di Pieve a Celle,
Via di Pieve a Celle 158,
51100 Pistoia

Tel	+39 0573 913087
Email	info@tenutadipieveacelle.it
Web	www.tenutadipieveacelle.it

Villa de' Fiori

With its formal rose gardens, immaculate lawns and neat box-hedged gravel paths, Villa de' Fiori lives up to its name. Pass through impressive gates and follow the cypress-lined drive to the main house, a renovated, 17th-century confection of peach and white with smart green shutters, a loggia for candlelit dining, terraces and, hidden beyond a high hedge, a pool with sophisticated white sun umbrellas, fringed with orange trees. Modernistic awnings provide cover for dining on the lawns. Inside, simple, uncluttered décor justifies the agriturismo status: vaulted sitting rooms, a music room, original geometric tiles, paintings, good solid furniture, high windows and massive fireplaces. There are seven rooms in the house, two of which are large, child-friendly family suites. The excellent restaurant is host to a dining club; yoga, ayurvedic treatments and Polynesian massage complete your relaxation; and the olive groves, woodland and vineyards are perfect for exploring – for child and adult alike.

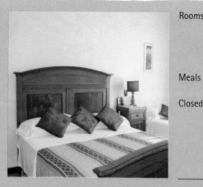

Rooms	4 doubles: €80-€140.
	2 family suites for 4: €110-€180.
	1 apartment for 3-5: €110-€165.
	Dinner, B&B €25 extra per person.
	Extra bed/sofabed €12-€25.
Meals	Dinner €20-€60. Wine €12-€150.
	Restaurant open to public.
Closed	January-March closed during the week.

Carla Silvestri
Villa de' Fiori,
Via Bigiano e Castel Bovani 39,
51100 Pistoia
Tel   +39 0573 450351
Email   info@villadefiori.it
Web   www.villadefiori.it

Villa Anna Maria

The wrought-iron gates swing open to reveal a strange but atmospheric haven. You feel protected here from the outside world, miles from the heat and bustle of Pisa. It is an intriguing place. Secret rooms lurk behind locked doors; some bedrooms seem untouched since the 17th century. They are all different, themed and with high ceilings, the most curious being the Persian and the Egyptian. The entrance hall is decked in marble, graced with columns and chandeliers; the library – a touch over the top for some – is in tune with the rest, and in tune, it must be said, with its eccentric owners. Claudio and his wife collect anything and everything and rooms are crammed with curios and collectibles. Yes, it's shambolic! Your host cares more about people than about money and there are no rules, so treat it as your home. There's a game room with billiards and videos (3,000 of them), table tennis, a garden with tall palms and woodland paths, a pool with piped music issuing from clumps of bamboo, a barbecue area for those who choose to self-cater, and a romping dog. *Minimum stay two nights. Rooms can be booked together as two apartments for two to eight.*

Rooms	6 doubles/triples: €120-€150.
	Singles €90.
	1 cottage for 2: €1,000 per week.
Meals	Dinner with wine, €40.
Closed	Rarely.

Claudio Zeppi
Villa Anna Maria,
SS dell'Abetone 146,
56010 Molina di Quosa
Mobile   +39 328 2334450
Email   zeppi@villaannamaria.com
Web   www.villaannamaria.com

Agriturismo Fattoria di Migliarino

On 3,000 farmed hectares between the Alps and the sea is a gated agriturismo run on well-oiled wheels. This is due to the indefatigable energy of Martino and Giovanna, a couple who understand families – they have four children themselves. The B&B rooms are in the main house, all great sizes, all different: Tuscan beds, soft wall lights and prints, mosquito-proofed windows, big arched sitting areas. There's a lovely communal sitting room with plenty of sofas, and a raftered dining room with two sociable tables. In the buildings beyond are 13 two-storey apartments of every shape and size, with terraces divided by hedges of jasmine so you may be as private or as sociable as you like. There's a pool open from June to September, fringed by neatly gravelled pathways and lawned spaces with sunloungers. On the Pisa road are restaurants, their farm shop – turkey, game, wine, vegetables, olive oil – and a well-being centre brimming with treatments. Football, tennis and ping-pong are on tap, riding and sailing can be arranged, and the sandy beaches are a bike ride away.

Rooms	5 doubles: €90–€110 per night. 4 triples: €130–€150 per night. 1 quadruple: €140–€180 per night. 6 apartments for 2; 5 apartments for 5; 2 apartments for 6; 1 apartment for 8; 1 apartment for 10: €380–€1,900 per wk. Sofabeds available.
Meals	Agriturismo's taverna 200m. Dinner (min. 15 people) on request.
Closed	Never.

Martino & Giovanna Salviati
Agriturismo Fattoria di Migliarino,
Viale del Mare 2,
56010 Migliarino
Mobile +39 348 4435100 / +39 335 6608411
Email   info@fattoriadimigliarino.it
Web   www.fattoriadimigliarino.it

Tenuta Poggio al Casone

You won't forget your first sight of this Tuscan villa, standing alone on top of the world. Alone but for the vast vineyards it oversees; this is wine country and the Castellani family have been in the business since Dante's time. The current generation cultivate organic chianti and now they've transformed the villa and two cottages into supremely elegant apartments. These would not look out of place in an Italian design fair, so sophisticated is their décor, so generous their space. Some apartments have mezzanine levels, others attics or terraces; yet others have jacuzzis and four-posters. The rooms are dressed in gorgeous fabrics and shades of soft ivory and latte, enlivened by splashes of aqua and Tuscan red. If the interiors are finely tuned, the views are utterly untouched. From organising wine tours and tastings to lake fishing and mountain biking, Michela and her team take care of you with consummate professionalism. Swim in the pool, fire up the barbecue, visit Pisa and the Etruscan coast. Fresh, stylish, memorable – a huge treat. *Minimum stay seven nights in high season.*

Rooms	5 apartments for 2 ; 2 apartments for 3; 2 apartments for 4; 1 apartment for 5: €630–€1,850 per week.
Meals	Self-catering.
Closed	Rarely.

Famiglia Castellani
Tenuta Poggio al Casone,
Via Volpaia 16,
56042 Crespina

Tel	+39 0506 42259
Email	resort@poggioalcasone.com
Web	www.poggioalcasone.com

Palazzo Cecchi Serragli

A lovely, lively, hilltop village immersed in rolling countryside, Palaia straddles two deep valleys. Negotiate the winding country roads, pull up in front of the big stone clock tower by the town hall and there it is – the unassuming façade which leads to Palazzo Cecchi Serragli. Through an inner courtyard, up 35 stone steps (no lift – this is for the sprightly!), to arrive on the second floor. Enter a living room with a sofa and two armchairs, and a state-of-the-art kitchenette set back under an arch. A staircase leads to a marble and stone bathroom and a pretty mezzanine. Two small, comfortable bedrooms and a further bathroom overlook the inner courtyard. Yet perhaps the greatest treat awaits beyond the mezzanine… up a further staircase, narrow and steep, and a further, even narrower, outside stair, to a roof terrace with a sensational view – to Pisa, Volterra and vine-braided hills. It's a heavenly spot for a bask in the sun, a glass of wine or a quiet read. Hike the marked trails, visit Tuscany's treasures, then back for a swim in the condominium's little garden, and a delectable wild boar casserole in Restaurant Bacciomeo. *Not suitable for children.*

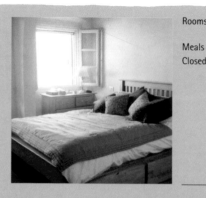

Rooms	1 apartment for 4: €550–€850 per week. Short stays available, €95–€125 per night.
Meals	Restaurants nearby.
Closed	Rarely.

Philip Doe
Palazzo Cecchi Serragli,
4 Palazzo Cecchi Serragli,
Via del Popolo 72,
56036 Palaia

Tel	+44 (0)20 7998 4972
Email	philipdoe@talktalk.net

Antica Dimora Leones

A labyrinth of vaulted ceilings, stone fireplaces and original frescoes in the heart of the medieval *borgo* of Palaia. The palazzo was restored in the 1800s but goes way back to 1000AD, when it formed part of the castle. Now it is an antique collector's paradise — which is no surprise: the owner's grandparents were antique dealers. It almost feels as though they are still here, wandering the historic corridors and rooms. Specialness is everywhere, from the high frescoed ceilings of the 'noble floor' to the bare beams and rooftop views of the characterful servants' quarters. Every floor (the lift is for luggage only) has a wonderful sitting room or library, with books, comfy chairs and something precious in each corner. A tray of drinks awaits your arrival; the buffet breakfast (salami, cheeses, homemade cakes) is served in the beamed dining room or under wisteria in the pretty garden. So much history, yet there are some winning modern touches — notably the seven-person hydropool. Restorative, soothing, special — head out to discover Tuscany and don't miss the lovely Etruscan town of Volterra.

Rooms	9 doubles; 1 single: €95–€120.
Meals	Lunch/dinner with wine, €35, on request (small groups only). Restaurant 100m.
Closed	Rarely.

Andrea Soldani
Antica Dimora Leones,
Via della Rocca 2,
56036 Palaia

Tel	+39 0587 622024
Email	info@leones-palaia.it
Web	www.leones-palaia.it

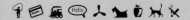

Castello Ginori di Querceto

Here's something for families who want the Tuscan sun but don't want to spend the earth. Querceto is a hamlet, a rambling medieval *borgo* on many levels, whose nucleus is a castle around which workers' cottages have evolved (and in the family since 1543!). Leave the car outside the walls and enter a timewarp; the Liscis may own 15 hectares of vineyards and produce a number of important red wines but no-one is in a hurry here. The apartments too will charm you: a clean plain décor in a rustic style, comfort without the frills. There are bright tartan cotton bedspreads, dark shutters to keep out the light, resuscitated floor tiles and nice old doors, simple kitchens with copper pans; the farmhouse sleeping eight (set apart with a small private pool) is brilliant value. The restaurant in the village sells fresh pasta and milk, fruit and vegetables, a bread van calls three times a week and the wine is on the spot. The grounds (not the gardens) are yours to roam, picnic spots are close and the big swimming pool is down the steep track, surrounded by olive trees.

Rooms	4 apartments for 2; 1 apartment for 3; 1 apartment for 4; 2 apartments for 6: €470–€1,550. 1 cottage for 8: €1,600–€2,000. 1 house for 6: €1,200–€1,500. Prices per week.
Meals	Self-catering.
Closed	January-February.

Cristina Sannazzaro
Loc. Querceto,
56040 Montecatini Val di Cecina
Tel   +39 0588 37472
Mobile   +39 335 5405006
Email   info@castelloginoridiquerceto.it
Web   www.castelloginoridiquerceto.it

La Fonte Villa

Deep in the Borgo Pignano estate grounds is this peaceful stone house converted as part of a bio-dynamic project. The large, long and arched ground floor, with French windows to the covered terrace and lake views, is a brilliant space for yoga, writing or dancing courses: off-white walls, wooden beams and floors, wood-burning stove. There's a separate study/dining room and you can really get to work in the excellent, professionals' kitchen with its central island for preparation and demonstration, hanging utensils and glass fronted cabinets so you can see where everything is, and huge semi-circular window to let the views in. Perfect! The style of the bedrooms is simple with colourful bedspreads, whitewashed beams and tiled floors. Some have mezzanine floors for extra beds and share practical, pristine bathrooms with showers. And there's room for three in the next-door detached annexe. Relax, explore, swim in the lake, head off to Florence or San Gimignano, or join what's on at the main villa at the centre of this unusual, beautiful and sustainably run Tuscan hamlet. *Due to remote location, a car is necessary during your stay.*

Rooms	1 house & annexe for 22: €5,000-€9,000 per week.
Meals	Borgo Pignano restaurant a 10-minute walk: dinner €30-€40, lunch €25. Restaurants 5km.
Closed	Rarely.

Camille Cazac
La Fonte Villa,
Località Pignano 6,
56048 Volterra

Tel	+39 0588 35032
Email	info@borgopignano.it
Web	www.borgopignano.it

Borgo Pignano

Perched on a hilltop, a magnificent 18th-century villa, a Tuscan dream, with 12th-century ramparts beautifully restored. Run with friendly flair by Camille and her team, this agriturismo hotel is integral to the eco-village lifestyle of the hamlet. And it's big, with elegant and frescoed bedrooms, princely limestone and marble bathrooms, and views to match – on a clear day you can see Corsica. The present peacefulness belies a turbulent past. You profit from the 19th-century conversion to a palatial country seat by the Marchese Ludovico Incontri and the addition of many seductions, including a saltwater infinity pool. Obviously you must have your wedding here, but what else to do? Take a painting or yoga class in the ballroom, listen to a pianist on the antique Bechstein, play billiards indoors, or bocce under the trees. Daydream, stargaze, watch a film, cycle to San Gimignano, shop in Florence, go truffle hunting or harvest olives. There's a crèche, a kindergarten… and fabulous buffet breakfasts, and candlelit dinners: feasts of local produce.

Rooms	4 doubles; 2 twin/doubles: €140–€310. 3 suites for 2: €300–€375. 1 family room for 2; 2 family rooms for 3; 1 family room for 4: €205–€360. Singles €205–€265. Extra sofabeds available in some rooms. Whole borgo €32,000 per week.
Meals	Lunch €25, dinner €30–€40, available on request. Restaurants 5km.
Closed	Rarely.

Camille Cazac
Borgo Pignano,
Loc. Pignano 6, 56048 Volterra

Tel	+39 0588 35032
Email	info@borgopignano.it
Web	www.borgopignano.it

Marignolle Relais & Charme

The best of two seductive worlds: a ten-minute drive brings you from the heart of Renaissance Florence to this classic country villa hotel. After a hectic day's sight-seeing it's heaven to unwind by the pool, facing olive groves and a cool wooded hillside, the scent of lavender, rosemary and roses rich in the air. Gracious Florentine hospitality from the Bulleri family is the memorable icing on the cake. Manager – and sommelier – Lorenzo organises and guides vineyard and general tours (it's only 30 miles to San Gimignano). Claudio loves to share his passion for golf. Paola, who has styled every room, runs brilliant cooking lessons with daughter Silvia. Buffet breakfasts are elegant in the glazed gazebo, with homemade cakes, local jams and breads; eggs and bacon too if you wish. A light Tuscan evening meal can be arranged if you'd rather stay put, perhaps lingering afterwards with a brandy by a winter fire. Children can let off steam in the family room. Traditional, super-comfortable and well-equipped bedrooms have parquet floors, coordinated floral fabrics and lovely spacious, white-tiled bathrooms. *Smoking area available.*

Rooms	8 doubles: €145-€275. 1 family room for 4: €235-€315. Singles €115-€180.
Meals	Light lunch & dinner available on request. Restaurant nearby.
Closed	Never.

Lorenzo Bulleri
Marignolle Relais & Charme,
Via San Quirichino 16, 50124

Tel	+39 055 2286910
Email	info@marignolle.com
Web	www.marignolle.com

Torre di Bellosguardo

Imposing, mellow buildings, exquisite gardens fashioned by a friend of Dante, and magical views of Florence: it is breathtaking in its beauty and ancient dignity. The entrance hall is impressive, glorious, with a frescoed ceiling and an ocean of floor; the view reaches through a vast splendid sun room to streams with stepping stones, lily ponds and hothouses of exotics. A water feature meanders along a stone terrace, a twisted wisteria shades the walkway to the potager, donkeys, goats, ponies graze, and cats doze. Amble round the lovely, flower-filled garden, find secret paths and hidden corners, pause by the pool for stunning views of the city. Each bedroom is different with its own character, most can be reached by lift but the tower suite, with windows on all sides demands a climb. The bedrooms defy modern convention and are magnificent in their simplicity, the furniture richly authentic and antique, the views sublime. With luck you'll meet Signor Franchetti whose manners and English are impeccable, and Coco Bello, his charismatic pink parrot. All this, and Florence a ten-minute cab ride down the hill.

Rooms	8 doubles: €300.
	7 suites for 2: €400.
	1 single: €160.
	Extra bed/sofabed available €50 per person per night.
Meals	Breakfast (included in winter only), €20. Restaurant 2km.
Closed	Never.

Amerigo Franchetti
Torre di Bellosguardo,
Via Roti Michelozzi 2,
50124 Florence

Tel	+39 0552 298145
Email	info@torrebellosguardo.com
Web	www.torrebellosguardo.com

Il Palagetto Guest House

A ten-minute bus ride from the main station, in a peaceful side street looking down on the city, is a small friendly guest house behind locked gates, owned by charming Tiziana. She and Ruggero live close by and come in to prepare breakfast each day – a big generous spread laid out on a polished bench-table – and to catch up with their guests. The villa – not so long ago used by the Uffizi to restore works of art – has been cosily and handsomely furnished. A landscape designer with a love of gardens, Tiziana has named the bedrooms after plants. There's spacious 'Gingko' for families, with a wrought-iron four-poster and orange taffeta curtains; bright light 'Primula', with plush pretty bedspreads; and 'Rosa', 'Clematis' and sweet 'Salvia', these three sharing a big bathroom (bathrobes are provided). Find new polished floor boards and lovely old terracotta tiles, wooden carvings by an artist from Mugello, and everything spotless and gleaming. There are books and guidebooks for the borrowing, you're a ten-minute walk into the centre of the city, and the WiFi is fast and free. *Minimum stay two nights. Pets by arrangement.*

Rooms	2 doubles (sharing bathroom with single); 1 twin/double: €49–€109. 1 family room for 2-4: €99–€149. 1 single (sharing bathroom with doubles): €39–€69. Extra bed/sofabed €20–€30.
Meals	Restaurants 10-minute walk.
Closed	Rarely.

Ruggero Bovelli
Il Palagetto Guest House,
Via Monte Oliveto 52, 50124 Florence

Tel	+39 0559 332257
Mobile	+39 335 7325593
Email	info@ilpalagettofirenze.it
Web	www.ilpalagettofirenze.it

Hotel Albion

Ten minutes from the heart of fashionable Florence (near the railway station) you're surrounded by shops, restaurants and apartments. In among the flashing scooters and cars find a three-storey 19th-century palazzo with pointed arch windows and pretty pots of flowers outside; there's no lift but friendly staff will heave the suitcases. Help yourself to a generous buffet breakfast at tables with bright yellow table cloths; you're bound to meet bubbly owner Sara and her dad. A bar area is crowded with tables, chairs and hand-written tourist information, perfect for a drink while deciding where to eat or to catch up with some work. All bedrooms (one on the ground floor) are comfortable and light with pristine en suite bathrooms; they have a family-home feel and the odd antique. A wide marble staircase shoots through the centre of the building (rather neglected but with a lovely bit of original fresco) leading to three big attic rooms and a small kitchen; some will adore it up here, others may feel cut off from the action. Saunter or cycle to museums, churches and markets from this friendly, buzzing place.

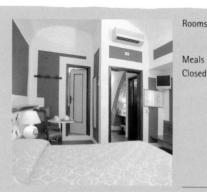

Rooms	7 twin/doubles: €90–€165.
	2 family rooms for 3-4: €130–€210.
	3 triples: €110–€185.
Meals	Restaurants within walking distance.
Closed	Rarely.

Sara Ravalli
Hotel Albion,
Via il Prato 22,
50123 Florence
Tel   +39 0552 14171
Email   sara@hotelalbion.it
Web   www.hotelalbion.it

Casa Howard Guest Houses

Strolling distance from bus and railway station is this handsome palazzo, the talk of the town. No reception staff, no communal space, just a big fur throw on a welcoming divan and smiling housekeepers who bring breakfast to your room. On each floor an honesty fridge carries soft drinks, wine and champagne, but best of all are the bedrooms, eclectic, original and humorous — and with heaps of style. If you can splash out on a larger, more lavish one, do, though all are delightful. One, with a sunken bath and Japanese prints on the walls, is a deep sensual red; another is 18th-century elegant with a black velvet sofa and gold taffeta curtains; off the patio is the Studio, an apartment with a chic kitchenette and a big bed above. There's one room for those who come with their best friend in tow (dogs' beds, baskets, large terrace), while the Play Room is for families (Disney videos, a climbing wall!). Bathrooms are memorable and nights are air-conditioned and peaceful, providing you keep windows shut. A breath of fresh air and two steps from the Duomo. *Minimum stay two nights at weekends in high season.*

Rooms	10 doubles; 2 suites for 2: €120–€250. 1 apartment for 2-3: €1,500–€2,200 per week.
Meals	Breakfast €12. Restaurants nearby.
Closed	Never.

Casa Howard
Casa Howard Guest Houses,
Via della Scala 18,
50123 Florence
Tel   +39 0669 924555
Email   info@casahoward.it
Web   www.casahoward.com

Be One

This small boutique hotel is perfectly tailored to its city centre location on the third floor of a five-storey palazzo. As people buzz in and out to the language schools and the Hard Rock Café next door, a subtle red carpet takes you off into the entrance hall and to cool modern interiors where designer furniture mixes with Italian art. Black and white prints of historic Florence adorn the halls and contrast with a crystal glass staircase that sweeps you up to the penthouse suite. This suite, with a remarkable corner kitchen and massage bath tub, may be the grandest of the rooms but the others almost trump it with their superior views. All of the rooms are decorated with elegance and style, skilfully blending modernity (the bathrooms are superb) with antiquity. The careful soundproofing throughout the building makes every room, including a communal sitting area that is flooded with light from its surround of windows, a perfect Florentine retreat. World-renowned galleries and glorious architecture are all around you, and this lavish lair sits at the heart of it all.

Rooms	7 doubles: €210–€350.
	1 suite for 4: €540–€660.
Meals	Restaurants nearby.
Closed	Never.

Antonio Tavera
Be One,
Via dei Brunellischi 1,
50123 Florence

Tel	+39 0552 19535
Email	reservation@b1florence.com
Web	www.b1florence.com

Palazzo Niccolini al Duomo

One minute you're battling with tourists in the Piazza del Duomo, the next you're stepping into a piece of history, this extraordinarily lovely palazzo. Take the lift to the *residenza*; two small trees, a brace of antique chairs and a brass plate announce the friendly reception. Built by the Naldini family in the 16th century on the site of the sculptor Donatello's workshop, the building has steadily grown in grandeur; the recent restoration hasn't detracted from its beauty, merely added some superb facilities. It's all you hope such a place will be – fabulously elegant and luxurious, with 18th-century frescoes, trompe l'oeil effects, fine antiques and magnificent beds… but in no way daunting, thanks to many personal touches; your host is a delight. The top suite looks the Duomo in the eye – staggering. Relax in the gracious drawing room with family portraits and books. Two signed photographs were sent in 1895 by the King of Italy to Contessa Cristina Niccolini, the last of the Naldini. She married into the current owner's family, bringing the palazzo as part of her dowry. An exceptional place.

Rooms	5 doubles: €150-€380. 5 suites for 2: €300-€500. Singles €130-€220.
Meals	Dinner available on request. Restaurants nearby.
Closed	Never.

Filippo Niccolini
Palazzo Niccolini al Duomo,
Via dei Servi 2,
50122 Florence
Tel   +39 0552 82412
Email   info@niccolinidomepalace.com
Web   www.niccolinidomepalace.com

Entry 157   Map 8

Le Stanze di Santa Croce

A great find, this very old *terratetto*, nestled between its neighbours on a small street off the Piazza Santa Croce – perfect for those who want to stay in the historic centre. There's attention to detail at every turn; everything has been thought through beautifully. The four elegant rooms, one with a four-poster, aren't large but are beautifully presented, each named after famous Florentine bells, each with its own refined identity. They provide sanctuary from the heat of the city, while the jasmine-garlanded breakfast terrace is the perfect place from which to enjoy Mariangela's baking. Your charming host runs her own highly acclaimed Tuscan cookery courses so make sure you book a lesson during your stay. Delectable cakes, homemade jams and a variety of teas are in constant supply. There's a cool lobby with comfortable seating and plenty of books, the internet and useful local info on where to go and what to see, and cheery Mariangela is always on hand to tell you more: the best markets, the artisan workshops, the hidden corners. Fresh and inviting.

Rooms	4 doubles: €145–€160. Ask about prices for singles.
Meals	Restaurant 50m.
Closed	Rarely.

Mariangela Catalani
Le Stanze di Santa Croce,
Via delle Pinzochere 6,
50122 Florence

Mobile	+39 347 2593010
Email	info@lestanzedisantacroce.com
Web	www.lestanzedisantacroce.com

Residenza Casanuova

Live like a Florentine in the heart of the city, high above the madding crowds. The top floor of this handsome palazzo belonged to Beatrice and Massimiliano's grandmother and is filled with her elegant taste. There are panelled doors and parquet floors, creamy walls and tall windows. Light-filled rooms are furnished with antiques, grand mirrors and pretty chandeliers, polished surfaces are dotted with china vases, walls hung with engravings, portraits and a collection of oils by great-grandfather. Calm, uncluttered bedrooms are soft and spacious, each with an amusing theme: a collection of umbrellas, hats or tin boxes. One has a magnificent Murano mirror. Breakfast on beautiful china in the handsome dining room or on the terrace before plunging into the city's museums, galleries and churches. The owners, with an apartment on the same floor, will help with tours, museums and shopping trips. Friendly and easy-going, they're on hand when you need them or happy to leave you alone. Return to a private terrace for a glass of wine and rooftop views.

Rooms	4 doubles: €129-€179. 1 single: €79-€92. Extra bed/sofabed available €30-€40 per person per night.
Meals	Restaurants within walking distance.
Closed	Rarely.

Beatrice & Massimiliano Gori
Residenza Casanuova,
Via della Mattonaia 21, 50121 Florence

Tel	+39 0552 343413
Mobile	+39 338 5450758
Email	info@residenzacasanuova.it
Web	www.residenzacasanuova.it

Entry 159 Map 8

1865 Residenza d'Epoca

Named after the era when the city was Italy's capital, this *residenza* is Florence at her best — authentic, graceful, and uncompromisingly chic. Michel and Cinzia (who, it's no surprise to learn, is a historian) have combined the elegance of 19th-century Florence with the comforts of 21st-century living. It works, beautifully. Frescos dance overhead, dark-stained floorboards gleam underfoot, chaise longues and other antique pieces sit comfortably alongside three-legged floor lamps, and there's fresh white linen on custom made beds — some with white cushioned headboards that stretch the length of the wall. Big marble bathrooms are state-of-the-art and filled with gorgeous smellies. The five bedrooms are named after writers who visited Florence in the 1800s — Dostoevsky, Henry James — adding to this B&B's quietly cultural air. There are bits that catch you by surprise too, such as the breakfast room with walls dressed in ruby red fabric. No outside space but open the windows for the green views and birdsong of the beautiful Wilson Gattai gardens. Florence's treasures lie at your feet!

Rooms	5 doubles: €175–€275.
Meals	Restaurants within walking distance.
Closed	Rarely.

Michel Sabatino
1865 Residenza d'Epoca, Via Luigi
Carlo Farini 12, 50121 Florence

Tel	+39 0552 340586
Mobile	+39 390 3838020
Email	michel.sabatino@gmail.com
Web	www.1865.it

Antica Dimora Firenze – Antiche Dimore Fiorentine

You'll reach the relaxed *residenza* via the small lift or the wide stone stairs, then come and go as you please – a friendly receptionist is here to welcome you. It's a treat to come back to a decanter of vin santo and a book of love stories by your bed. If it's not a four-poster you'll have a jasmine-scented balcony... Italian love of detail is evidenced by rose-pink and pistachio-green walls, luscious fabrics woven by local artisans, striped sofas, silk curtains and little vases of dried lavender. Black and white 19th-century prints and antique tiled floors combine beautifully with waffle towels and walk-in showers, modems and satellite TV: the best of old and new. Settle down in the sitting room, dip into almond biscuits and a cup of tea and plan where to have dinner; all the info's there. Browse a glossy book or a magazine, choose a DVD, be as private or as sociable as you like. There are homemade cakes and jams at breakfast, you are on a quietish street near the university and it's great value for the centre of Florence.

Rooms	3 doubles; 3 twins: €90–€150.
Meals	Restaurant 30m.
Closed	Never.

Lea Gulmanelli
Antica Dimora Firenze –
Antiche Dimore Fiorentine,
Via San Gallo 72, 50129 Florence

Tel	+39 0554 627296
Email	info@anticadimorafirenze.it
Web	www.anticadimorafirenze.it

Antica Dimora Johlea – Antiche Dimore Fiorentine

A cross between B&B and hotel – no room service but a friendly face on reception all day – the *residenza* idea is perfect for the independent traveller. Lea Gulmanelli has got her *residenze* down to a fine art and what's special about this one is the roof terrace. Weave your way past antiques tucked under sloping ceilings and up to a wide, sun-flooded, pergola'd space for breakfast and sundowners with a classic panorama of Florence – thrilling at night! The entire top floor of this restored 19th-century palazzo feels bright, light and inviting. Furnishings are colourful and fresh, bedrooms – some lofty, some more intimate – have beautiful silk-canopied four-poster beds, delicate prints on walls and mozzie-protected windows. Luxurious extras include radios, WiFi and satellite TV, there's an honesty bar for drinks and polished tables for breakfast. Romantics could ask for a room with a balcony. Michelangelo's David is at the Accademia round the corner, the Duomo is a ten-minute walk.

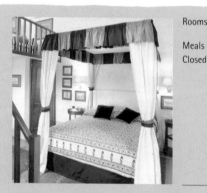

Rooms	2 doubles; 2 twins; 1 triple: €100–€170. 1 single: €75–€120.
Meals	Restaurant 30m.
Closed	Never.

Lea Gulmanelli
Antica Dimora Johlea –
Antiche Dimore Fiorentine,
Via San Gallo 80, 50129 Florence

Tel	+39 0554 633292
Email	anticajohlea@johanna.it
Web	www.johanna.it

Residenza Johanna I – Antiche Dimore Fiorentine

Astonishingly good value in the historic centre of Florence – and what an attractive, friendly place to be. You really feel as though you have your own pad in town, away from tourist bustle. Owner Lea has several other *residenze* (see previous entries). They were such a success that she and Johanna opened this one in a lovely 19th-century palazzo, shared with notaries and an embassy. Take the lift or marble stairs to a big welcome on the first floor from staff, keen to make your stay a happy one. Graceful arches, parquet floors and soft colours give a feeling of light and space to the two corridors, classical music wafts past and there are plenty of books and guides to browse through. The bedrooms are airy and cool, silk beautifies beds (some four-posters) and give the rooms a feeling of charm and elegance. All have good, stylish bathrooms. There's a new breakfast room, too. Slip out to a bar for a cappuccino before wandering happily off to the Duomo, the San Lorenzo market and the Piazza della Signora. *Free WiFi. Bike hire available nearby.*

Rooms	5 doubles; 4 twins: €71–€140.
	1 single: €50–€90.
Meals	Restaurants nearby.
Closed	Never.

Signora Ilanit
Residenza Johanna I –
Antiche Dimore Fiorentine,
Via Bonifacio Lupi 14, 50129 Florence

Tel	+39 0554 81896
Email	lupi@johanna.it
Web	www.johanna.it

Relais Villa Antea

A peaceful 1900s villa a 15-minute walk from Piazza San Marco – with parking! Off a leafy residential square, close to restaurants, antique shops, botanic gardens and Russian Orthodox church, is a friendly Italian-family concern, a lovely little find. The Antea is overseen from early morning until 8.30 at night by owner Dileita, her sister Serena and mascot Marta (the Jack Russell); when they go home, Florina takes over. Enjoy continental breakfast with fruits in season – and perhaps homemade *bombolone* (mini doughnuts) – served at tiny round tables in the elegant dining room. Up the white stone stair are big airy bedrooms with tall windows and timeworn parquet, lavish silken drapes in yellows and greens, net curtains, pristine covers, walk-in wardrobes, posies of plastic flowers. Extras include air con, mini bar, WiFi and a restaurant guide put together by Dileita. Beds are extra-king in size and bathrooms are vast, with hydromassage showers. Through the side gate is a courtyard shaded by horse chestnut trees; a further pebbled courtyard makes a tranquil spot for an aperitivo before a night on the town.

Rooms	6 doubles: €100–€180.
Meals	Restaurant 2-minute walk.
Closed	Rarely.

Dileita Lenzi
Relais Villa Antea,
Via Puccinotti 46,
50129 Florence

Tel	+39 0554 84106
Email	info@villaantea.com
Web	www.villaantea.com

Villa La Sosta

It's a five-minute bus ride to the Duomo, yet the 1892 villa on the Montughi hill stands in large landscaped gardens where songbirds lull you to sleep. The mansard-tower sitting room with sofas, books, billiards and views is a lofty place in which to relax. Bedrooms, with large windows and wooden shutters, are equally stylish with striking toile de Jouy, checks and dark Tuscan pieces. Interesting, too, are the artefacts – wooden statues and innumerable ivory carvings – gathered from the Fantonis' days in Africa; the family ran a banana plantation there. Simple breakfast is served outside under an ivy-covered pergola in summer or in the dining room, just off the family's bright sitting room; over coffee the young, affable Antonio and Giusi – a brother-and-sister team – help you plan your stay. If the city's treasures start to pall they will organise a day in the vineyards or local pottery villages. There's parking off the main road and the number 25 bus, which stops outside the gates, will ferry you into the city or up into the hills.

Rooms	3 doubles: €75–€130.
	1 triple: €99–€160.
	1 quadruple: €100–€120.
	Singles €70–€105.
Meals	Restaurants 800m.
Closed	Rarely.

Antonio & Giuseppina Fantoni
Villa La Sosta,
Via Bolognese 83,
50139 Florence
Tel   +39 0554 95073
Email   info@villalasosta.com
Web   www.villalasosta.com

Il Fornaccio

Half way up the hill, high above the Mugnone valley, is this blissful and bucolic spot; you could be miles from anywhere. But no: there's a pizzeria you can walk to and Florence can be glimpsed through the trees. Surrounded by olive orchards and fields, Il Fornaccio (the 'bread oven') is a 16th-century farmhouse whose oak and chestnut beams and terracotta floors have been beautifully restored. Loredana lives here with young daughter Eleonora, loves company (and dogs: meet the elderly German shepherd), gives you private sunbeds and tranquil seating corners and prepares breakfasts of homemade cakes, yogurts, fruits and jams before she leaves for work. Bedrooms feel lived in and loved, one reached via the living room, the other below, with a private kitchenette and a charming courtyard under the spreading linden tree: perfect for families. Both rooms have spectacular views. On cooler days you can share Loredana's books, fire and CDs; in summer you be sitting at the rustic stone table in the shade of the ancient oak, or plucking cherries and figs from the trees. *Sofabeds available.*

Rooms	1 double; 1 twin (with kitchenette & separate bath): €80–€120. Discounts on week-long stays.
Meals	Dinner with wine, on request. Restaurant 1km.
Closed	Rarely.

Loredana Pecorella
Il Fornaccio,
Via di Campolungo 297/B,
50036 Florence
Mobile   +39 348 7723629
Email   info@ilfornacciofirenze.com
Web   www.ilfornacciofirenze.com

Villa di Campolungo Agriturismo

Described as an 'elegant residence' in 1427, this secluded farm manor in the hills of Fiesole makes you feel you've stepped back 600 years. Its bold yellow façade peeks out from 1,500 organic olives which, thanks to friendly Silvia, produce extra virgin olive oil and olive soaps. Passionate about sustainability, Silvia and her husband renovated the building the traditional way: local *pietra serena* and limestone, Tuscan fabrics, mosaics. Intact are the stable doors and mangers, trussed beams, oil jars, steps and terracotta that give each spacious room its character. The rest is fresh and modern, from slinky sinks and cylindrical showers to monogrammed linen on big comfy beds. Silvia's homemade cakes at breakfast might tempt you to book a Tuscan cooking course or dinner on the terrace, whose views tumble over olive groves towards Florence. Vegetables are from the garden, water from the spring, heat from a ground source pump, energy from the sun... You can take a train to the city centre, carry a picnic into the hills or wander through Fiesole, whose history dates to the Etruscans. *Courses & short stays available.*

Rooms	7 doubles (extra bed available): €110–€180.
Meals	Dinner on request. Restaurant 1.5km.
Closed	Rarely.

Silvia Cantini
Via Campilungo 1, Località Querciola,
50010 Fiesole Caldine

Tel	+39 0550 515250
Mobile	+39 348 4950083
Email	info@villadicampolungo.it
Web	www.villadicampolungo.it

Casa Palmira

A medieval farm expertly restored by charming Assunta and Stefano who, being Italian, have a flair for this sort of thing. You are immersed in greenery yet half an hour from Florentine bustle. The views on the road to Fiesole are stunning; Stefano will ferry you around neighbouring villages in his mini-van, or you could hire mountain bikes and take one of Assunta's picnic baskets with you. For lazier days, the wonderful pool beckons. The log-fired sitting room sets the tone: the *casa* has a warm, Tuscan feel, and bedrooms open off a landing with a brick-walled 'garden' in the centre – all Stefano's work. Two have four-poster beds dressed in Florentine fabric, all have polished wooden floors and pretty views, onto the gardens where Stefano grows herbs and vegetables. You are 500 metres above sea level so... no need for air conditioning, no mosquitoes! Breakfast on seasonal fruits and Assunta's tasty scrambled eggs; dine on delicious Tuscan food. There is also an excellent restaurant up the road. *Minimum stay two nights. Kitchen available at additional cost.*

Rooms	4 twin/doubles: €80–€110.
	1 single: €60–€70. 1 triple: €110–€130.
	1 apartment for 3: €120–€130;
	€700–€850 per week.
Meals	Picnic available.
	Dinner with wine, €30.
	Restaurant 700m.
Closed	10 December to 10 March.

Assunta & Stefano Mattioli
Casa Palmira,
Via Faentina 4/1, Loc. Feriolo,
Polcanto, 50030 Borgo San Lorenzo

Tel   +39 0558 409749
Email   info@casapalmira.it
Web   www.casapalmira.it

Casa Valiversi

Perched on a hill, painted in pretty pink, this distinctive, distinguished B&B was once, incredibly, a laboratory. Just four rooms – one with a balcony, one with an open fire – and Mirella, warm, friendly and living next door. Tired of commuting to Florence every day, she opened her *casa* to guests, popping in to serve generous breakfasts. Inside are 20th-century antiques from her years of dealing, sprinkled over three floors with originality and taste. Armchairs range from cream 30s Art Deco to 60s bubblegum pink, bold art beautifies pale walls, a white 50s lamp dominates the glass dining table, the six dining chairs are immaculately upholstered. Bedrooms are serene spaces that breathe comfort and class and monogrammed linen while big arched windows overlook groves of olives. For self-caterers, the kitchen is fitted in contemporary style (plus one perfect antique cupboard from France), opening to the lovely garden, rose-climbed pergola and large terrace. Here in the hillsides of Sesto Fiorentino, five miles from Florence's centre, is a relaxing, refreshing and peaceful place to stay.

Rooms	4 twin/doubles: €100-€120. Whole house €3,000-€5,000 per week.
Meals	Use of kitchen €10. Restaurants 1km.
Closed	Never.

Mirella Mazzierli
Casa Valiversi,
Via Valiversi 61,
50019 Sesto Fiorentino

Tel	+39 0553 850285
Email	mirella@casavaliversi.it
Web	www.casavaliversi.it

Entry 169   Map 8

Azienda Agricola La Capannaccia

Constructed in 1753, revived phoenix-like from an 18th-century fire, commandeered by the Americans in WW2, and renovated over a period of 30 years by the current family, this country pile of an agriturismo (Chianti grapes, organic olive oil) is steeped in history and character. No pool but a large lawned garden with a hot tub to share, heaps of olive groves and vineyards to stroll, farm machinery all around and a stunning view from the top of the hill. As for the apartments, two occupy an extended wing, the other is in the main house. They exude an elegant simplicity with their solid wrought-iron beds, new fireplaces, mottled, clotted cream paint schemes, cotta floors, and classic, cosy kitchens. The apartment in the main house is decoratively busier, with its many antiques and Murano glass chandeliers. Your hosts, the charming Luca and his parents, are warm, fun, love horses (the stables house six, plus two shaky-kneed foals when we visited) and happy to advise on everything; they'll even drive you to the restaurant down the road. Beautifully positioned for day trips to Florence, and a riding school nearby. *Minimum stay two nights.*

Rooms	2 apartments for 2; 1 apartment for 4: €560–€1,750 per week.
Meals	Self-catering.
Closed	Rarely.

Luca Bini
Azienda Agricola La Capannaccia,
Via delle Selve 5, 50018 Scandicci
Tel   +39 0552 41839
Email   info@lacapannaccia.com
Web   www.lacapannaccia.com

La Canigiana Agriturismo

With Florence's Duomo glistening in the distance across a carpet of olive groves, this Tuscan farmhouse has the best of both worlds. Set amongst the sparkling air of the Chianti hills, it is 15 minutes from that glorious city. Producing organic olive oil, the farm has been in Alessandra's family for over 100 years. Her family and father still live on the estate — let yourself to be swept into their warm embrace. The apartments (with private entrances) share those glorious views. A cut above those of the average agriturismo, the bedrooms here are country comfortable with colourful bedspreads, wrought-iron beds, posies of fresh flowers and prints on white walls. Traditionally tiled floors, beams and shuttered windows add charm. Kitchen areas incorporated into the living room are fine for holiday cooking and there are pretty tablecloths for dinner; choose the ground-floor apartment for its lovely terrace, or take the two together. Those Tuscan jewels — Pisa, Lucca, Siena, Florence — are under an hour away, and there's an orchard-enclosed pool for your return. Bliss. *Minimum stay two nights, seven nights in high season.*

Rooms	2 apartments for 2: €490-€840 per wk. Extra bed/sofabed €10.
Meals	Self-catering.
Closed	Never.

Alessandra Calligaris
La Canigiana Agriturismo,
Via Treggiaia 146, 50020 La Romola

Tel	+39 0558 242425
Mobile	+39 339 4463483
Email	info@lacanigiana.it
Web	www.lacanigiana.it

Il Poggetto

A deliciously green and sunny Tuscan hilltop, surrounded by vineyards and olive groves. Once through the electronic gates, you'll be captivated by the views. The gardens are delightful, too: three hectares of rose-filled lawns, fruit trees, azaleas and heather (always something in flower), with pines and cypresses for shade and a terrace dotted with lemon and mandarin trees. Ivana and her family moved to the 400-year-old *casa colonica* in 1974 and have renovated beautifully, using original and traditional materials. The apartments are attractive, uncluttered and full of light. All have big comfortable beds, antique furniture and private patios. 'La Loggia' was once a hay barn; the huge, raftered living/dining area is superb and the old triangular air bricks are still in place. 'La Cipressaia', characteristically Tuscan in style and very private, is a conversion of the stable block, and sleeps five. 'Il Gelsomino', named after the jasmine outside the door, and 'La Pergola' join each other. Everyone has use of the pool, which is set apart in a stunning position: you can watch the sun rise and set from your lounger. *Minimum stay three nights on weekdays, seven nights in high season.*

Rooms	2 apartments for 2; 1 apartment for 4: €490–€1,092. La Cipressaia for 5: €994–€1,393. Prices per week. Extra bed/sofabed available €10 per person per night.
Meals	Self-catering.
Closed	Rarely.

Andrea Boretti & Ivana Pieri
Il Poggetto,
Via del Poggetto 14,
50025 Montespertoli

Mobile	+39 339 3784383
Email	info@poggetto.it
Web	www.poggetto.it

Dimora Storica Villa Il Poggiale

Where to start? This historic 16th-century Tuscan villa is so serenely lovely. Breathe in the scent of old-fashioned roses from a seat on the Renaissance loggia. Wander through olive trees to the pool. Retreat to the house for some 1800s elegance. Much loved, full of memories, this is the childhood home of brothers Johanan and Nathanel Vitta, who devoted two years to its restoration. Rooms are big, beautiful, full of light, and everything has been kept as it was. An oil painting of their grandmother welcomes you as you enter; a portrait of Machiavelli by Gilardi hangs in the salon. Bedrooms are all different, all striking. Some have frescoes and silk curtains, others have fabrics commissioned from a small Tuscan workshop. The attention to detail is superb but in no way overpowering. The independent apartment is a restored farmhouse with original fireplace and stunning views over the rose garden. The staff clearly love being here and want you to love it too. Breakfast is a generous buffet, dinner is in the restored olive store and Florence is a 20-minute drive.

Rooms	21 doubles: €130–€240.
	2 suites for 2: €195–€240.
	1 apartment for 5: €310.
Meals	Dinner €30. Wine from €8.
	Restaurants 300m.
Closed	9 January to 9 February.

Monica Cozzi
Dimora Storica Villa Il Poggiale,
Via Empolese 69,
50026 San Casciano in Val di Pesa
Tel   +39 0558 28311
Email   villailpoggiale@villailpoggiale.it
Web   www.villailpoggiale.it

Candida's Country House

Candida is a lady of many talents: gardener, furniture restorer, milliner, jeweller, painter and fabulous cook. Her creativity shines throughout house, be it in a beautiful painted landscape, sculpted hat-cum-art pieces, or in the food, much of which has come from her own allotment. Breakfast on fresh croissants and homemade jams while putting the world to rights in Candida's kitchen – and when the Tuscan sun shines (which is most of the time!) take your coffee to the rose-filled garden. The warmth and character continues in bedrooms that have delicate tapestries and richly coloured throws, terracotta floor tiles and small windows looking out to undulating hills; wonderful shower rooms with piles of soft towels complete the set. This is a house that wears its age with dignity, a fine Italian country home set amongst the olive groves with a view to Val di Pesa. It's only half an hour from Florence but such is the peace that you can feel a million miles from anywhere. A special slice of *la dolce vita* that Candida has made all her own. *10% discount in January-March & October-December. Smoking permitted in the garden.*

Rooms	3 doubles: €95.
Meals	Dinner with wine, €30, by arrangement. Restaurants 1km.
Closed	Rarely.

Candida Bing
Candida's Country House, Montepaldi 1,
50026 San Casciano in Val di Pesa

Tel	+39 0558 228109
Mobile	+39 360 888253
Email	candidabing@libero.it
Web	www.candidabing.it

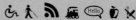

Fattoria Le Corti – Principi Corsini

The 17th-century Villa Le Corti is one of the noblest in Tuscany; the land, in the Corsini family since 1427, has been producing *chianti classico* and rich olive oil since the beginning of time. There are cellars to visit, wines to taste, horses to ride, and fascinating tours of the *orciaia*, the most beautiful oil store in Tuscany; find, too, cookery classes in historic kitchens, a cosy restaurant above the shop, and holiday houses scattered about. It's a working estate with a wonderful buzz. Go B&B, or come with a party and have a whale of a time in 'La Gugliaie', a big rambling farmhouse with two sitting rooms and bedrooms dressed in lovely fabrics and colours; discover steps, nooks, crannies, beams and polished wooden floors made from old wine barrels. The garden begins at the swimming pool and ends in the olive grove, with wondrous far-reaching views. Bake bread in an old wood-oven, take a soak in a hidden bath, sip a glass of chianti on your bedroom balcony. All this and a situation to dream of: posh but friendly San Casciano is the nearest village, Florence is a bus ride away. *Minimum stay seven nights in high season.*

Rooms	7 doubles; 1 single: €100–€140. Whole house €4,000–€5,800 per week (sleeps 12–14).
Meals	Breakfast from €9 for self-caterers. Restaurant on site.
Closed	Rarely.

Duccio Corsini
Via San Piero di Sotto 1,
50026 San Casciano in Val di Pesa

Tel	+39 0558 29301
Mobile	+39 348 7215125
Email	info@principecorsini.com
Web	www.principecorsini.com

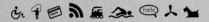

Entry 175   Map 8

Locanda le Boscarecce

A sparkling star in Tuscany's firmament. Susanna is full of life and laughter, her daughter Swan is equally warm – and an accomplished sommelier. Susanna concocts dishes that people travel miles to discover. Fruit, vegetables, herbs and olive oil are all home grown, there are plenty of wines in the cellar and, outside, the biggest pizza oven ever. The 200-year-old *locanda* is on a ridge, embracing fields and farms and heavenly sunsets. Bedrooms in the farmhouse are part rustic, part refined, with bold colours and pretty lace at the windows, each space unique. Beds are modern and comfortable, furniture 18th and 19th century, bathrooms have bath tubs and showers, and some rooms have kitchenettes. Tennis, cycling, swimming in the saltwater pool with its panoramic view – all are possible; or simply relax under the dreamy gazebo and dip into an art book from the library. Even the geography is enticing, in the charmed triangle formed by Florence, Siena and Pisa. Heart-warming, creative and definitely special.

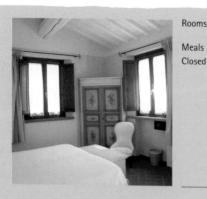

Rooms	8 doubles; 3 triples;
	1 quadruple: €100–€145.
Meals	Dinner €25. Restaurant 3km.
Closed	10 November to 15 March.

Susanna Ballerini
Locanda le Boscarecce,
Via Renai 19,
50051 Castelfiorentino

Tel	+39 0571 61280
Email	info@leboscarecce.com
Web	www.leboscarecce.com

Entry 176   Map 8

Fattoria Barbialla Nuova

An organic farm specialising in Chianina cattle, fragrant olive oil and white truffles; utter tranquillity one hour from Florence. Delightful Guido and others have worked hard to provide somewhere stylish, bio-sensitive and beautiful to stay on this 500-hectare nature reserve/farm. Three farmhouses here, all with sweeping views. 'Le Trosce' – one floor but several levels – is for one big party. 'Doderi' is divided into three apartments, simple and minimalist; Gianluca's bedcovers and 60s retro furniture add style, originality and colour. The apartments in 'Brentina', deeper in the woods, are a touch more rustic – designers will love their whitewashed simplicity. All have books, music and delicious bathrooms. Outside: chic patios and pools. Down at the farm: a vegetable and herb garden, orchards, pigs, hens and a very warm reception. Nature trails entice you to explore, so forage in the cool shade of the woods in the truffle zone or stumble upon a ruined *casa colonica*. Lovely old Montaione, San Miniato and Certaldo Alto have festivals throughout the year. *Minimum stay three nights, seven nights in high season. Pets by arrangement.*

Rooms	2 apartments for 2; 3 apartments for 4; 2 apartments for 6: €560-€1,500. Le Trosce for 8: €1,790-€2,350. All prices per week. Extra bed/sofabed €15.
Meals	Self-catering.
Closed	31 December to 13 March.

Guido Manfredi
Fattoria Barbialla Nuova,
Via Casastrada 49, 50050 Montaione

Tel	+39 0571 677259
Mobile	+39 335 1406575
Email	info@barbiallanuova.it
Web	www.barbiallanuova.it

Country House Nazzano – Rondine, Lucciola, Libellula

A couple of miles up from Certaldo Basso, through vines and olives and a private road, is a pretty cluster of farm buildings on a gentle rise. In the tall pale stone farmhouse is 'La Rondine' (Swallow), a lovely big ground-floor apartment for two, full of light and charm. In the ochre-hued haybarn, beautifully renovated with brick vents intact, are three more. (Each apartment is independent but all interconnect – great for one big party.) Families can choose between 'La Lucciola' (Firefly) and 'La Libellula' (Dragonfly), while 'La Coccinella' (Ladybird) is a sofa-bedded studio for two. Expect character and cosiness, soft colours and old beams, pretty kilims on gentle terracotta, well-equipped little kitchens and lovely country antiques. 'Libellula' is on the first floor – with an extra dining space outside – and 'Lucciola' is the largest, with a great sitting-dining room and a Tuscan fireplace, and a glazed arched window that glides open to a loggia. All have views sweeping over the valley to the famous towers of San Gimignano. Friendly Miriam meets and greets and knows all the history; her husband is delightful too. *Min. stay four nights on weekdays, five in high season.*

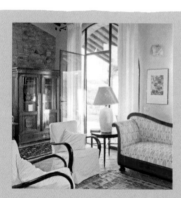

Rooms	1 apartment for 2-4; 2 apartments for 4: €420–€850. 1 studio for 2 (1 double sofabed): €350–€450. Prices per week. Extra charge for heating, depending on consumption.
Meals	Restaurants 4km.
Closed	Never.

Miriam Mocarini
Loc. Sant'Andrea a Gavignalla,
50050 Gambassi Terme

Tel	+39 0571 666578
Mobile	+39 347 7520860
Email	info@countrydomus.com
Web	www.countrydomus.com

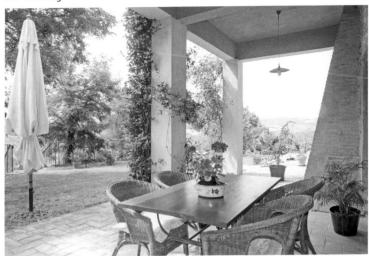

Country House Nazzano – Usignolo & Pettirosso

You're more or less midway between Pisa, Florence and Siena – and your delightful hostess knows the area inside out. Up from Certaldo Basso, through vines and olives along a private road, is this pretty cluster of farm buildings on a gentle rise. In the big stone farmhouse owned by the Mocarini sisters are these apartments charmingly furnished by Patrizia – one up ('Pettirosso'), the other down ('Usignolo'). First-floor 'Pettirosso' is ideal for a family – a big floral sofa and a Tuscan fireplace, ceiling beams and touches of exposed stone, and a charming wicker furnished balcony-terrace (you also get your own seating area in the olive tree grounds). Ground-floor 'Usignolo', a retreat for two, has a big double bedroom and a lofty dining room/ kitchen with a fabulous open fireplace… and, through a wide arch, a sitting room with a divan bed (fine for a child) and a loggia for sun and shade. Certaldo Basso, a five-minute drive down the hill, is great for restaurants and bars, and the funicular to lovely hilltop Certaldo Alto. As for the views, they stretch across the valley to the towers of San Gimignano, thrillingly floodlit at night.

Rooms	1 apartment for 2; 1 apartment for 4: €330–€560 per week.
Meals	Restaurants 4km.
Closed	Rarely.

Patrizia Mocarini
Loc. Sant'Andrea a Gavignalla,
50050 Gambassi Terme

Tel	+39 0571 666264
Mobile	+39 338 3450124
Email	pineltard@alice.it

Casa al Cantone

You approach along the beautiful winding road, surrounded by hills, cypresses, farmhouses... in the distance bristle the 15 towers of San Gimignano. Then up to hilltop Certaldo Alto and the cobbled *centro storico*, to unload near the 12th-century Palazzo Pretorio. Opposite is a medieval house behind whose unassuming façade two attractive apartments lie. Ideal for couples (and, thanks to sofabeds in sitting rooms, small families) they're connected by a staircase and can be rented as one. The slightly smaller 'Fiammetta' is on the ground floor, with a view over the Via Boccaccio. Above is lovely light-filled 'Terrazza', with a plant-potted roof terrace, a gorgeous panorama and a big parasol for the shade. Inside are old terracotta floors, wicker chairs, country antiques, heaps of charm; and, in both, tiny shower rooms and basic kitchens. Step straight onto the pedestrianised cobbles of Certaldo, catch the funicular down to good restaurants and bars. There's an occasional Sunday flea market, from spring to autumn, and the Mercantia Festival in July. Lovely owner Miriam lives close by. *Small pets welcome.*

Rooms	2 apartments for 2-4: €350-€550 per week.
Meals	Restaurants nearby.
Closed	Never.

Miriam Mocarini
Casa al Cantone,
50050 Certaldo Alto

Tel	+39 0571 666578
Mobile	+39 347 7520860
Email	info@countrydomus.com
Web	www.countrydomus.com

Castello di Pastine

Enthroned on an olive-terraced hill in a Chianti vineyard sea, this 14th-century castello encloses a number of comfortable self-catering apartments in two big ancient buildings and a house tucked away in the woods. Acres of landscaped grounds, wonderfully magical, perfectly maintained, have long and spectacular views past statues and cypresses, secret hideaways and jogging trails. There's a huge pool with snazzy parasols and pergolas, multiple terraces with barbecues, slides, swings, ping pong, volleyball and floodlit tennis, and a hot tub for the lazy. All feels nicely countrified and cared for, with terracotta floors, exposed brickwork, plentiful beams, big sofas piled with cushions, eclectic prints – testament to family travels – and well-stocked kitchens. 'Casa Colonica' can be rented as a single unit but our favourite is the house for six that hides in the woods; one wall was once part of a cave. Young Guido knows all the secrets and stories: the Castello is his pride and joy. Cycle tours of vineyards beckon, San Gimignano is close, Florence is half an hour. A paradise for families.

Rooms	3 apartments for 2; 2 apartments for 4; 1 apartment for 5; 1 house for 6; 1 apartment for 8: €392–€1,806 per week.
Meals	Self-catering.
Closed	Rarely.

Guido Materi
Castello di Pastine,
2-4 Strada di Vico – Pastine,
50021 Barberino Val d'Elsa

Tel	+39 0558 075176
Email	castellodipastine@gmail.com
Web	www.pastine.it

Villa Le Barone

The late Marchesa wrote a delightful book about her passion for this lovely old manor with its maze of stairs and crannies, in the family for 400 years. A gorgeous, genuinely unspoilt place, it has old-fashioned comforts. Staff bustle with easy-going friendliness under the guidance of the owners, an elegantly charming couple who spend part of the year here. Bedrooms vary, some in the villa, others in outbuildings; some small, others on a grand scale; most with fantastic fabrics, prints, oil paintings and pretty antiques; all have warm Tuscan style. In the drawing room you'll find the irresistible comfort of a log fire on chilly nights and vast coffee-table books to whet your appetite for Italy. The airy dining room, once the wine store, is a proper setting for superb, leisurely Tuscan dinners and wines. The gardens are no less appealing, full of roses, olive trees and lavender; there's tennis and a training track for the active, a parasoled terrace for the idle and a pool that is far too seductive for anyone hoping for a cultural holiday. That said, do visit the exquisite church of San Leolino, a step away.

Rooms	23 twin/doubles: €195–€350. 5 suites for 2: €315–€370. Dinner, B&B €110–€190 p.p.
Meals	Light lunch €20. Dinner €45. Wine from €20. Restaurants 1km.
Closed	Only 3 rooms available (for self-catering) from November to March.

Aloisi de Larderel
Villa Le Barone,
Via San Leolino 19,
50022 Panzano in Chianti

Tel +39 0558 52621
Email info@villalebarone.com
Web www.villalebarone.com

Hotel

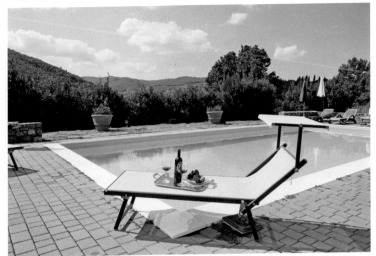

Villa Rosa di Boscorotondo

As you follow the winding Chiantigiana road, keep your eyes peeled for the Villa Rosa; in spite of its colour it is easy to miss! Once you've found it, the parking is opposite, a dash across the road. Your hosts work hard to make their guests happy and Sabine will give you a big welcome, along with handsome dog Baba. This is a quaint, friendly hotel with 11 rooms and a history, built by a Frenchman in 1905, attracted by the area's wines. And there at the back is Tuscany: sloping vineyards, olive groves, young cypresses, and the villa's grounds with terraces and box hedges where children and dogs safely play. The pool is up a bit, in a bright sunny spot (loungers, no parasols), with a wooded area close by for shade. Inside: a ground floor living area flooded with light, a cosy sitting room upstairs, and two floors of bedrooms, the quietest and smallest facing the vines. Expect elegant wrought-iron beds, modest bathrooms and polished red floors; some rooms come with big balconies and forest and road views. Set off to discover wineries and villages, return to Sabine's much-loved dinners.

Rooms	7 doubles: €70-€100.
	2 triples: €90-€130.
	2 quadruples: €100-€160.
	Singles €60-€90.
Meals	Dinner €26. Restaurants nearby.
Closed	Easter & 1st week of November.

Neri Avuri
Villa Rosa di Boscorotondo,
Via San Leolino 59, Località Panzano
in Chianti, 50022 Greve

Tel	+39 0558 52577
Email	info@resortvillarosa.it
Web	www.resortvillarosa.it

Fattoria Viticcio Agriturismo

You're on a hill above Greve, in *chianti classico* country. Alessandro's father, Lucio, bought the farm in the 1960s and set about producing fine wines for export. It was a brave move at a time when people were moving away from the countryside. Now the vineyard has an international reputation. Visit the vaults and taste for yourself. Nicoletta (also a sommelier) runs the agriturismo, helped by their daughters. The apartments are named after them – Beatrice, Arianna, Camilla – and lie at the heart of the estate. Much thought has gone into them. Plain-coloured walls, brick arches, beams and terracotta floor tiles give an attractively simple air, furniture is a charming blend of contemporary and antique pieces; kitchens are superb. One pool rests in a walled garden, with a small play area for children; a second lies within the olive groves. You may hear the occasional tractor – this is a working estate – but the farmyard is tidy and well-kept, with tubs of flowers everywhere. There's a family atmosphere, too, and wonderful views. *Minimum stay two nights, one week in apartments. Nightly rate available in studio apartment.*

Rooms	4 apartments for 2; 2 apartments for 4-6: €700–€1,290 per week.
Meals	Breakfast €5. Restaurants 1km.
Closed	Rarely.

Alessandro Landini & Nicoletta
Florio Deleuze
Fattoria Viticcio Agriturismo, Via San
Cresci 12a, 50022 Greve in Chianti

Tel	+39 0558 54210
Email	info@fattoriaviticcio.com
Web	www.fattoriaviticcio.com

Palazzo Malaspina B&B

A special find. The medieval walls of San Donato are tucked away behind an arch, while the Renaissance façade belies a modern and spacious interior. Enter the big hall with its fine wooden doors and stylish staircase, sense the history. The palazzo is a listed building and Maria is enthusiastic about all she has to offer. She was born here (in Room 3), and now lives in the apartment downstairs with her pet dog. Breakfast – in your bedroom, or at a huge table with white runners and china – includes fruits, cheeses, croissants, jams. You can also request a full English; the guest book says it is sensational. Each of the bedrooms has a classic Tuscan charm with family antiques and fabrics from Busatti of Anghiari. Luxurious bathrooms have mosaic tiles and huge white towels bearing the palazzo's emblem; three have a jacuzzi. From some of the rooms you can just glimpse the towers of San Gimignano, from others, little gardens that guide the eye to the countryside beyond and its treasures. There's a huge cherry tree in the small back garden. Drop your baggage off outside; car parks are a five-minute walk. *Welcome bottle of wine & tea, coffee, cake and biscuits on arrival.*

Rooms	3 doubles; 2 twin/doubles: €90-€115.
Meals	Restaurant next door.
Closed	Rarely.

Maria Pellizzari
Palazzo Malaspina B&B, Via del Giglio
35, 50028 San Donato in Poggio
Tel   +39 0558 072946
Mobile   +39 339 4114711
Email   info@palazzomalaspina.it
Web   www.palazzomalaspina.it

B&B Del Giglio

Fall under Del Giglio's spell. With the beauty, the history and your hosts' warmth and zest, you won't have a chance of resisting. In the delightful walled borgo of San Donato is this 12th-century house; Roberto and Laura fell in love with it years ago and have been working on it devotedly ever since. Today polished antiques and Roberto's works of art blend beautifully with white walls and chunky rafters. The bedrooms are simple, comfortable, the bathrooms shine, and a delicious continental breakfast is served on the little veranda on sunny days. Downstairs, through a courtyard with an ancient wine cellar attached, is a neat and secluded lawned garden, complete with tortoises and glorious views; spot the towers of San Gimignano. There are some good little restaurants in the borgo, but if you don't want to eat out, you don't need to; there's a barbecue under the old olive trees and a guest kitchen if you stay three or more nights. For a couple or a small family, it's an exceptional place to stay, and once through the gate, there's walking for miles. Chianti lies at your feet. *Minimum stay two nights.*

Rooms	2 doubles: €75–€95 for 2; €170 for 4. Guest kitchen for longer stays.
Meals	Restaurants 50m.
Closed	Rarely.

Roberto Cresti
B&B Del Giglio,
Via del Giglio 78,
50028 San Donato in Poggio

Tel	+39 0558 072894
Email	info@delgiglio.it
Web	www.delgiglio.it

Entry 186   Map 8

Sovigliano

A stone's throw from Tavarnelle, down a country lane, this ancient farmhouse stands among vineyards, olives, cypresses and pines. Though the setting is secluded you are in the middle of some of the most popular touring country in Italy; on a clear day, you can see the towers of San Gimignano. Every view is breathtaking. Sovigliano has been renovated by the family with deep respect for the architecture and traditional materials. The self-catering apartments – one palatial, with a glorious stone fireplace – are most attractive, all white walls, ancient rafters, good beds and country antiques. If you choose to go B&B, the double rooms are equally charming. The big rustic kitchen, with a private fridge for each guest, makes it easy to meet others should you wish to do so, or a delicious dinner can be arranged. Breakfast under the pines in the garden, take a lazy dip in the pool, work out in the exercise area (here children must be supervised), enjoy a pre-dinner drink. Vin Santo, olive oil and grappa are for sale. Signora is most helpful and will insist you return!

Rooms	2 doubles; 2 twins: €120–€175. 4 apartments for 2-4: €770–€1,780 per week.
Meals	Dinner with wine, €35.
Closed	Rarely.

Patrizia Bicego
Sovigliano,
Strada Magliano 9,
50028 Tavarnelle Val di Pesa

Tel	+39 0558 076217
Email	info@sovigliano.com
Web	www.sovigliano.com

Le Muracce di Sotto

One minute you're on the main road, the next, parked under bamboo in the middle of the olive groves... then down a little path to the rambling stone farmhouse. The owners live at the 'new' end, tenants live at the other, and you are in the 1600s middle. It's a two-floor apartment full of colourwash and character, a quaint bolthole for two. Up the outside stone stair, enter the kitchen, the hub of the house – great open fireplace, big square table, comfy sofas, cushioned seat under the window. Up the steps... more paintings, more books, a divan bed in the sitting room, Tuscan colour on the walls, and a bedroom, welcoming and inviting, with a pretty bedspread, an antique bed and lush garden views. The bathroom, lilac, hand-tiled, with a big tub and a shower above, is a beauty. The owners – he American, she Italian, both charming – have created gardens for all to share: brimming borders of English and Mediterranean colour, a perfect little playhouse, a freshwater pond for wildlife swims, terraces for picnics and views. Golf is up the road, Florence is a hop away.

Rooms	1 apartment for 2-4 (1 double, 1 sofabed): €300-€350 per week.
Meals	Restaurants 1.5 km.
Closed	Rarely.

Bryan Moore
Le Muracce di Sotto,
Via della Montagnola 174,
50027 Strada in Chianti
Tel   +39 0558 588686
Email   b.moore@tin.it

Locanda Casanuova

'The beauty of simplicity' is their motto. Casanuova was once a monastery, then an orphanage… now the Besançons work hard for the production of their organic wine and olive oil here, along with cookery and yoga classes. They're a hospitable family: fresh menus are chalked up on the board each day; meals, served at large tables under the vines, are happy events, open to the public. Off the refectory is a library where you can pore over trekking maps at a big round table. Just a short stroll from the house are two apartments for self-caters, one up, one down. But we recommend the B&B rooms, spotless and charming, furnished with natural fabrics (no TVs) and with a serenely monastic air; bathrooms are equally delightful. This is a real family business: Ursula and Thierry have made it what it is today and their sons will create the future. Wander the delightful garden with its green corners, inviting terraces and a 'secret' herb garden. Best of all, in a clearing in the woods, is an enchanting swimming 'pond', a natural, self-cleansing pool with lily pads, surrounded by decking.

Rooms	12 doubles: €100-€154. 4 singles: €80-€100. 1 apartment for 2; 1 apartment for 4: €80-€200.
Meals	Breakfast €10 for apartments. Dinner €30-€35. Wine €12-€50. Restaurant 7km.
Closed	November-March.

Famiglia Besançon
Locanda Casanuova,
San Martino Altoreggi 52,
50063 Figline Valdarno
Tel   +39 0559 500027
Email   locanda@casanuova-toscana.it
Web   www.casanuova.info

Podere La Casellina Agriturismo

Come here for life's slow rhythm – and for this warm, honest and lovely family. The grandparents arrived in 1936, when the little church put the *podere* into their hands; they and young Michelangelo have worked the land ever since. Anyone wishing to experience 'real' Italian peasant life (*vita del contadino*) should come here; so little has changed at La Casellina, inside or out. Simple spotless bedrooms, in the old hayloft and stables, have very comfortable beds and views of San Pietro al Terreno church. All the food, oil and produce is deliciously Slow, while the landscape, between Chianti and Valdarno, is exquisite; you have the chestnut woods of the Chianti mountains to one side, oaks, cypresses and olives to the other. Learn to prune vines and pick olives on the farm; gather chestnuts and wild mushrooms in the woods. Go riding or biking, then return to Grandma's recipes – the grape flan is scrumptious and there's passion fruit for breakfast. Michelangelo is a dear who talks to the animals as though they were family and speaks brilliant English.

Rooms	3 doubles: €60–€72.
	Dinner, B&B €48–€56 p.p.
Meals	Lunch with wine, €16.
	Dinner with wine from €18.
	Restaurant 2km.
Closed	Rarely.

Michelangelo & Silvia Bensi
Podere La Casellina Agriturismo,
Via Poggio alla Croce 60,
50063 Figline Valdarno

Tel	+39 0559 500070
Email	poderelacasellina@tin.it
Web	www.poderelacasellina.it

La Libellula

Your room in this solid former convent, with its fabulously fecund garden, is appealingly quirky and cosy. The ground floor entrance leads to it through Anna's second kitchen and your sitting/breakfast room, once stabling, with arched windows. Gaze up from your bed – which belonged to film director Klaus Maria Brandauer – to ancient oak beams, light terrazzo tiles, a west-facing window, antique chairs and linen curtains, a sewing machine bedside table and, behind the armoire, a simple white-tiled shower room; no window, nice toiletries. Friendly and outgoing Anna is a professional cellist and a passionate and outstanding cook – her pastry alone deserves the detour! She makes the most delicious croissants, bread and fruit preserves using all things local and organic, and will prepare memorable dinners for you to eat under the vine pergola, or by the scintillating pond. Head for Florence under an hour away, or walk the hills and visit other towns in the Mugello; Vicchio has a good swimming pool. Not the easiest approach but well worth it.

Rooms	1 double (sofabed available): £95-£120.
Meals	Dinner on request €28-€30.
	Restaurants 3km.
Closed	Mid-November to mid-March.

Anna Pegoretti
La Libellula,
Fraz. Orticaia 9,
50062 Dicomano

Tel +39 0558 387752
Email lalibellula.bandb@gmail.com

Le Due Volpi

Twenty miles from Florence, yet utterly unspoilt: the gentle hills of the Mugello valley have escaped development and the drive from Borgo is truly lovely. At the end of a long white track is a big house strewn with ivy; outside two snazzy little foxes – *le due volpi* – splash water into a trough. Step into spaciousness and light and a charming Tuscan interior. Heidi is Italian, well-travelled and speaks perfect English; Lorenzo has a passion for old radios and antiques. They are naturals at looking after guests, love cooking on their Aga, dispatch meals to the loggia in summer and are embarking on a greener lifestyle, introducing solar panels and wood-fired central heating. The bedrooms, with their wooden floors and chunky rafters, couldn't be nicer. Beds are large and lighting soft, wood-burners keep you cosy in winter, Chini-tiled shower rooms have a stylish rusticity. Note that the two top-floor rooms are reached via several stairs. Vicchio, full of history, is a ten-minute drive and there's a riding stables down the road. Bliss. *Whole house available June to October (on self-catering basis). Minimum stay two nights on weekdays. Children over 10 welcome.*

Rooms	3 doubles (1 with kitchenette); 1 twin: €80–€120. Extra bed €20–€30.
Meals	Dinner with wine from €25. Light meals from €15. Restaurant 3km.
Closed	Rarely.

Heidi Flores & Lorenzo Balloni
Le Due Volpi, Via di Molezzano 88,
50039 Vicchio

Tel	+39 0558 407874
Mobile	+39 338 6220160
Email	info@leduevolpi.it
Web	www.leduevolpi.it

Villa Campestri Olive Oil Resort

Truffle expeditions, olive oil tastings, outdoor massages – this is a sensuous place to stay. Campestri is the world's first Olive Oil Resort (2,000 olive trees in seven hectares of land) so don't miss the *Oleoteca*, and Gemma's tastings: her knowledge is inspiring. Pass the frescoes by a pupil of Giotto and the 14th-century chapel; observe the wooden ceilings and the old terracotta tiles; contemplate the indoor well, the ultimate in ancient 'mod-cons'. Bedrooms, some in the main house, the rest in the farmhouse and dairy, are somewhat more luxurious, with their antique pieces, rich fabrics, white towels in immaculate bathrooms and, from upper floors, amazing views (no air con, but the fresh mountain air is so much better!). One suite has a sensational canopied bed, each floor has its own big sitting room; outside is a turquoise pool. Much of the food is home-grown with a local following, and the dining room, with its 17th-century frescoes and Art Deco windows, is a great backdrop for it. The entire place is a testament to Viola's gentleness and to her diligent, contented team.

Rooms	10 doubles: €103–€172. 8 suites for 2-4: €140–€227. 3 family suites for 4: €184–€238. 1 single: €80–€135. 3 triples: €159–€213. 1 apartment for 4: €203–€257.
Meals	Dinner €35–€52. Restaurants 6km.
Closed	15 November to 15 March.

Famiglia Pasquali
Villa Campestri Olive Oil Resort,
Via di Campestri 19/23,
50039 Vicchio di Mugello

Tel	+39 0558 490107
Email	villa.campestri@villacampestri.it
Web	www.villacampestri.com

Agriturismo Fattoria I Ricci

Down winding Tuscan lanes with perfect Tuscan views, through wrought-iron gates that glide open to greet you... to pull up to a courtyard between an old mill and a 16th-century villa. Discover majestic cedars in the garden, a spacious pool surrounded by lawns, smartly furnished patios scattered here and there and the Cecchinis' olive groves beyond: the first impression is wonderful. And then there's Caterina, who looks after you all with her big open smile. Welcome to self-catering with a difference: breakfast, served at large tables beneath chunky beams, is included in the price, and lunches and dinners are on request (gluten-free if you wish). All feels genuine, friendly and family-run, with two generations living in the main villa and the old mill beautifully renovated: guest apartments above, dining areas below. The apartments are Italian traditional, each individual and pleasing, with pretty curtains and peaceful colours, each as neat as a new pin. 'La Cascina', a Hansel and Gretel cottage in the garden, is the choice of romantics — and free bikes for guests are a boon.

Rooms	2 apartments for 2-3; 2 apartments for 4-5: €500-€1,400. Whole house available for 12: €3,200-€3,700. Prices per week.
Meals	Breakfast included. Lunch & dinner on request.
Closed	Rarely.

Caterina Cecchini
Agriturismo Fattoria I Ricci,
Via Rostolena 14, 50039 Vicchio
Tel   +39 0558 44784
Mobile   +39 347 7920638
Email   info@fattoriairicci.it
Web   www.fattoriairicci.com

Porcigliano

The kitchen is the hub of the house – and Gabbriella, smiling, welcoming, in a neat pink and white pinny, is the sort of hostess who can rustle up a supper of eggs, ham and home-grown toms for late arrivals and make you feel totally at home. Having been in travel all her working life, she knows the area intimately – make the most of her good knowledge. The drive up through woodland above Polcanto brings you – finally! – to an eco restoration with spectacular views, best enjoyed from the conservatory with a glass of Gabbriella's limoncello. Lavender and rosemary border the terrace below and beyond is her husband's haven: a mini vineyard and olive grove. Throughout, modern art posters grace rag-rolled walls and floral curtains dress windows. Bedrooms, reached via a spiral stair, are homely, fresh and inviting; two have views of the hills, all have bright and distinctive bathrooms. Wake to the prospect of homemade jams and *mortadella di Bologna*, spend the day in Florence, hike or bike to the villas and castles of the Mugello, and return to a garden scented with roses. *Minimum stay two nights.*

Rooms	2 doubles: €68–€85.
	1 triple: €95–€115.
Meals	Restaurant 500m.
Closed	Rarely.

Gabbriella Bartolozzi
Porcigliano,
Via Tassaia 46B, Polcanto,
50032 Borgo San Lorenzo

Tel	+39 0558 409903
Email	info@porcigliano.it
Web	www.porcigliano.it

Podere Capitignano

Welcome to the Mugello valley! Up a country lane, at the end of a cypress-lined drive, is a peaceful Tuscan farmstead with far-reaching views over the Apennines. A farmhouse and outbuildings make up this neat and tidy complex – much-loved and sympathetically restored. Let the caretakers settle you in – or the owners, generous, energetic and in residence part-time. With its 400 olive trees and small vineyard, Capitignano feels like a farm, with the added luxuries of tennis court and pool. The 'Fienele', a converted old hay barn, makes a roomy holiday home, with its big friendly living room and French windows to two terraces below and a large living space above. If you're a big party the 'Fattoria' is for you, all exposed beams and vaulted ceiling, smart kitchen, large terrace and private courtyard. 'La Stalla', an old stable, is bright and spacious and sleeps up to five; 'La Casetta' is a neat stone cottage on a hill, with terraces front and back, a charming bolthole for two. There's a library with WiFi, DVDs and open fires for all. So much to see and do – and a train nearby that whisks you to Florence in half an hour. *Min. stay two nights, seven in high season. Pets by arrangement.*

Rooms	1 house for 2; 1 house for 4;
	1 house for 5; 1 house for 6-8;
	1 house for 9: €490–€1,680 per week.
Meals	Self-catering.
Closed	Never.

Lynn Fleming Aeschliman
Podere Capitignano, Via San Cresci 48,
50032 Borgo San Lorenzo

Tel	+39 0558 495600
Mobile	+41 (0)79 200 4222
Email	lfa@tasis-schools.org
Web	www.capitignano.org

Il Fienile di Scarperia

Scarperia is famous for its Mugello race track and colourful festivals, but Il Fienile (the haybarn) is tucked over the hill in a quiet pocket of Tuscan countryside. Here is Italian family life at its most genuine and welcoming. Francesca brims with enthusiasm for the corn-yellow stone house and neat gardens which she, Paris, their two young children (and fluffy little dog) share happily with guests. There are four cosy chunky-beamed guest rooms here; one is tinged in dusky pink with shuttered windows and fancy new shower; another is smaller but just as homely, with a claw-foot bath. Like many in this foodie region, Francesca loves to cook. Tuck into dinner by a roaring fire in a vaulted country kitchen hung with Tuscan crockery; on summer mornings, taste Grandma's jams out on the garden terrace. Beyond the rustic wooden fence lie rolling hills, bike trails, a sailing lake, championship golf course and horse riding ranch; Francesca will help with maps and bookings. A short stroll takes you to town and a bus whisks you south: you can be in Florence in 40 minutes. A genuine, family-run B&B.

Rooms	1 double; 2 twin/doubles; 1 twin/double with separate bath: €75–€95.
Meals	Dinner with wine, €25.
Closed	Never.

Francesca Parigi
Il Fienile di Scarperia,
Via della Resistenza, 15/F,
50038 Scarperia

Tel	+39 0558 430578
Email	info@ilfieniledidiscarperia.it
Web	www.ilfieniledidiscarperia.it

Locanda Senio

Food is king here – Slow food – Roberta's genuine home cooking with home-grown fruit and veg and, in the restaurant, Ercole's gastronomic fare. Echoing the movement to revive lost medieval traditions, they are passionate about wild herbs and 'forgotten' fruits. Take a cookery course (included if you stay three nights or more). The prosciutto from rare-breed *Maiale Medievale* is delicious; breakfast is a feast of homemade delights; dinner a leisurely treat served in the cosy little log-fired restaurant. The inn occupies a stunning spot in a quiet town in the Mugello valley, surrounded by rolling hills… there are guided walks through the woods, gastronomic meanders through the valley. Bedrooms are comfortable and pretty with country antiques – but splash out on a suite if you can; they're in the 17th-century building with original fireplaces. Roberta and Ercole are very proud of their wellbeing centre, too – jacuzzi, sauna and Turkish bath. Steps lead up to a pool with an amazing view; body and soul are nurtured; walkers are in heaven. Special indeed.

Rooms	6 twin/doubles: €115–€145. 2 suites for 2-3: €155–€175. Dinner, B&B €100–€145 per person.
Meals	Dinner from €35. Wine from €10.
Closed	Rarely.

Ercole & Roberta Lega
Locanda Senio,
Via Borgo dell'Ore 1,
50035 Palazzuolo sul Senio

Tel   +39 0558 046019
Email info@locandasenio.com
Web   www.locandasenio.com

Odina Agriturismo

You are 650 metres above sea level and feel on top of the world – the Arno valley reaches out before you and the air is pure. Paolo is a talented gardener and each bush, tree and herb has been chosen with care, posing magnificently next to the solid, blue-shuttered house. The interiors of the house and apartments are delightfully rustic and contemporary. Each is different: kitchen surfaces are of granite, or local *pietra serena*, bathroom walls are softly ragged in varying shades. All have French windows to a patio with wooden outdoor furniture. Oil, vinegar, sugar, coffee, salt and washing-up liquid are provided; ask in advance and they'll provide more (for which you pay). The reception is in a beautifully restored, deconsecrated chapel, with an old bread-making chest and a 'shop' selling Odina olive oil, honey, lavender and beans. Take a dip in the pool, go for long, lazy walks in the olive groves and chestnut woods, prepare a barbecue. Garden courses and visits – highly recommended – are held here in May. *Minimum stay two nights, seven nights in high season. Pets by arrangement.*

Rooms	1 cottage for 2; 2 cottages for 4; 1 cottage for 5: €600–€1,850. 1 house for 8: €2,100–€4,100. Prices per week. Extra bed/sofabed available at no charge.
Meals	Self-catering.
Closed	Mid-January to end of February.

Paolo Trenti
Odina Agriturismo,
Loc. Odina, 52024 Loro Ciuffenna

Tel	+39 0559 69304
Mobile	+39 333 9556699
Email	info@odina.it
Web	www.odina.it

Borgo Iesolana Agriturismo

At the centre of an immaculate patchwork of fields, vineyards and woods, this irresistible group of old buildings. Mellow stone and warm brick blend, flowers tumble from terracotta pots, arches invite you in out of the sun, a pool beckons. Giovanni and Francesco inherited the estate from their grandfather and live here with their young families. They have created 11 apartments from the farm buildings, and it is a solid, sensitive conversion. The décor is an upmarket, uncluttered mix of traditional and new: good beds and fabrics, super kitchens, thoughtful lighting. And if you prefer not to self-cater, you can breakfast in the 'wine bar' across the way. This, too, is an impeccable restoration, with modern Italian furniture and big windows. Lunch and dinner are available on request: local produce and traditional Tuscan fare. The farm is beautifully run (even the vines are edged with roses) and produces wine, olive oil, grappa and honey. It lies alongside an old Roman road that once linked Siena with Florence, with views on all sides of Chiantishire.

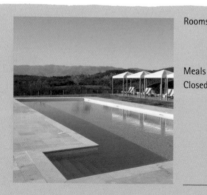

Rooms	3 apartments for 2; 3 apartments for 4; 3 apartments for 6; 2 apartments for 8: €770–€2,940 per week. Two nights low season: €130–€180.
Meals	Self-catering.
Closed	December-February.

Giovanni & Francesco Toscano
Borgo Iesolana Agriturismo,
Loc. Iesolana,
52021 Bucine
Tel   +39 0559 92988
Email   info@iesolana.it
Web   www.iesolana.it

Castello di Gargonza

Intriguing, delightful: a fortified Romanesque village in the beauty of the Tuscan hills, whose 800-year-old steps, stones, rafters and tiles remain virtually intact. Today it is a private, uniquely Italian marriage of exquisitely ancient and exemplary modern. Seen from the air it is perfect, as if shaped by the gods to inspire Man to greater works: a magical maze of paths, nooks and crannies, castellated tower, great octagonal well, a heavy gate that lets the road slip out and tumble down, and breathtaking views. You're given a map on arrival to help you navigate your way round. No cars, no shops, but a chapel, gardens, pool and old olive press for meetings, concerts and breakfasts by the fire. The old storeroom is now a spacious and airy restaurant with wooded hillside views. As for the Count and Countess, they and their staff look after you beautifully. Bedrooms and apartments are 'rustic deluxe' with smart modern furnishings, white-rendered walls, superb rafters, open fireplaces, tiny old doors reached up steep stone staircases. There's an ancient ambience, as if time has stood still.

Rooms	20 doubles: €150-€190.
	13 apartments for 2-10: €735-€2,275.
	Extra bed €130-€145. Cot €10.
	Prices per week.
Meals	Breakfast €9 for self-caterers.
	Lunch/dinner with wine, €25-€35.
Closed	10 January to 1 March.

Elisa & Neri Guicciardini
Castello di Gargonza,
Loc. Gargonza,
52048 Monte San Savino

Tel	+39 0575 847021
Email	info@gargonza.it
Web	www.gargonza.it

Casa Bellavista

A glass of wine at a table in the orchard. Birdsong for background music – or occasionally foreground, if the family rooster is feeling conversational. And a panorama of Tuscan landscape. Bellavista is well-named: its stunning all-round views take in Monte Amiata, Foiano della Chiana and the old Abbey of Farneta. There was a farm here for 200 years but the house was extensively restored about 30 years ago. It still has the original brick exterior, now softened by creepers, and a welcoming, family atmosphere: lovely Simonetta and Guido have two teenage children. There's an assured, uncluttered country elegance to the rooms, while pretty, airy bedrooms are furnished with family antiques and interesting textiles; two have their own balcony with views onto the garden. Simonetta's kitchen has a huge marble table top for kneading bread and she cooks farmhouse food for her guests: delicious; breakfasts are lavish, cookery lessons are a treat. Roam the Arezzo province in true Italian style: vespas and bikes are free and there's a beautiful 65km route to test them on. Italian family B&B at its finest.

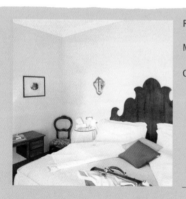

Rooms	2 doubles; 2 twin/doubles: €100–€149.
Meals	Dinner €35, by arrangement. Wine from €19.
Closed	Rarely.

Simonetta Demarchi
Casa Bellavista,
Loc. Creti C.S. 40, 52044 Cortona

Tel	+39 0575 610311
Mobile	+39 335 6383377
Email	info@casabellavista.it
Web	www.casabellavista.it

Casa Capanni

Remember sociable holidays with idle fantasies of clubbing together to buy the place? Here it happened, at this elegant green-shuttered *casa padronale*. It's run by a rotating group of Dutch friends (humorous Alexandra and Rosie are staples), and you are greeted with open arms and perfect English. Inside the symmetrical 1600s building are rooms punctuated with candles, light scents and huge character. Fireplaces fill walls, beams heave with history and lamplight dapples the walls of a cherished home. Breakfast is a riotous buffet of crusty breads, prosciutto and juicy fruits; tables pock the garden and four courses of goodies frequently grace the dining table. Calming colour-themed bedrooms named after grand masters have Gustavian-style furniture, sumptuous linen, antique touches; 'Raphael' comes with a huge Indonesian four-poster. The high-hedged garden has a pool amid olive, fig and hazelnut trees – snooze in the shade of a muslin-swagged gazebo. Art and nature aficionados will love Cortona and Perugia, and all summer's festivals.
Minimum stay two nights, three nights in high season. Children over four welcome.

Rooms	6 doubles (4 with separate bathrooms); 1 twin: €110–€160. 1 family room for 4: €200–€230. Family deal available (1 double, 1 twin sharing bathroom): €150–€160.
Meals	Dinner on request €20. Restaurants 5km.
Closed	November–March.

Rosanne van Cruyningen
Casa Capanni, Loc. Monsigliolo 31-32,
52044 Cortona

Tel	+39 0575 62268
Mobile	+39 327 5872232 / +31 6 3100 3967
Email	info@capanni.eu
Web	www.capanni.eu

Il Pero

Horses, dogs, cats, chickens and a pool with long views – this is a brilliant place for families, lived and worked in by delightful William and Miranda. With their two daughters, they have poured their hearts into a new life in Italy. Il Pero is a work in progress, a lovely old Tuscan farmhouse (1782) set in a flat plain and surrounded by barley and sunflowers, plus a haybarn, an olive press (they produce their own oil) and a kitchen garden where you can help yourself. There are four super apartments with good kitchens, cheery bright bedrooms, big wet rooms and little pergolas for private outdoor spaces – and a romantic bedroom in the square tower with an ancient wine barrel for the shower! All is new or cleverly recycled, from the adjustable mattresses to the lovely old floorboards from a nearby convent. Don't miss the minstrels' gallery, lit by a 120-candle chandelier (a wow for big celebrations) or the pizza evenings – great fun. As for cobbled hilltop Arezzo, it is stuffed with fine churches and frescoes, pretty shops and irresistible *gelati*.

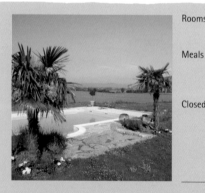

Rooms	1 double: €150.
	1 apartment for 6; 1 apartment for 5;
	2 apartments for 2: €800–€1,500 per wk.
Meals	Breakfast €15 for self-caterers.
	Welcome pack.
	Occasional dinner with wine, €30.
	Restaurants 5km.
Closed	Rarely.

Miranda Taxis
Il Pero,
Loc. Manziana 15,
52100 Policiano

Tel	+39 0575 979593
Email	info@ilpero.com
Web	www.ilpero.com

Villa La Lodola

One of the warmest, most generous and inviting places we know. The moment you pass through the wrought-iron gates you leave the outskirts of town and the main road behind: welcome to La Lodola. Hard to believe that livestock once lived downstairs: now low velvet sofas sprawl on polished terracotta floors and interesting pictures dot rose colour-washed walls. You'll like the huge fireplace you can actually sit in, the multi-drawed sideboards, the honey-bricked arches, the rustic 18th-century beams. Bedrooms – four upstairs – are a feast for the eyes, with heavy swagged curtains and some playful trompe l'oeil; those at the back have views. Gentle Mario is head of the family, his son cooks in the Osteria, his wife and daughter sell antiques. Mario's delicious cakes are served with fruits, cheeses and hams under your chosen pergola in summer – chase the morning sun – and the cookery courses are a treat: find the best produce in the market, then bring it home. Olives, pomegranates, lemons, vines flourish here so linger in their shade, then wander down to the pool for a long valley view. *Minimum stay three nights.*

Rooms	2 doubles; 1 twin/double: €120–€140.
	2 suites for 2: €150–€170.
	Singles €100–€150.
	Extra bed/sofabed €20–€35.
Meals	Lunch on request.
	Dinner with wine from €30.
Closed	Never.

Mario Porcu
Villa La Lodola,
Via Piana 19, Foiano della Chiana,
52045 Arezzo

Tel	+39 0575 649660
Email	info@lalodola.com
Web	www.lalodola.com

Villa I Bossi

Fifty people once lived on the ground floor of the old house and everything is as it was – the great box that held the bread, the carpenter's room crammed with tools, the robes hanging in the sacristy, the oven for making charcoal… Francesca loves showing people round the house that has been in her husband's family since 1240; it is brimful of treasures. There's even a fireplace sculpted by Benedetto da Maiano in the 1300s – his 'thank you for having me' to the family. Sleep in faded splendour in the main villa or opt for the modern comforts of the orangery: simple and beautiful. This is a magical place, full of character and memories, overseen by the most delightful people. As for the park-like gardens… set among gentle green hills, they have been enriched over the centuries: to one side of the swimming pool, a hill covered in rare fruit trees, to the west, Italian box hedges and camellias, peonies and old-fashioned roses, avenues, pond, grassy banks and shady trees, enticing seats under arching shrubs, olives and vines… And they make their own chianti and oil.

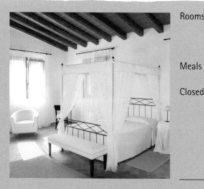

Rooms	2 doubles; 2 doubles (Orangery); 2 twins; 2 triples (Orangery); 2 quadruples (Orangery): €125-€165. Extra bed €10.
Meals	Dinner, 4 courses with wine, €35, by arrangement. Restaurant 100m.
Closed	January-February.

Francesca Vignali Albergotti
Villa I Bossi,
Gragnone 44/46,
52100 Arezzo

Tel	+39 0575 365642
Email	franvig@ats.it
Web	www.villaibossi.com

Galealpe Agriturismo

The road winds ever higher to an olive farm on the top of a hill, surrounded by Tuscan beauty. The olives are organically farmed, the house has been restored with local materials. The two apartments, bright and country simple, each with its own entrance and a private spot in the garden, have new bathrooms and well-kitted kitchens, comfy sitting rooms and wood-burners for chilly evenings. Bedrooms are a good size, and charming. New owners, Martin and Dorothee, are trained naturopaths and offer a range of relaxing treatments. Try out archery, or practice your short golf game in a specially fenced-off area. A delicious four-course dinner is served once a week. Tour the chianti region, hike in the Prato Magno range, or visit Florence (just an hour away and perfect for a day trip) then cool off in the lovely eco pool in among the papyrus and the water lilies. A ten-kilometre drive brings you to Arezzo and its Saturday market where you can stock up with cheeses, hams, breads, tomatoes, then head for the hills and a picnic. Or take it back to your terrace overlooking the garden and valley views that reach to Arezzo's Duomo.

Rooms	1 apartment for 4; 1 apartment for 5: €90–€140; €665–€980 per week. Sofabeds available. Additional cleaning charge of €50 for stays of 1–3 nights.
Meals	Restaurants 5km.
Closed	Rarely.

Martin & Dorothee Saunders
Galealpe Agriturismo,
Pieve San Giovanni 76, 52010 Arezzo

Tel	+39 0575 1785611
Mobile	+39 329 8283949
Email	info@galealpe.com
Web	www.galealpe.com

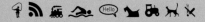

Casa Simonicchi

A magical spot from which to absorb the stillness that these hills evoke. After a blissful drive through the Casentino National Park you arrive at this stone farmhouse with a barn attached, made comfortable to the point of luxury by sculptress Jenny. In the top barn (six entrance steps only) is a family apartment, simple and charming: Italian and English pieces, natural colours, paintings and sculpture. The bedrooms, each with a shower, are placed at either end; the spacious sitting room and well-equipped kitchen lie between. Best of all is your roof terrace with its breathtaking panorama of sweet-chestnut forests. Bask in the sun or the shade, take a cool shower, dine al fresco, stargaze from the jacuzzi – or the telescope. Steeply below are wonderful terraces, lavender, irises, olives, pergola and small sculptures. Jenny also does B&B in the farmhouse and gives you a suite, with one bedroom romantically over the arch: beams, antiques, a huge fireplace. Warm, generous Jenny can tell you about the historic towns, the countryside of Michelangelo and St Francis of Assisi – and the welcoming taverna down the road. *Minimum stay two nights. Fans available at no extra charge.*

Rooms	1 suite for 2 (with kitchen): €175 per night. 1 apartment for 4: €675–€975 per week.
Meals	B&B on request. Dinner with wine from €30, by arrangement. Restaurant nearby.
Closed	Christmas–April.

Jennifer Frears–Barnard
Casa Simonicchi,
Via Simonicchi 184,
Caprese Michelangelo, 52033 Arezzo

Tel	+39 0575 793762
Email	jennifer.barnard6@gmail.com
Web	www.simonicchi.com

The Tuscan Mill

The bucolic valley is edged with woods – so peaceful you could hear a pin drop. Such is the setting for this ancient water mill. Owner Lulu lives in part of the house, is kind and charming and has done a terrific job of preserving the mill's inner workings through the creative use of thick glass and clever lighting. Much of the furniture has been brought from England and the slight English country-house feel is enhanced by some horsey paintings (a reminder of Lulu's past as a point-to-pointer) alongside the traditional arches, beams and cotto floors so typical of rural Italy. The treehouse in the lawned garden is heaven for children and not bad for adults either, as you watch your energetic little ones clambering about: you can enjoy an aperitivo on the terrace. Dine out here, too; as night falls and the stream is lit up, you'll be hard pressed to think of anywhere you'd rather be. But go out you must, particularly as Sansepolcro, birthplace of Renaissance genius Piero della Francesca, is a ten-minute drive. Arezzo with its lively, monthly antiques market is not much further. *B&B option available.*

Rooms	1 house for 4: €700–€900 per week.
Meals	Restaurants 1km.
Closed	Rarely.

Lulu Primavera
The Tuscan Mill,
Il Mulino, Tavernelle 21, Anghiari,
52031 Arezzo
Mobile   +39 334 2119170
Email   luluprimavera@gmail.com
Web   www.thetuscanmill.co.uk

Casa della Portaccia

The rosy terraced town house stands near the entrance to a medieval hilltop town: you're 50 metres from the main square with its restaurants and bars, yet have open views over the valley and space for parking. The two lower floors are yours, fresh and minimalist with bright artworks on white walls and a collection of eye-catching antiques and ornaments. Two sitting rooms – one up, one down – are cosy with squishy white sofas, wicker chairs and lamps. Fling open shutters to bucolic views. Upstairs, a stone fireplace flanked by oil paintings; downstairs, a well-equipped kitchen and big white table for family dinners. Original cotto bricks, tiles and beams remind you of the house's age, but most is modern, including white-dressed beds and shower rooms. You can sit out with a drink on a small terrace by the entrance – and really, there's so much to do in eastern Tuscany you won't miss a garden. Sansepolcro, 15 minutes away, holds Renaissance paintings by Piero della Francesca; Florence is only an hour. Wine tasting, horse riding? Ask friendly Lulu, English and always on hand.

Rooms	1 house for 4 (2 doubles; 2 shower rooms): €750–€950 per week.
Meals	Restaurant 50m.
Closed	Never.

Luca Vichi
Casa della Portaccia,
Via dell'Intoppo,
52031 Anghiari
Mobile   +39 334 211 9170
Email   lucavichi2@gmail.com

Borghetto Calcinaia

Over the hill to be blown away by the views, a lake surrounded by dense trees and olive groves; the setting is magnificent. Charming English owners live in the main house and guests live to the side, in a wonderful old house, 'Casa Mandorlo,' that sleeps nine. 'Casa Olivetto', an ancient, restored barn for two with spectacular views of Lake Montedoglio and the Apennines, can be rented as an annexe in the summer. At the back is the barn with a ground-floor for two plus two (ideal for extra grandparents, children, teenagers). Imagine real old cotto floors, mellow dressed stone, sand-blasted beams… a Tuscan dream. The big house has two storeys linked by wide stairs, a sitting room with books and sofas, a stylish kitchen with a farmhouse table, and antiques from far-flung travels. Bedrooms have simple blinds, good shutters, cushions made by friends, lovely mellow bathrooms. Buy the owners' olive oil; treat yourself to their jams. Children can run around to their hearts' content, the fruit tree'd gardens are safely enclosed, and the pool is positioned for the views. *Casas Susinetto & Olivetto can be booked separately October-April. Minimum stay three nights.*

Rooms	Mandorlo for 9: €2,100-€3,750. Susinetto for 2-4 (with sofabed); Olivetto for 2: €1,750. Prices per week. Cots available.
Meals	Dinner on request €25. Restaurants 3km. Chef available for in-house dinners & cookery courses.
Closed	Rarely.

Dennis Sullivan
Borghetto Calcinaia,
Sigliano 120/122,
52036 Anghiari

Tel	+39 0575 791249
Email	calcinaia@me.com
Web	www.tuscanparadiso.com

Casa Singerna

The hamlet is known as Castro and has three residents... including the owner of this villa in 23 acres of Tuscany, with its own vineyard and olive grove. The surrounding fields sway with golden grain, brilliant poppies, fragrant alfalfa or sunflowers, so pick your season. Although it has come a long way from humble beginnings, this solid 300-year-old house keeps its original character: chestnut beams, handmade ceiling tiles, stone window surrounds. Step in to find a big open-plan ground-floor space filled with light. There's a table of solid chestnut, two plump sofas, a corner kitchen to keep sociable cooks happy, and an archway with glass doors to frame the breathtaking view. Uncluttered bedrooms, one off the terrace, four upstairs, will charm you, one with beautiful antique wardrobes. Generous Susan offers babysitting and six bikes – spin off down the white road for lunch in the village where Michelangelo was born. Hilltop Anghiari, also close, is another jewel. Come home to chilled wine on the terrace or a swim in the pool.

Rooms	1 house for 10: €1,850–€3,990 per week.
Meals	Restaurants 2km.
Closed	Rarely.

Susan Hill
Casa Singerna,
214 Via Castro,
52033 Caprese Michelangelo

Tel	+39 0575 791166
Email	info@casasingerna.com
Web	www.casasingerna.com

Casa Mila

You park outside the walls of the town of Sansepolcro, and the owners meet you by the Duomo. This charming old merchant's house (it dates to 1390) stands in the *centro storico*, behind the museum that guards the paintings of Piero della Francesca, and the moment you enter you can see the garden beyond; Casa Mila is a welcoming sanctuary. There are two apartments here, the larger one up a steep flight of stairs with an amazing roof terrace for sunsets and views, and the smaller one on the ground floor, opening to a Italian garden shaded by a big magnolia, which Val and Colin happily share. All is contemporary and comfortable inside, with whitewashed ceilings and white beams, original fireplaces and tiled floors, Colin's watercolours on the walls, wine on the table, books on the shelves: there's a rustic simplicity, a Tuscan authenticity. No need for a car; you have exceptional produce on your doorstep, little bars and restaurants to discover, and a crossbow competition in September! (Fly to Rome to get here, then catch the bus.) If you do have a car, you can visit Anghiari, Monterchi, Citerna…

Rooms	1 apartment for 2; 1 apartment for 6: €540–€1,290 per week. Whole house available, €1,130–€1,900 per week. Apartment for 2, €100 per night. Apartment for 2-6 €90–€215 per night.
Meals	Restaurants nearby.
Closed	Rarely.

Val Stevens
Casa Mila, Via della Firenzuola 49,
52037 Sansepolcro

Tel   +39 0575 733 477
Mobile   +39 338 1608607
Email   info@casamila.it
Web   www.casamila.it

Il Palazzetto

An unassuming barn conversion up a steep drive, this self-catering treat combines traditional architecture with fresh homely furnishings and underfloor heating. A 2.5-acre garden of fruit orchards and olives with long vistas to ancient hill-topped Tuscan towns ensures birdsong and herb-tinted peace and tranquillity. Bedrooms are understated, simple and comfortable with plenty of wood and natural colours. The spacious sitting room is made snug by an open fire in winter, while French windows keep it breezy in summer. Behind the house is a rose-rambled terraced dining area and a wisteria-covered pergola; down some steps through the olive trees to the field below lies a lovely large saltwater infinity pool, a secluded sun trap for relaxing with far-reaching views. There's loads to do in the area, from truffle snuffling, fishing and riding to meandering through the alley'd mazes and markets of nearby medieval towns Città di Castello, Sansepolcro and Anghiari. A well-converted, well-furnished space with beautiful gardens. *Minimum stay one week.*

Rooms	1 house for 8: €900–€2,200 per week.
Meals	Self-catering.
Closed	Never.

Diane Noel
Il Palazzetto,
Loc. Borgacciano,
52031 Monterchi

Mobile	+44 (0)7956 841895
Email	diane@noelfamily.co.uk
Web	www.il-palazzetto.com

Le Caviere

What's lovely about this tranquil place – apart from the luxuries within – are the long dreamy views and the pool that's your own. You have utter privacy from the main house, in a creamy limestone hay barn with lots of garden in a lovely untouched corner of Tuscany. It's a superb renovation, awash with space and light, true to the building's age yet the finest of contemporary. Enter an open-plan living area with rustic terracotta floors and soothing biscuit shades, deep white sofas, art, books, antiques and flowers. Off which: an immaculate kitchen, a wisteria draped terrace, and a bathroom, surely the most delicious in Italy... impeccable white fittings, vast rain heads suspended from an ancient brick arch, an olive ladder on which to sling a luxurious towel. Then it's up the open stone stair to Busatti linens and a sumptuous bed. Sansepolcro, six miles off, is a draw for art lovers but has chic shops and restaurants too – or fire up the barbecue or the old pizza oven. The owners will also cook on request: the home-grown vegetables, raspberries and olive oil are the biggest treat.

Rooms	1 barn for 2: €1,300–€1,500 per week.
Meals	Self-catering.
Closed	Rarely.

Kate Middleton
Le Caviere,
Azienda Agricola Le Caviere,
52036 Pieve Santo Stefano

Mobile +39 347 8990137
Email kate@oliveoilandraspberries.it
Web www.oliveoilandraspberries.it

Agriturismo Vecchia Quercia

If you're the lucky person who has been put in charge of hunting down a gorgeous place for a group of friends – or a family reunion – you can expect lavish praise when you arrive at La Vecchia Quercia. Set high on a hill above medieval Poppi where a gentle breeze deflects the hottest excesses of the Tuscan sun, the estate is private, beautifully maintained and big enough to get lost in. You have enough bedrooms and bathrooms to avoid a coin toss, a state-of-the-art kitchen, a harmonious and contemporary décor and – best of all – a lovely owner on hand. Francesca can arrange trips around the farm (including a *nero estivo* hunt in the newly planted truffle wood), restaurant recommendations, cookery lessons and discounted visits to the nearby golf course. You can text her in the evening and she'll drop off fresh bread and croissants in the morning. Make sure that you ask her mother Novella to cook at least one evening meal for you all – it's always nice to have dinner taken care of as you doze on a chic lounger by a sublime pool knowing that everyone else is happy too. *Total possible capacity 20.*

Rooms	1 house for 11; 1 apartment for 4; 1 barn for 2: £1,845-£3,690 per week. Extra beds available.
Meals	Restaurants nearby.
Closed	November–January.

Francesca Panci
Agriturismo Vecchia Quercia,
Colle Ascensione 159,
52014 Poppi
Mobile   +39 348 3637186
Email   info@agriturismovecchiaquercia.it
Web   www.agriturismovecchiaquercia.it

L'Ultimo Mulino

The sense of space is stunning – the vast, medieval hall, the lofty ceilings, the stone walls, the flights of stairs… a fairy tale. Original arches give glimpses of passageways beyond and many of the rooms are connected by little 'bridges' with the millstream far below. Outside the restored watermill there's a large terrace for delicious breakfasts, a lovely long pool, and a small amphitheatre where the odd concert is held. You're in the middle of nowhere, surrounded by trees and it's immensely quiet – just the sound of water and birds. All feels fresh and clean, the atmosphere is welcoming and informal, and nothing is too much trouble for the staff. Sparsely, elegantly and comfortably furnished, the great hall makes a cool, beautiful centrepiece to the building – and there's a snug with a fireplace where you can roast chestnuts in season. Excellently equipped, smallish bedrooms have terracotta tiled floors and good, generously sized beds. You dine in the conservatory overlooking the stream, on mainly Tuscan dishes – be tempted by truffles and local delicacies. Historic Radda is a ten-minute drive.

Rooms	12 doubles: €112-€203.
	1 suite for 2: €324-€370.
Meals	Dinner €35-€45. Wine €15-€80.
Closed	Mid-November to mid-March.

Massimo Rossinelli
L'Ultimo Mulino,
Loc. La Ripresa di Vistarenni,
53013 Gaiole in Chianti

Tel	+39 0577 738520
Email	info@ultimomulino.it
Web	www.ultimomulino.it

Castello di Spaltenna

Come, if not for the church, the food and the stunning buildings, for the classic Chianti views. The castle, with its neighbouring bell-towered church, was the centre of a medieval hamlet and still feels feudal. Walls are solid, doors are carved, ceilings beamed and vaulted, and passageways dotted with armour, wall sconces and cushioned seats in arched alcoves. The tapestry-hung dining room, originally a refectory when the castle was a monastery, is hung with papal portraits. The 400 wines are perhaps a papal tradition too. There is nothing medieval about the comfort; luxurious bedrooms have been designed into the grand spaces, the feel being more Italian country-castle than swish hotel. Fabrics are rich – silks, bold stripes, soft muslins – and each room is different; some have four-posters, others have beds on a dais, perhaps a fireplace, wooden ceiling, stone wall or archway. The two pools (one indoor), sauna, gym and Turkish bath should be enough for most of us. You can gaze over the Chianti valley, play tennis, stroll to the village bars, dine – superbly – in the candlelit courtyard.

Rooms	30 doubles: €190–€330. 8 suites for 2: €380–€500. Singles €150–€190. Child 6-12, €25 per night. Extra bed €50.
Meals	Dinner €55–€70. Restaurants nearby.
Closed	Rarely.

Alessandro Ercolani
Castello di Spaltenna,
Via Spaltenna 13, Località Pieve di
Spaltenna, 53013 Gaiole in Chianti

Tel	+39 0577 749483
Email	info@spaltenna.it
Web	www.spaltenna.it

Borgo Argenina

Soft striped hillsides of vineyards, the occasional signature farmhouse with a cypress by its side – not a shadow of doubt you are in Chianti! Winding roads a short distance from Siena lead to the borgo Elena bought 25 years ago, then had restored under her impeccable supervision. Cascading red geraniums accent windows and roses glow in every corner. A bundle of energy and enthusiasm, a former fashion designer from Milan, she is a hostess par excellence so join in! As she cooks in the evening you may drink local wine and chatter with fellow guests. Feast on fresh coffee cakes and bucolic views at the start of the day, end it with a Tuscan meal by the open fire; if you stay in one of the villas you may cook for yourself. Elena has furnished the six B&B rooms in country style, with patchwork quilts on white wrought-iron beds and feminine florals in celestial blues. Floors are rustic brick, beams are chunky and your hostess's colourful artistry has brought discarded objects back to life. Forget your established itineraries and let Elena guide you, to villages and wineries bordered by Siena and Florence.

Rooms	4 doubles: €170.
	2 suites for 3: €200–€240.
	1 villa for 4-5: €480.
	2 villas for 2-3: €240–€300.
	Singles €130. All prices per night.
Meals	Restaurants 1.5km.
Closed	15 November to 10 March.

Elena Nappa
Borgo Argenina,
Loc. Argenina, San M. Monti,
53013 Gaiole in Chianti
Mobile   +39 345 3537673
Email   info@borgoargenina.it
Web   www.borgoargenina.it

17 Via dei Goti

Just south-east of Siena, this medieval hill town buzzes with its weekly market and year-round inhabitants. Catch brilliant views of surrounding hills through entrance arches in ancient walls; Porta dei Tintori is a fine place to sit with a glass of wine in the evening. Your perfect townhouse is tall and narrow, on four floors, cool in the summer yet cosy in winter; rusts, blues and whites bathe its walls. You enter the open-plan dining area off the street; through an arched wall is a fully-stocked kitchen. (Take what you need – wine included – then simply replace.) On the first floor are a double bedroom and an elegant living room with a beamed ceiling, an open fireplace, a cream sofa and chairs, lovely art work and books galore. A second salon and another bedroom are on the third floor, then right at the top (not for the un-nimble) is the master bedroom, splendid with its French antiques and embroidered linen curtains and sheets. The bathroom has a claw-foot bath from which you may gaze over rooftops, and candles are waiting to be lit. Fabulous.

Rooms	1 house for 6: €450–€850 per week.
Meals	Self-catering.
Closed	Rarely.

Sheri Eggleton & Charles Grant
17 Via dei Goti,
53040 Rapolano Terme

Tel	+44 (0)117 9081949
Mobile	+44 (0)7932 186096
Email	sherieggleton711@googlemail.com
Web	www.17viadeigoti.co.uk

Laticastelli Country Relais

In the fresh, clean air of a forested hilltop, this medieval hamlet once guarded Siena from marauding invaders. Now it's a charming hotel, with space to relax and a restaurant in the wine cellar. Rolling green views – pure Tuscany – are best enjoyed from the infinity pool, set amid flowers, lush grass and big old trees; bliss. Meals may be taken on the terrace at sunset, or cosily under rustic brick arches; food is fresh, local, and again, pure Tuscany. If you feel the belt tightening, use the communal kitchen to prepare your own snack, then settle on the sofa by an enormous stone fireplace. Two sitting rooms are dotted with eye-catching paintings and books – great conversation-starters in this sociable place. With the motorway close by, you can zip everywhere; or ask Giancarlo about wine tours, horse riding, polo lessons, hot springs. Wake to a slow buffet breakfast and take your turn guarding Siena, from the comfort of that heavenly pool. And when night and peace fall, trot across to big, bold bedrooms with chunky wood beams, terracotta floors, deep chic baths and huge walk-in showers.

Rooms	21 doubles: €166–€185.
	4 family rooms for 4: €238–€280.
	2 singles: €81–€90.
Meals	Lunch/dinner €30. Wine €15–€400.
	Guest kitchen. Restaurant 3km.
Closed	Christmas & New Year;
	10 November to 1 April.

	Giancarlo Lorizzo
	Laticastelli Country Relais,
	53040 Rapolano Terme
Tel	+39 0577 724419
Email	contact@laticastelli.com
Web	www.laticastelli.com

Podere Patrignone – Villa & Apartments

Wine festivals, music festivals, sunsets galore: Tuscan heaven! After a stupendous drive along the road between Florence and Siena you descend, through dappled woodland, to Patrignone, high on a hill, with spectacular views. Simon and Verity, charismatic and open-hearted, live in the main farmhouse of a 15th-century cluster of buildings linked by flagstone courtyards and jasmine-strewn terraces. Paths lined with lavender lead to Verity's herb garden, while an 18th-century olive crusher stands witness to 30 hectares of olive groves; some trees are 250 years old, others are exceedingly rare. You can do B&B or be independent and self-cater; each apartment feels nicely secluded. One is reached by outside steps and delights in its own balcony, another has an open fireplace, bliss on autumn days. The largest, 'Terrazza', is the oldest and, in summer, the coolest. Imagine stone walls and chunky beams, walnut veneer beds, painted cupboards and lovely old lace at windows. Then its off to the trampoline, treehouse and unfenced pool, or for a waggy walk in the woods with Lola and Charlie. *Minimum stay four nights. Capacity may include child's bed.*

Rooms	2 apartments for 2; 1 apartment for 4; 1 apartment for 5; 1 apartment for 7: €125–€250; €120–€1,530 per week. 1 house for 8-14: €735–€880; €3,755–€4,525 per week. Whole estate available (sleeping 33) €8,940–€10,735 per week.
Meals	Restaurant 5-minute drive. Once weekly 4-course Tuscan banquet, €40, children €20. Breakfast by arrangement.
Closed	November-March.

Simon Zimbler
Podere Patrignone – Villa & Apartments,
Loc. Patrignone 3,
Castellina in Chianti
Mobile   +39 331 7338442
Email   enquiries@patrignone.com
Web   www.patrignone.com

Fattoria Tregole

A vineyard and a private family chapel. What could be more Italian? The delightful Kirchlechners – he an architect, she a restorer – make *chianti classico* and olive oil from their Tuscan manor farm. They spent seven years restoring the buildings, keeping original features – raftered ceilings, terracotta floors, large fireplaces – and furnishing with a light, country-house touch. The airy apartments and the bedrooms, including a ground-floor suite with a terrace, feel like the family's rooms; all are lovely. Walls are eye-catching with Edith's hand-painted stencils, painted brass bedsteads are cleverly restored; there are traditional lampshades, dried flowers, patchwork quilts and crochet cushions. It is light, warm and inviting. Have your breakfast in the sunny dining room or on the patio, whilst the on site restaurant serves traditional Tuscan dinners. Guests can learn to recreate recipes in cookery classes or sample wines from the Tregole cellars. A beautiful pool, quiet views over olive groves and vine-clad hills, a garden with shady nooks, a tiny Renaissance chapel – it is intimate and homely. *Minimum stay three nights in apartments.*

Rooms	4 doubles: €130–€150.
	1 suite for 2: €180.
	1 apartment for 5; 1 apartment for 4:
	€220–€360. Prices per night.
Meals	Dinner €35, book ahead.
	Wine from €10. Restaurants 4km.
Closed	Rarely.

Edith Kirchlechner
Fattoria Tregole,
Loc. Tregole 86,
53011 Castellina in Chianti

Tel	+39 0577 740991
Email	fattoria-tregole@castellina.com
Web	www.fattoria-tregole.com

Locanda dell' Artista

In 40 rolling acres, with views across vineyards and olive groves to San Gimignano, is an immaculate restoration of a Tuscan farm. Your hosts employed a team of talented local builders to combine modern architectural flourishes with traditional design, and the results are enticing. Off the country road, through the wrought-iron gates, down the gravelled pathways, to find whitewashed beams, cotto floors and a big wonderful welcome. Your hosts – Baker, a film producer for Disney, and Cristian, owner of a fashion accessories business in Bergamo – are loving their new adventure, and will no doubt be having a few star-spangled friends to stay (who's heard of Elton John?). Inside all is spacious and stylish, with soft lighting, fine fabrics, beautiful books, art from their collections and … a green baby grand! Listen to the monks chanting prayers in the Abbey of Sant'Antimo, enjoy personal vineyard tours and lunches, visit a pecorino farm in Pienza. Bliss to come home to a lap in the pool, a relaxed meal on the terrace, and a bed dressed in Italian linen, perhaps with a view of those famous towers. *Minimum stay two nights. Children over 12 welcome.*

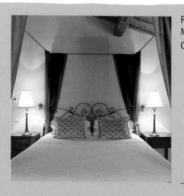

Rooms	5 doubles; 1 twin/double: €160–€245.
Meals	Restaurants 4km.
Closed	November–February.

Baker Bloodworth & Cristian Rovetta
Locanda dell' Artista,
Loc. Canonica-Lucignano 43,
53037 San Gimignano

Tel	+39 0577 946026
Email	info@locandadellartista.com
Web	www.locandadellartista.com

La Locanda

Admire the view from the pool – both are stunning. This is a magical place; a soft green lawn edged with Mediterranean shrubs slopes down to the pool, a covered terrace overlooks medieval Volpaia. (Some of the best chianti is produced here; the village itself is a 20-minute walk.) The house vibrates with bold colour and lively fabric. The beautiful raftered living room, with open fireplace, big, stylish sofas and pale terracotta floor, reveals photos of Guido and Martina, he from the South, she from the North. They scoured Tuscany before they found their perfect hotel, renovated these two houses and filled them with fine antiques, delightful prints, candles and fun touches. There's a library/bar where you can choose books from many languages and where Guido is generous with the grappa. The bedrooms, some with their own terraces, are in a separate building and have big beds, great bathrooms and whitewashed rafters, as was the custom here. Martina cooks and gardens while Guido acts as host – they are a charming pair. Once settled in you'll find it hard to stir. *Minimum stay two nights.*

Rooms	3 doubles; 3 twins: €220-€290.
	1 suite for 2: €310.
	Singles €190-€250.
Meals	Dinner €35 (Mon, Wed & Fri).
	Wine €18-€70. Restaurants 4km.
Closed	November to mid-April.

Guido & Martina Bevilacqua
La Locanda,
Loc. Montanino,
53017 Radda in Chianti

Tel	+39 0577 738832/3
Email	info@lalocanda.it
Web	www.lalocanda.it

Palazzo Leopoldo

In a corner of the hall is a stone carving of a swaddled baby – 14th-century evidence of the hospital this once was. For the last few centuries Palazzo Leopoldo has been a manor house. It's surprisingly peaceful here, in the middle of beautiful, hilltop Radda, strolling distance to several *enoteche* – taste the fine chiantis. The whole house, on several levels and teeming with nooks and crannies, has a delightful feel: the hall is light, with white-painted arches and old tiled floor, there are bright rugs and fresh flowers. Stroll onto the terrace for sensational Tuscan views. Bedrooms range from suites to doubles up under the roof, all generously equipped and with a rustic-rich Tuscan feel. Some have the old bell-pulls for service, others the original stoves and frescoes; there's a beautiful elegance. A remarkable breakfast is served in a remarkable kitchen, replete with 18th-century range: the best-ever setting for a cookery class. Add to that an indoor pool and spa, a restaurant serving delicious food, and delightful staff. More than worth the steep and winding road to get here!

Rooms	14 doubles: €113–€225.
	5 suites for 2: €315–€394.
Meals	Breakfast €9.90. Lunch €25.
	Dinner €35.
Closed	January–February.

Massimo Rossinelli
Palazzo Leopoldo,
Via Roma 33,
53017 Radda in Chianti
Tel   +39 0577 735605
Email   info@palazzoleopoldo.it
Web   www.palazzoleopoldo.it

Antico Borgo Poggiarello

Totally unspoilt, with stunning views over the hillsides to San Gimignano and Volterra, this tucked-away 17th-century *borgo* has been transformed into an utterly charming 'holiday village' linked by a circuit of paths. Poggiarello is a family set-up: Signora Giove does the cooking, sons Roberto and Paolo do front of house, while their father, Nino, is there when you need him. You can self-cater or do B&B here: the arrangements are flexible. Most apartments are for two; some interconnect and are ideal for eight. Rooms are big and comfortable with wrought-iron beds, cream curtains and covers, tiled floors; all have patios and great views and one is excellent for wheelchair-users. Days are spent lolling by the pool, evenings sunset-gazing on the terrace. You'll find it hard to leave, even though the treasures of Siena, Monteriggioni and Volterra lie a short drive away. Note the beautiful Roman bath housed in a cave that's heated all year to 38 degrees (extra charge) and the terraced restaurant in the stables where you can sample the best of Tuscan home cooking.

Apartments can interconnect.

Rooms	1 apartment for 4; 2 apartments for 2; 1 apartment for 6: €100–€240. €100–€140 for 2 per night.	
Meals	Breakfast €9. Dinner, 5 courses, €31, by arrangement. Wine from €13. Half board extra €37 p.p.	
Closed	20-27 December.	

Nino Giove
Antico Borgo Poggiarello,
Strada di San Monti 12,
53035 Monteriggioni

Tel	+39 0577 301003
Email	info@poggiarello.com
Web	www.poggiarello.com

Bichi Borghesi Scorgiano

A clutch of 17th-century buildings — some beautifully restored, others ageing gracefully — make up this glorious wine estate half an hour from Siena. The hamlet is full of life: tractors trundle around the country lanes, estate workers throw you a cheery 'Buongiorno!', dogs scamper around your feet on arrival. Despite the activity, this is a refined, relaxed place to stay. Archways, formal gardens and courtyards beg exploration, and there's a delightful pool to laze away the afternoon by... masses of space at every turn. There's always stuff going on here too: cookery courses in the kitchens, wine and olive oil tasting in the old stables, trips to neighbouring towns and vineyards. The comfortable apartments are set back away from all the hubbub. Traditionally furnished and wonderfully spacious, they have antique pieces, exposed brickwork and strong colours on the walls — ochres, terracottas, lemon yellows. Petite, sparkly-eyed Paola throws masses of energy into everything she does; she and Vittorio are a great team and will look after you perfectly. You won't want to stir. *Minimum stay two nights.*

Rooms	2 apartments for 4; 1 apartment for 7: €570–€1,070 per week.
Meals	Self-catering.
Closed	Casa Rufini: Jan to mid-April. Cocchieri & Fattoria: Jan to mid-March.

Paola & Vittorio Mereu
Bichi Borghesi Scorgiano,
53031 Casole d'Elsa

Tel	+39 0577 301020
Email	info@bichiborghesi.it
Web	www.bichiborghesi.it

Rocca di Castagnoli

Max truly wants this place to shine, and shine it does. Ancient Rocca di Castagnoli, one of Chianti's most prestigious wine-producing estates, is a one-thousand-year old hilltop castle with an attached hamlet and – off a courtyard with time-polished cobbles – some swooningly beautiful self-catering apartments and rooms. Immaculately designed interiors with beamy ceilings and ancient cotta floors offset the sharply defined opulence of sleek modern fixtures, royalty-sized draped beds, gold embroidered curtains, mountains of cushions and perfectly placed antiques. Bathrooms have huge whirlpool showers and snazzy products. Kitchens and sitting rooms follow flawless suit. A communal billiards room opens onto a terrace with stop-and-stare views that are shared from the pool in the garden below. Breakfasts are predictably perfect; and there's an exquisite inn, Osteria al Ponte, a stroll away. Tour the vineyards and cellars, dig into your pool-side sunspot, let dashing manager Max advise you – in perfect English – on wine trails in Chianti. Postpone the return home. The place is a dream!

Rooms	6 doubles: €125–€210 per night. 5 apartments for 2; 2 apartments for 4: €515–€955 per week.
Meals	Breakfast €8–€13. Restaurant 5-minute walk.
Closed	Rarely.

Max Adorno
Rocca di Castagnoli,
Loc. Castagnoli,
53013 Siena

Tel	+39 0577 731909
Email	info@roccadicastagnoli.com
Web	www.roccadicastagnoli.com

Santa 10

Friendly owners Elisa and Gianni, with their two kids in tow, made the move here in 1996, to this breezy hill outside Siena; the city's medieval towers dominate the horizon – and there's a 1,000-year-old tower right here. It was only after the renovation of this old farm had begun that they discovered the *cantina* underground. Now they are in the wine business too, and vines stretch out along the valley in both directions. There's just one bedroom, round the back, with views to Siena. It's simple, countrified and extremely comfortable, with flashes of blue and gold on the walls, waxed floorboards underfoot, and some lovely family pieces dotted around. The colourful bathroom has a huge shower and a handsome gilt mirror and a little porthole through which you can espy the pool and gardens. Next to the house, what was once a lemon house is now a beautiful, naturally restored apartment. Gianni and Elisa are a kind, interesting, loveable couple who want you to enjoy their life as much as they do. Breakfast in their kitchen or in your room – and don't leave without a bottle of Santa 10 in your suitcase!

Rooms	1 double: €120.
	1 apartment for 4 (2 doubles on mezzanine): €1,120 per week.
Meals	Restaurants within 1km.
Closed	Rarely.

Gianni & Elisa Massone
Santa 10,
Strada di Santa Regina 10/A,
53100 Siena

Tel	+39 0577 43566
Email	elisa@santa10.it
Web	www.santa10.it

Frances' Lodge Relais

You stay in a converted hilltop lemon house, a ten-minute bus ride into the city. Catch your breath at views that soar across olive, lemon and quince groves to Siena's Torre del Mangia. The old farmhouse was built by Franca's family as a summer retreat. Now she and Franco – warm, charming, intelligent – have filled the lofty, light-filled *limonaia* with beautiful things: an oriental carpet, a butter-yellow leather sofa, family antiques, potted plants and vibrant art by Franca. In the cooler months, guests may take breakfast in this lovely living room which is divided by a glass partition etched with a lemon tree from the kitchen, Franca's domain. And the first meal of the day – in the historic garden in summer – is to be lingered over: Tuscan salami and pecorino, fresh figs, delicious coffee. Bedrooms burst with personality and colour – one, funky and Moroccan, another huge, white and cream, with an outside area with a view. Chic coloured bed linen, huge walk-in showers, a fridge stocked with juice and water. A special place with a big heart. *Minimum stay two nights. Over 18s only.*

Rooms	5 doubles: €180–€220. 1 suite for 2-4: €240–€380.
Meals	Restaurant 800m.
Closed	10 January to 10 March.

Franca Mugnai
Frances' Lodge Relais,
Strada di Valdipugna 2,
53100 Siena

Mobile	+39 337 671608
Email	happyiwan@gmail.com
Web	www.franceslodge.it

Entry 231 Map 8

Campo Regio Relais

In bustling, beautiful Siena, step straight in from a quiet cobbled street to marble floors, frescoed walls, fine antiques and wonderful paintings. A first-floor sitting room gleams with leather sofas and vases of fresh flowers, there are striped cloths on the tables where copious breakfasts are taken, and the terrace looks over rooftops to the Duomo: an incomparable cityscape. This building, which dates from the 16th century, has its own peculiar architecture. One bedroom has a private terrace and that view, another, the view from its bed; all are generously sumptuous with monogrammed sheets, taffeta curtains, soft creams and pale lilacs, buckets of smellies and big-mirrored bathrooms; totally pampering. The charming owners live upstairs and are unintrusively present. It's a stroll to restaurants, shops, street life and the great sights. Then back for a nightcap from the honesty bar in the candlelit salone as you watch the twinkling lights of the city below. Honeymooners will find it irresistible, architecture buffs will swoon, children may prefer somewhere a touch more robust.

Rooms	6 twin/doubles: €190-€650.
	Singles €150-€300.
Meals	Restaurants nearby.
Closed	Beginning of January to mid-March.

Livia Palagi
Campo Regio Relais,
Residenza d'Epoca,
Via della Sapienza 25, 53100 Siena

Tel	+39 0577 222073
Email	relais@camporegio.com
Web	www.camporegio.com

Agriturismo Podere Di Santa Maria

The restoration of this old farm has created a pretty cluster of weathered stone dwellings with wide and lovely views over thickly wooded hills. The garden is mostly laid to grass with olive and acacia trees, lavender borders and higgledy old walls topped with pots of geraniums. The ingenious saline swimming pool is a delight; it could be hard to leave its side – perhaps just for the ten minute stroll along the medieval walled lane for lunch in Cicciano? You can help yourself from charming Gianna's vegetable plot and each apartment has a decent kitchen. 'Casa Ada' and 'Gualdi' are on one floor, 'Casa Erina' is on two, in the former hay barn. Bedrooms are traditional and simple with rosy pink or yellow walls, modern floor tiles, dark wood furniture, wrought iron beds – it's more about being out and about here. It's easy to visit Siena, Florence and San Gimignano; you're only an hour from the coast and there's stacks to do locally: visit the ruined abbey of San Galgano, go biking, hiking or riding, or try a spot of speleology in the ancient mineral and metal mines of the Colline Metallifere – this is a beautiful area.

Rooms	1 apartment for 2; 2 apartments for 4: €500–€850 per week. Extra beds available.
Meals	Restaurants 10-minute walk.
Closed	December-February.

Gianna Corsi
Località Santa Maria a Cucinato,
Ciciano, 53012 Chiusdino

Tel	+39 0577 750641
Mobile	+39 347 1937052
Email	info@poderedisantamaria.it
Web	www.poderedisantamaria.it

Poggio Boldrini

Poets, dreamers, lovers will find inspiration here, high in the olive-grove'd hills. Sue, the English artist owner, has beautifully and sustainably restored an abandoned olive farm. Your little Hayloft stands 200m from the main house, truly secluded, with its own loggia and garden. Enter to find a kitchen cum sitting room with big windows for the view – spectacular in the day time and magical at night: San Giovanni's castle is illuminated. Your little bedroom and bathroom are equally fresh and simple: a white throw on a double bed, chunky beams, contemporary tub, floaty curtains, Sue's abstracts on the walls. And, should you fancy a winter stay, warm toasty floors. Best of all, a private path leads down to a fabulous infinity pool in terraced gardens, yours for half a day, everyday. Sue's artistry is not confined to painting and ceramics and her garden is a year-round joy, a-tumble with lavender and roses in summer. Beauty and serenity surround you, and you can walk to tiny Chiusure, an ancient hilltop village founded by the Etruscans.

Rooms	1 apartment for 2: €500–€900 per week.
Meals	Restaurants 1km.
Closed	Rarely.

Ryan & Sue Law
Poggio Boldrini,
53020 San Giovanni d'Asso
Mobile   +39 347 8812709
Email   kennington.sue@gmail.com
Web   www.poggioboldrini.com

Bosco della Spina

The road sign for 'pizzeria' is misleading: nothing so mundane here. Tables overlook a magical garden of pergolas, waterfalls, vines and wisteria; Castle Murlo hangs in the distance. Imaginatively restored and landscaped, these former farmhouse cellars in medieval Lupompesi have strikingly modern interiors and old Tuscan beams and terracotta; architecturally it is an interesting restoration. The restaurant, a cool space of open arches, raftered ceiling and sleek furniture, serves classic regional dishes (pizza in the summer only) accompanied by 180 wines. Reached down a series of impersonal corridors, the super comfy suites, each with fridge, sink and dual hob, have terraces, big divans and furniture made by local craftsmen. Blankets are neatly rolled, colours white and conker brown, beds hi-tech four-poster, bedcovers faux suede, shower rooms designery. All this and a wine bar, library, small gym, slimline pool (suitable for lengths only) and garden spots filled with tinkling water and views. A smoothly run and relaxed operation, popular with wedding parties, too.

Rooms	6 suites for 2; 3 suites for 4: €115–€300.
	4 apartments for 2; 1 apartment for 4:
	€70–€370.
	Sofabeds available. Pets €5.
Meals	Dinner €30. Wine from €7.
Closed	6 November to 28 March.

Brigida Meoni
Bosco della Spina,
Lupompesi, 53016 Murlo

Tel	+39 0577 814605
Email	bsturist@boscodellaspina.com
Web	www.boscodellaspina.com

Castelnuovo Tancredi

From the town of Buonconvento you wend your way up the hillsides to eight hectares of vineyards and olive groves, and an illustrious house. Continue down the road to a hamlet built in 1832 where the farmers and the livestock once resided: a cluster of rustic outbuildings that make up Borgo di Castelrotto. Surrounded by a natural garden of lavender, rosemary and roses, each house has its own pergola for meals. A pool on the hill overlooks a perfect Tuscany valley, the air is fresh and the silence is golden. Step inside to find original brick floors and chunky beamed ceilings, wrought-iron beds and country antiques, and unfussy kitchens and bathrooms; an engaging simplicity remains. The two largest apartments are on the first floor, reached via outside stairs, with big inviting rooms and huge fireplaces. The smallest is in a separate, charming house with a super-private patio outside and a second bedroom in the hayloft. Gracious owner Guido (fourth generation) and his amicable wife Lee offer a welcome brunch on Sunday mornings and can prepare private wine tastings in their historic, architect-designed Cantina. *Minimum three nights in low season, four in high season.*

Rooms	1 house for 4; 2 apartments for 8: €1,100–€1,950 per week.
Meals	Dinner on request. Restaurants 2km.
Closed	Mid-January to mid-March.

Guido & Lee Venturini del Greco
Az. Agr. Castelnuovo Tancredi, Borgo
Castelrotto, 53022 Buonconvento

Tel	+39 0577 806090
Mobile	+39 335 7410549
Email	amministrazione@castelnuovotancredi.it
Web	www.castelnuovotancredi.it

Podere Salicotto

Watch sunsets fire the Tuscan hills; catch the sunrise as it brings the valleys alive. Views from this hilltop farmhouse roll off in every direction. It is peaceful here, and beautiful. Breakfast is a delicious feast that merges into lunch, with produce from the organic farm, and Silvia and Paolo, a well-travelled, warm and adventurous couple, are happy for you to be as active or as idle as you like. Eat breakfast in the big farmhouse kitchen or under the pergola, as deer wander across the field below. Paolo is full of ideas and will take you sailing in his six-berth boat that has crossed the Atlantic – or organise wine-tasting and cycling trips. The beamed and terracotta tiled bedrooms are airy and welcoming, full of soft, Tuscan colours and furnished with simplicity but care: antiques, monogrammed sheets, great showers. B&B guests are in the main house (private entrance) while the studio is in the converted barn. Visit Siena, medieval Buonconvento, Tuscan hill towns. Come back and laze around the pool with a glass of wine and a fabulous view. *Min stay two nights, three nights in high season. Children over 12 welcome.*

Rooms	6 doubles: €168–€254; €1,060–€1,600 per week. 1 studio for 2: €1,320 per week. Whole house available on self-catering basis (27 December to 7 January only). Sofabeds available.
Meals	Guest kitchen & barbecue. Wine from €7. Restaurants 300m.
Closed	3 November to 16 April.

Silvia Forni
Podere Salicotto,
Podere Salicotto 73,
53022 Buonconvento

Tel	+39 0577 809087
Email	info@poderesalicotto.com
Web	www.poderesalicotto.com

Castello di Ripa d'Orcia

As you drive up the long, long white road, the castle comes into view: a thrilling sight. Ripa d'Orcia is 800 years old and one of Siena's most important strongholds. The battlemented fortress (closed to the public) dominates the *borgo* encircled by small medieval dwellings. The delightful family are descendants of the Piccolomini who acquired the estate in 1484 and are naturally proud of their heritage. Grand banquets and knights in shining armour come to mind... it's gloriously, romantically atmospheric. Rooms and apartments have huge raftered ceilings and are furnished simply and well; most have breathtaking views. There's also a dayroom, filled with wonderful furniture and heaps of books to browse. You breakfast in a small annexe off the main restaurant, there's a cellar for wine tastings and a shop for you to stock up on your favourites. A pool too, and a beautiful chapel in the grounds. The area is a paradise for walkers and there is enough on the spot to keep lovers of history and architecture happy for hours – before the 'official' sightseeing begins. *Minimum stay two nights, three nights in apartment.*

Rooms	6 twin/doubles: €110–€150. 3 apartments for 4; 5 apartments for 2: €110–€190. All prices per night.
Meals	Dinner from €12. Wine from €10. Closed Mondays.
Closed	November–March.

Famiglia Aluffi Pentini Rossi
Castello di Ripa d'Orcia,
Loc. Ripa d'Orcia,
53027 Castiglione d'Orcia

Tel	+39 0577 897376
Email	info@castelloripadorcia.com
Web	www.ripadorcia.it

Il Rigo

The fame of Lorenza's cooking has spread so far that she's been invited to demonstrate her skills in the US (she runs courses here, too). So meals in the big, beamed dining room at pretty check-clothed tables are a treat. Irresistible home-grown organic produce, 60 local wines to choose from and a gorgeous Tuscan setting. There are two houses on the family farm, named after the stream running through it. 'Casabianca', reached via a cypress-flanked drive, is ancient and stone built. A vine-covered pergola shades the entrance; beyond the reception area is a courtyard full of climbing roses. The second house, 'Poggio Bacoca', is about 600 metres away. Once home to the farmworkers, it's red-brick built and has two sitting rooms and panoramic views. You walk to 'Casabianca' for those wonderful meals. Bedrooms are homely, pretty and inviting; all have embroidered sheets, appealing colour schemes and matching bathrooms. No televisions: it's not that sort of place. Lorenza and Vittorio hope and believe that their guests will prefer a relaxed chat over a glass of wine.

Rooms	15 doubles: €100–€124.
	Dinner, B&B €144–€170 for 2.
Meals	Lunch/dinner €22–€25, by
	arrangement. Wine from €12.
	Restaurant 4km.
Closed	Never.

Vittorio Cipolla & Lorenza Santo
Il Rigo, Podere Casabianca,
53027 San Quirico d'Orcia

Tel	+39 0577 897 291
Mobile	+39 342 3735370
Email	info@agriturismoilrigo.com
Web	www.agriturismoilrigo.com

Casa Lemmi

Swoop south from Siena into a gentle Tuscan valley whose tree-lined hills and picturesque towns inspired many a Renaissance artist. Park below the fortified walls of San Quirico d'Orcia to find the Lemmi-Menesini family's 12th-century palazzo opposite the magnificent Collegiate. An old pilgrims' stopover and Templar lodge, the sandstone house holds many secrets – not least ancient brick cellars that may have been a pagan temple. Now, for a small fee, you may luxuriate under the arches in a slim heated pool and jacuzzi. Above ground, the palazzo is split in two, with steep stairs to big, airy, beamed rooms and rather dated bathrooms. All are a cosy mishmash of strong colours, carved armoires, quirky lamps, rugs and antique radios. Fling open shutters to glorious views over the piazza, rooftops and church (bells chime hourly). If you find the sitting room and breakfast tables just too teensy, take your coffee and homemade cakes out to the patio's geraniums and vines. Scale Monte Amiata, soak in the hot springs of Bagno Vignoni, take a lazy lunch in hilltop Montalcino and Pienza.

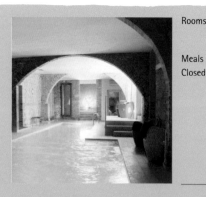

Rooms	4 doubles: €69-€109.
	5 suites for 2: €89-€149.
	Singles €69-€89.
Meals	Restaurants nearby.
Closed	Rarely.

Stanko Brnjac
Casa Lemmi,
Via Dante Alighieri 29,
53027 San Quirico d'Orcia
Tel   +39 0577 899016
Email   info@casalemmi.com
Web   www.casalemmi.co.uk

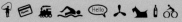

Terre di Nano

Along the rolling *strada bianca* through vines, olives, oak woods, down the cypress-lined drive (the family's vineyards on either side), through stone gates... to an elegant, well-proportioned country villa and heart-stopping views. The ochre walls have mellowed over time and the outbuildings glow in the evening sun. Ilaria (receptionist) or Giorgio (chef and wine expert) – or Marco the owner – will greet you and take you to your room. It will be chestnut-beamed, furnished in relaxed style and overlooking a hill town of your dreams (Montepulciano, Montecchiello, Pienza). Mouthwatering aromas assail you so make sure you've booked in for dinner, served at pink-clothed tables in an intimate dining room on the first floor or on the gravelled terrace. Sample too the estate's excellent wines. There's no communal sitting room but bedrooms are large enough to have seating areas or terraces, and bathrooms flourish thick white towels (and, in one, British fox hunting scenes!). In the gardens are two swimming pools, boules, pots spilling flowers, and seats for incomparable views.

Rooms	3 doubles: €110–€180.
Meals	Dinner on request. Restaurants 2km.
Closed	Rarely.

Ilaria de Pieri
Terre di Nano,
Località Nano,
53026 Monticchiello di Pienza
Tel   +39 0578 070115
Email   info@terredinano.com
Web   www.terredinano.com

Terre di Nano

Close to some of the finest hilltop towns in Tuscany, at the top of the winding white road – ah, the breezes! – is a well-proportioned 19th-century villa with Giotto-esque views. Through impressive stone gates are ochre walls that have mellowed with time, and outbuildings that glow in the sun. When the owners are not here, Ilaria and Giorgio usher you in and show you the self-catering options, of which there are five. 'Terrazza' is above the cellar, with a vast terrace for an even vaster view; single-storey 'Casetta' is traditional-new, with its own little garden and gazebo; 'Fornace' is in a renovated outbuilding, with a chunky beamed country kitchen and two big floors. Rustic 'Torrino' and 'Bellavista' are in the main villa. The décor is traditional, comfortable, relaxed – a leather sofa here, an antique bread chest there, swagged cream curtains, a painted door as a bedhead, a marble fireplace for winter. You're ten minutes from Montecchiello for provisions, but why not book in for dinner here? Warm, friendly Giorgio is an excellent cook and he also takes care of the wines (they're delicious).

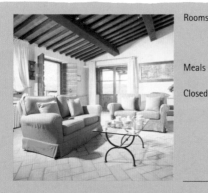

Rooms	2 apartments for 4: €960–€1,680.
	2 houses for 4: €960–€3,150.
	Prices per week
	Nightly rates €160–€450.
Meals	Breakfast €12. Dinner on request.
	Restaurants 2km.
Closed	Rarely.

Ilaria de Pieri
Terre di Nano,
Località Nano,
53026 Monticchiello di Pienza
Tel   +39 0578 070115
Email   info@terredinano.com
Web   www.terredinano.com

Follonico

Dog, horse, hens, donkey, three little children and Fabio and Suzanne: all live in harmony at this Tuscan *casale*. Follonico sits in a bucolic valley surrounded by grassy garden and some of the most beautiful scenery in Italy, and gazes up to Montepulciano. Weathered old doors have been kept and used as shutters, an old jug stuffed with flowers sits in a niche, agrarian implements are propped against walls. It is a lesson to all, in how to restore a property so it doesn't look restored. The living space where you breakfast on fruits, frittatas and breads (homemade) is all you'd hope for: rustic beams and worn terracotta, a great fireplace hung with chestnut roasting pans, a white sofa splashed with cushions, books piled on a reclaimed table. Your Italian-Dutch hosts – relaxed, welcoming and in love with this region – have created four beautiful suites in the house and two in an outbuilding: big, simple, charming, with chunky beds on pale stone floors, lights recessed in bare plaster walls, delicious mattresses and a choice of pillows, and retro objets to feast the eyes on. Bathrooms are bliss. Inspirational.

Rooms	6 suites for 2: €135–€250.
Meals	Restaurants 4km.
Closed	Never.

Fabio Firli
Follonico,
Torrita di Siena,
53049 Monte Follonico
Tel   +39 0577 669773
Email   fabio@follonico.com
Web   www.follonico.com

San Gallo Agriturismo

On Fridays they invite you to lunch with their friends – a generous gesture typical of a this family. The setting is bucolic, made up of vineyards, olive groves and views that sweep up to San Biagio and lovely Montepulciano – two kilometres away. This is a simple Tuscan farmhouse whose ground floor housed the animals and whose living quarters, dominated by big country fireplaces, were upstairs. Today the house sits in spacious gardens with mature trees for shade and benches for views. As for the apartments, these are all in the house, those on the upper floor air conditioned for hot nights; thick walls keep lower floors cool in summer. Kitchenettes, all bar one, have hobs not ovens; fabrics are plain and traditional; tiled floors and cream walls are pristine; bathrooms are in perfect order. The 20-hectare estate includes a small lake populated by ornamental ducks (not for the pot!) and a big pool surrounded by rosemary, roses and pergolas for sunloungers: comfort reigns supreme. Architecture and archaeology abound as does the lush and unsung Vino Nobile; make the most of San Gallo's tastings.

Rooms	5 apartments for 2; 1 apartment for 3: €750–€900 per week.
Meals	Restaurants in Montepulciano, 2km.
Closed	Never.

Olimpia Roberti
San Gallo Agriturismo, Vie delle
Colombelle 7, 53045 Montepulciano

Tel	+39 0578 758330
Mobile	+39 339 7769444
Email	info@agriturismosangallo.com
Web	www.agriturismosangallo.com

Montorio

As you pootle up the drive, you will be inspired by the Temple of San Biagio. A Renaissance masterpiece designed by Antonio Sangallo the Elder, it is an unforgettable backdrop to Montorio. The house stands on top of its own little hill, 600m above sea level, overlooking a vast green swathe of Tuscany. Made of warm stone walls and roofs on different levels, it was once a *casa colonica*. It is now divided into five attractive apartments, each named after a celebrated Italian artist or poet, each with a well-equipped kitchen and an open fire. White walls, beams and terracotta floors set a tone of rural simplicity; antiques, paintings and wrought-iron lights crafted by Florentines add a touch of style; leather chesterfields and big beds guarantee comfort. The terraced gardens – full of ancient cypress trees, pots of flowers and alluring places to sit – drop gently down to olive groves and vineyards. Stefania's other villa, Poggiano, is five minutes away and historic Montepulciano, full of shops and eating places, is close enough to walk.

Rooms	3 apartments for 2; 2 apartments for 4: €600-€1,650 per week.
Meals	Self-catering.
Closed	December/January.

Stefania Savini
Montorio,
Strada per Pienza 2,
53045 Montepulciano

Tel	+39 0578 717442
Email	info@montorio.com
Web	www.montorio.com

Entry 245   Map 12

Fattoria San Martino

The track to San Martino is surrounded by wild roses, lavender and birds. Dutch Karin, warm and full of life, lives with her family in harmony with nature and gives you fine vegetarian dinners at a long table beneath an antique chandelier; or under the pergola in summer. This soft ochre-hued fattoria, restored with earth-tone pigments and immersed in garden, feels as though it is part of the landscape. Inside is as special. Expect limewash, wood, beeswax and stone; feast on the simplicity, indulge the senses. The feel is rustic, creative, eclectic, inventive. Bedrooms — with views that sweep in every direction — have electric-current disjoiners that come into play as soon as the last light is turned off, and beds positioned according to electromagnetic fields: your sleep will be deep. Wake to scrumptious spreads of yogurt, honey, cake, muesli, marmalade and bread — home-grown, homemade and biodynamic. Look forward to a day of Tuscan treats, from visits to hilltop towns, churches and monasteries to wine tastings of Vino Nobile di Montepulciano. It's as close to heaven as heaven gets. *Whole house available.*

Rooms	1 double: €140.
	3 suites for 2-4: €180.
	Reduced rates for weekly stays.
Meals	Dinner €35. Lunch & dinner by arrangement. Restaurant 1.5km.
Closed	Rarely.

Antonio Giorgini
Fattoria San Martino,
Via Martiena 3,
53045 Montepulciano

Tel   +39 0578 717463
Email   sanmartino@montepulciano.com
Web   www.fattoriasanmartino.it

Casa Fabbrini

There's fine food at this superb place; it probably hosted pilgrims on the Via Francigena. Paola is up at dawn making strudel or crostata for breakfast – a lavish affair with fresh ricotta, homemade yogurt, jams and jellies. Dinners are wonderfully convivial; watch or help with the preparation of the day's Tuscan menu – pastas a speciality – using their own wine, fruit and veg. Then feast together at the rustic tables that migrate out under the loggia when the weather's good (it's fine to ask for a separate table). In serious Siena olive-growing territory, the Casa itself is surrounded by mature oaks and lavender and you'll be met by three generations of dachshunds! The ground floor of the main house gets a 'wow-plus': a huge space divided by arches and a metal hanging fireplace opens into fabulous cooking, eating and living areas. There are soft cashmere throws and colourful cushions, and a dozen pots of orchids catch the light. Bedrooms and bathrooms are smallish, coloured and striped, with white piqué bedspreads, wrought-iron beds and soft white towels. And there's a 20-metre saltwater swimming pool. *Small pets welcome.*

Rooms	8 doubles: €220–€300. Singles €77–€105. Extra bed available in some rooms.
Meals	Dinner with wine included.
Closed	Never.

Booking Enquiries
Casa Fabbrini,
Podere Ceppetto,
53040 San Casciano dei Bagni

Tel	+39 0578 56130
Email	info@casafabbrini.it
Web	www.casafabbrini.it

Poderi Firenze

Throw open your shutters to a rich panorama – up here, on top of the world. Ascend 20 hectares of vineyards… until you reach the farmhouse dominating its hill, the valley sweeping below. Flavia, a designer, welcomes you in, then it's up the sober 18th-century staircase to bedrooms on the second floor, and an minimalist, rustic-Tuscan perfection. Walls are exposed stone, rafters are high, floors are beautiful worn terracotta, shower stalls are ultra modern, and the suite has its extra beds on the mezzanine. Gianluigi looks after the vineyards – taste the wines – while the agriturismo is Flavia's new venture; both live just down the hill. Buffet breakfasts are laid out in a serene room with darkwood tables, a stone resin floor and a wonderful view-filled window. Tuck into fresh orange juice, eggs with bacon and homemade cakes before you set off for the wild hilly landscapes of the Maremma Grossetana or the Saturnia hot springs. Two very old olive trees guard the entrance to the west, a large flagged terrace overlooks the pool to the east and the views are enchanting from wherever you stand. *Minimum stay two nights.*

Rooms	2 doubles; 1 twin: €80–€90. 2 suites for 3: €130–€170.
Meals	Lunch/dinner occasionally available, €15. Restaurants 8km.
Closed	October–March.

Flavia Tagliabue
Poderi Firenze, Loc. l'Abbandonato,
58031 Stribugliano Arcidosso
Tel   +39 0564 967271
Mobile   +39 335 6888609
Email   info@poderifirenze.it
Web   www.poderifirenze.it

Pian del Colombaio

A well-hidden treasure in the Tuscan countryside that sociable folk will be delighted to discover. A stone-built terrace of apartments looks across the river Orcia to Monte Amiata, surrounded by olive groves – a deeply rural scene. These once dilapidated farmhouse buildings have been rescued and revived with Italian vitality, so you can gather together and relax on the terrace or by the pool, and then retreat to the privacy of your apartment. All three are spacious and simply dressed: wooden beams, white walls, elegant fabrics. Two have vaulted ceilings, all have contemporary bathrooms and kitchens. The owners visited on a whim seven years ago and fell in love with the tranquillity – now they delight in sharing it all, and offer courses to guests. Yoga groups can spread out on the veranda, there are courses for budding photographers, and wine tasting trips too; massage, aromatherapy and art courses are in the offing. There's something for everyone here, all delivered with warmth and humour from two generations of the charming McCrackens. *Pets welcome, but not in the bedrooms.*

Rooms	1 apartment for 2 ; 1 apartment for 4; 1 apartment for 5: €125; €650–€1,200 per week.
Meals	Restaurants 5km.
Closed	Rarely.

Alexander McCracken
Pian del Colombaio,
Montenero d'Orcia 36, 58033 Grosetto

Tel	+39 0564 954151
Mobile	+39 388 9082826
Email	info@piandelcolombaio.com
Web	www.piandelcolombaio.com

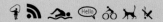

Pieve di Caminino Historic Resort

A fallen column lying deep in the grass, woods, a quiet lake... so peaceful it's hard to believe what a history this settlement has had since it was first recorded in 1075. It is set in a huge natural amphitheatre, ringed by hills and medieval fortresses, and has its own magic spring. Once you've driven through the big rusty gates and down the tree-lined drive, you'll be greeted by your hosts in an 11th-century church – part of their private quarters. It's the most lovely, airy space, with battered columns, soaring arches and elegant furniture – a subtle study in cream, gold and brown. The suites (one a romantic cottage) and the apartments are beautiful too. Each has its own terrace or balcony and is simply furnished with family antiques and fine old paintings. Enchanting windows look over the grounds, the massive walls are rough stone or plaster, the ceilings beamed or vaulted. The 500-hectare estate has been in Piero's family since 1650 and produces its own olive oil and wine. The beautiful panoramic pool has distant views to the isle of Elba. *Minimum stay three nights in high season.*

Rooms	5 suites for 2-3: €110-€170; €600-€900 per week. 2 apartments for 4-5: €180-€250; €900-€1,300 per week.
Meals	Breakfast €10. Restaurant 5km.
Closed	Never.

Piero Marrucchi & Daniela Locatelli
Pieve di Caminino Historic Resort,
S.P 89 snc,
58036 Caminino

Tel   +39 0564 569736
Email   caminino@caminino.com
Web   www.caminino.com

Quercia Rossa

The farmhouse sits on an estate of oak and cypress-scudded fields of wheat; olive groves and vineyards sweep down to the Tyrrhenian Sea. Loll on poolside loungers, soak up the peace. It's wonderfully laid-back, yet classy and romantic at the same time. As for the interiors, they are quirky and design-mag cool. A huge communal Maremma table beneath antique oil-lamps in a stunningly elegant dining room forms the focus of meals enriched by stylish young Alessandro; the chef bakes fresh cakes for breakfast each day. Fabulous furniture from Victorian voyager Augusta Belloc (daughter of Hilaire) – bought blind as a 'job lot' – catches the eye throughout: big gold mirrors and pretty gilded sconces; cherrywood pieces, intricate swans carved into their legs; a huge mahogany four-poster; an ornate bathroom mirror above an ancient marble basin; and, in the red and white-tiled sitting room, beautiful antique armchairs in deep rich blue and gold. Try to peel yourself away: medieval towns, beaches and the thermal baths at Saturnia are close. A special, unusual and remote place – made magical by Alessandro.

Rooms	6 doubles: €81-€143.
Meals	Dinner with wine, €25-€35. Restaurant 5km.
Closed	Rarely.

Alessandro Bonanni
Quercia Rossa,
Montemerano, Santarello 89,
58014 Manciano
Tel +39 0564 629529
Email info@querciarossa.net
Web www.querciarossa.net

Locanda Rossa

Through the gates, down the straight white road, to a super-stylish retreat, an oasis in the middle of the Maremma, with long green views to far-off hills. Locanda Rossa, with its indoor and outdoor spaces, its soothing suites, its wine bar, restaurant, beautiful pool and intimate spa, runs on well-oiled wheels – all thanks to the manager, Barbara, with boundless energy and a smile for all. Welcome to a terracotta-red complex of Tuscan buildings (some old, most new), elegant, harmonious and impeccable in every way. Not just a sophisticated, grown-up place, it is, cleverly and unobtrusively, family-friendly to a fault; away from the main complex – yet not too far – is an area devoted to children. And when they've tired of the football pitch, the Miss Kitty playhouse, the wonderful games and the infant pool, you can whisk them off to beaches and a boat from Argentario to the isles of Giglio and Giannutri, or a tour of the glittering mosaics of Niki de Saint Phalle. Return to modern bedrooms in tasteful hues – greys, whites, creams, browns – each with its own identity, many with private terraces. *Minimum stay two nights, three nights in high season.*

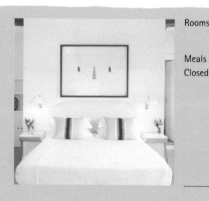

Rooms	10 doubles: €120–€325. 1 suite for 2 (with kitchenette); 2 suites for 2: €160–€425.
Meals	Restaurant on site.
Closed	3 November to Easter.

Barbara Valleggi
Locanda Rossa,
Strada Capalbio Pescia Fiorentina 11b,
58011 Capalbio

Tel	+39 0564 890462
Email	info@locandarossa.com
Web	www.locandarossa.com

Locanda Rossa

Through the gates to a super-stylish retreat, an oasis in the middle of the Maremma, with lovely views to distant hills. Locanda Rossa, with its indoor and outdoor spaces, its B&B rooms and its independent apartments, its wine bar, restaurant, spa and pool, runs on friendly and well-oiled wheels. It's a terracotta-red complex of Tuscan buildings (some old, most new), harmonious, elegant and impeccable in every way, and, with a discreet play area devoted to children, is manna from heaven for families. If you wish to self-cater, there are four swish apartments, each on three floors, each with a big fenced garden — but if you come with a crowd, take the villa for ten, a hop away in the hills. Renovated in ultra-slick Italian style it comes with its own pool, a romantic view of medieval Capalbio, a soothing décor and a housekeeper/chef who can cook as much or as little as you like. It's wonderfully swish! Catch a boat from Argentario to the isles of Giglio and Giannutri, bask on stylish beaches, visit the glittering mosaics of Niki de Saint Phalle. Unwind…

Rooms	4 apartments for 6 (2 doubles, 1 twin): €1,700–€3,400. 1 house for 10 (2 doubles, 3 twins): €5,500–€9,500. All prices per week.
Meals	Restaurant on site.
Closed	3 November to 11 April.

Barbara Valleggi
Locanda Rossa,
Strada Capalbio Pescia Fiorentina 11b,
58011 Capalbio

Tel	+39 0564 890462
Email	info@locandarossa.com
Web	www.locandarossa.com

Il Pardini's Hermitage

The quickest way to arrive is by water taxi; the €25 trip (for one or two) takes 20 minutes. And if the seas are too choppy, you set off by foot, a one-hour hike uphill. (There are plenty of little areas to sit and catch your breath along the way!) Isola del Giglio is a glory of flora and fauna – peregrine falcons, kestrels, buzzards, wild flowers – and the views to the peninsula are spectacular. The 50-year-old villa of the charming Pardinis, embraced by eucalyptus and pine, offers a near-vertical layout and utter seclusion. Bedrooms – some in the house, some in wooden huts – are small, simple, spotless and endowed with excellent air con; all but the single rooms have a sea view. The delightful gardens are full of cacti and flowers, there's a platform for diving, and the azure waters are a snorkeller's dream. Paint, pot, sail, meet the animals (pigs, goats, donkeys, hens), book in for a massage, enjoy the seawater jacuzzi, walk to Giglio Castello, or dream. Delicious, sociable meals are taken at set times: simple breakfasts and salads from the garden, their own meat, cheese and ricotta… dinner is a tad more formal. A rare place. *Minimum stay three nights.*

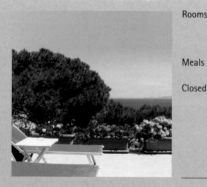

Rooms	10 doubles: €240-€380.
	1 suite for 2: €280-€420.
	2 singles: €120-€190.
	All prices full-board.
Meals	Half-board or full-board only.
	Wine from €15 (included in low season).
Closed	October-March.

Federigo & Barbara Pardini
Il Pardini's Hermitage,
Loc. Cala degli Alberi,
58012 Isola del Giglio

Tel	+39 0564 809034
Email	info@hermit.it
Web	www.hermit.it

Villa Bengodi

A family house where you feel you've stepped back to a gentle age of old-fashioned charm and peace. Great-aunt Zia Ernesta lived in the room with the angel frescoes for most of her life. Catarina now oversees the running of the villa. Bedrooms are generous, light and spotless and house a hotchpotch of furniture from past decades; some have ceilings painted in 1940, another a terrace; all have original floor tiles in varying patterns. Modern bathrooms are excellent, views are to the garden or the sea. The villa and its grounds are the owners' pride and joy. While away the days in the enchanting palm-fringed garden or on the terrace where you might see Corsica on a clear day. Beaches and mile upon mile of surf are a hop away – or you could walk the full mile to Talamone, where a family friend takes you out on his boat to fish and swim; then eat what you've caught. The apartments, separate from the villa, have their own gardens. Dine al fresco in summer; in winter under a chandelier made of antlers and pine cones. An unusual, warmly personal house in a magical setting. *Minimum stay three nights.*

Rooms	6 doubles: €110–€170. 3 apartments for 2-4: €800–€1,500 per week.
Meals	Dinner with wine, €30, by arrangement. Restaurant 1km.
Closed	Rarely.

Famiglia Orlandi
Villa Bengodi,
Via Bengodi 2, Loc. Bengodi,
58010 Fonteblanda

Mobile	+39 335 420334
Email	info@villabengodi.it
Web	www.villabengodi.it

Boccadalma

Follow the umbrella pines from the Maremma coast to meet friendly hosts Ellen and Luciano. Soak up the essence of their 200-year-old farmhouse at breakfast in the stables, alongside the old wooden drinking troughs. Homemade cakes, jams, honey from the local beekeeper and good Italian coffee set you up for a day's Etruscan sightseeing and beach swimming – or decadent idling around the grassy open terrace, amid acres of olive groves and fig and plum orchards. Views are of the Alma valley, the breezy sea and fields where wild boar roam. This renovated home on a hillock has solar power and upscale appliances, tricks like skylights and glass bricks let light flood in, and 18th-century prints and Navajo rugs top wrought-iron beds in rooms named after the Tuscan archipelago: Capraia, Elba, Giglio. Local organic smellies rest on modern square sinks in huge bathrooms and your private terrace has furniture for sun and shade; listen to the crickets, donkeys, wind in the pines. A four-star campsite nearby has social cafés, shops and bike hire. Best of all, the exquisite sands of Cala Violina cove are a short stroll. *Minimum stay two nights.*

Rooms	1 double; 1 double; 1 twin/double; 1 twin/double (with separate bath): €95-€145. Singles €75-€90. Whole house available for large groups on self-catering basis, €2,500-€2,800 per week. Sofabeds available in some rooms.
Meals	Campsite café 1.5km.
Closed	Rarely.

Ellen Sutherland & Luciano Burgalassi
Boccadalma,
Podere Binacco 23, 58020 Scarlino

Mobile	+39 328 8396352 / +39 347 7971593
Email	info@boccadalma.com
Web	www.boccadalma.com

Relais Vedetta

Anna greets you with a glass of prosecco and it just gets better from there. Her makeover has transformed the rustic red farmhouse into a place of elegance and glamour: chestnut floors, cacti in an old manger, an honesty bar in an antique dresser. Bedrooms are styled after eccentric family members. Flirtatious 'Libertine' has sensuous his-and-hers chairs, a round mosaic bath, deep red silk curtains – one can only imagine! Linger in the loggia over imaginative dinners, mostly organic and home-grown. Folding glazed windows mean that in winter you still feel like you're outdoors. And that outdoors is seriously beautiful, with views sweeping down to Follonica then out to the Tyrrhenian Sea. You can enjoy the view from a shapely saltwater pool or from vast, sloping gardens dotted with eucalyptus and ilex trees. Hike or horse-ride the wooded trails of Maremma or pop down to the coves of Cala Violina and Cala Civette; the ferry at Piombino will take you to Elba for the day. Return, up the bumpy winding track, to a place of peace where you can sit out under a parasol, birdsong and the breeze. *Children under six free.*

Rooms	1 double: €130-€200.
	7 suites for 2 (1 in annexe): €220-€420.
	Whole villa available to rent
	1 Nov-30 April, €1,000 per night.
	Extra beds available.
Meals	Dinner €35-€40.
Closed	15 November to 15 February.

Anna Barberini
Relais Vedetta,
Poggio la Forcola 12,
58020 Scarlino
Tel   +39 0566 37023
Email   info@relaisvedetta.eu
Web   www.relaisvedetta.eu

Entry 257 Map 11

I Monti Agriturismo

Between Siena and the sea, on a high grassy knoll with stupendous views, this handsome old farm is approached up a white road twisting steeply through chestnut woods. Its position is ideal for capturing solar energy and environmentalists Lucia and Emilio set out to make it zero-impact. Water is either spring or rain and the garden produces masses of organic vegetables – guests can take their pick. Recycling is high on the agenda so reclaimed beams, stone and other local materials were used in the renovation, and to build the large swimming pool. Three of the apartments are on the ground floor of the house ('Val di Merse' is the biggest with the best kitchen). Two are on the first floor of the old hay barn and can be easily joined. The style is simple, traditional and unfussy with white walls, modern floor tiles, some bare stone and open fires. Kind Lucia's welcome basket is a treat; ask about oil and wine and helping with the haymaking or chestnut harvest. Great for children who can run around safely, for walkers and geologists fascinated by the Colline Metallifere area; its mines have been worked since Etruscan times. *Short stays available.*

Rooms	4 apartments for 2; 1 apartment for 4: €450–€750 per week.
	1 suite for 2: €80–€120 per night.
Meals	Restaurants 4km.
Closed	Never.

Lucia Minocci
I Monti Agriturismo,
Località i Monti,
58026 Montieri
Mobile   +39 335 5487777
Email   info@imontiagriturismo.com
Web   www.imontiagriturismo.com

Poggio ai Santi

Journalist and TV producer Dominique knows what people yearn for when they're away. At Poggio ai Santi, he and his wife are channelling all their imagination and flair into providing it. Here are three buildings – the main house 19th-century, the other two modern – set among roses and with spellbinding sea views. Uneven paths wind through fabulously relaxing gardens planted with a hundred exotic trees; there's even a painting hut – help yourself to art supplies and have a go at capturing the views. You breakfast on the magnificent terrace in summer with its gorgeous views: much is home-grown in a buffet of sweet and savouries including home-baked bread. Bedrooms are cool, Asian-chic and luxurious, bathrooms are astonishingly lush and the biggish suites have magnificent terraces and ingenious wardrobes opening to mini-kitchens. Enter the 'Royal Mare' and you find a vast free-standing bath on the corner of your terrace… drink a toast to your good fortune as you soak, gazing across the sea to the isle of Elba. *Minimum stay two nights May-September.*

Rooms	12 suites for 2: €149-€428.
Meals	Dinner €35-€40. Wine €10-€100.
Closed	Ask for winter closing dates.

Francesca Vierucci
Poggio ai Santi,
Via San Bartolo 100,
57027 San Vincenzo

Tel	+39 0565 798032
Email	poggioaisanti@toscana.com
Web	www.poggioaisanti.com

Entry 259 Map 11

La Casetta

Up a little road dotted with houses is a handsome *colonica* with a view of the sea. Entertaining, sprightly Adriana welcomes you in perfect English to a delightful terrace with a big table, wicker chairs and dreamy wisteria. This is where you breakfast in summer, on local breads and homemade cakes, delicious coffee and fruity teas. Inside are vaulted ceilings, chunky beams and rooms awash with light and artistic colour: beiges, whites, creams; chartreuse cushions; lavender-painted doors. In the hall: a big table for leaflets and books; up the stairs: a guest sitting room with bedrooms off it. Be charmed by comfy sofas, family antiques, books on low shelves, rugs on painted wooden floors, and the occasional fine watercolour or oil. Bathrooms are filled with light and stocked with towels; fresh bedrooms have blue and white spreads and lovely views (two have a view of the sea). There are several resorts within an easy drive, fish restaurants in little Bolgheri and history in medieval Castagneto Carducci. Return to super grounds with huge ancient olives, delectable peaches and a tucked-away pool.

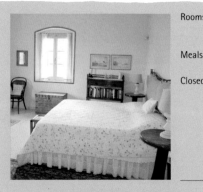

Rooms	1 double; 1 twin/double with separate bath; 1 single: €90–€130. Discounts for stays of 7 or 15 days.
Meals	Dinner €24. Wine €10. Restaurant 4km.
Closed	Rarely.

Adriana Milla
La Casetta,
Loc. Vallone Segalari 175,
Bolgheri, 57022 Castagneto Carducci

Tel   +39 0565 763525
Mobile   +39 339 1286330
Email   milla.adri@alice.it

Podere Le Mezzelune

A treat to find this house in the north Maremma. After a long winding track, two big wooden gates; ring the bell and they swing open to reveal a tree-lined drive. This is a typical Tuscan, late 1800s farmhouse turned into a delightful B&B and you feel as though you are visiting friends. Downstairs, a huge dining table for breakfasts of fresh, home-baked pastries and seasonal fruits, and an open fire for winter. Upstairs are the bedrooms, two looking out to sea, all with their own terrace and a view. Painted white and cream, they have linen curtains, wooden floors, furniture made to the owners' design, candles, fresh fruit and vintage wooden pegs hung with an antique shawl. Bathrooms, too, are perfect. For longer stays there are two little cottages in the garden, comfortable with open fires, dishwashers and beams. You are surrounded by cypresses, vines, flowers, herbs, 2,000 olive trees and seven hectares of woodland. This is a magical place, five minutes from the historic centre, 15 minutes from the sea and blissfully free of newspapers and TV. *Minimum stay three nights in cottages.*

Rooms	4 twin/doubles: €160-€180. 2 cottages for 2-3: €180-€200. Sofabeds available.
Meals	Breakfast €15 for self-caterers, by arrangement. Restaurants 3km.
Closed	15 December to January.

Azienda Agricola Le Mezzelune
Podere Le Mezzelune,
Loc. Mezzelune 126,
57020 Bibbona

Tel   +39 0586 670266
Email   info@poderelemezzelune.it
Web   www.mezzelune.com

Umbria

Sambuco

In the absence of an invisibility cloak, the next best thing: a lovely old Etruscan farmhouse hidden among rolling pasture... yet you can pop into Orvieto for the Christmas Jazz Festival. With no one else in sight, the party starts as soon as you see the kitchen, fully rigged with the latest gear including a 'cucina economica'. Chefs will agree that big wine goblets by the fire look as good as they do on the elegant dining table, situated in the former stables and complete with mangers along one side. For fresh produce, step into the enormous vegetable garden, where Sandro is happy for guests to pluck at will; and look out for old Emilio who discreetly tends the garden. Otherwise the nearest shop is only a kilometre away. Bathrooms are classy, while flame-coloured bedrooms luxuriate in wrought iron, the grandest with its own terrace and outside stair. Bookworms can disappear to the downstairs sitting room with its dramatic bottle-green walls, or to the stripy sofas upstairs; if you seek complete privacy, find the caves behind the orchard and infinity pool when the barbecue on the loggia is in full swing. *Short stays available.*

Rooms	1 house for 10: €2,100–€4,900 per wk.
Meals	Restaurants 4km.
Closed	Never.

Sandro Ligossi
Sambuco,
Torre San Severo, 05018 Orvieto

Tel	+39 0759 306157
Mobile	+39 345 3513087
Email	info@pereto.eu
Web	www.vocabolosambuco.it

Entry 262 Map 12

Locanda Palazzone

An imposing palazzo in the Umbrian countryside, Locanda Palazzone is full of contrasts. Built by a cardinal as a resting place for pilgrims to Rome, it was designed with urban sophistication: buttressed walls, mullioned windows, vaulted hall. Later, it fell from grace and became a country farmhouse – until Lodovico's family rescued it, planting vineyards and restoring the buildings. Despite the rustic setting, the interiors are cool, elegant, chic. The light and airy sitting room, once the Grand Hall, has huge windows overlooking the garden. Bedrooms – split-level suites, mostly – are understatedly luxurious, their modern and antique furnishings set against pale oak floors, cream walls, exposed stone. Red, claret and purple cushions add warmth; white linen sheets, Bulgari bath foams and specialist herb soaps soothe. Meals, both regional and seasonal, are served on rainbow china on the terrace, accompanied by the estate's wines. Your generous hosts are eager to please, the pool is surrounded by delphiniums and roses, and views sweep to vineyards and forests. A remarkable place. *Minimum stay two nights June-September.*

Rooms	5 suites for 2; 2 suites for 4: €172–€410. Extra bed/sofabed €50.
Meals	Breakfast €9; free for children under 9. Dinner, 4 courses, €43, by arrangement.
Closed	10 January to 20 March.

Lodovico Dubini
Locanda Palazzone,
Loc. Rocca Ripesena,
05010 Orvieto

Tel	+39 0763 393614
Email	info@locandapalazzone.com
Web	www.locandapalazzone.com

Locanda Rosati Agriturismo

From the moment you turn off the road – whose proximity is quickly forgotten – the atmosphere is easy. The house has been gently modernised but remains firmly a farmhouse; the summer-cool rooms on the ground floor, with open fires in winter, have been furnished with an eye for comfort rather than a desire to impress, and wild flowers, books and magazines are scattered. Dinner is the thing here; it's rustic, delectable and Giampiero and Paolo are natural hosts, full of stories and enthusiastic advice on what to do and where to go. Tables are laid with simple cloths, glass tumblers and butter-coloured pottery, the recipes have been handed down the Rosati generations, the ingredients are home-grown and the wines come from a cellar carved out of the tufa seven metres below ground. Bedrooms are simple, with new wooden beds, pristine bed linen, spotless showers. Much of the furniture comes from the famous Bottega Michelangeli in Orvieto, whose jigsaw-like carved animal shapes characterise this region. From the gardens you can see the spiky skyline of Orvieto: delightful.

Rooms	4 doubles;
	5 family rooms for 4: €110-€150.
	1 single: €90-€110.
	Half-board option available.
Meals	Dinner with wine, €37.50.
Closed	7 January to February.

Giampiero Rosati
Locanda Rosati Agriturismo,
Loc. Buonviaggio 22,
05018 Orvieto

Tel	+39 0763 217314
Email	info@locandarosati.it
Web	www.locandarosati.it

Tenuta di Canonica

The position is wonderful, on a green ridge with stunning views. The house was a ruin (17th century, with medieval remnants and Roman foundations) when Daniele and Maria bought it in 1998. Much creativity has gone into its resurrection. There's not a corridor in sight – instead, odd steps up and down, hidden doors, vaulted ceilings, enchanting corners. Cool, beautiful reception rooms are decorated in vibrant colours, then given a personal, individual and exotic touch: family portraits, photos, books... there's even a parrot. The bedrooms are vast, intriguingly shaped and opulent, with rugs on pale brick or wooden floors and gorgeous beds and fabrics. The dining room opens onto a covered terrace surrounded by roses and shrubs, a path sweeps down to the pool – oh, the views! And there's walking on the 24-hectare estate. This is a hotel that reflects its owners' personalities. Daniele and Maria are vivid, interesting and well-travelled. While they are away, Christin and Maurizio are on hand, to welcome guests to the rich tapestry of rooms.

Rooms	11 doubles: €180–€260 per night. 2 apartments for 3-4: €250–€300; €1,100–€1,350 per week.
Meals	Dinner €40. Wine €10–€40. Restaurants 6km.
Closed	1 December to 15 March.

Daniele Fano
Tenuta di Canonica,
Vocabolo Casalzetta 75,
06059 Todi

Tel +39 0758 947545
Email tenutadicanonica@tin.it
Web www.tenutadicanonica.com

La Palazzetta del Vescovo Relais

Only the bells from a nearby convent or the hum of the tractor will disturb you. Paola and Stefano love to pamper their guests and there's a 'wellness' room in the cellar. Widely travelled and from the corporate world, they decided in 2000 to hang up their business suits and do something different. They bought this 18th-century hilltop palazzetta – once a summer residence for bishops, utterly abandoned in the 1960s – and restored it to its former glory. An informal elegance prevails. The four sitting rooms are cool, elegant and inviting; the bedrooms, each individual, each lovely, are composed in subtle, muted colours: pale walls, fine rugs, muslin'd four-posters, antique Neapolitan beds. What they have in common is a matchless view over steeply falling vineyards and the Tiber valley. On a clear day you can see as far as Perugia. The newly planted gardens and the pool make the most of the outlook, too – as does the terrace, where you can enjoy an aperitif before Paola's Umbrian cuisine. She, like her house, is a delight – serene, smiling and friendly. *Minimum stay two nights.*

Rooms	9 doubles: €190–€270.
	Singles from €160.
Meals	Light lunch from €15.
	Dinner, 4 courses, €38.
	Wine from €12. Restaurant 4km.
Closed	November–February.

Paola Maria & Stefano Zocchi
La Palazzetta del Vescovo Relais,
Via Clausura 17, Fraz. Spineta,
06054 Fratta Todina

Tel	+39 0758 745183
Email	info@lapalazzettadelvescovo.it
Web	www.lapalazzettadelvescovo.com

Entry 266   Map 12

Casale Campodoro

This restored 18th-century building has been embellished inside with style and a quirky humour: imagine an Indonesian hippo's head over a fireplace and a plastic goose as a lamp. Piero, a gentle, humorous and intelligent man, lives here with warm-hearted Carolina, four cats, some geese, a pony and three daft, friendly and boisterous dogs. In one shower room, a muscular plaster-cast juts out of the wall as a towel rail; elsewhere, scary Scottish grandmother's clothes – lace interwoven with scarab beetles – have been framed. By the pool are plastic yellow Philippe Starck sofa and chairs; on the walls, religious icons. The garden sits on an Umbrian hillside and has little steps leading to hidden corners and a large aviary whose birds escape and return at night. There are lovely views across to an old abbey, and other, more edible delights: warm, fresh, homemade bread and tasty jams for breakfast. Once a week, guests get together for dinner with everyone contributing a national dish. If you like animals and don't mind the odd bit of peeling paint, this is a kind, joyously individual and eccentric place.

Rooms	3 doubles: €70–€80.
	2 apartments for 3; 1 apartment for 5: €80–€110; €500–€700 per week.
Meals	Restaurants 2km.
Closed	Rarely.

Carolina Bonanno
Casale Campodoro, Fraz. Viepri 106,
06056 Massa Martana

Tel	Please enquire by email.
Mobile	+39 333 3875740
Email	info@casalecampodoro.com
Web	www.casalecampodoro.it

La Licina

Just beyond the outskirts of Spoleto you find yourself in winding leafy country lanes. And there is 'La Licina', tucked into a fold of the hills, a mini *borgo* at the end of the track. Friendly open Ludovico and Francesca live in the main house, guests live in the ochre-washed stables a pace away. 'Ginestra', on the ground floor, may be where the horses slept but you wouldn't know it now, though the brick inner arch and the chunky beams remain. This simple, spotless, open-plan space opens to its own grassy garden with a round table, a barbecue and gentle green views. 'Tartufo', which lies above, is similarly comfortable, with slightly more workspace in its kitchen and a step away from its own elevated, furnished patio with pretty views. Lots to love: a pool, pines and hosts who give you figs, plums and pears from their garden, and all the local info you desire. The position is fantastic: you are walking distance from civilised Spoleto, and a three-minute stroll through the olive groves to a pizzeria… life in the slow lane, and you can pat the neighbours' donkeys on the way!

Rooms	1 apartment for 4; 1 apartment for 5: €700–€1,000 per week. Extra bed/sofabed available at no charge.
Meals	Self-catering.
Closed	Rarely.

Ludovico Angelini Rota
La Licina,
Loc. La Licina 9, 06049 Spoleto

Tel	+39 0743 49323
Mobile	+39 349 5834907
Email	info@lalicina.it
Web	www.lalicina.it

Entry 268   Map 12

Le Terre di Poreta – Borgo della Marmotta

No one fuses the past with the present so perfectly as the Italians. This venerable 150-hectare estate, in the family since 1673, lies in a landscape of beauty and tranquillity. Approach through olive groves with valley views, wash up at a *borgo* in the hamlet of Poreta. The square, the stables, the sheepfold, the granary, the mill – all have been exquisitely revived. Two friendly dogs and owner Filippo, tall, languid and charming, live in the villa up on the hill and welcome you on board. The *borgo* exudes exclusivity yet feels unexpectedly relaxed. Imagine exposed stones and rustic rafters, colourwashed walls in muted earth tones, elegant rugs on terracotta floors, four-posters draped in soft cotton, upholstered bedheads, ancient doors, a sunken bath tub like a Turkish hamman: these are spaces to linger in. With a dining room and a multi-sofa'd *salotto*, a sauna, a kitchen for cookery courses and a trio of pools, it's a resort of the classiest kind. They're into Slow Food here and breakfasts are plentiful, served under the pergola in summer. Good value, too.

Rooms	7 doubles; 4 twin/doubles: €120–€180. 1 apartment for 4; 6 apartments for 2-4: €180–€260; €820–€1,140 per week.
Meals	Breakfast €10 for self-caterers. Dinner €30, lunch €18 (on request). Restaurant 2km.
Closed	Easter & Christmas.

Filippo Montani Fargna
Le Terre di Poreta –
Borgo della Marmotta,
Poreta 74, 06049 Spoleto
Tel   +39 0743 274137
Email   info@leterrediporeta.it
Web   www.leterrediporeta.it

Le Terre di Poreta – Villa della Genga

Up near Pope Leone XII's ex-hunting lodge (the Fargna family home) are five solid estate buildings – homes of rustic sophistication and rare beauty. First 'La Colombaia', its brick staircase leading to a bedroom in the tower, a wonder of ancient beams and arches, doves' perches and niches. Then 'Il Grottone', whose cave-like living room wall stands in stark contrast to its fabulous ultra-chic décor. From 'Gli Ziri' a glass door faces the sunsets; the roof garden of 'Casa Nello' pulls the outside in. And everywhere: sumptuous fabrics, hand-made tiles, beautiful antiques, elegant lighting, and glorious kitchens that combine Italian modernity with rustic ceramics: ancient and modern go hand in hand. The estate produces organic beans, chickpeas, lentils and olive oil – note the delicious hand-made soaps – and the swimming pool is chemical-free. What to do? Learn to prune olives, help in the harvest, go truffle hunting, enjoy the family's restaurant nearby. Lovely hilltop Spoleto has its summer music festival and Assisi its Basilica di San Francesco; linger a while after the crowds have gone home.

Rooms	Gli Ziri for 4; Il Grottone for 4; Casa Nello for 4; La Colombaia for 6; Mattutuccio for 10: €750–€1,950 per week.
Meals	Self-catering.
Closed	Easter & Christmas.

Filippo Montani Fargna
Le Terre di Poreta – Villa della Genga,
Poreta 74, 06049 Spoleto

Tel	+39 0743 274137
Email	info@leterrediporeta.it
Web	www.leterrediporeta.it

Pianciano

The old *borgo* buildings (some 16th century) are now self-contained apartments; come for deep delicious comfort on a working, self-sufficient estate. Wander down the terraced orchards to a huge pick-your-own vegetable garden overlooking a steam bath and sleek pool – and tables and chairs under a vine canopy, an idyllic setting for lunch. Beyond are olive groves, vineyards and pastures – space galore to explore. Lavender-scented bedrooms are touched with elegant details: jade-coloured vases arranged just so, divine hand-detailed linen, old doors mounted as headboards, antique frames holding romantic paintings. Neutral coloured throws complement beamed ceilings, terracotta floors and sturdy wooden pieces, bookshelves hold handsome tomes, framed copies of old letters and antique architectural plans dot walls. High-ceilinged sitting rooms and a cavernous dining room hewn from the hillside provide heart-warming living space; knock-out views across the valley mean you'll keep the curtains open. Visit the wonderful little villages of the Valnerina, fall in love with this magical place.

Rooms	2 apartments for 6; 1 apartment for 8: €800-€2,000 per week.
Meals	Self-catering.
Closed	Never.

Francesco Bachetoni
Pianciano,
Loc. Silvignano,
06049 Spoleto
Mobile   +39 339 3091290
Email   pianciano@pianciano.it
Web   www.pianciano.it

Casa del Cinguettio

A winding road leads up into the hills and the rewards on arrival are great. Tucked out of sight from the village street, beneath a medieval castle, this beautifully restored barn appears to hang on to the side of the hill – and the views, from pool and terrace over the Spoleto valley, are stupendous. A night swim almost leaves you feeling suspended in space! As for the recently refurbished, split-level interiors, they combine traditional, solid, cave-like Umbrian architecture with funky modern touches. Slabs of wood from the wall make a glass-bannistered staircase, there are cream marble floors, a glass-topped dining table, a groovy, steep-stepped mezzanine area where children can sleep, state of the art showers; the contrasts and colours are gorgeous. Ethnic spreads, an oriental rug and a corner fireplace add warmth to the sitting room on cool evenings in, while the fully kitted kitchen leads onto a barbecue terrace for lazy lunches under the olives trees. Herbs scent the air. The hills are laced with walking and riding paths, the area is rich with history, Assisi is a short drive.

Rooms	1 house for 6-8: £950-£2,200 per week.
Meals	Self-catering.
Closed	Rarely.

	Berenice Anderson
	Casa del Cinguettio,
	06042 Campello Alto
Tel	+44 (0)1865 553244
Mobile	+44 (0)7713 638627
Email	berenice@campello.me.uk
Web	www.casadelcinguettio.com

I Mandorli Agriturismo

I Mandorli is aptly named: there's at least one almond tree outside each apartment. The blossom in February is stunning and, in summer, masses of greenery shades the *casa padronale*. Once the centre of a 200-hectare estate, the shepherd's house and the olive mill in particular are fascinating reminders of days gone by. Mama Wanda is passionate about the whole lovely rambling place and will show you around, embellishing everything you see with stories about its history. Widowed, she manages the remaining 47 hectares, apartments and rooms, and cooks, aided by three charming daughters: home-grown produce and excellent gnocchi every Thursday. Bedrooms are sweet, simple affairs with new wrought-iron beds and pale patchwork quilts; small bathrooms are spotless. Children will love the wooden slide and seesaw, the old pathways and steps on this shallow hillside and the new pool – wonderful to return to after cultural outings to Assisi and Spoleto. This is olive oil country so make sure you go home with a few bottles of the best.

Rooms	1 twin/double; 2 triples: €45-€90; €300-€650 per week.
	1 apartment for 2; 2 apartments for 4: €70-€150; €400-€700 per week.
Meals	Restaurants 500m.
Closed	Rarely.

Famiglia di Zappelli Cardarelli
I Mandorli Agriturismo, Loc. Fondaccio 6,
06039 Bovara di Trevi

Tel	+39 0742 78669
Mobile	+39 333 498309
Email	info@agriturismoimandorli.com
Web	www.agriturismoimandorli.com

Brigolante Guest Apartments

In the foothills of St Francis' beloved Mount Subasio the 16th-century stone farmhouse has been thoughtfully restored by Stefano and Rebecca. She is American and came to Italy to study, he is an architectural land surveyor – here was the perfect project. The apartments feel very private but you can always chat over an aperitif with the other guests in the garden. Rooms are light, airy and stylishly simple, combining grandmother's furniture with Rebecca's kind touches: a rustic basket of delicacies from the farm (wine, eggs, cheese, honey, olive oil, homemade jam), handmade soap and sprigs of lavender by the bath. Pretty lace curtains flutter at the window, kitchens are well-equipped, and laundry facilities are available. This is a farm with animals, so ham, salami and sausages are produced as well as wine. Feel free to pluck whatever you like from the vegetable garden – red peppers, fat tomatoes, huge lettuces. Warm, lively, outgoing and with two young children of their own, your hosts set the tone: a charming place, and bliss for families and walkers.

Rooms	3 apartments for 2: €400–€600 per wk.
Meals	Self-catering.
Closed	Rarely.

Rebecca Winke Bagnoli
Brigolante Guest Apartments,
Via Costa di Trex 31,
06081 Assisi
Tel   +39 0758 02250
Email   info@brigolante.com
Web   www.brigolante.com

Romantik Hotel Le Silve & Agriturismo

The setting, deep in the heart of the Umbrian hills, takes your breath away. It's as beautiful and as peaceful as Shangri-La – so remote you'd do well to fill up with petrol before leaving Spello or Assisi. The medieval buildings have been beautifully restored and the whole place breathes an air of tranquillity and exclusivity. Superb, generous-sized bedrooms have stone walls, exquisite terracotta floors, beautiful furniture, old mirrors and (a rarity, this!) proper reading lights. Bathrooms are similarly rustic with terracotta floors and delicious pampering extras. The apartments are spread across three converted farm buildings. We loved the restaurant, a brisk walk: intimate and inviting indoors and out. The produce is mostly organic, the bread is homemade, the cheeses, hams and salami are delectable. There's tennis and table tennis, an enormous new pool on the edge of the hill, a hydromassage and a sauna, and hectares of hills and woods in which to walk or ride: pick an estate horse. A delightful, friendly place, and popular – be sure to book well in advance. *Minimum stay two nights in apartments.*

Rooms	20 doubles: €130-€300. Dinner, B&B €210-€300 for 2. 13 apartments for 2-4: €100; €600 per week.
Meals	Breakfast €10 for self-caterers. Dinner €40. Wine from €10. Restaurants 12km.
Closed	Hotel closed from November to March. Agriturismo open all year.

Marco Sirignani
Romantik Hotel Le Silve & Agriturismo,
Loc. Armenzano,
06081 Assisi

Tel	+39 0758 019000
Email	info@lesilve.it
Web	www.lesilve.it

Casa Rosa

Once you've wrenched your gaze from pool-side panoramas over the forested flanks of Mount Subasio National Park, and had your senses tickled by the sweet orchestra of lavender, Russian sage and Mediterranean herbs that assail you – strategically planted to waft their perfumes into the apartments – let wonderful host Jennifer welcome you in. An expat artist whose mural and decorative work embellishes these homely, colourful, bohemian interiors, she will relate Elysian tales of living off the land and raising a family on the 17-acre farm estate. Antique kettles and pots, bunches of dried herbs suspended from ceilings, well-stocked wine racks and flora 'n' fauna painted surrounds to mirrors and French windows, all lend themselves to a relaxed vibe, while an organic vegetable garden, and a yurt tucked away in the woods, add to the communal, convivial idyll. There's WiFi if you need it but it won't distract you from the views; lap them up from your balconied terrace. Better still, take the book of local walks provided, add a picnic, and head for the wooded hills.

Rooms	2 apartments for 2; 1 apartment for 4; 1 apartment for 5: €380–€1,090 per week.
Meals	Self-catering.
Closed	Rarely.

Jennifer Holmes
Casa Rosa,
Santa Maria Lignano,
06081 Assisi

Tel	+39 0758 02322
Email	jennifer@casa-rosa.it
Web	www.casa-rosa.it

Agriturismo Alla Madonna del Piatto

You'll be jolly glad you're in a hired car! A bumpy track leads through woods to a simple, centuries-old farmhouse in a hidden corner of Umbria. The position is stupendous. Views stretch over olive groves and forested hills to Assisi and its basilica, yet you are an easy distance from Perugia, Assisi, Spoleto. The farmhouse was abandoned for decades until these Italian-Dutch owners fell in love with the view, then restored the building with sympathy and replanted the olive groves, for oil which is organic and delicious. Bedrooms are airy, uncluttered, their country antiques mixed with Mediterranean delights picked up on Letizia's travels; one room has a loo with a view. Lovely Letizia joins you for breakfast (her own breads and jams) in a fresh, modern space of white and rose walls, with sofa and open fire. She and husband Ruurd are squeaky green, approachable and share their home gladly, letting you make your own salad, cheese and wine dinner on the terrace if you can't tear yourself away. There are walks, medieval hill towns and all of Umbria to explore. *Minimum stay two nights in high season, three nights over bank holidays.*

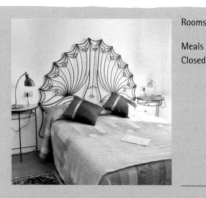

Rooms	5 twin/doubles;
	1 family room for 3: €90–€95.
Meals	Restaurant 1km.
Closed	Beginning of November to end of March.

Letizia Mattiacci
Via Petrata 37, Pieve San Nicolò, 06081 Assisi

Tel	+39 0758 199050
Mobile	+39 328 7025297
Email	letizia.mattiacci@gmail.com
Web	www.incampagna.com

Entry 277   Map 12

Casale Santa Maria Nuova

All you hear is cicada hum on this vast old hunting estate – 600 hectares of cultivated fields, olive groves and tranquillity, with views to Umbria to one side, Tuscany to the other. Wash up in front of a big rosy-brick house and converted tobacco-drying tower, and a warm, effusive welcome from multi-lingual Milena. There are four apartments here, three on the ground floor opening to the garden, the fourth (sleeping ten) spread across the top floor and reached via an outside stair. Thanks to Milena, interiors are spic, span, contemporary and classy, furnished in creamy shades with shots of colour. There are ceiling fans and cool floors, thick bathrobes and white kitchenettes, the occasional wall hanging or beautiful cow hide rug. It's a civilised spot for sybarites, and heaven for nature lovers, too: hedgehogs, hares, badgers, roe deer, all drop by. The gardens are well-tended, two trees are slung with hammocks, there's a long communal table under the pergola, delicious rattan sofas, white parasols, and a large pool. Arezzo, Montepulciano and Lake Trasimeno lie over the hill. *Payments accepted via Paypal.*

Rooms	2 apartments for 2; 1 apartment for 4; 1 apartment for 10: €590–€2,530 per week. Singles €15. Extra bed/sofabed available, €15.
Meals	Restaurants 3km.
Closed	Rarely.

Milena Bono Parodi
Località Val del Sasso, 18,
06061 Castiglione del Lago

Tel	+39 0759 527360
Mobile	+39 388 0493940
Email	info@casalesantamarianuova.com
Web	www.casalesantamarianuova.com

Mazzarelli 2

On the edge of a truly tiny village is a century-old house in one beautiful untamed acre. With loungers in the shade of a willow and a small slender pool, it is one of the most charming we have seen. Across the lawn: olive trees, vegetables, hens and a few rows of vines. Annie and her husband moved from Scotland to create a characterful Italian home; they're there when you need them, disappear when you don't and you couldn't hope to meet a nicer pair. Downstairs, with its own entrance and orchard garden, is a super apartment for two, an eclectic mix of old and new. You have an elegant blue and white living room, a romantic white bed, a library of books and DVDs, and Annie's paintings on exposed stone walls. There's a super bathroom with a big bath and a deluge shower, a dear little kitchen too, a welcome pack of local goodies... and heaps of good, well-priced restaurants nearby. Catch the train from Chiusi to Florence or Rome, go watersporting on Lake Trasimeno. Then it's back to your very own terrace and a dip in the pool — all yours between ten and five.

Rooms	1 apartment for 2: €660–€810 per wk.
Meals	Restaurants 2km.
Closed	Rarely.

Annie Robertson
Mazzarelli 2,
06060 Paciano

Tel	+39 0758 30441
Mobile	+39 339 4161263
Email	anniebr50@gmail.com
Web	www.justfortwoitaly.co.uk

Relais Mastro Cinghiale

Through sweeping, swooping countryside with views to far-off hills, you reach the fortified walls of Paciano – and this magnificent edifice. With one side facing the tiny street and the other the hills, it's a historic, grand and friendly house, and in the family for 200 years. Young, warm, gentle Flaminia, her family and her charming red setter, divide their time between Paciano and Rome, and will delightedly show you around. You have a vast salon on the first floor with swagged curtains and big comfy sofas, and a triple-arched sitting room below, cosy and homely, its great fireplace stacked with logs. One arch is filled with Piemonte wines (the family's own), another opens to a library (take your pick) and the doors lead to a gravelled terrace scattered with arbours of wisteria. As for the bedrooms, unfussy but comfortable, you can rent some or all, including a loft room with its own sitting area. Paciano is a lovely little town, close to Panicale with its jewel-like theatre and Città della Pieve, famous for saffron. The kitchen is for cooks, the welcome basket includes delectable jams, and the parking is easy, just outside the wall.

Rooms	1 house for 12: €2,000–€4,000 per wk.
Meals	Restaurants nearby.
Closed	Rarely.

Flaminia Muratori
Relais Mastro Cinghiale,
Via Rossini 12,
06060 Paciano

Email   info@relaismastrocinghialepaciano.com
Web   www.relaismastrocinghialepaciano.com

Relais Mastro Cinghiale

Through sweeping, swooping countryside with views to far-off hills, you reach the fortified walls of Paciano — and this magnificent edifice. With one side facing the tiny street and the other the hills, it's a historic, grand and friendly house, in the family for 200 years. Young, warm, gentle Flaminia, her family and her charming red setter, divide their time between Paciano and Rome, and welcome you into their lovely home. You have a vast salon on the first floor with swagged curtains and big comfy sofas, and a triple-arched sitting room below, its great fireplace stacked with logs. Breakfast here (or on the terrace on sunny days) at one large, convivial table: sumptuous homemade cakes and jams, local organic apple juice, yogurts. Sleep peacefully in bedrooms which face the village or garden: all are comfortable with antiques, flower prints, pretty bedside lamps; a loft room has its own sitting room. Paciano is a lovely little town, close to Panicale with its jewel-like theatre and Città della Pieve, famous for saffron. Parking is easy, just outside the wall, you can walk to restaurants or ask to eat in.

Rooms	3 doubles; 2 twins; 1 suite for 2: €100–€170.
Meals	Restaurants nearby.
Closed	Rarely.

Flaminia Muratori
Relais Mastro Cinghiale,
Via Rossini 12,
06060 Paciano
Email info@relaismastrocinghialepaciano.com
Web www.relaismastrocinghialepaciano.com

La Casetta Nel Bosco

For nature lovers, cyclists and walkers – this remote little house in the woods has mind-clearing views of thickly wooded hills, olive groves dotted with farms and a distant backdrop of high mountains. It's only 30km from Perugia but the long and winding *strada bianca* to get here makes you feel a long way from anywhere; best stock up and stay put – that hammock needs occupying! The Casetta is a re-built outbuilding of the farmhouse where Jascha, quietly passionate about his area, lives with his girlfriend and parents. You share their garden and can help yourselves to fruit and vegetables. And you've a barbecue and a smallish swimming pool – also with lovely views – next to their house. Inside your rustic building all is simple, bright and colourful. Plain white walls; bold and stripy fabrics; stylish mosaic floors; light and functional furniture with wooden pieces from Jascha's company: there's a retro 70s feel. You walk straight in to the sleeping/sitting room of the lower apartment; the upstairs one is split level with a steep metal staircase (fun but could be tricky). Simple good value in deepest Umbria. *Min. stay two nights, seven in high season.*

Rooms	2 apartments for 2; 1 apartment for 4: €70-€98; €450-€610 per week. 5% discount for stays of more than 2 weeks or 1 week when renting 2 apartments. Sofabed available.
Meals	Breakfast goodies provided. Restaurants 10km.
Closed	Rarely.

Jascha Rose
La Casetta Nel Bosco,
Monte Vibiano Vecchio 1,
06072 Mercatello

Tel	+39 0758 787026 / +39 0758 783218
Email	info@lacasettanelbosco.it
Web	www.lacasettanelbosco.it

Villa Aureli

Little has changed since the Villa was built in the 18th century and became the country house of the Serègo Alighieri family 100 years later. The ornamental plasterwork, floor tiles and decorative shutters reflect its noble past, it is known to all the locals and is full of precious and historic treasures (walled up by a perspicacious housekeeper during the Occupation) which inspire the interest, attention and care of Signor Sperello. The house in fact has its origins in the 16th century, and the grounds are suitably formal – overgrown here, tamed there, with lemon trees in amazing 18th-century pots in the *limonaia* and a swimming pool created from an irrigation tank. The apartments are big and beautiful, the one on the second floor the largest and grandest, with balconies and views. Floors have mellow old tiles, ceilings are high and raftered, bedrooms are delightfully faded. You are a step away from the village, so can walk to the few shops and bar. A quietly impressive retreat, wonderfully peaceful – and special.

Rooms	1 apartment for 4; 1 apartment for 5; 1 apartment for 8: €700–€2,025 per week.
Meals	Self-catering.
Closed	Never.

Sperello di Serègo Alighieri
Villa Aureli,
Via Luigi Cirenei 70,
06132 Castel del Piano
Mobile   +39 340 6459061
Email   villa.aureli@libero.it
Web   www.villaaureli.it

Villa Rosa

The beautifully restored farmhouse looks out over fields and farms to the villages of Solomeo and Corciano, with Perugia in the distance. Distant church bells, the hum of a tractor, the bray of a donkey... yet you are only five kilometres from the superstrada. You couldn't find a better spot from which to discover Tuscany and Umbria. Megan, who is Australian, and Lino are a hospitable couple, and will help you enjoy every aspect of your stay: hunt for truffles (or cashmere, in Solomeo!), book in for occasional cookery courses, with them (or a smart chef!), take advantage of a personalised tour. For a family, the two-storey *casetta* at the end of the garden is perfect – a delightful mix of recycled beams and terracotta tiles, with open fire, air con, jacuzzi and perfect views. The flat on the ground floor of the farmhouse is similarly good – new bunk beds in the living area, cool in summer, a great terrace. There's a saltwater pool to cool you down, and the views from two of the apartments are wonderful. *Minimum stay three nights. Pets by arrangement.*

Rooms	1 apartment for 3; 1 apartment for 4: €450-€800. 1 barn for 2: €350-€550. 1 cottage for 6: €600-€1,200. Singles €350. All prices per week.
Meals	Meals available on request. Breakfast from €5, dinner from €25.
Closed	Rarely.

Megan & Lino Rialti
Villa Rosa, Voc. Docciolano 9,
Montemelino, 06060 Magione

Tel	+39 0758 41814
Mobile	+39 329 6154531
Email	meglino@libero.it
Web	www.villarosaweb.com

San Lorenzo della Rabatta Agriturismo

Near Perugia but in another world, this tiny medieval hamlet is guarded by densely wooded hills. The houses congregate around a central space, their walls covered with ivy, wisteria and roses. This is a good place to bring children – pleasant, practical – and they'll be entertained by the agricultural touches: the rickety farm stools, the cattle stall converted into a seat, the wine barrel acting as a side table. One bed has an old gate for a bedhead and there are some four-posters too (draped in white nylon). The living spaces are open-plan, with gingham much in evidence; most have a fireplace and a big rustic basket of wood. The kitchen areas and bathrooms are small and basic but clean and adequate. Outside, narrow steps bordered with miniature roses lead you down to the pool and lovely views to the hills. There's also table tennis and a small play area for children set amongst the olive trees. It's all wonderfully peaceful, but more apartments are planned. Teodora, who lives on site and has a lovely smile, will, given a day's notice, cook you a five-course meal.

Rooms	4 apartments for 2; 2 apartments for 4; 1 apartment for 6; 1 apartment for 8: €560–€1,680 per week.
Meals	Breakfast included mid-June to mid-September. Dinner, 5 courses, €20.
Closed	January/February.

Paola Cascini
San Lorenzo della Rabatta Agriturismo,
Loc. Cenerente, 06134 Perugia

Tel	Please enquire by email.
Mobile	+39 331 6768889
Email	info@sanlorenzodellarabatta.com
Web	www.sanlorenzodellarabatta.com

Castello di Petroia

Brave the loops of the Gubbio-Assisi road to arrive at the castle at dusk. The front gate is locked, you ring to be let in; an eerie silence, the gates creak open. Inside, dim lighting, stone walls, a splendid austerity. Come morning, you will appreciate the vast-fireplaced magnificence of the place, and the terrace that catches the all-day sun. The restaurant is open to the public now and the food is something to write home about; dinner is candlelit, refined, and sociable when presided over by Carlo, your gracious tweed-clad host. Then it's up the stairs – some steep – to bedrooms with beeswax polished floors and shadowy corners, aristocratic furniture and elegant beds, the swishest with hydromassage baths. (Ask for bathside strawberries and cream for the ultimate romantic escape!). The castle is set on a hillock surrounded by pines in beautiful unpopulated countryside with a marked footpath running through it. Walk to Assisi – it takes a day – then taxi back. Or take the bus into Gubbio and the funicular into the hills: the views are stupendous. A privilege to come home to this 900-acre estate.

Rooms	4 doubles (1 in tower): €120-€180.
	4 suites for 2: €180-€260.
Meals	Dinner with wine, €30-€38.
	Restaurant 5km.
Closed	January-March.

Carlo Sagrini
Castello di Petroia,
Scritto di Gubbio,
06020 Gubbio

Tel	+39 0759 20287
Email	info@petroia.it
Web	www.petroia.it

Entry 286 Map 12

Agriturismo Val di Boccio

Massimo and Lucia are a charming young couple, full of energy for their agriturismo adventure. The renovated farm sits on a hillside surrounded by olive trees, oaks, laurels and lavender, the main building houses the B&B, the attached one is for self-caterers, and the family lives just up the hill. All around: 170 acres of farmland and woods, and the sweet hills of Umbria. The hillside is quite precipitous but if you keep an eye on the toddlers, this is heaven for children. There are four ponies, two donkeys, one cow, goats, sheep, pigs, hens, a squeaky new play area and a beautifully landscaped pool – imagine diving into that on a hot day. The guest rooms and apartments are pleasant and spotless: floors newly tiled, beds of wrought iron, bedspreads coloured and patterned, and, for the B&B guests, a big comfy sitting room with books, cards, games, toys and an aromatic fire in winter. Dinners? They're a highlight, delivered to long tables in a rustic dining room: rich pasta sauces, gnocci and ravioli with black truffles, wild boar in season, Lucia's almond biscuits… and seconds for everyone. *Short stays available.*

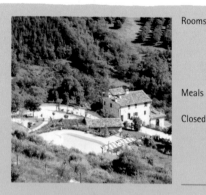

Rooms	4 doubles; 1 double with separate bath: €60–€80. 1 triple: €80–€100. 1 quadruple: €80–€110. 1 apartment for 5; 1 apartment for 3: €80–€160.
Meals	Dinner with wine, €19. Restaurants 1km.
Closed	Rarely.

Massimo Passeri
Agriturismo Val di Boccio,
Località Caresto 13,
06024 Gubbio
Email   agriturismovaldiboccio@gmail.com
Web   www.agriturismo.umbria.it

Villa Pian di Cascina

An amazing surprise at the top of the hill: an old farmhouse in acres of land with heavenly views and broom on the breeze. Isabel and Paul are hugely family-friendly but don't ignore the grown ups! As well as all you could possibly need for children there's an adult chill-out zone with a hammock, massage and beauty treatments and gorgeous Italian food if you don't want to bother with cooking. Three self-catering houses stand in a row, each with a barbecue terrace: two-storey 'Cascina', characterful 'Villetta' and cosy little 'Cantina'. The barn, 'Granaio', has been converted into four ground-floor apartments, and interiors are fresh and immaculate. Find sofas, armchairs, log-burning stoves, excellent kitchens and wrought-iron beds, tiled floors, rustic walls, the odd beam. Read a book, listen to music, cool off in the pool, play ping pong or volley ball... it's family heaven. Wander the organic gardens planted with cherries, apricots and almonds, take the old unsignposted mountain road to Assisi for stunning views, drop in on Bevagna's gorgeous churches. Magic in Umbria. *Whole place available for groups of up to 30. Short breaks available (min four nights).*

Rooms	1 house for 2 (with cot); 1 house for 4; 4 apartments for 2-6; 1 house for 8: €650-€2,199. Extra bed €100. All prices per week. Sofabeds available.
Meals	Dinner, 4 courses, €30. Children's menu €12 (under 10s). Restaurants 10-minute drive.
Closed	November-Easter.

Paul & Isabel Farber
Villa Pian di Cascina,
06024 Gubbio
Mobile   +39 334 1810602 / +39 338 3068307
Email   info@avillainumbria.com
Web   www.avillainumbria.com

Vaccaria

In the epicentre of Renaissance Italy, surrounded by hills, is this magical place. John and Janice, who have lived and worked all over the world, are vegans with a taste for Italy and for food grown with love (vivacious Janice is a wonderful cook) and it is no surprise they have landed here, in among 20 acres of wildlife, waterfalls and acacia groves; catch your breath at the views. In their glowing renovation of an old monastery – natural pigments, reclaimed materials – are polished concrete and ancient terracotta, huge cream sofas heaped with cushions, Chinese lacquer cabinets and Tibetan antiques, paintings, books and winter fires, and a salon for thought-provoking workshops, painted a stunning jade. Each bedroom is beautiful – one very private in a chapel that opens to the garden, one under the eaves, another in a tower – all with chunky beams, delicious beds, jugs of flowers. Fall asleep to the sound of the wind in the cypresses; wake to crêpes, chapattis and fresh fruits served in the sun. If the food is not home-grown it comes from the farmers' market in lovely hilltop Gubbio. Beyond are Perugia, Arezzo, Assisi… *Minimum stay two nights at weekends.*

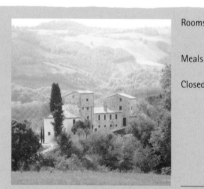

Rooms	2 doubles: €140–€160. 1 single (extra bed available): €80. 1 tower for 2; 1 tower for 4: €140–€180.
Meals	Dinner €25–€30. Vegan lunch or picnic available on request.
Closed	Rarely.

John & Janice Lapin
Vaccaria,
Fraz Colpalombo, 06024 Gubbio

Mobile	+39 392 8992192
Email	nardostachys57@yahoo.com
Web	www.metamorefosi.com

Locanda del Gallo

A restful, almost spiritual calm emanates from this wonderful home. In a medieval hamlet, the *locanda* has all the beams and antique tiles you could wish for. Light, airy rooms with pale limewashed walls are a perfect foil for the exquisite reclaimed doors and carved hardwood furniture from Bali and Indonesia; your charming hosts have picked up some fabulous pieces from far-off places and have given the house a colonial feel. Each bedroom is different, one almond with Italian country furniture, another white, with wicker and Provençal prints; some have carved four-poster beds. Bathrooms are gorgeous, with deep baths and walk-in, glass-doored showers. A stunning veranda wraps itself around the house: doze off in a wicker armchair, sip a drink at dusk as the sun melts into the valley. The pool is spectacular, like a mirage clinging to the side of the hill; and there's a huge lime tree. Jimmy the cook conjures up food rich in genuine flavours, with aromatic herbs and vegetables from the garden; he and his wife are part of the extended family. Paola and Erich are interesting, cultural and warm. *Minimum stay two nights in high season. Pets by arrangement.*

Rooms	9 doubles: €140–€160.
	Dinner, B&B €95–€100 p.p.
Meals	Lunch €12. Dinner €25–€28.
	Wine from €10.
Closed	Rarely.

Paola Moro & Erich Breuer
Locanda del Gallo,
Loc. Santa Cristina, 06020 Gubbio

Tel	+39 0759 229912
Email	info@locandadelgallo.it
Web	www.locandadelgallo.it

Le Cinciallegre Agriturismo

This was once a tiny 13th-century hamlet on an ancient crossroads where local farmers met to buy and sell their produce. It's an incredibly peaceful spot, overlooking valley, meadows and woods, reached via a long, unmade road. English-speaking Fabrizio was an architect and his conversion of these old houses is inspired: all feels authentic. In the cool, beamed living room, comfy seats pull up around a 200-year-old wood-burning stove, there's rustic furniture and a fine old dresser. The simple, comfortable bedrooms, named after birds, have their own terrace areas and immaculate bathrooms. You can cook in the outhouse but Cristina can also recommend places for real country food and Umbrian wines so you have plenty of choice. Fabrizio is a local expert and will point you in the direction of the most beautiful medieval towns and wonderful walking and, very importantly, knows when to avoid the crowds. This is a warm and hospitable place, looked after by a couple who are passionate about the environment, their lovely natural garden, and ten organic hectares of wildlife. Heaven for independent couples. *Minimum stay two nights, three in high season. Children over six welcome.*

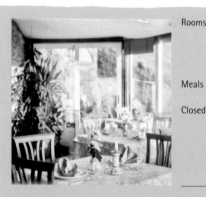

Rooms	3 doubles: €70-€80.
	1 family room for 4: €80-€120.
	1 single: €40.
	2 triples: €80-€100.
	Extra bed/sofabed €20.
Meals	Outdoor kitchen & barbecue.
	Local produce tasting €20.
Closed	October-March.

Fabrizio & Cristina de Robertis
Le Cinciallegre Agriturismo,
Fraz. Pisciano, 06024 Gubbio

Tel	+39 0759 255957
Mobile	+39 340 8986953
Email	cince@lecinciallegre.it
Web	www.lecinciallegre.it

Entry 291   Map 9

La Cuccagna

A big, solid, traditional style farmhouse – meticulously restored after the Assisi earthquake – with chestnut windows, shutters, doors, and achingly beautiful panoramas across wooded hills, farmland, olive groves and the odd tower-topped hamlet; you feel on top of the world. Paved paths lead through old olive and cherry trees, lavender and herbs (plus a little veg patch for guests to raid) to a hammock, pergola and exquisitely sited infinity pool. The cowshed cottage is cosy; the bedrooms in the farmhouse are simple and spare, with their tiled floors, beamed ceilings, locally made fabrics and ceramics, and memory foam mattresses to ensure deep sleep. Everywhere, lots of child-friendly space. Your lovely eco-conscious hosts Salvatore and Sarah ensure a special stay and think of every last detail: lavender bags, flowers, their own olive oil, truffle and asparagus foraging tips, local lore; pizza and pasta making (and eating), too. Sip Sal's homemade limoncellos over sublime sunsets on the terrace, gaze at the stars. And look forward to your discovery of this history steeped, culturally rich region. *Minimum stay three nights.*

Rooms	2 doubles (1 with child's bed); 2 twin/doubles (1 with extra bed): €90–€110. 1 suite for 2-4: €100–€150. 1 cottage for 2-3: €90–€110.
Meals	Dinner €25. Restaurant 1.5km.
Closed	January to mid-March.

Salvatore & Sarah Marano
La Cuccagna,
Fraz. S. Cristina 22, 06024 Gubbio

Tel	+39 0759 20317
Mobile	+39 348 7792330
Email	info@lacuccagna.com
Web	www.lacuccagna.com

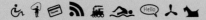

La Cuccagna

Achingly beautiful panoramas take in wooded hills, farmland, olive groves and the odd tower-topped hamlet – feel on top of the world! La Cuccagna (the cowshed) stands behind the main farmhouse, a snug retreat for two, with its own pergola and paving for wining and dining. Step in to find two bright rooms, an open plan living space in one (corner kitchen, check-clothed table, little sofabed) and a simple bedroom with a lovely beamed ceiling in the other, plus a top-notch shower. Outside, your own outdoor space for eating leads to paved paths through a garden of old olive and cherry trees, lavender and herbs (plus a little veg patch for guests to raid) to a hammock, and exquisitely sited infinity pool – yours to share. Owners Salvatore and Sarah live in the main farmhouse and have thought of every last detail: their own olive oil and limoncello to buy; truffle and asparagus foraging tips; horse riding and paragliding; pizza making (and eating), too... feel free to join in. Good restaurants are bountiful and near, Perugia, Assisi and Gubbio are within a 45-minute drive.

Rooms	1 cottage for 2: €650–€700 per week.
Meals	Self-catering.
Closed	January to mid-March.

Salvatore & Sarah Marano
La Cuccagna,
Fraz. S. Cristina 22, 06024 Gubbio

Tel	+39 0759 20317
Mobile	+39 348 7792330
Email	info@lacuccagna.com
Web	www.lacuccagna.com

Santa Chiara

Umbria is known as 'the green heart of Italy'. As you gaze out from your private terrace to olive groves and wooded hills, in the midst of hibiscus, lavender and oleander-filled gardens, you'll know why. With two young children of their own, Anita and Paul (who live in the apartment downstairs) know just what parents need on a precious break and have thought of everything, from hand-blenders and night lights to a safely fenced pool... no need to travel with 100kg of excess baggage! Those without children in tow will love these spaces too, their rough stone walls, new rustic terracotta floors and lively splashes of magenta and carmine in soft furnishings adding a contemporary edge. And this is a great place to stay with an extended party, as the apartments can be linked yet everyone keeps their independence. Walks from the door along the river are dreamy and if you can tear yourselves away, Perugia with its July jazz festival is only 20 minutes. Umbertide, even closer, is a great little place for restaurants and shops. Take a book to the hammock, raise a glass to Umbria. *Minimum stay seven nights in high season. Short stays available.*

Rooms	1 apartment for 2; 2 apartments for 4: €570–€1,450 per week.
Meals	Restaurants 2km.
Closed	Rarely.

Anita Harrington
Santa Chiara,
Via Case Sparse 24,
06015 Pierantonio
Mobile   +39 349 8132297
Email   info@tuscanyumbriaholidays.com
Web   www.tuscanyumbriaholidays.com

Casa San Gabriel

Enjoy David's wine on arrival, absorb the view of cultivated and wooded hills and unwind. Chrissie and David, warm, generous, thoughtful, bought the farmstead in a ruinous state and did it all up in under a year. The little 'houses', private but close, each with its own terrace, are suitable for singles, couples or families. For further space there's a living room in the main house with books and board games. The restoration is sympathetic, unpretentious, delightful, the off-white décor and soft furnishings enhancing undulating beams and stone walls; the bathrooms are so lovely you could spend all day in them. Supplies are left for breakfast on your first morning and should last until you're ready to venture out. You may also pick produce from the vegetable gardens or feed a fluffy alpaca. David cooks on Tuesdays, and Thursday is pizza night – your chance to use an original wood-fired oven. Bliss to have Perugia so near by – a 20-minute drive – and to return to a pool with views down the valley all the way to Assisi, a bottle of chilled Orvieto by your side. *Minimum stay two nights October-May.*

Rooms	1 apartment for 2; 2 apartments for 4: €450–€1,295 per week. Double room €95 per night.
Meals	Self-catering.
Closed	Rarely.

Christina Todd & David Lang
Casa San Gabriel, CP No 29, V.
Petrarca No 2, 06015 Pierantonio

Tel	+39 0759 414219
Mobile	+39 338 8916641
Email	chrissie@casasangabriel.com
Web	www.casasangabriel.com

Chiesa del Carmine

Streams of light reflect the Romanesque calm of a 11th-century church, whose nave makes a beautiful, lofty sitting room. Gnarled beams tangle overhead, and ancient stone pediments support a glass dining table with long views south towards Monte Subasio. Every stone, tile and wooden door has been sensitively restored by English owners, and a modern country kitchen comes with a double oven, marble sink and espresso machine. You can sip a cool drink by the slim outdoor pool, barbecue on a pergola-shaded terrace, and spend cosy nights around the wood-burner and grand piano. You sleep not in the church but in the farmhouse next door, whose elegant simplicity extends through multi terracotta-floored bedrooms, many with a terrace. Graceful wrought-iron beds carry memory-foam mattresses, antique wardrobes are meticulously restored and bathrooms have travertine showers and elegant round basins. Managers Chrissie and David help with the organic olives, vines and truffle woods, as well as a veg garden you're welcome to sample. There are wild carp in the lake, trails from the gate, and picnics to be relished in the hills.

Rooms	1 house for 14: €4,000-€8,000 per week.
Meals	Restaurants 2km. On site catering available on request.
Closed	Rarely.

Christina Todd & David Lang
Chiesa del Carmine,
06015 Pierantonio

Tel	+39 0759 414219
Mobile	+39 338 8916641
Email	info@chiesadelcarmine.com
Web	www.chiesadelcarmine.com

Entry 296   Map 9

Prato di Sotto

The visitors' book glows: some have called Prato di Sotto 'heaven on earth'. Penny has nurtured the hilltop farmhouse and its 14th-century outbuildings resplendently back to life – French beams were imported for the ceilings, the doors leading to the library come from a monastery, some fireplaces are Umbrian. Sri Lankan armchairs live harmoniously alongside antique mirrors, deep sofas, cushions, kilims and deliciously comfortable beds, and the kitchens have been designed with serious cooking in mind – one of Penny's passions. 'Casa Antica' is deeply luxurious with many bedrooms and bathrooms, a dining terrace and an upstairs balcony/terrace with stupendous views. 'La Terrazza' has a large terrace draped in wisteria and white roses; the ancient olive mill is a romantic studio with a huge veranda; the cottage, too, has a private terrace and a glorious view. Borrow a friendly dog for your rambles across the hills, swim in the fabulous infinity pool, relax in gorgeous gardens and total peace. Penny cares for you as family friends and provides fresh-laid eggs and organic homemade jams for breakfast. *Minimum stay three nights. Pets by arrangement.*

Rooms	1 apartment for 4; 1 apartment for 8: €800-€2,750. 1 cottage for 2: €700-€950. 1 studio for 2: €500-€850. All prices per week.
Meals	Breakfast & dinner on request. Restaurants 20-minute drive.
Closed	December-March.

Penny Radford
Prato di Sotto,
Santa Giuliana, 06019 Pierantonio
Tel   +39 0759 417383
Mobile   +39 335 5866792
Email   peneloperadford@gmail.com
Web   www.umbriaholidays.com

Villa Piantoni

A small slice of heaven for outdoorsy types: you stay on the Castello di Antognolla estate with its medieval castle, 600-hectare nature reserve, 18-hole golf course and hiking/biking trails. The architect, who owns the adjoining house (you share the pool), has carefully revived this solid 1600s farmhouse. Inside is deliciously peaceful with rich fabrics, rustic brick floors and beamed ceilings. Bedrooms, two in the house, one in a separate 'cottage', are beautifully furnished with good art and windows framed in antique lace have colourful potted geraniums on the sills. Bathrooms are prettily tiled and gleaming. The open-plan kitchen/diner/living room is a lovely space to hang out with its corner fireplace, tapestry wall hanging, books, games and iPod dock. Lavender, rosemary and roses run riot, you can whip up meals and eat under the vine-covered pergolas or the very good restaurant on the estate will deliver if you fancy a night off. Chrissie or David, who live nearby, meet you and can arrange activities or just let you get on with lounging around in the infinity pool and soaking up the valley views. Lush. *Pianetta Cottage available for separate rental from October to April.*

Rooms	1 house for 4; 1 cottge for 2: €500-€1,450. House and cottage together €1,200-€1,700. All prices per week.
Meals	Restaurants 2km.
Closed	Rarely.

Patricia Bernstein
Villa Piantoni,
Loc. Antognolla, Strada San Giovanni
del Pantano, 06133 Pierantonio

Tel   +1 719 598 4960
Email   Info@villapiantoni.com
Web   www.villapiantoni.com

Relais l'Antico Convento

Climb up through scrubby oak woodland and the Convento appears above you on the ridge – a lovely pile of elegant stone buildings around a central courtyard with views in all directions. Dating from the 12th century, the building was rescued from a dilapidated state by previous owner Joan, a New Yorker with an eye for design. The apartments, each named after a tarot card (a pack was found in a niche during the restoration) wouldn't look out of place in an interiors magazine. A classy minimalism of stark walls and old brick floors combines with luxurious detail: quality linens on deep mattresses, light muslin at windows, delicate ironwork, fresh flowers, dark wood antiques. It feels pleasantly exclusive here but in no way pretentious – just relaxingly country-chic. In front of the Convento is a large terrace with weathered terracotta pots while a bank of lavender and a sweep of gravel steps leads to the pool area for some serious basking. Courteous, smiling Antonietta will show you around and if you need a bit of action, Umbertide, Perugia and Assisi, and their festivals, are not far.

Minimum stay three nights on weekdays, seven nights in high season. Pets by arrangement.

Rooms	6 apartments for 2; 1 apartment for 4: €540-€1,480 per week. Sofabed available in some rooms. Ask for rates for stays under a week.
Meals	Restaurants 4km.
Closed	Rarely.

Antonietta
Relais l'Antico Convento,
Racchiusole 467, 06019 Umbertide

Tel	+39 0759 413048
Email	info@relaislanticoconvento.it
Web	www.relaislanticoconvento.it

Racchiusole

Visiting families barely leave this peaceful, hilltop estate. With such comfortable child-friendly villas, rolling acres to explore, private pools with views and shared astroturf tennis court, it is tempting to simply stay put – though there's sailing on Lake Trasimeno, a well-rated golf course nearby and Perugia 30km away. The Russells' careful conversion of 'Scopetaccio' (on two floors) and 'Calachiesa' (on three, with one room in a separate lodge) combines traditional materials (stone, wood, terracotta), loggias and outside stairs with contemporary comfort in English country-house style: plump seating, open fires, heated floors, modern prints, heavy curtains, top-quality bathrooms, family pictures (and ornamental hippos!), and kitchens equipped for cooks. Both villas have wonderful views and scented gardens (jasmine, roses, lavender), built-in barbecues and loggia-covered dining areas. If you don't feel like cooking Ann can prepare a meal for you, or arrange for a chef. She and Tony live on the estate – handy if needed but they seem to have thought of everything. An Umbrian dream.

Rooms	2 houses for 10: €2,000-€4,500 per wk.
Meals	Dinner on request, €15.
	Restaurant 4km.
Closed	Rarely.

Tony Russell
Racchiusole,
06019 Umbertide

Tel	+44 (0)20 7993 2064
Email	tr@racchiusole.com
Web	www.racchiusole.com

Entry 300   Map 9

Ca' di Gosto

You know you've stumbled across something special when you enter, on arrival, a room of beaming guests. The chunky-beamed sitting room is the hub of the house, mellow, beautiful with a touch of Englishness about it: a rose-coloured sofa piled high with cushions, a coffee table laden with books on art, and every inch of white wall hung with handsome paintings. The rest of the house is equally gorgeous. Big bedrooms on the first floor have colourful rugs and family pieces, fresh-cut flowers on deep sills, Sicilian-tiled bathrooms with antique taps; climb the creaky staircase to the tower for green views on all sides and a roll top bath next to the bed. As for David and Jenny, you couldn't be in the hands of a more creative or thoughtful pair; what's more, Jenny is an exquisite chef so don't miss out on dinner. Breakfast includes fruits, freshly baked bread and eggs from fluffy-footed bantams. David is a film producer but is happier, so he's discovered, renovating Umbrian farmhouses. Outside: a natural pool, young vines (their own) that roll down to the valley, and a shady terrace with a centuries-old tree.

Rooms	4 doubles: €170-€200.
Meals	Dinner with wine, €60.
	Restaurant 4km.
Closed	Rarely.

David Nichols
Ca' di Gosto,
Leoncini 14, 06019 Umbertide
Mobile   +39 348 3236704
Email   david.nichols@mac.com
Web   www.slowcooking.homestead.com

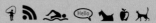

Il Vecchio Porcile

Was there ever a more perfect little nest for honeymooners? The blush-coloured *porcile* (our trotter'd friends moved on some time ago) has views across vines to distant Umbrian hills, a four-poster on a little mezzanine, and a country kitchen (downstairs, along with your bathroom) with sage-green cupboards and a scrubbed wooden table for dinners in. Through French windows enter a sloping beamed sitting room – most unusual – with a grand stone fireplace framed by comfy sofas, shelves stacked with books, and plenty of light; a room created with perfect relaxation in mind. Cross the cotta floors and head up three wooden steps, through a low gate (a reminder of a former farmyard life) to the bedroom, where floral curtains hide you away from the main room at night. David and Jenny live in the big farmhouse where they run B&B and will be as on hand as you want them to be, but don't miss the opportunity to sample Jenny's fabulous dinners. You have your own terrace with clambering roses, and acres of grounds to share with the others, including a wonderful natural pool.

Rooms	1 cottage for 2 (with cot/child bed on request): €150; €1,050 per week. €25 per child.
Meals	Breakfast optional for self-caterers. Dinner with wine, €60. Restaurant 4km.
Closed	Rarely.

David Nichols
Il Vecchio Porcile,
Leoncini 14, 06019 Umbertide
Mobile   +39 348 3236704
Email   david.nichols@mac.com
Web   www.slowcooking.homestead.com

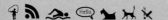

La Molinella

Eat, sleep and dream in the little old watermill in the Umbrian hills – an enchanting bolthole for two. Though you can reach Perugia in under an hour it is fairly remote; but the hiking and riding are easy. Potted lavender, herbs and tidy vines are plentiful, and apple trees and a few olives up by the cool circular pool (all yours, with views)… the 'shabby chic' of the interior repeats itself outside so you barely notice where the gardens end and nature begins. Loveliest of all is the dappled veranda complete with daybed for outdoor R&R. Back inside, ceilings are low, floors are old wood or terracotta, beams are rustic, pale blue paintwork is deliberately worn, and the kitchen, with its antique marble-topped table and old-fashioned pellet stove in one corner, will make you giddy with delight. (It also has loads of workspace and a modern oven.) Owner Annie is here when guests arrive, lives nearby should you need her, and moves back in in winter! At the top is the snug bedroom with romantic bed and sweet white linen, below is a sitting room with deep sofa and open fire. Honeymoon heaven.

Rooms	1 house for 2: €995-€1,195 per week.
Meals	Self-catering.
Closed	November-April.

The Owner
La Molinella,
Voc. La Molinella,
06010 San Leo Bastia
Mobile   +39 340 6349783
Email   lamolinella2012@googlemail.com

La Preghiera Residenza d'Epoca

This glorious 12th-century monastery, hidden in a wooded valley near Gubbio and Cortona, was a pilgrim's resting place. The Tunstills, an architect and interior designer, have restored it with English country-house flair and Italian attention to detail. The big sitting and dining rooms are elegantly scattered with sofas, paintings and antiques; there is a billiard room and a library. Bedrooms combine original features — beamed and raftered ceilings, terracotta floors, wooden shutters, exposed stone — with sophistications such as cotton and silk bed linen, handmade furniture, wardrobes with interior lights, marbled bathrooms. Outside are shady terraces, a sunken garden, a flower-filled loggia, a private chapel and a second villa that sleeps an extra six. Have breakfast on the terrace, tea by the pool, dine by candlelight on local boar and truffles. There are vintage bikes to borrow, horse riding and golf nearby, medieval hilltop towns to visit, lovely staff to look after you. You can even book a massage by the pool. *Whole villas available or individual rooms.*

Rooms	1 villa for 18: €4,000–€5,000.
	1 villa for 6: €1,000–€1,800.
	Whole place: €5,000–€6,800.
	Prices per week.
	Extra beds available. Individual rooms on request (min. 3 nights).
Meals	Breakfast on request. Dinner with wine, 4 courses, €50, by arrangement. Restaurant 1km.
Closed	December–February (open on request).

Liliana & John Tunstill
La Preghiera Residenza d'Epoca,
Via del Refari, 06018 Calzolaro

Tel	+39 0759 302428
Mobile	+39 333 1855737
Email	info@lapreghiera.com
Web	www.lapreghiera.com

Entry 304   Map 9

L'Ariete

Well-travelled Martina and Andreas from Vienna are full of love for their new venture: a restaurant with apartments (and two rooms) in Umbria. It's a *casa padronale* plus outbuildings, above which teeters lovely Montone on its hill. The apartments are in the main house, spread over the first and second floors, most with a big open fireplace, all with a kitchenette or kitchen. Find original beams and terracotta floors, charming wrought-iron beds and antique chandeliers, embroidered white cotton and light-filled bathrooms that range from small to vast: there's a fresh and beautiful simplicity. The rustic restaurant in the old stables is the perfect setting for seasonal regional fare in Slow Food style, where ingredients are home-grown or from the local farms and the dishes are delicious Umbrian (with apple strudel for pudding if you're lucky); there's a grocer's shop, too. Montone is a joy to explore: atmospheric churches and cobbled squares, cafés, bars and a film festival in July. Wend your way back down the hill to a garden of sunflowers and birds, lawns mown by sheep and a charming pool. A gem! *Min. stay two nights, seven in high season. Pets by arrangement.*

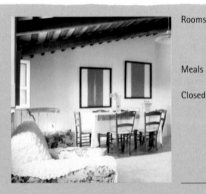

Rooms	2 doubles (can interconnect): €60–€100. 1 apartment for 4; 3 apartments for 2: €590–€1,050 per week. Singles €60–€90.
Meals	Breakfast €15 for self-caterers. Dinner, 3 courses with wine, from €30.
Closed	Rarely.

Andreas Sax
L'Ariete,
06014 Montone
Mobile   +39 339 2909493
Email   andreas@lariete.org
Web   www.lariete.org/en

Podere Cardaneto

Warm, welcoming, enticing, a delight for the senses and with spellbinding views. The 14th-century look-out tower is the oldest part of this mellow stone *podere*; the house is for B&Bers, the barn apartment for self-caterers. To a backdrop of ancient beams and flagstone floors, intriguing arches, undulating walls and small deep-set windows (some framing views of Montone on the hill) is an elegant and inviting décor: a huge fireplace with a 16th-century fireback, mismatched sofas heaped with cushions, side tables here and there with magazines to browse, a collection of hats, books galore (vintage and new), a standard lamp of antlers... and fabulous idiosyncratic antiques: your hosts are in the trade in Milan. Cultured, gentle, quietly spoken, they are hugely accommodating to people's wants and needs, give you big beautiful bedrooms (one with a stand-alone bath), homemade cakes at breakfast and jams in season. For shops, bars and dining, Montone is a mile away. Classical music wafts in summer to pergolas entwined with wisteria and vines; seats are of wicker or wrought-iron. Irresistible, enchanting!

Rooms	5 doubles; 1 twin: €130-€180.
	1 apartment for 8: €600-€2,500 per week.
Meals	Restaurants 1.5km.
	Dinner available on request.
Closed	Rarely.

Maurizio Munari
Podere Cardaneto,
06014 Montone

Tel	+39 0759 306453
Mobile	+39 337 688137
Email	maurizio@cardaneto.it
Web	www.cardaneto.it

Casa delle Grazie

Skirt upwards around the edge of the lovely old town walls of Montone to find an ancient stone farmhouse and enthusiastic owners Aine and Fabio; three holiday homes form part of a long, low barn opposite. 'La Stalla' and 'La Cantina' are single storey; 'La Torretta', in the middle, has two floors. All is new inside with open-plan living/kitchen areas with simple wooden tables, eco-heated floors, beamed ceilings and white walls. Bedrooms are simple and stylish, with pretty rose-pink quilts and good mattresses; the upstairs bedroom in 'La Torretta' has the best views, but all are bright and airy. Bathrooms are spacious with good big showers and warm biscuit coloured tiles. You have your own terracotta terrace with comfortable furniture and a pergola for shade; privacy is provided by hedging and a high trellis with roses. Supplies are left for breakfast on your first morning and you have your pick of the vegetable garden. Explore the area: the walks are sublime and there's a film festival in July. *Minimum stay seven nights in high season. Pets by arrangement.*

Rooms	1 apartment for 2; 2 apartments for 4: €500–€1,250 per week.
Meals	Self-catering.
Closed	Rarely.

Aine Browne & Fabio Urso
Casa delle Grazie,
Via Case Sparse 19, 06014 Montone
Mobile +39 331 9862638
Email aine@casadellegrazie.com
Web www.casadellegrazie.com

La Locanda del Capitano

Wend your way up to the fortified village of Montone, closed to traffic and impeccably preserved. On one of its steepest alleys is the locanda of the 'Captain', Giancarlo Polito – economist, photographer, hotelier and *chef straordinario*. Passionate about life, history, everything, he adores showing off his village and his home, loves talking about food and knows every producer in Umbria. Enter the wrought-iron gate off the street and trot up the steps to reception. Spill onto the front terraces for conversation, relaxation and the sound of the church bells, feast on wines and cheeses in Tipico, their 'cave' next door, or set sail for the dining room, elegant and charming, with bow-backed chairs and an antique piano. The food is beautiful and full of surprises, combined tastes to awaken the senses accompanied by 400 wines. Cooking classes, truffle hunts, visits to wineries and producers, Perugia, Assisi, Bevagna and Montefalco: history and gastronomy combine. Then it's back to decorative iron beds on parquet floors and salmon and soft-green hues. Ask for a room with a balcony and a view.

Rooms	10 doubles: €100-€130.
	2 triples: €120-€150.
	Singles €80-€100.
Meals	Dinner €30-€50. Restaurants nearby.
Closed	January/February.

Giancarlo Polito
La Locanda del Capitano,
Via Roma 5/7, 06014 Montone

Tel	+39 0759 306521 / +39 0759 306455
Email	info@ilcapitano.com
Web	www.ilcapitano.com

Pereto

Don't make elaborate sightseeing plans before you go: the moment you clap eyes on the wisteria-clad farm buildings, the hammocks hanging temptingly from the gables on the terrace, and the lavender and rosemary-fringed pool, any itineraries involving time away from Pereto will vanish. Sandro and Bruna ("utterly *simpatici*" says our inspector) have transformed the old stable and tobacco-drying barn into gorgeously rustic yet refined retreats. Incredibly old and slightly wonky throughout, they have dark chunky beams, low deep-sill windows, and flagstones shiny and worn from 400 years of farmyard activity; and there's something baronial about the drying barn's sitting room with its handsome stone fireplace and worn leather armchairs. Walls are rich in colour (ochre, olive, burnt terracotta), brass pans decorate kitchen walls, nooks are crammed with books. Find homemade essential oils in the bathrooms, honey from the bees in the welcome hamper, bikes to borrow. And if you really must venture beyond the farm's 450 acres, Perugia, Montone, and Assisi are close by. Heavenly. *Short stays available.*

Rooms	1 house for 4; 1 house for 6: €1,800-€3,400 per week. Houses can be booked together for groups of up to 10, €3,600-€5,000 per week.
Meals	Restaurants nearby.
Closed	Never.

Sandro Ligossi
Pereto,
Zona Carpini 48, 06014 Montone
Tel   +39 0759 306157
Mobile   +39 345 3513087
Email   info@pereto.eu
Web   www.pereto.eu

Monte Valentino Agriturismo

On top of the world in Umbria, woods fall away, hills climb to snow-scattered heights. It's the perfect escape, the only route in a steep, winding, two-kilometre track. All around you lie 60 hectares of organically farmed land – mushrooms are gathered from the woods, cereals and vegetables from the fields, fruit from the trees, water from the spring. These new apartments are contemporary yet cosy and comfortable with simple wooden furniture, tiled floors and throws on striped sofas. All have small balconies and kitchens and clean, fresh shower rooms; two have access to beautifully designed brick terraces where the views sweep and soar away. Surrounded by deck chairs and olive trees, the pool is delightful. Fabrizia, who lives next door, is enthusiastic and charming with an engaging smile, and proud of her venture – meet her over a simple breakfast in her homely kitchen. This is perfect cycling terrain – if you're tough! You can also swim in the river, horse riding is six miles away, cookery lessons can be arranged and Nicola will give you archery lessons if you fancy something different. They are lovely people.

Rooms	2 apartments for 2; 2 apartments for 2-3: €70-€80; €450-€560 per week.
Meals	Breakfast included. Restaurants 12km.
Closed	Never.

Fabrizia Gargano & Nicola Polchi
Monte Valentino Agriturismo,
Loc. Monte Valentino,
06026 Pietralunga
Tel   +39 0759 462092
Email   info@montevalentino.it
Web   www.montevalentino.it

Villa Solferino

In the land of gentle hills and valleys, 11th-century frescoes, Renaissance palaces, chamber music, truffles and porchini, is a handsome house in an enviable setting. Its owner is Simon who resides in Monterchi; having lived in Umbria for 23 years he happily shares his knowledge. Through the gates, up the drive and there is a big ochre house with pale grey shutters on a hill, surveying a fabulous panorama. Step in to find three floors of comfort and light, and an authentic Tuscan décor: arches, beams, balconies, a vast stone fireplace, and elegant sofas on terracotta floors. The kitchen, big, friendly and fun to cook in, leads to dining areas on two sides: one out under the arches, the other in. Bedrooms are large and lovely, with chestnut wardrobes, walnut dressing tables, perhaps an Art Deco bed or a vintage chandelier. Bathrooms are fresh, simple and contemporary. You're near the hilltowns of Città di Castello and Montone, steeped in medieval history – don't miss the convent and cloisters of San Franceso. After a day's hiking or biking in the upper Carpina valley, make a splash in your 50-foot pool.

Rooms	1 house for 10: €1,300–€3,500 per week. Discount on last minute bookings.
Meals	Free dinner one night a week. Restaurants 3km.
Closed	Rarely.

Simon Mather
Villa Solferino,
Loc. Pino, Petrelle,
60012 Città di Castello
Mobile   +39 348 7830344
Email   info@villasolferino.com
Web   www.villasolferino.com

Agriturismo Campara

In spring and summer you swim amongst irises and lilies. No salt, no chlorine in this 'bio lake', just lovely clear water, a small cascade and the odd friendly frog. Children adore it and the setting is sweet, 500 metres above sea level and never too hot. As you approach up a winding tarmac road the house suddenly appears above on the side of the hill. Delightful Margherita lives here with her artist husband, plus cats, hens, rabbits and children, growing their own olives, fruits and veg. If you ask, she will happily cook you dinner and bring it to the garden. You have a choice of three apartments here: 'Ninfea' (upstairs) and 'Davina' (down), twin homes in a peachy 60s villa; and 'Ginestra', older, snugger, beamier, more characterful, attached to the farmhouse. All have patios or a terrace with views and all are really well furnished: find colourful rugs on spotless floors (lovely old terracotta ones in 'Ginestra'), light cotton curtains at sturdy windows and well-dressed wrought-iron beds. Borrow rods for the lake, play on the swings or visit Cortona, Perugia, Arezzo for classic Umbrian magic. *Minimum stay two nights, seven nights in high season.*

Rooms	3 apartments for 4: €385–€665 per wk. Extra bed/sofabed available at no charge.
Meals	Self-catering.
Closed	Rarely.

Margherita Cerrai
Agriturismo Campara, Voc. Campara 84,
Loc. Volterrano, 06010 Città di Castello

Tel	+39 0758 574136
Mobile	+39 339 2610973
Email	info@campara.it
Web	www.campara.it

Cinque Querce & Mezzo

At the end of a short country road… a dream of a house in dreamy grounds. Mirrors dance from trees, shells clink softly in the wind and views stretch for miles. Hillside villages to one side, long plains to the other, gentle valley in front of you, and almond trees, cypresses, gazebos and terraces all on different levels. As for the house, it is equally enticing, with four storeys, big stairs sweeping you up and down, and fascinating Roman cellars below. Ask Dennis and Gilly about wine tastings – no request is too great for this lovely English couple who live near by. You get a big kitchen at the top and a small kitchen down – both geared up for good chefs – and a pizza oven and a huge barbecue. And Gilly's veg patch to plunder. Floors are old terracotta, bathrooms have great big mirrors and bedrooms are beautiful with wood floors and pastels. Sofas, books, games, iPod dock, satellite TV – all yours, and a divine pool. You're right in the centre of a protected nature reserve yet thrillingly close to Città di Castello (shops, restaurants, bars), and the path taken by St Francis on his walk from La Verna to Assisi.

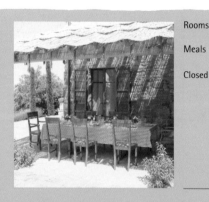

Rooms	1 house for 8: €2,000–€3,600 per week.
Meals	Restaurants 2km. Chef available for in-house dinners & cookery courses.
Closed	Rarely.

Dennis Sullivan
Cinque Querce & Mezzo,
06012 San Giustino

Tel +39 0575 791249
Email calcinaia@me.com

Marche and Molise

Photo: istock.com

Locanda della Valle Nuova

In gentle, breeze-cooled hills, surrounded by ancient, protected oaks and on the road that leads to glorious Urbino, this 185-acre farm produces organic meat, vegetables and wine. Three self-catering apartments are bright and colourful with comfortable beds and very well-equipped kitchens. Each has a terrace so that guests can eat outside, one has a particularly beautiful view of the 'Montefeltro' Marche landscape, another is more shaded in summer and closer to the swimming pool. It is an unusual, unexpectedly modern place whose owners have a special interest in horses and in the environment: solar panels for heating, photovoltaic panels for electricity. For B&B guests, the conversion has given La Locanda the feel of a discreet modern hotel, where perfectly turned sheets lie on perfect beds, and most of the rooms have views. The riding school has a club house for horsey talk and showers; there are two outdoor arenas as well as lessons and hacks, and a fabulous pool. If you arrive at the airport after dark, Giulia kindly meets you to guide you back. *Children over 12 welcome. Short stays available.*

Rooms	2 apartments for 2; 1 apartment for 4: €600–€980 per week. B&B €86 p.p per night. Minimum stay 2 nights. Sofabed available. Check prices for longer stays.
Meals	Dinner €30 (twice a week). Wine from €9. Restaurant 2km.
Closed	Mid-November to May.

Giulia Savini
Locanda della Valle Nuova,
La Cappella 14,
61033 Sagrata di Fermignano,

Tel	+39 0722 330303
Email	info@vallenuova.it
Web	www.vallenuova.it

La Casetta

The pretty twin bedroom once housed the wood oven. La Casetta dates back to the 1700s and has been seamlessly extended by Peter and Richard – it is simple, unpretentious, charming. Separate from the main house, it faces the opposite way, with rolling views across farmland and to mountains. It is bliss to spill into your own private garden with a pergola covered in roses and a fig tree to plunder; all this yours, and – beyond a leafy arch – box hedges guarding herbs and lavender. Back inside are peachy curtains and two checked sofas, an open fireplace and lovely low beams: a warm and inviting place to hole up in in winter. The kitchen is proper country-style, a delight to work in, but if you wish to shed your chef's apron there are restaurants in Frontone – and medieval Cagli, three miles away. Urbino and Gubbio, sensational 'città d'arte', are a half-hour drive, and beaches not much further. Peter and Richard, who have written guides about Italy, have a big library of books for guests to borrow. Hard to imagine more generous – or good-humoured – hosts. *Minimum stay seven nights in high season.*

Rooms	1 apartment for 4: €780–€880 per wk.
Meals	Self-catering.
Closed	January-March.

Richard Dixon & Peter Greene
La Casetta, San Cristoforo,
Strada Santa Barbara 5, 61043 Cagli,

Tel	+39 0721 790215
Mobile	+39 339 2411737
Email	mail@le-marche.com
Web	www.sancristoforo.info

La Pieve

It is spacious, arched and lofty; the former sacristy is a bedroom (serene, simple, charming) and the confessional still stands in a corner. La Pieve was a chapel that dates from the 1700s. Colours are warm, floors are modern tiled, the shower is roomy and there's so much space you each have your own sofa! It's cosy for winter (books to borrow; a wood-burning stove) and gorgeous in summer, with French windows opening to a private little garden with luscious views; sit out midst the lavender and raise a glass to the vines. Richard and Peter live and share this 'dolce vita' with two gentle dogs on the other side of metre-thick walls. Cultured and humorous, happy to lend you chicken-bricks or juniper berries, they are conscious of their guests' privacy but on hand if required. Come for wild flowers in May, river swims in summer, funghi and truffles in autumn (visit the truffle fair at Acqualagna) and the gutsy, restorative cuisine of the Marche all year round. Look out for posters advertising the local 'sagra': a festival dedicated to a town's particular speciality — a foodie's delight. *Minimum stay seven nights in high season.*

Rooms	1 apartment for 2: €550–€630 per wk.
Meals	Self-catering.
Closed	January-March.

Richard Dixon & Peter Greene
La Pieve, San Cristoforo, Strada Santa
Barbara 5, 61043 Cagli,

Tel	+39 0721 790215
Mobile	+39 339 2411737
Email	mail@le-marche.com
Web	www.sancristoforo.info

Villa Giulia

Place and people have extraordinary charm. Pines, cypress oaks and roses surround the Napoleonic villa, wisteria billows over the lemon house, the gardens merge into the family olive groves and an ancient wood. No formality, no fuss, just an easy, gracious and kind welcome from Anna, who lives here with her youngest son. The villa was named after an indomitable great-aunt (the first woman to climb Mont Blanc!) and the family furniture is perfect for it – big wood-framed mirrors, stunning antiques – along with a candle burn on the mantelpiece left by the Nazis. Bedrooms, the best and most baronial in the villa, have shutters and old-fashioned metal beds; one noble bathroom has its own balcony, another is up a winding stair. The two suites in La Dependenza have kitchenettes while the apartments proper are divided between the Farmhouse and the Casa Piccola. Sitting rooms are grand but easy, dining room chairs are gay with red checks, summer breakfasts are taken at pink-clothed tables on a terrace whose views reach to the Adriatic (the beach is a mile away). Atmospheric, historic, beautiful, and good for all ages.

Rooms	6 doubles; 5 suites for 2: €120–€260. 4 apartments for 2; 1 apartment for 4: €800–€1,800 per week. Sofabed available.
Meals	Dinner €30–€50. Wine €8–€36. Restaurant 2km.
Closed	January–March.

Anna Passi
Villa Giulia, Via di Villa Giulia,
Loc. San Biagio 40, 61032 Fano,

Tel	+39 0721 823159
Mobile	+39 347 0823935
Email	info@relaisvillagiulia.com
Web	www.relaisvillagiulia.com

Castello di Monterado

Orlando's great-great-grandfather bought the Castello, parts of which date from 1100. The renovation continues, and is glorious. Orlando and Kira, quietly spoken and charming, are deeply passionate about the family home whose exquisite revival has been achieved floor by floor. The Music Room is a living museum; its terrace overlooks the new, azure, arc-shaped pool, a foil to the grand park and its ancient trees and, in the distance, the Caseno valley and the Adriatic. The Library combines vast armchairs with ancient tomes, there are frescoes on every wall and ceiling, antiques, works of art, chandeliers – the sheer beauty will thrill you. There's a lovely balcony for fresh-air breakfasts and a dining room for drearier mornings (overseen by Bacchus and Ariadne, of course). Bedrooms, all vast, all generously different, ooze splendour; cherubs chase each other across ceilings, beds are soberly but beautifully dressed, cupboards have been crafted from the cellar's barrels, one suite has its hydromassage bath positioned so you gaze on gardens as you soak. Very special, and good value. *Minimum stay two nights in high season. Pets by arrangement.*

Rooms	4 suites for 2: €110–€180.
Meals	Restaurants within walking distance.
Closed	Rarely.

Orlando & Kira Rodano
Castello di Monterado,
Piazza Roma 18, 60010 Monterado,
Tel   +39 0717 958395
Email   info@castellodimonterado.it
Web   www.castellodimonterado.it

Castello di Monterado – Apartments

Cut off from western Italy by the Apennines is the region of Le Marche; peaceful, charming and unsought-out. At the top of a steep wooded hill is Monterado, a small medieval town of cobbled streets and fabulous views. Beyond is the sea. On a small square in town, opposite the Castle of Monterado is a solid old stone building housing six apartments with a contemporary and luxurious feel. One is on the ground floor, two are on the first and two are on the second; 'Anemone', the largest, spreads itself over two levels. Lofty walls are plastered white, floors are polished parquet, styling is minimalist, classy and sleek. Guests in the apartments can use the pool in the castle gardens. In the town are a handful of restaurants and shops, tennis courts and, in May, a hog roast festival to which locals flock, the region is the home of *porchetta*. If you want beach resorts with a Sixties feel, then head west for the resorts of Le Marche. After a day's touring, return to the peaceful garden of the Castello, with its cedar trees and scented roses and, beyond, a landscaped woodland with winding paths. *Min. stay seven nights in high season. Pets by arrangement.*

Rooms	2 apartments for 2-5; 3 apartments for 2-4; 1 apartment for 4-6: €420–€756 per week.
Meals	Self-catering.
Closed	Never.

Orlando & Kira Rodano
Castello di Monterado – Apartments,
Piazza Roma 26, 60010 Monterado

Tel	+39 0717 958395
Email	info@castellodimonterado.it
Web	www.castellodimonterado.it

Monastero di Favari

Through the handsome wrought-iron gates that come from a convent in Tuscany, up the winding drive, to a villa built for a 17th-century nobleman, recently and beautifully restored. Behind is a young vineyard; to the side, a simple chapel, an enchanting place for a wedding. Whether you come in summer for pool and gardens, or winter for heated floors and log fires, there's masses of space for a party. Find two sitting rooms, seven bedrooms and three storeys linked by a dramatic circular stair, dazzling white walls, sweeping floors in pale terracotta, chunky wooden ceilings (some sloping, some with a chandelier), and elegant pale painted furniture. New mattresses top antique bedsteads, cream sofas are deep, bathrooms are gorgeous. As for the views, they bring joy all year round. There's ping-pong and football on the grass, golf on the craggy Conero peninsula (unlike Le Marche's gentle Riviera) and a riding stables in Apiro. Restaurants are close, a cook can be provided, and the region has been dubbed Italy's Garden of Eden. We love it. Don't miss it! *Short stays available.*

Rooms	1 house for 15: €1,500–€4,000 per wk. Double sofa bed available.
Meals	Restaurants nearby.
Closed	Rarely.

Camilla Wood
Monastero di Favari,
Contrada Favari 6, 62021 Apiro

Mobile	+44 (0)7717 396635
Email	monasterofavari@gmail.com
Web	www.monasterofavari.com

La Serendipita

Welcome to an ancient house in super-sleek style, owned by an English couple. It's sandwiched between two others in the ancient walls of the town, and stands on a street reached by 39 steps (you'll probably leave fitter than you arrive!). The front door opens to an Italian showhome kitchen with a glass-top table and modern stairs up and down. Up: an immaculate bedroom in whites, greys and splashes of red, with a heart-shaped chair, a state-of-the-art sauna and a mountain view. Down: the perfect place for a game of Scrabble on a cosy night in, with a chic leather sofa, a bio-ethanol fire, books, DVDs. Off here is the balcony, small, soaked in sun, with beanbags, barbecues and views. Close to the central piazza (butcher, greengrocer, weekly market) La Serendipita is brilliantly sited; you can dine out deliciously, too. Head off for the Sibillini mountains or the Adriatic sea, the caves at Frassasi, the opera at Macerata, or a splash in the owners' pool equipped with a shower, changing room and a sensational view: it's worth the 40-minute drive. *Sunday start date only. Minimum stay one week.*

Rooms	1 apartment for 2: £380–£525 per wk. Discounts available for stays over 2 weeks during low season.
Meals	Restaurants nearby.
Closed	Rarely.

Carole Chapman
La Serendipita,
62100 Treia

Tel   +39 0733 433508
Email   la.serendipita@yahoo.co.uk

La Casa degli Amori

When Sandy and Laurence found this honey-coloured farmhouse with glorious views they could hardly believe it had lain empty for 30 years. Now it embraces four sun-lit guest bedrooms, their beds decked in white linen, their pretty, rustic furniture chosen with care. Each has its own fresh clean bathroom, sparkling with travertine tiles. Two cosy first-floor sitting rooms and the entire open-plan ground floor are yours to relax in, so wander at will. In the garden, the scent of roses, wisteria and lavender hangs on the breeze, and the vegetable garden, fruit trees and olive grove give bumper harvests. Your hosts greet you with prosecco and antipasti; they love to please. Chef Sandy ensures breakfasts on the terrace (or by the sparkling pool) are a joyous array of local or homemade breads, cakes, fruit, yogurt, omelettes and cereals… with a bit of notice, she'll magic up a full English for you, or lunch, or a three-course dinner. Laurence is a wrought-ironsmith with his workshop in the garden – drop by. All this just five minutes from Treia, one of Italy's most beautiful towns. *Minimum stay two nights, three nights in high season.*

Rooms	4 doubles: €85–€95.
	Extra bed/sofabed available.
Meals	Dinner, 3 courses with wine, €25.
	Lunch on request. Restaurants 1.5km.
Closed	Rarely.

Sandy Love
La Casa degli Amori,
Contrada Conce 11, 62010 Treia

Mobile	+39 338 1700977
Email	sandyloveitaly@gmail.com
Web	www.casadegliamori.com

Caserma Carina Country House

Nothing is too much trouble for Lesley, whose easy-going vivacity makes this place a delight, while Dean gardens immaculately. Cots, toys, DVDs, a bottle of wine at the end of a journey, a welcoming smile – she and Dean provide it all. The apartments are immaculate, the gardens prettily landscaped, the pool has long views. A 15-minute walk down the hill from historic Mogliano (three restaurants, shops, banks and bars) is this magnificent 19th-century country house, its new apartments spanning three floors. The unrestored part sits quietly, rustically alongside. Inside, all is new, inviting and spotlessly clean. Showers have cream tiles and white towels, kitchens are quietly luxurious, sofas gleam in brown leather, cushions add splashes of red, wooden furniture is stylish and new, indoor shutters cut out early morning light, and views are of rolling hills. You are in the heart of the lovely, unsung Le Marche, an easy drive from historic Macerata and not much further from the Adriatic coast. Couples love it, and families, too. A year-round treat. *Minimum stay three nights, seven nights in high season.*

Rooms	1 apartment for 2-3; 1 apartment for 4: £475-£1,045 per week.
Meals	Self-catering.
Closed	Rarely.

Lesley McMorran
Caserma Carina Country House,
Contrada Mossa 16, 62010 Mogliano

Tel	+39 0733 557990
Mobile	+39 366 1822519
Email	info@caserma-carina.co.uk
Web	www.caserma-carina.co.uk

Casa Nobile

From the ancient pink-brick'd town of Loro Piceno the road winds down for a kilometre to a beautifully restored farmhouse set in idyllic countryside. It is a comfortable, spacious, well-proportioned house with an open ground-floor layout: a wide arch links the dining room to the high-raftered kitchen (with an extravagant stone sink), which opens to a wonderful terrace. Lovely to dine al fresco at the big glass-covered dining table or sink into deep armchairs – then to drift across to the glittering saltwater pool: super-smart, with Roman steps and loungers. A charming friend of the Canadian owners meets and greets, while a cleaner pops by to change sheets and towels. Up the stairs you pass a portrait of Giuseppe Verdi – rumour has it he once stayed here – to three bedrooms with sprung mattresses, crisp white linen, ceiling fans and gentle views. The master en suite has an open fire and dressing room, the twin is under the rafters. Walking sticks in the hall hint at the proximity of the Sibillini mountains. The less sporty will love Loro Piceno, a historian's delight – and festival-home to sweet velvety Vino Cotto.

Rooms	1 house for 8: €1,800-€2,400 per wk.
Meals	Self-catering.
Closed	End of October to end of March.

Margaret Rose
Casa Nobile,
Contrada Salsaro Ete 49,
62020 Loro Piceno
Email   mrose_1344@hotmail.com

Casa Ginestra

Classic Marchegiana views of hilltop towns and steep valleys roll out in front of you as you dangle your toes in the pool. Behind you is the pale stone farmhouse of Casa Ginestra. Here you feel at home, in the heart of Italy. The casa's renovation has been thorough and the house has a swish, contemporary feel. Soft beige tones and a sweeping dark leather sofa in one of the two living rooms complement the original roof timbers, echoed in the kitchen furniture and the wood-framed beds. Two of the bedrooms are tucked up in the eaves on the third storey, their floor-level windows creating a shaded light, their beams making a romantic canopy. The well-equipped kitchen can easily handle the task of supplying the long dining table, but if you aren't up to it, then housekeepers Renzo and Simona, who greet you on arrival, can organise just about anything. The area is great for hiking and history: the Sibillini Mountains National Park has miles of trails and incredible flora and fauna, while the Marche towns sport medieval forts and a rumoured campsite of Hannibal and his elephants at Porto Recanati. *Smaller groups can rent two rooms only (except July/August).*

Rooms	1 house for 8: £1,400-£2,000 per week.
Meals	Restaurants 3km.
Closed	Rarely.

Amanda Gresham
Casa Ginestra,
Contrada San Venanzo,
62020 Monte San Martino

Tel	+44 (0)1394 461368
Email	agresham@talk21.com
Web	www.casaginestra.com

Hotel Leone

The owners have poured love and soul into this beautiful hotel – and it shows. There are fabulous views over the Marchegiana countryside to the Adriatic Sea, and the pretty courtyard garden that overlooks the pool is idyllic… the cool, relaxing atmosphere is most refreshing on a hot summer's day. Inside, you'll find a unique blend of cultures and styles, from 15th-century features to Art Deco furniture. Bedrooms are boutique in style, but intimate, and have personal touches. There's even a collection of novels to pore over, and restored antique furniture here and there to complete the effect. The en suite bathrooms are shiny-new with elegant cream tiles and fragrant bath products, and after you've scrubbed up, you can look forward to dinner, cooked by chef-patron Tim. Ingredients are fresh and local, recipes are too – along with a few far-flung eastern numbers. What's more, a wood-fired oven and a local chef are to hand for pizza lovers! If you manage to tear yourself away from this blissful spot, there are guided walks, music festivals and local food markets to keep you busy all summer long.

Rooms	4 doubles; 2 twin/doubles: €125–€140; 1 suite for 2; 1 suite for 4: €170–€220. Singles €103–€125. Extra bed/sofabed €40. Prices per night. 1 apartment for 4: €595–€795 per week.
Meals	Dinner, B&B €25 extra per person. Full-board €35 extra per person.
Closed	Mid-January to mid-March.

Madeline & Tim Jones
Hotel Leone,
Via Vittorio Emanuele II 60,
63853 Montelparo

Tel   +39 0734 782041
Email   info@hotelleone.it
Web   www.hotelleonemarche.com

Agriturismo Contrada Durano

Spend a few days at this tranquil agriturismo and you may never want to leave. The hillside farm, built in the late 18th century as a refuge for monks, has been lovingly restored by its generous, delightful and energetic owners: Englishman Jimmy and Italian Maria Concetta. No clutter, no fuss, just tiled floors, white walls, dark furniture. The bedrooms are simple and some are small, but the bar and sitting areas have masses of space. If you want a view – of olive groves, vineyards and perched villages – ask for rooms 1 or 2. There's dinner most evenings: Maria's food will make your heart sing, the produce home-grown in their wonderful kitchen garden or local and organic prosciutto, pecorino, and their own bread and wine. As you feast your eyes on distant mountains from all three dining rooms you may ask yourself, why eat elsewhere? In spring and summer, walk through wild flowers up to the village of Smerillo. And do visit the *cantina* and stock up with Durano bounty: olives, preserved apricots and beetroot, wines from Le Marche and homemade passata – an Italian summer in a bottle. *Minimum stay two nights, three nights in July/August.*

Rooms	7 doubles: €90-€110. Singles €50-€60. Dinner, B&B €80-€85 p.p.
Meals	Dinner with wine, €38.
Closed	Rarely.

Maria Concetta Furnari
Agriturismo Contrada Durano,
Contrada Durano,
63856 Smerillo
Tel +39 0734 786012
Email info@contradadurano.it
Web www.contradadurano.it

Villa Marziali

It takes a while to wind your way up to the village Montefalcone... once there, you are rewarded with a view that reaches to the Sibillini mountains. And there's a similar panorama from the villa that lies just beyond. It's mesmerizing at all hours, even at night when you can see Montefalcone's church illuminated through the trees. The British owners, who fell in love with the area many years ago, totally renovated this turn-of-the-century house; now it gleams inside and out. The old wine-making cellars have become open-plan living spaces, well-equipped and cool (the kitchen has two sinks, two ovens, two fridges), and the en-suite bedrooms are spread over two floors above. Original tiles are berugged, antiques are from the area and match the period of the house, and the elegant master bedroom has a fine decorative ceiling. You can stroll to the village for coffee and brioche, do the serious shopping in Comunanza, bask on the sands at San Benedetto, or hike in the mountains. Pick your own aubergines, cherries and figs, listen to the fountain play, fire up the barbecue, take a splash in the delicious long pool. *Minimum stay seven nights in high season.*

Rooms	1 house for 12: £2,250–£3,600 per wk. Sofabed available.
Meals	Restaurants nearby.
Closed	Rarely.

Clare Robertson–McIsaac
Villa Marziali,
63855 Montefalcone Appenino

Tel	+44 (0)191 212 1234
Email	clare.robertson-mcisaac@rmib.co.uk
Web	www.marziali.co.uk

Casa San Ruffino

In a land that venerates the 'bella figura', Claire and Ray Gorman, transplants from London, keep their rural B&B running on perfectly oiled wheels and a huge dose of style. The four smart guest rooms in their recently renovated 19th-century farmhouse are decorated in neutral tones in sympathy with clean white walls, beamed ceilings and beautiful old terracotta floors. Beds with crisp white linen, neatly folded fuzzy blankets and four lush pillows will cradle you to sleep, while pinch-me views from sparkling French windows will welcome you in the morning. Plan your day over homemade breads and cakes in the neat, chic breakfast room or outside at your own little garden table. The medieval towns of Montegiorgio and Fermo, and the Adriatic beaches, are a short drive. If, however, you can't tear yourself away from this glorious country spot, trot down the gravel path, past sweet-smelling lavender and perfectly potted lemon trees, to the pool, and take your fill of the rolling vineyard hills, the silvery olive groves and the distant snow-capped mountains. Who would not fall in love with this place? *Children over 14 welcome.*

Rooms	4 doubles: €140–€150.
Meals	Restaurants 3km.
Closed	1 November to 31 March.

Ray & Claire Gorman
Casa San Ruffino,
Contrada Montese 13,
63833 Montegiorgio
Tel   +39 0734 962753
Email   info@casasanruffino.com
Web   www.casasanruffino.com

Vento di Rose B&B

House, orchards, breakfasts, roses, owners... in the foothills of Monterubbiano, ten minutes from the sea, these all add up to unexpected treasure. Your gentle, happy, delightful hosts, with a little English between them, fill the house with artistic flourishes and love doing B&B. Emanuela's sunny personality infuses everything and on the first night Emidio will take you to a local restaurant to see you don't get lost. The kitchen/breakfast room, authentically Italian, is all blues and creams, its lace tablecloth strewn with rose petals then laden with garden cherries, peaches, pears, fresh frittata of artichokes, mulberry fruit tarts, warm bread from Moresco – a different treat every day. Too much? Borrow a picnic basket and take some for lunch. Shady bowers are scented with roses, honeysuckle and jasmine; views are long; pillows carry sprigs of lavender at night. Bright airy bedrooms, each with a sitting area, have pale colourwashed walls and embroidered linen; and you're welcome to share the *salone*. A paradise of peace, hospitality and blissful breakfasts.

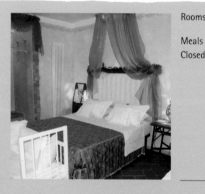

Rooms	1 double; 2 family rooms for 2-4: €90–€100.
Meals	Picnic available. Restaurants 3km.
Closed	January-February.

Emidio di Ruscio
Vento di Rose B&B, Via Canniccio 7
(Via Pozzetto), 63026 Monterubbiano

Tel	+39 0734 59226
Mobile	+39 348 7761166
Email	ventodirose@libero.it
Web	www.ventodirose.it

Agriturismo Ramuse

Sign up on a blackboard if you're staying for dinner – and why wouldn't you when the menu is so tempting? Everything here is produced locally or on the farm (including Mama's plum jam); Paolo's enthusiasm for his venture is intoxicating. He once used to nip between Italy and London with a precious cargo of truffles for top chefs – and some of those chefs have stayed here: *Gennaro's Contaldo's Italian Year* features a Ramuse recipe. Since then, he's been busy restoring his grandparents' old farm and creating this rustic haven. Find traditional interiors, stepped vine-clad terraces, nesting boxes for birds and a beautiful oval pool. Bedrooms are warm and cosy with beamed ceilings, beds are in keeping with the country style, and there's rosy brick flooring throughout. A summer day spent lolling in hammocks by the stream – raising yourself for the odd game of badminton – would be sublime! As would a foraging visit in autumn or winter… and coming home to sausages cooking over the dining room fire. If you can tear yourself away, the Sibillini mountains and the Adriatic coast are close. Slow heaven. *Minimum stay three nights.*

Rooms	2 twin/doubles: €60–€90.
	2 apartments for 4–6:
	€980–€1,190 per week.
	For 2: €560–€1,190 per week
	(Saturday–Saturday).
Meals	Dinner by arrangement, €18.
	Wine €8–€20. Restaurant 6km.
Closed	12 November to February.

Paolo Ciccioli
Agriturismo Ramuse,
Loc. Casette 3,
63045 Force

Mobile	+39 328 6291859
Email	agriturismoramuse@gmail.com
Web	www.ramuse.it

Dimora del Prete di Belmonte

The old palace hides among the cobbled streets of the medieval centre – a gem once you step inside. Venafro, a Roman town, lies in the lovely valley of Monte Santa Croce, ringed by mountains. The first thrill is the enchanting internal garden with its lush banana palms and citrus trees, where a miscellany of Roman artefacts and olive presses lie scattered among tables and chairs. Next, a frescoed interior in an astonishing state of preservation; painted birds, family crests and *grotteschi* adorn the walls of the state rooms and entrance hall. Bedrooms are furnished in simple good taste, one with a big fireplace and a sleigh bed, another with chestnut country furniture, most with views. Shower rooms are small – bar one, which has a bath. Dorothy is a wonderful hostess and has fantastic local knowledge; she and her son are a great team. They also run an organic farm with 1,000 olive trees (many of them over 400 years old), vines, walnut-trees and sheep. An area and a palace rich in content – and relaxed, delicious dinners do full justice to the setting. Breakfasts are as good.

Rooms	5 doubles; 1 family room for 2 (1 double, 2 single sofabeds); 1 apartment for 2-4: €100. Singles €80. Extra person €30. Apartment €500 per week (€200 for weekend).
Meals	Breakfast €10 for self-caterers. Lunch/dinner with wine, €30.
Closed	Never.

Dorothy Volpe del Prete
Dimora del Prete di Belmonte,
Via Cristo 49, 86079 Venafro

Tel	+39 0865 900159
Email	info@dimoradelprete.it
Web	www.dimoradelprete.it

Lazio

Agriturismo Pulicaro

Free-ranging animals, a bountiful veg garden, fruit trees and 2,000 olives: it's easy to share Chiara and Marco's enthusiasm for their 24-acre organic farm. Solar panels heat water and generate electricity, grey water is collected and soon there will be a space for cookery and yoga courses. The stunning brick and stone house, parts of which date back to Barbarossa's time, now has simple self-catering apartments – one in the oldest part of the house with a garden view, another with a stunning stone vaulted ceiling – and equally unfussy B&B rooms with super comfy mattresses, tiled floors and beamed ceilings. Generous buffet breakfasts, laid out on gingham tablecloths, include homemade breads and jams, local organic meats and cheeses. Dinner is a convivial affair: guests mingle; your hosts sit down and chat. Afterwards you can unwind in an elegant sitting room in front of a big open fire. Head out to discover Etruscan tombs, glide above the Alfina plateau; boat on Lake Bolsena; or stay put, pick fruit and turn it into ice cream with help from Chiara's father who was a master ice cream maker.

Rooms	2 doubles; 2 twin/doubles: €60–€85. 2 apartments for 2-5 (extra beds available): €65–€160. Singles €55–€70.
Meals	Dinner available.
Closed	Rarely.

Chiara & Arianna
Agriturismo Pulicaro, Azienda Agricola
Pulicaro, 01021 Torre Alfina
Tel   +39 0763 716757
Mobile   +39 329 9512418
Email   info@pulicaro.it
Web   www.pulicaro.it

Casa Corona

Step back in time to the sleepy village of Castel Cellesi, and this adorable little house. It sits on the main square, pretty in pale blue, with a climbing red rose and a bench out front from which you can catch the last of the sun's rays. And chat with your neighbours; next door lives the owner, warm, elegant Tellervo. Inside find a fresh blue and white kitchen/dining room, and a sitting room beyond a charming sliding screen: an inviting cream sofa, rugs, lamps, and a secret little jasmine-scented terrace. Upstairs is the cosy bedroom – roses on the bedspread, pink swags – and a second sitting room in white and blue, with a big comfy sofabed and painted beams, and a terrace with a boldly striped canopy. Little shower rooms, one up, one down, are spotless and bright. There's a conglomerate of seven restored houses in this village, sharing a lovingly tended garden, with a swish pavilion for drinks (and meals) and a splendid pool on the lawns. This may be off the beaten track but you're close to Renaissance gardens, Etruscan sites and the largest volcanic lake in Europe, for blissful swims in crystalline waters. *Minimum three nights.*

Rooms	1 house for 2-4: €120; €910 per week. Sofabed available.
Meals	Restaurants 8km.
Closed	Rarely.

Tellervo Puuri
Casa Corona,
Piazza della Repubblica 14,
01022 Castel Cellesi

Tel   +39 0761 790323
Email   tellyitaly@libero.it
Web   www.italianvacationvillage.com

Casa Amorosa

Wind through high rolling countryside – with far-reaching views – to the end of the road and a village set in time. Castel Cellesi (two piazzas, a parish church, a post office, an *alimentari*, a bar) is home to a tiny conglomerate of restored houses of which Amorosa is one. All share a manicured lawned garden of fruit trees, roses and lavender, a swish pavilion for drinks (and meals: a lady cook can be arranged) and a splendid pool. Casa Amorosa, down a cul de sac behind the main square, is a spotless former farmer's house, whose stone steps and dark ceiling beams remain. Walk in off the street to a sitting/dining/kitchen area that feels traditional, welcoming and homely: lace curtains at windows, a sofa patterned with roses, a pendant lamp in old-fashioned style. The kitchen is country-simple and well-equipped, there's a 'cave' below and bedrooms above, one opening to a bright canopied terrace, the other to a balcony with views. The charming Finnish owner will tell you of Renaissance gardens and Etruscan sites to visit, and can arrange shiatsu and massage to come to the house. *Minimum stay three nights.*

Rooms	1 house for 4: €150; €1,040 per week.
Meals	Restaurant 8km.
Closed	Rarely.

Tellervo Puuri
Casa Amorosa,
Piazza della Repubblica 14,
01022 Castel Cellesi

Tel	+39 0761 790323
Email	tellyitaly@libero.it
Web	www.italianvacationvillage.com

Relais Villa La Trinità

A short drive from Rome on the ancient Roman road, beyond towering cypresses and pines, is a stately villa built in 1889, surrounded by gardens of lavender and roses. The Lazzè family from Rome have restored it to perfection and now its three floors shine. With living rooms, studies and six bedrooms it's a big generous house for a two-family holiday or a special occasion. Enter to find a lofty beamed sitting room with great big sofas and a sober stone fireplace, a dining room that seats 14, a breakfast room for ten, a cosy study, a large bathroom and a big Italian country kitchen ideal for cookery demonstrations (yes, they hold them). Sweep up the travertine staircase to bedrooms with brick floors, beamed ceilings, fine fabrics and elegant antiques. Bathrooms too are individually styled, with marble basins and stencilled corners, and there's a great cellar for entertainments. Midway between Lakes Vico and Bracciano, the area is the heart of Etruscan civilization, so don't miss the amazing frescoes of Cerveteri and Tarquinia. Come home to a dip in the pool.

Rooms	1 house for 10: €3,500–€6,500 per wk. B&B €120–€180 per night.
Meals	Restaurants nearby.
Closed	15-28 February & 1 November to 15 December.

Michela Lazzè
Relais Villa La Trinità,
Località La Trinità,
01012 Capranica
Mobile   +39 329 7196711
Email   info@villalatrinita.com
Web   www.villalatrinita.com

Lazio

B&B

La Torretta

Casperia is a joyful, characterful, car-free maze of steepish streets in the Sabine hills. La Torretta has the dreamiest views from its terrace, and easy interior spaces that have been wonderfully designed by architect Roberto. A huge ground-floor sitting room with beautiful frescoes around the cornicing welcomes you… an old stone fireplace, modern sofas and chairs, books, paintings, piano. The upper room – opening onto that terrace – is a stunning, vaulted, contemporary space with an open stainless-steel kitchen and views through skylights to the church tower and valley. Maureen, warm-hearted and hospitable, is passionate about the region and its food. She arranges cookery courses and will cook (on request) using the best olive oil and whatever is in season – mushrooms, truffles, wild boar. Whitewashed, high-ceilinged bedrooms are charming in their simplicity; beds are made and towels changed regularly; bathrooms are a treat. Don't worry about having to leave your car in the square below the town: Roberto has a buggy for luggage. Fine breakfasts, too – among the best in Italy!

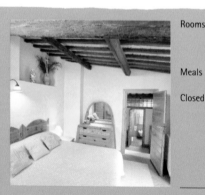

Rooms	5 doubles: €90. 1 family room for 4 (1 family room with 2 connecting rooms): €150. 1 single: €70.
Meals	Dinner with wine, €30, by arrangement. Restaurant 100m.
Closed	Rarely.

Roberto & Maureen Scheda
La Torretta,
Via G. Mazzini 7, 02041 Casperia

Tel	+39 0765 63202
Mobile	+39 338 1451859
Email	latorretta@tiscali.it
Web	www.latorrettabandb.com

Azienda Agrituristica Sant'Ilario sul Farfa

Friendly, for families, no frills. Half an hour by train from Rome (an hour by car) so here you can combine city culture with a rural retreat. The little farm sits high on one of the steeply terraced hills above the river Farfa: the views are incredible. The approach along a steep tarmac track is marked by that typically Italian juxtaposition of swish modern gates and an olive tree of great antiquity. Susanna is a creative hostess whose dinners – delivered on request from organic farm produce – are brilliant value. Bedrooms in two ranch-like single-storey farm buildings, white with wooden shutters, are snug and wood-panelled with some fine antique bedheads, white walls and showers. The three apartments in the main house have small kitchens – great for families. A pleasing tangle of trellises extends across the farmyard garden. Take a dip in the pool or the river, knock a ball around the football pitch or court (tennis 100m), Visit nearby medieval villages, book into yoga or an olive or grape harvesting weekend. There are painting classes for grown-ups, cookery and craft classes for children. So much to do!

Rooms	4 doubles; 2 family rooms for 4: €80.
	Dinner, B&B €55–€60 p.p.
	1 apartment for 3, 1 apartment for 4;
	1 apartment for 5-6: €480–€880 per wk.
Meals	Dinner with wine, €25.
Closed	Rarely.

Susanna Serafini
Azienda Agrituristica Sant'Ilario sul Farfa
Via Sant'Ilario,
02030 Poggio Nativo
Tel +39 0765 872410
Email info@santilariosulfarfa.it
Web www.santilariosulfarfa.it

Dependence Luca

Past the lake, through olive and hazelnut groves, up the track into undulating farmland… and there is the house above, in splendid isolation 30 minutes from Rome. Built 20 years ago for the National Park, it is weathered and softened by jasmine and wisteria. The Dependence is all yours and it connects to a delightful overspill Studio. Inside is light, bright, spacious and beautiful, with a stylish Nordic feel and luscious Indian touches. Living areas are upstairs, cocoon-like bedrooms are below, opening to a long brick-paved loggia and gardens with a cushioned pergola (dine under the stars), a divine pool and a gentle view of lake and hills. The main bathroom is clad in green mosaics, towels spill from baskets, rich curtains sweep the floors. Upstairs: a light-filled space of high-pitched ceilings, big square windows, a red rug on a black floor, L-shaped seating, book-filled niches, a vast rustic table, a stunning open-plan kitchen. As for Trevignano Romano, it's awash with pretty restaurants so choose a table by the lake and toast your good fortune.

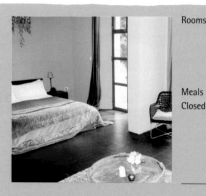

Rooms	1 house for 10 (3 doubles, 2 sofabeds): €1,695–€1,995 per week. Studio annexe for 4 (1 double, 1 sofabed): €795 per week. Studio not let independently. Cots available.
Meals	Restaurants 3km.
Closed	Rarely.

Stina Boman
Dependence Luca,
Via Fonte Termini 9,
00069 Trevignano Romano

Tel	+46 767 129864
Mobile	+39 342 3747740
Email	stina@wittich.se

Hotel

Relais Teatro Argentina

Five-star service with family charm and the elegance of a vintage palazzo – the best of all worlds in central Rome. This boutique hotel, run by gentle Paolo and his niece Carlotta, is steps from Largo Argentina's ruined temples and the spot where Julius Caesar met his fate, an easy walk from the Campo dei Fiori fruit and veg market, the glorious Pantheon and Rome's backstreet art galleries. Ring the bell at the imposing doorway and ascend the pale marble stairs to the warm red reception. Gilt-framed mirrors and chandeliers give a taste of what's to come in palatial bedrooms: wallpapers of pale green willow or rose-pink, king-size beds and parquet floors, antique tables, long draped curtains and gleaming windows. Bathrooms are shiny-new and modern. All is refined and restful, a grand hideaway for a special stay. Fresh pastries, fruit and Italian coffee arrive on a breakfast trolley; no bar/lounge, but you can take a drink out to the little terrace overlooking Rome's rooftops. Paolo and Carlotta are like your personal concierges (but much more friendly!), arranging transport, guides, opera tickets and more.

Rooms	1 double; 3 twin/doubles; 2 triples: €143–€265.
Meals	Restaurants nearby.
Closed	Rarely.

Paolo & Carlotta Fè d'Ostiani
Relais Teatro Argentina,
Via del Sudario 35, 00186 Rome

Tel	+39 0698 931617
Mobile	+39 331 1984708
Email	info@relaisteatroargentina.com
Web	www.relaisteatroargentina.com

Entry 340   Map 12

My Navona

Beware the urge to stay for weeks! Visit Rome's highlights then return to lose yourself in the thrub of fascinating, twisting streets of this colourful, characterful neighbourhood: Via dei Coronari, Piazza Navona, Via del Governo Vecchio. The best view from this peachy, classic 18th-century palazzo is from the smallest room facing the beautiful Bramante church. Your gracious, knowledgeable hosts (interior designer and architect – obviously!) couldn't be more helpful. Their third-floor guest rooms are in two adjacent apartments, each with a foyer sitting area. One is more contemporary with stripped doors, framed black and white photographs and architectural drawings, brown suede and grey flannel headboards, modern lighting, light grey walls. The other has teal blue walls, period paintings, antiques on parquet floors, gorgeous fabrics for curtains, bedspreads and cushions. Bathrooms are designer modern with grey glass mosaics and locally made soaps. You breakfast royally in your room, on a large trolley with porcelain cups, cake, toast, homemade jams, yogurt and cereal. A real Roman treat of a place.

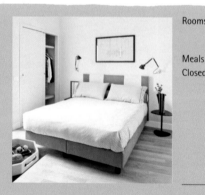

Rooms	4 doubles: €100–€250.
	1 suite for 2-3: €130–€205.
	Singles €80–€170.
Meals	Restaurants nearby.
Closed	Rarely.

Alessandra Bruti Liberati
My Navona,
Via Tor Millina 35,
00186 Rome

Mobile	+39 334 6034288 / +39 345 8525339
Email	mynavona@gmail.com
Web	www.mynavona.com

Casa Trevi I & II

A hop, skip and a jump from the world's most famous fountain, the Casa Trevi is a treasure. Find yourself in an astonishingly peaceful courtyard, all olive trees, scented oranges and a fountain inhabited by small turtles. Though you're in Rome's most vibrant heart, not a sound penetrates from outside. The apartments are on the ground floor of one of the old buildings and open directly off the courtyard. Interiors are bright, soothing and minimalist in the most beautiful way: white walls and terracotta, glass shelving and concealed lighting, a mix of modern and brocante finds. There are no windows as such but the double glass-paned doors let in plenty of light. Hobs and fridges are provided in the airy, white kitchens, but serious cooking is not catered for (who wants to eat-in in Rome?). Shower rooms are gorgeous. On three sides are 17th-century buildings in yellows, ochres and reds; on the fourth, a modern monstrosity. Marta could not be sweeter, and the security – a big plus – is excellent, with a porter and security camera in the main entrance. Good value for central Rome.

Rooms	2 apartments for 2: €840–€1,400 per week. Sofabeds available.
Meals	Restaurants nearby.
Closed	Rarely.

Marta Nicolini
Casa Trevi I & II,
Via in Arcione 98,
00187 Rome
Mobile +39 335 6205768
Email info@casatrevi.it
Web www.casatrevi.it

Casa Trevi III

This, too, is five minutes from the Trevi Fountain – most breathtaking by night – but in a separate street from Casas Trevi I and II. Marta – full of warmth, a busy bee – has waved her stylish wand again and created a deeply desirable place to stay. She employed one of the top restoration experts in Rome to make ceiling beams glow and terracotta floors gleam – and the result? Old Rome meets new. Up a tiny lift to the third floor and into an open-plan sitting, dining and kitchen area – black, white, grey, chic, with a polished wooden floor. A discarded shutter for a frame, an antique door for a bedhead, air con to keep you cool, double glazing to ensure quiet. The white-raftered twin and double rooms share a sparkling, 21st-century shower in beige marble. Modigliani prints beautify cream walls, mirrored doors reflect the light, silk cushions sprinkle the sofa and shutters are painted dove-grey. Never mind the tourists and the street vendors, Rome lies at your feet. And you have the unassuming Trattoria della Stampa, where the locals go, in the very same street.

Rooms	1 apartment for 4: €980–€1,400 per week. Sofabed available.
Meals	Restaurants nearby.
Closed	Never.

Marta Nicolini
Casa Trevi III,
Via dei Maroniti 7,
00187 Rome

Mobile	+39 335 6205768
Email	info@casatrevi.it
Web	www.casatrevi.it

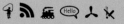

Hotel Modigliani

There's a sense of anticipation the moment you enter the marble hall, with its deep, pale sofas and fresh flowers – Marco's wide smile and infectious enthusiasm reinforce the feeling. This is an unusual, delightful place, hidden down a side street just five minutes' walk from the Spanish Steps and Via Veneto. The house belonged to Marco's father, and Marco and Giulia (he a writer, she a musician) have turned it into the perfect small hotel. Marble floors and white walls are a dramatic setting for black-and-white photos taken by Marco, their starkness softened by luxuriant plants. The bread oven of the 1700s has become a dining room – all vaulted ceilings, whitewashed walls, cherrywood tables, fabulous photos. Bedrooms are fresh and elegant; some have balconies and wonderful views, all have small, perfect bathrooms. There's a lovely new sitting room and bar for guests to use. The whole place has a sweet, stylish air, it's unusually quiet for the centre of the city and there's a patio scented with jasmine. Marco and Giulia will tell you about Rome's secret corners – or grab a copy of Marco's new guide and discover Rome for yourselves.

Rooms	20 twin/doubles: €90–€205.
	2 suites for 2: €208–€340.
	1 family room for 4–6: €330–€440.
	1 apartment for 6; 1 apartment for 3: €200–€250.
Meals	Restaurant 10m.
Closed	Never.

Giulia & Marco di Tillo
Hotel Modigliani,
Via della Purificazione 42,
00187 Rome

Tel	+39 0642 815226
Email	info@hotelmodigliani.com
Web	www.hotelmodigliani.com

Entry 344   Map 12

66 Imperial Inn

Gracious owner Francesca is on hand in the mornings; three others are around all day long, manning the desk and helping you with itineraries, tickets, transfers and all things Roman: the service here is second to none. This peach-coloured, turn-of-the-century building is a ten-minute walk from the Termini Station so the location is hard to beat. Up the stairs – or tiny antique elevator – to the fourth floor to discover Francesca has a passion for decoration. Brightly hued papers decorate bedroom walls in harmony with oriental cushions and runners, while vintage bedside tables are brought to life with colourful touches. Three bedrooms face the Via del Viminale (ask for these if you need WiFi), two are at the back, and the triples are on the floor below. All have deliciously comfortable beds, immaculate hydro-jet showers and double paned windows to banish street noise. Help yourself to a good continental breakfast (at smart glass-topped tables or in your room), then set off for the ancient Forum and Colosseum, the contemporary Teatro dell'Opera or the super cool Monti quarter right next door.

Rooms	3 doubles: €79–€155.
	3 triples: €109–€175.
	1 quadruple: €139–€199.
	Singles €79–€155.
Meals	Restaurants nearby.
Closed	Never.

Francesca Adilardi
66 Imperial Inn,
Via del Viminale 66,
00184 Rome
Tel +39 0648 25648
Email info@66imperialinn.com
Web www.66imperialinn.com

B&B di Piazza Vittorio

A marquis built this Cuban-style palazzo in the 1880s and Alessandra's fifth-floor B&B retains its noble sense of style. A former journalist, she has turned her energy and enthusiasm to this spacious, airy apartment, where light floods through large windows and family antiques rest on pale wooden floors. All is classic, calm, cool, and white predominates. 'Suite G' has two romantic rooms linked by an arched doorway, one with a sofabed, desk and windows catching the morning sun over via Machiavelli. 'Koko' has shelves of travel books, chess, family mementoes. Single travellers like 'Magnolia' with its French double bed and antique desk; it shares a bathroom with Alessandra. She'll bring continental breakfast to your door or serve up in the modern little kitchen and, if you wish, wrap a lunch panini for later. Best is the position, in cosmopolitan Esquilino on the highest hill in Rome. You're 500 metres from the Colosseum and a few steps from humming Piazza Vittorio for restaurants and delis. Alessandra is a mine of information and quirky ideas, from a city tour in a classic convertible to a trip down the Tiber. *Minimum stay two nights.*

Rooms	1 twin/double: €105–€175.
	1 suite for 2-4: €126–€206
	1 suite for 3: €158–€258
	1 suite for 4: €125–€250.
	1 single with shared bathroom: €85–€140.
	Extra bed/sofabed €20–€30.
Meals	Packed lunch available on request. Restaurants nearby.
Closed	Rarely.

Alessandra Daveri
B&B di Piazza Vittorio,
Via Machiavelli 60, 00185 Rome

Tel	+39 0645 502561
Mobile	+39 340 8605321
Email	info@bebdipiazzavittorio.com
Web	www.bebdipiazzavittorio.com

Caesar House Romane

A calm, comfortable and welcoming oasis above the Roman din. The Forum can be glimpsed from one window, elegant cafés, shops and restaurants lie below, the Colosseum is a five-minute stroll. Take the lift to the second floor of the ancient palazzo, where grand reception doors open to a bright welcoming space. Charming, stylish sisters Giulia and Simona run things together with the help of their mother: a family affair. Bedrooms, named after celebrated *italiani*, have warm-red floors, heavy curtains in maroon or blue, matching sofas and quilted covers, a choice of blankets or duvets, vestibules to keep luggage out of the way and every modern thing: air con, minibar, internet, safe, satellite TV. You breakfast in your room – it's big enough – or in the pretty dining room with its tables draped in cream linen and modern art dotted here and there. There's even a gym for those who have surplus energy after a day's sightseeing among the city's ancient ruins. The service here is exemplary – maps, guided tours, airport pick up, babysitting, theatre booking, bike hire. It's thoroughly professional, and personal too.

Rooms	4 doubles; 2 twins: €120–€230. Singles €100–€200. Extra bed €20.
Meals	Restaurants nearby.
Closed	Never.

Giulia & Simona Barela
Caesar House Romane,
Via Cavour 310,
00184 Rome

Tel	+39 0667 92674
Email	info@caesarhouse.com
Web	www.caesarhouse.com

  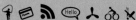

Villa Giulia Suites

Up and away from bustling bars and hooting vespas, this is peaceful: the odd car passing, the odd screech from a free-ranging parrot! On one of the Eternal City's seven hills: fresh air and pretty buildings, cobbles and umbrella pines, and fabulous views across the rooftops of Rome. Enter a large palazzo dating back to the 1940s, trip down a short flight of stairs, step into a small light lobby off which three apartments lie. 'Rosso' is the largest, 'Verde' the smallest and 'Marrone' is the one with the bath. 'Marrone' also connects with 'Verde' through a bookshelf/door in the dressing room… Each is stylish and modern, bright and inviting: a window seat here, a carved headboard there, elegant little kitchens and thick luxurious curtains. Best of all, each apartment has its own pretty outside seating area just below the big spreading garden; there's a gazebo for aperitivi, a proper barbecue, a veg plot from which you can choose herbs. The delightful Mila settles you in, then it's off to discover Testaccio, Trastevere, the Colosseum – and, round the corner, Gregorian chant in the Church of Sant'Anselmo all'Aventino.

Rooms	3 apartments for 2: €980–€1,680 per week. Sofabed available.
Meals	Self-catering.
Closed	Rarely.

Anna Passi
Villa Giulia Suites,
Via Marcella 2, 00153 Rome

Tel	+39 0721 823159
Mobile	+39 347 0823935
Email	info@relaisvillagiulia.com
Web	www.villagiuliaroma.com

Guest House Arco de' Tolomei

Up the sweep of the dark communal wooden staircase into another world, a fascinating little B&B in the peaceful old Jewish quarter of Trastevere. The house has been in Marco's family for 200 years and those sedate gentlemen on the blue walls are the previous inhabitants. Marco and his wife Gianna, great travellers and anglophiles, have filled the family home with bits and pieces from their journeys abroad. Floor to ceiling shelves heave under the weight of books in the red drawing room, gorgeous pieces of art and sculpture beautify walls and tables, and floors are laid with exquisite parquet; there's plenty of dark wood and every square inch gleams. The convivial oval dining table awaits guests eager to sample Gianna's lavish breakfasts. Bedrooms, reached through a guest sitting room, have bold flowers or pinstripes on the walls, a backdrop to handsome bedsteads and great little bathrooms, while the best have miniature staircases up to private terraces with views that roll over Trastevere's terracotta roofs and fascinating web of streets below.

Rooms	3 twin/doubles: €140-€205. 3 triples: €165-€230. Singles €125-€180.
Meals	Restaurants 50m.
Closed	Never.

Marco Fè d'Ostiani
Guest House Arco de' Tolomei,
Via dell'Arco de' Tolomei 27,
00153 Rome

Tel	+39 0658 320819
Email	info@bbarcodeitolomei.com
Web	www.bbarcodeitolomei.com

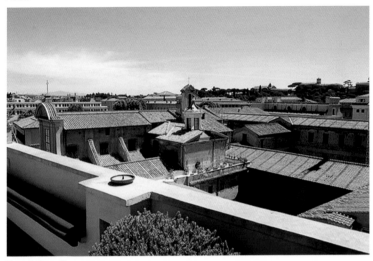

Hotel San Francesco

Trastevere – Rome's stylish and bohemian quarter – is at its best on a sleepy Sunday morning when the flea market unfurls and the smell of spicy *porchetta* infuses the air. But first, enjoy a generous Italian breakfast (forget about toast, indulge in cakes), served by ever-friendly staff in a long, light room that overlooks a 15th-century cloister complete with friar, garden and hens... Built in 1926 as a training school for missionaries, this young hotel runs on well-oiled wheels. There's a black and white tiled sitting room with black leather armchairs, big white lilies and a piano, and a stylishly furnished roof garden with canvas parasols and views to the Vatican; gorgeous by day, ravishing by night. Marble stairs lead to carpeted corridors off which feed small, comfortable bedrooms – lined curtains at double-glazed windows, fabulous bathrooms, garden views at the back. Pop into the Santa Cecilia next door for a peep at Bellini's Madonna, stroll to the sights across the river, rent a bike. Not truly central – you'll be using the odd taxi – but a very pleasant springboard for discovering the city.

Rooms	24 doubles: €69–€310.
Meals	Restaurants nearby.
Closed	Never.

Daniele Frontoni
Hotel San Francesco,
Via Jacopa de' Settesoli 7,
00153 Rome

Tel	+39 0658 300051
Email	info@hotelsanfrancesco.net
Web	www.hotelsanfrancesco.net

Kimama

On a tree-lined street on the edge of atmospheric Trastevere is a cheerful, cosy and practical place for visiting Rome – with queen-bedded rooms for couples and a small apartment that works for families. Raffaella speaks English and is a warm, enthusiastic host. The first floor (with lift) of this handsome five-storey building was once her home and she sees that everything runs like clockwork, from good things for breakfast popped in fridges each morning to WiFi, air con and satellite TV. The marble-floored green B&B room is the more spacious, with a street-facing window and a small shower room, while the orange room has wooden floors, a window onto the quiet internal courtyard and a bigger bathroom, in travertine with a tub. The large-windowed apartment also overlooks the street and has a decent-sized, well-equipped kitchen. There's a colourful, cobble-streeted open-air food market just around the corner, shops, restaurants and bars aplenty – but you're set back from the hubbub. You can walk to many sights and there is good transport to others. Book that city break now!

Rooms	2 doubles: €75–€110.
	1 apartment for 3: €100–€160.
	Singles €60–€95.
Meals	Restaurants nearby.
Closed	Never.

Raffaella Benvenuto
Kimama,
Via Emilio Morosini 18,
00153 Rome
Mobile +39 339 3858509
Email kimamabb@gmail.com
Web www.kimama.it

Hotel Santa Maria

Breakfast is a feast, fittingly for Trastevere – a neighbourhood of Rome renowned for its trattorias and outdoor eateries. In warm weather you can eat under the orange trees in a quiet central courtyard, in winter by a roaring fire under the arch of an ancient artisan's workshop. Each evening, this space transforms into a private bar where regional wines and finger foods are served – a great place to meet other guests and chat with utterly delightful owners, Paolo and Valentina, and their team of staff. Ground level bedrooms and family suites wrap around the courtyard, shielded somewhat from Rome's bustle and with most opening directly out to a wooden portico. A sunny, natural feel pervades, with yellow walls, pretty stencilling and street scenes by a local artist on the wall. Up on the roof, a sun deck dotted with umbrellas and chairs. You're a block from Santa Maria square with its ancient church. Bring comfy walking shoes or borrow a free bike: you can cross the bridge for Campo de' Fiori, turn right for the Forum and Colosseum, and follow the Tiber north to St Peter's and the Vatican. *Children under three free.*

Rooms	9 doubles: €99–€230.
	4 triples: €149–€280.
	1 quadruple: €179–€310.
	1 suite for 6; 4 suites for 4: €229–€460.
	Cot available.
Meals	Restaurants nearby.
Closed	Never.

Paolo Vetere
Hotel Santa Maria,
Vicolo del Piede 2, 00153 Rome

Tel	+39 0658 94626
Email	info@hotelsantamaria.info
Web	www.hotelsantamaria.info

Buonanotte Garibaldi

Cross the Tiber into maze-like Trastevere. Turn right for boisterous bars, left for cobblestoned tranquillity. Here lies a place that is small and special – an artistic find behind solid green doors. Fashion and textiles designer Luisa, as welcoming as can be, has transformed her studio and home into a vibrant three-bedroom B&B. Built around a beautiful sun-dappled courtyard, it is a showcase for her creations. Two bedrooms, Orange and Green, are on the ground floor opening to the courtyard (orange trees and magnolias, a marvel in spring) while the Rome room is above with its own big terrace, heaven for honeymooners. Walls are clean and minimalist, bathrooms mosaic'd and sparkling; splashes of colour come from hand-painted organza. Yours to retire to – a winter treat – is a salon with stylish settees and books on art and Rome. Charming staff, friendly and discreet, serve breakfast at an oval dining table surrounded by silk panels: fresh fruits, breads, meats, eggs how you like them, lavender shortbread, baked peaches; a wonder. All this in Rome's old heart – and Luisa's lovable dog, Tinto.

Rooms	3 twin/doubles: €180–€280.
Meals	Restaurants within walking distance.
Closed	2 January to 15 February & 15 August to 31 August.

Luisa Longo
Buonanotte Garibaldi,
Via Garibaldi 83, 00153 Rome

Tel	+39 0658 330733
Email	info@buonanottegaribaldi.com
Web	www.buonanottegaribaldi.com

Casa in Trastevere N.2

Wend your way through Trastevere's buzzing streets, past old palazzi to a quiet alley leading to the Aurelian walls of Rome. Just before the ancient stone, spy a more modern – 15th-century! – rose-clad building. Fold back the wooden doors with a whoosh to the 21st century: a swooping space of white and glass, lofty beams and brick. All is light and city-chic, from sisal mats on shiny floors to modern lights illuminating violet sofabeds and Marta's abstract photos. Behind thick glass, a pristine kitchen. Bedrooms contrast bright white walls with streaks of brick; peep out over pretty window boxes to a convent. The all-white bathroom is just as modern, with a rectangular sink, mosaic shower and glinting spotlights. Trastevere hums with life: organic food shops, trendy boutiques, bars and restaurants – but its shady squares are far from touristy and you may find yourself chatting with locals over an aperitivo. Peek into the (very) old church of Santa Maria, or that of Cecilia, patron saint of musicians. Warm, cultured Marta will tell you of local events. The Vatican is a 20-minute walk – and then there's all of Rome. *Minimum stay four nights.* .

Rooms	4 apartments for 4-6: €150-€200; €1,050-€1,400 per week. Sofabed available.
Meals	Restaurants nearby.
Closed	Never.

Marta Nicolini
Casa in Trastevere N.2,
Vicolo Moroni 12, 00165 Rome

Mobile	+39 335 6205768
Email	info@casatrevi.it
Web	www.casaintrastevere.it

Casa in Trastevere

If you're independent souls, fortunate enough to be planning more than a fleeting trip to Rome, this apartment is a great base, a ten-minute walk from the old quarter of Trastevere. The area, though residential, has a great buzz at night and the shops, bars and restaurants are a treat to discover. Signora Nicolini, once a specialist restorer, has furnished this sunny first-floor flat as if it were her own home. She has kept the original 19th-century red and black terrazzo floor and has added contemporary touches: a cream sofa, an all-white kitchen (no microwave or oven, but you won't mind, with so many tempting restaurants on your doorstep), kilims and modern art. You have a large open-plan living/dining room with screened kitchen, a double and a twin bedroom, each with a white bathroom, and an extra sofabed. All is fresh and bright, and the big bedroom is very charming with its hand-quilted bedspread. Marta is a delight and does her best to ensure you go home with happy memories. Put your feet up after a long day, pour yourself a glass of wine… then set off to explore some more of this magical city.

Rooms	1 apartment for 4-6: €1,050-€1,400 per week. Sofabed available.
Meals	Restaurants nearby.
Closed	Rarely.

Marta Nicolini
Casa in Trastevere,
Vicolo della Penitenza 19,
00165 Rome

Mobile	+39 335 6205768
Email	info@casatrevi.it
Web	www.casaintrastevere.it

B&B Cristiana

A fresh arty vibe sweeps through Flaminio, tucked in a fold of the Tiber as it meanders north of Rome. Steps from the concerts and contemporary art of Auditorium Parco della Musica and MAXXI, Cristiana's apartment exudes an unruffled peace. Hugging a rosy-stone courtyard of mosaics and magnolia, the apartment has a cool, contemporary air with parquet floors and big ceiling fans. There's a cosy kitchen where you're welcome to brew a quick cuppa and browse piles of books, and just two bedrooms, simple yet pristine with colourful fabrics and wood. Quirky caricatures of conductors leap over the white walls of 'Musica', while 'Foglia' lives up to its leafy name with pretty prints of plants and herbs. The latter harks back to Cristiana's profession as a herbalist. So expect unusual teas at breakfast, along with delicious home-baked treats. Pizzerias and bars buzz around Ponte Milvio, whose ancient stones are worn down by love padlocks. There are trams to Trastevere, buses to the Vatican, and a flea market to browse on Sundays. For anything else, Cristiana and Angela act as your personal concierges.

Rooms	2 doubles: €80-€100. Singles €70-€100.
Meals	Dinner available on request when same party is renting both rooms. Restaurants nearby.
Closed	Rarely.

Cristiana Ligi
B&B Cristiana,
Via Guglielmo Calderini 68,
00196 Rome
Mobile   +39 333 9392323
Email   bbcristiana@gmail.com
Web   www.bbcristiana.com

Quod Libet

Have breakfast in bed in this zany-bright B&B, high in a 19th-century palazzo near the Vatican. Gianluca and Consolata deliver a tray piled with eggs and fresh bread from the gorgeous-smelling bakery downstairs – and if you don't fancy crumbs in the sheets, each big bright double room has space for a table and chairs. Shiny-new bedrooms are themed by season – spring rose-pink, summery yellow, frosty blue-grey – and overlook a wide plane tree-lined viale leading to the river. Families will choose the chocolatey red of 'Autunno', with its sofabed, bath and windows over a quiet inner courtyard. Canvas paintings are by Gianluca, owner, artist and computer whizz; he and Consolata will share a welcome drink and tips on the best local markets, restaurants, nightlife. Best of all, it's a five-minute walk to Saint Peter's and the Vatican Museums, perfect for early tours before the crowds. Ottaviano-San Pietro metro station is a block away and you're a pleasant 30-minute stroll to most of Rome's delights. A superb addition to Rome's B&Bs: as fresh, bright and cheerful as its owners. *Parking €4 per day.*

Rooms	4 doubles: €70-€220.
	Singles €60-€100. Sofabed available.
Meals	Restaurants within walking distance.
Closed	Rarely.

Consolata Sodaro
Quod Libet,
Via Barletta 29, 00192 Rome
Mobile +39 347 3355160 / +39 347 1222642
Email info@quodlibetroma.com
Web www.quodlibetroma.com

Torretta de' Massimi

Imagine visiting Rome in the summer and coming home to cool woods and a pool. Imagine visiting at any time of year. The set-up is unique, two properties on a 150-hectare hillside within the city's boundaries. Ring at the isolated green iron gate to enter, then climb the road through woods of cork oak, olive, cypress and pine to arrive at a fascinating group of restored houses and a tower, part of an operating farm. Prince Ottavio Lancellotti is your delightful host and loves getting involved with his English speaking guests; ask him about his 'secret Rome'. You can rent the elegant five-bedroom villa or the medieval tower for four, or bring the whole family and take it all. Interiors have been done in smart country style: shining tiled floors, stippled ochre walls, good antiques, modern metal furniture, and a superb white kitchen for the villa. Both houses have shaded patios and the elegant pool is to share, along with a lovely garden protected by high shrubs. There are logs for winter, ping pong for kids, babysitting and bikes, and a regular bus to take you into town.

Rooms	Villa for 10; Tower for 4: €1,300–€5,000. Villa & Tower can be rented together, €5,000–€6,000 per week; €800–€1,000 per night. Villa's attic has extra room for 4 children (price on request).
Meals	Restaurants nearby.
Closed	Rarely.

Ottavio Lancellotti
Torretta de' Massimi,
Via della Pisana 600,
00163 Rome
Email   info@torrettademassimi.it
Web   www.torrettademassimi.it

Casa Mary

Seasonal fruits in the hamper, Roman ruins all over the place, heavenly views from wherever you stand. Welcome to a fabulous house built into the hillside in the park of Campo Soriano. The once-derelict farmhouse, surrounded by figs, lemons, lavender and 400 olive trees, has been revived by its English owner – beautifully. Inside all is fresh, uncluttered and Italian, with terracotta floors and soft colours and walls a metre thick (keeping you cool in summer). The bedrooms are delightful, the bathrooms are en suite and the kitchen, rustic-contemporary and very well equipped, opens to the terraced gardens; help yourself to herbs. Further provisions are a 15-minute drive away, in the wonderful market at Terracina; you're close to a good supermarket, too. Bliss to dine on the terrace, in the shade of the olive tree by day, under the stars by night. History buffs can visit the Cistercian Abbey at Fossanova – a must-see – while families will head off for the beaches at Sperlonga (itself enchanting) and Sabaudia; the house information booklet is a boon. Then there's Pompeii, Naples, Rome… a treat.

Rooms	1 house for 8: €1,300–€1,750 per week. Extra charge for central heating.
Meals	Self-catering.
Closed	December–March.

	Mary Tucker
	Casa Mary,
	Via Campo Soriano Snc, Cascano,
	04010 Sonino
Email	marytucker0609@aol.com

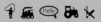

Campania

Country House Giravento

Stay here and tread lightly on the planet. Sweet Serena is a passionate environmentalist – but never sacrifices comfort. The new handsome pink farmhouse oozes character and charm. Built to high environmental standards (local bricks, naturally treated wood floors, old-fashioned terracotta tiles) on a site surrounded by olive groves and orchards with views of the Taburno Camposauro regional park, the whole place is a paradise for birds, wild flowers and animals. Bedrooms, with private entrances, are light, airy and thoroughly natural: voile curtains, stripped floors, eco lighting, solid country furniture, and jewel-like splashes from rugs and bed throws. Heaps of space and walk-in showers, too. Flop around the pool, find a shady spot of your own among the olive trees, relax in the open-plan living area with those views across the valley. Share a meal around the table and discover Serena's passion for cooking – and her delectable, delicious slices of tart apples dipped into bitter chocolate. Raise a glass and watch the magical fireflies perform.

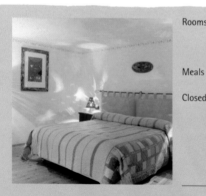

Rooms	1 double: €90–€100.
	1 triple: €135–€150.
	1 quadruple: €180–€200.
	Singles €60.
Meals	Summer brunch €15. Dinner with wine €30, by arrangement.
Closed	1 October to 31 May.

Serena Bova
Country House Giravento,
Via Castagneto 7, Contrada Nido,
82030 Melizzano Benevento

Mobile	+39 347 2708153
Email	info@giravento.it
Web	www.giravento.it

Il Cortile Agriturismo

Special place, special people, and, behind the plain brown door, a verdant surprise. Off the suburban street is a stunning flagstoned courtyard rich in jasmine and oranges – ravishing in spring. Now this historic villa, built as a summer retreat for the forebears, offers two sober, uncluttered and charming B&B rooms, one facing the courtyard with its own secluded entrance, the other in a building just beyond the garden gates. This is a delightful two-bedroom family suite with views onto the lush and lovely garden of Il Cortile. Dutch Sijtsken is charming and thoughtful, serves delicious meals in the vaulted cellar – a stunningly atmospheric dining room – and is aided in her enterprise by daughters Giovanna (trainee sommelier) and Alessandra (dessert chef extraordinaire). As for the *giardinello delle delizie* – the 'little garden of delights' – it is far from small; indeed weddings are held here in the summer, in among the date palms and the magnolias, the glistening roses and the camellia. Find a deckchair and dream. The family delight in sharing their table and their home with guests – wonderful.

Rooms	1 suite for 2-4: €70-€75 for 2; €110 for 3; €120 for 4. 1 family room for 3: €110.
Meals	Dinner €25. Wine from €5.
Closed	Never.

Sijtsken, Giovanna & Alessandra Nucci
Il Cortile Agriturismo,
Via Roma 43, 80033 Cicciano

Tel	+39 0818 248897
Email	info@agriturismoilcortile.com
Web	www.agriturismoilcortile.com

Luna Caprese

A five-minute stroll from Naples' romantic waterfront, this fourth-floor palazzo apartment, reached via a smart central courtyard, is tucked away in charmingly posh Chiaia. The feeling is one of refined 19th-century elegance and your friendly, time-generous host Arnaldo has a passion for art: a lavish collection of paintings, photos and sculptures adorn this sophisticated apartment. The snazzy reception recalls a gentleman's club: high ceilings, wooden floors, beautiful rugs, Neapolitan furniture; deep, comfy sofas everywhere, soft lighting, fine paintings, sculptures and floor-to-ceiling books. Restful colours — beige, wine, terracotta, cream — add to the feeling of elegance and a genteel way of life — with every modern luxury added. Bedrooms are spacious and light, with fine cotton sheets, old style bedsteads, terracotta floors and private balconies. Arnaldo's love of Naples is infectious, so take advantage of his local knowledge and of tours to the Aeolian Isles. Note you are wonderfully placed for the Via Morelli and its fabulous antiques — browse or buy!

Rooms	3 doubles; 3 twin/doubles: €110–€130.
	Singles €85–€100.
	Extra bed/sofabed €20–€30.
Meals	Restaurants within walking distance.
Closed	Rarely.

Arnaldo Cotugno
Luna Caprese,
Via Chiatamone 7, 80121 Naples
Tel   +39 0817 646383
Email   info@lunacaprese.net
Web   www.lunacaprese.net

La Murena Bed & Breakfast

Views from the rooftop terrace stretch to chestnut forests and the Gulf of Naples below. Here, high on the slopes of Vesuvius, the peace is palpable and the air cool and pure. Giovanni and his son live on the ground floor of this modern house and you have the option of self-catering (shops are very near) or B&B. The three bedrooms, kitchen and huge terrace are upstairs, and guests are welcome to share Giovanni's living room below; this is where he serves a delicious breakfast of peaches, apricots and oranges from the garden, cheeses and homemade jams. There's also a large outside area for children to romp in. The big, light and airy bedrooms are very traditional – beds may be of wrought iron, writing desks are antique with marble tops and floor tiles are patterned blue. The kitchen, too, is well equipped and prettily tiled, there's blue glassware in a sea-blue cupboard, a white-clothed table and no shortage of mod cons. A dream for lovers of archaeological sites – Herculaneum, Pompeii, Torre Annunziata, Boscoreale. Naples is a short train ride away. *Minimum stay three nights.*

Rooms	2 doubles; 1 triple: €80 B&B per night. Whole house €240; €1,500 per week.
Meals	Restaurants nearby.
Closed	Rarely.

Giovanni Scognamiglio
La Murena Bed & Breakfast,
Via Osservatorio 10,
80056 Herculaneum

Tel	+39 0817 779819
Email	lamurena@lamurena.it
Web	www.lamurena.it

Villa Giusso

An intriguing place, and quite a challenge to reach, but once there you fall into the staggering view — and know why you came. Originally a monastery (1600s), it stands high on a promontory overlooking the bay of Naples and the Sorrento coast. The whole place could be a Fellini film setting. After an effusive welcome from Erminia, Giovanna and the rest of the Giusso family, you will settle into your rooms — romantic with vintage iron beds, quirky antique furnishings and old paintings. Two are in the old monks' quarters, the others overlook the courtyard where a couple of friendly dogs welcome you. The sitting rooms include a wonderful salon (wisely roped off) full of collapsing antique sofas and heirlooms. Dinner, biodynamically home-grown and delicious, is served at a vast communal table in the vaulted, ancient-tiled kitchen — an occasion to relish. At breakfast of fruit, fresh ricotta and homemade cakes, plan an exciting day in Naples, to return to a blissfully peaceful stroll through the estate's vines and olive groves then a glass of homemade walnut liqueur on the terrace — with that view. *Minimum stay two nights.*

Rooms	5 doubles; 1 double with separate bath; 1 suite for 4: €90–€130.
Meals	Dinner €28 (except Mondays). Restaurants 2km.
Closed	November–Palm Sunday.

Famiglia Giusso Rispoli
Via Camaldoli 51, Astapiana,
Loc. Arola, 80069 Vico Equense

Tel	+39 0818 024392
Mobile	+39 329 1150475
Email	astapiana@tin.it
Web	www.astapiana.com

Villa Oriana Relais

Leave Sorrento's pizzazz far below. Sweep through the gates, down the lemon groves, and breathe in the scent of jasmine and honeysuckle. A 15-minute climb (or nippy taxi ride) from town, this feels like a world away. On arrival you are drawn to the main terrace with its spectacular bay-of-Naples panorama; the public rooms – uncluttered spaces of white walls and terracotta floors – lie above the bedrooms to make the most of the views. This sleek white villa, decked with terraces like a cruise ship – will enfold you in coolness and calm. And hospitality: family warmth fills the place, thanks to Pasquale and his mother Maria. What a way to start the day, feasting on homemade breads, jams, juices and flans! Bedrooms are cool and airy, furnished in a mix of antique and modern – linen curtains and Murano chandeliers, a walnut writing table, a lacy cover – while marbled bathrooms are lavish and pristine. Restaurants are an easy walk down, a steep climb up (ask about the free shuttle) – treat yourself to a swirl in the rooftop jacuzzi on your return. The sunsets are a dream.

Rooms	3 twin/doubles: €59–€210. 1 suite for 2: €90–€290. 2 family suites for 4 (1 double, 1 twin/double): €90–€315.
Meals	Dinner available on request. Restaurants nearby.
Closed	Never.

Famiglia d'Esposito
Villa Oriana Relais,
Via Rubinacci 1,
80067 Sorrento

Tel	+39 0818 782468
Email	info@villaoriana.it
Web	www.villaoriana.it

Azienda Agricola Le Tore Agriturismo

Vittoria is a vibrant presence and knows almost every inch of this wonderful coastline – its paths, its hill-perched villages, its secret corners. She sells award-winning organic olive oil, vinegar, preserves, nuts and lemons on her terraced five hectares. The cocks crow at dawn, distant dogs bark in the early hours and fireflies glimmer at night in the lemon groves. It's rural, the sort of place where you want to get up while there's still dew on the vegetables. The names of the bedrooms reflect their conversion from old farm buildings – Stalla, Fienile, Balcone – and are simply but solidly furnished. We are told by those who stay that dinners are abundant and delicious, so do eat in, and get to meet Vittoria and your fellow guests. Breakfast is taken at your own table under the pergola, and may include raspberries, apple tart and fresh fruit juices. You must descend to coast level to buy postcards, but this is a great spot from which to explore, and to walk – the CAI 'Alta via dei Lattari' footpath is nearby. Le Tore is heaven to return to after a day's sightseeing, with views of the sea.

Rooms	4 doubles; 1 twin; 1 family room for 4: €90. 1 apartment for 6: €700–€1,000 per week.
Meals	Dinner €25, by arrangement. Restaurant 5-minute walk.
Closed	November–Palm Sunday (apartment available all year).

Vittoria Brancaccio
Via Pontone 43, Sant'Agata sui due
Golfi, 80064 Massa Lubrense

Tel	+39 0818 080637
Mobile	+39 333 9866691
Email	info@letore.com
Web	www.letore.com

Boccaccio B&B

Between the post office and the hardware shop, climb the marble staircase, step into your room and your heart will skip a beat at the view. Just the other side of the busy road, one thousand feet below, is the dizzying curve of the Bay of Salerno. Vineyards, lemon groves, white houses, all cling to the steep valley in apparent defiance of gravity; it is almost impossible to pull yourself away and all but one room has the view. Boccaccio is a family affair; grandmother had these rooms and the family still live on the upper floor. They have refurbished the house in a clean-cut, understated modern style that has the virtue of simplicity (as does the breakfast): beechwood furniture, crisp bed linen, sleek lighting and sunny, hand-painted Vietri floor tiles. Bathrooms are spotless, with all necessary fittings. Two minutes from Ravello's picture-perfect piazza (a tourist trap in season), and the Rufolo and Cimbrone gardens, Boccaccio's position is enviable. Your host worked in the film industry for 35 years, and appears still to be very busy in the village.

Rooms	4 twin/doubles: €75–€95. Discounted parking: book ahead.
Meals	Restaurants 100m.
Closed	Rarely.

Antonio Fraulo
Boccaccio B&B,
G. Boccaccio 19,
84010 Ravello

Tel	+39 339 2037006
Email	boccaccioravello@gmail.com
Web	www.boccaccioravello.com

Hotel Villa San Michele

Utterly, unashamedly romantic. Stone steps tumble down from terrace to terrace past lemon trees, palms, bougainvillea and scented jasmine to the rocks below, and a dip in the deep blue sea. It's a treat to stay in this small, intimate, family-run hotel, with the most delightful staff to minister to you and the most sublime views – watch the ferries slip by on their way to Positano or Capri. San Michele may stand at an apparently busy road junction but its hanging gardens and bedrooms turn towards the sea and you live in perfect tranquillity. The hotel building is at the top – light, airy, cool; almost every room has a balcony or terrace and you are lulled to sleep by the lapping of the sea. Cool floors are tiled in classic Amalfi style or white, beds have patterned bedcovers. All is charming and unpretentious and that includes the striped deckchairs from which you can gaze on one of the finest views in Italy. Delectable aromas waft from a cheerful kitchen where Signora is chef; the menu is short, the food delicious. Atrani and Amalfi are walkable, though traffic is heavy in summer; for the weary, a bus stops outside. *June-Sept half-board only.*

Rooms	12 doubles: €100–€170. Dinner, B&B €95–€110 p.p.
Meals	Dinner €28. Wine from €15. Restaurants 500m.
Closed	7 January–14 February; 7 November–25 December.

Nicola Dipino
Hotel Villa San Michele,
SS163 Costiera Amalfitana,
Via Carusiello 2, 84010 Ravello

Tel	+39 0898 72237
Email	smichele@starnet.it
Web	www.hotel-villasanmichele.it

Entry 368   Map 13

Villa en Rose

Get a feel here of what life must have been like before roads came to these hillsides; this is a place for walkers. And for some of the most stupendous views in Italy; you are halfway between Minori and Ravello on a marked footpath that was once a mule trail. In fact, the only way to get here is on foot, with about 15 minutes' worth of steps down from the closest road. (Lugging provisions up here could be a challenge in bad weather.) The open-plan apartment is modern-functional not aesthetic, and spotless; its bedroom is in an alcove off the sitting room, its views from arched windows are a glory and you are surrounded by terraced lemon groves. It feels a world away from the crowds down on the coast, and the secluded little pool means you are not obliged to climb miles down to the beach. The second, much smaller apartment is on the owner's floor above, with no sitting space as such: very basic. If you don't feel like cooking, hot-foot it up to the main square in ravishing Ravello; heaps of restaurants to choose from. Don't miss the glorious gardens of the Villas Rufolo and Cimbrone. *Minimum stay three nights.*

Rooms	2 apartments for 2: €700–€750 per week.
Meals	Self-catering.
Closed	Rarely.

Valeria Civale
Villa en Rose,
Via Torretta a Marmorata 22,
84010 Ravello

Mobile	+39 333 8779628
Email	valeriacivale@yahoo.it
Web	www.villaenrose.it

Agriturismo Biologico Barone Antonio Negri

Monica's grandfather, the Barone Antonio, was a much-loved mayor and the piazza named in his honour is a fine place for an evening passeggiata amongst the locals. The farm has been in the family for 150 years, but it's only once you pass the high gates and approach the house that you appreciate the far-reaching views toward Salerno – the sunsets are divine. Positioned on various levels, each of the good-sized and individually decorated Provençal style rooms, some sporting modern frescoes, keeps its original tiles and surveys nine hectares of nut, fruit and olive trees and vines; enjoy a morning stroll before cooling off in the pool. The exuberant Monica offers cookery classes using regional ingredients, and dinner on the terrace (or in the restaurant) is delicious: local mozzarella, just-picked tomatoes, chicken cooked to grandmother's recipe, and always, a dessert extravaganza. It's wonderful being high and cool and within easy reach of the Amalfi coast, but for children it's the animals who steal the show; everyone loves the donkey Serafina who has her own knowing call for Monica.

Rooms	2 doubles; 2 twin/doubles; 1 family room for 2-4: €90-€110. Singles €80-€100. Dinner, B&B €70-€80 p.p.
Meals	Dinner with wine, €25. Restaurants 5-minute walk.
Closed	Rarely.

Monica Negri
Via Teggiano 8,
Gaiano di Fisciano, 84084 Salerno
Tel   +39 0899 58561
Mobile +39 335 6852140
Email   info@agrinegri.it
Web   www.agrinegri.it

Borgo la Pietraia

The colourful building that awaits at the top of a hill climb is the only ostentatious thing you'll find here, where nothing has been designed to come between you and relaxation. The entire site has a feeling of space, especially embodied in the junior suites. Lined up like a curved terrace of houses – with gaily painted front doors – the interior proportions are immense, with big double beds lost on one side and each bay-side wall a sweep of glass framing sea and hills bookended by towering mountains. Outside, the patios are screened from one another with wicker divides – as if you could take your eyes off the view! The smaller bedrooms have the same spectacular panorama and all share a high standard of minimal, comfortable design. Breakfast is served at a scattering of small tables in the main building and features homemade cake – the hotel's first step in a plan to produce their own food (and toiletries). After you've eaten you could venture out to historic sites or bike down the mountain, but, as your genial host Signor Scariati admits, most of his guests just "read, read, read."

Rooms	4 doubles: €90–€150. 8 suites for 2: €110–€250. Singles 15% discount. Extra beds available.
Meals	Lunch €20. Dinner €30. Lunch & dinner available April-October. Restaurants 1.5km.
Closed	Rarely.

Arianna Scariati
Borgo la Pietraia, Via Provinciale 13 snc,
84047 Capaccio-Paestum

Tel	+39 0828 1990285
Mobile	+39 320 9216382
Email	info@borgolapietraia.com
Web	www.borgolapietraia.com

Il Cannito

Down the *strada bianca*, through the maquis where lizards scuttle and owls hoot... to Cannito, immersed in wilderness. Once the summer residence of friars, now it is wondrously restored – a heart-warming place. Food is prepared with love, and style; bedrooms are immaculate havens; bathrooms are sanctuaries to linger in. The Gorga family – mother, son, two daughters – greet you warmly and nothing is too much trouble. Two of the rooms sit below the main building, reached by shallow steps lit at night, sharing a furnished stone terrace. All have big beds, modern art, designer chairs, beautiful linen (three have hydromassage baths). Visit stunning Paestum and its temples, and the clifftop villages of the Cilento National Park; or take a boat tour to hidden caves and coves. Return to 15 hectares of shimmering butterflies and centuries-old oaks, exceptional views to the Isle of Capri, perhaps lunch by the infinity pool and a sundowner from a lounger. The day starts with breakfasts of homemade cakes and jams, local mozzarella and salami, fruits from the kitchen garden. Special.

Rooms	4 doubles: €250.
	Singles €50. Extra bed/sofabed €50.
Meals	Dinner from €35. Restaurants 5km.
Closed	End of October to the end of February.

Antonella Gorga
Il Cannito, Via Cannito,
84047 Capaccio-Paestum
Tel +39 0828 1962217
Mobile +39 333 365 2324
Email antonella@ilcannito.com
Web www.ilcannito.com

Domus Laeta

The 'Happy House' is in the charming village of Giungano, at a high altitude and with views down to the sea and Paestum. It oozes history and lovely owner Camilla's family have owned it since the 1600s – the common rooms overspill with family portraits, antiques and a library filled with books and documents (ask to visit). A huge open fire welcomes you in colder months, breakfasts are special and locally sourced, dinner is by arrangement – outside on the terrace or inside at an optional communal table. Bedrooms (cool even in summer months) are colourful and vary in size. The first floor rooms have views to the sea and their own private terrace; family rooms are in the mansard and are more modern in style, but all have views and their own bathrooms. The garden is enchanting with arches, internal courtyards, plenty of space, a swimming pool all in stone and restful places to sit. Walkers will be in heaven, with the Cilento National Park to amble (or yomp) through, the village is unchanged with little shops and restaurants, staff are friendly and helpful. You are well looked after here. *Minimum stay four nights in August.*

Rooms	5 doubles: €90–€120.
	1 suite for 4: €160–€120.
	2 family rooms for 4: €130–€200.
Meals	Occasional dinner €30.
	Restaurants nearby.
Closed	May.

Camilla Aulisio
Domus Laeta,
Via Flavio Gioia, 84050 Giungano

Tel	+39 0828 880177
Mobile	+39 339 8687983
Email	info@domuslaeta.com
Web	www.domuslaeta.com

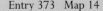

Casa Albini

Trickle down a side street strangely full of elegant, crumbling palazzi to the Albini family's charming palazzo where stunning views sweep over valley and hills to the sea beyond. On a clear day you can see as far as Capri. Step into a cool courtyard and all is reassuringly welcoming, in this civilised old home where your cultured hosts (keen foodies) live as an extended family. Guest bedrooms are tile-floored and elegantly understated with swagged curtains, lofty ceilings, no TVs. Plump for the suite that looks onto the rose garden where you breakfast amid shady cypresses – or tuck yourself away in the stable with its downstairs sitting room. Pamper yourself in the Turkish bath, book in for a beauty treatment, amble to the village for supper, then back for a film in the little cinema. Expect breathtaking sunsets from the garden, pomegranates and lavender, hikes through valleys of wild orchids – and the best home-made crostata ever! Never mind the odd bit of peeling paint, this is a welcoming base for the Ancient Greek colony of Velia and the Charterhouse in Padula. Don't miss Thursday's market in Agripoli. *Children over 11 welcome. Short stays available.*

Rooms	2 twin/doubles: €90-€120.
	1 suite for 2 (1 twin/double, 1 sofabed);
	1 suite for 2 (1 twin/double, 2 sofabeds):
	€100-€140.
	Singles €45-€65.
Meals	Restaurants nearby.
Closed	31 October to 29 March.

Anna Albini
Casa Albini, Vittorio Emanuele 5,
Copersito Cilento, 84076 Torchiara

Tel	+39 0974 831392
Mobile	+39 346 1641633
Email	info.casa.albini@gmail.it
Web	www.casaalbini.it

Borgoriccio

All the pleasures of a Slow holiday in Italy. A quiet hilltop village in the Cilento National Park; a beautiful house hugged by olives, figs, flowers; a local restaurant (special deal for guests) serving regional wines; a *via verde* through the stunning scenery of Torchiara. Angela has rebuilt an old family home in a traditional style. 'Casa Bassa' (the old olive press) has country-style suites in the landscape's warm browns and bright yellow-greens. 'Casa Alta' (on the terrace above) holds more bedrooms, a large, fire-warmed sitting room, a small library, a dining room with country antiques, a small tower for reading and reflection. Outside, a swimming pool basks in southern Italian sunshine, a jacuzzi bubbles and gardens sprawl; views stretch over Cilento's forested hills. Feisty Angela knows the area's best spots while Michaela looks after guests with homemade cakes, fresh juice and a warm smile. It's a seven-minute drive to Agropoli for blue flag beaches and near to Palinuro, Amalfi and Positano. If archaeology is your thing then head for Paestum, Velia, Pompeii and Ercolano. Enchanting, carefree, delightfully Slow.

Rooms	7 doubles: €90–€125.
	1 suite for 3: €110–€150.
	Singles €72–€100.
Meals	Restaurants 5-minute walk.
Closed	Rarely.

Angela Riccio
Borgoriccio,
Strada Provinciale 86, n° 56,
84076 Torchiara

Tel	+39 0974 831554
Email	info@borgoriccio.com
Web	www.borgoriccio.com

Marulivo Hotel

Cool – in both senses of the word. Metre-thick walls give the whole place that delicious damp-ancient smell, a constant reminder that you are staying in a 14th-century monastery. Architect Lea, and Massimo, lovely people, have revived the ruin after 100 years of abandonment. Open to the elements, its topsy-turvy layout is intriguing, the kind of place that cries out to be explored the moment you duck under the archway. Gorgeous bedrooms have exposed brickwork, terracotta floors, balconies and super beds with curly-whirly headboards, and heaps of individual touches: dividing the bedrooms of one suite is the 'window' of a confessional unearthed during the restoration. The terraces, the numerous steps and the blue views will leave you giddy; sink into a cushioned wicker sofa and toast the beauty with a lovely glass of the local greco. This is a place that won't play on your eco conscience either; they've won awards for their green efforts. Potter around exquisite, car-free Pisciotta, scramble down through the olive groves to the harbour, visit the famous grottos. New to us, but a favourite already. *Minimum two nights in cottages.*

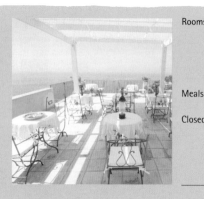

Rooms	9 doubles: €70–€210.
	2 suites for 2: €130–€210.
	2 cottages for 2-3; 1 cottage for 2-6: €60–€150; €400–€1,050 per week.
	1 house for 5: €140–€215; €1,000–€1,500 per week.
Meals	Breakfast €10 for self-caterers. Restaurant 40m.
Closed	November–February.

Lea Pinto
Marulivo Hotel,
Via Castello,
84066 Pisciotta

Tel   +39 0974 973792
Email   info@marulivohotel.it
Web   www.marulivohotel.it

Locanda San Fantino

Do not follow the sat nav to get here – the owner will come and find you, in little San Giovanni a Piro! The roads wind up into the mountain countryside, the sea glistens in the distance, and cherry trees line the dusty track… we've never tasted fruit so delicious. The estate is self-sufficient (jams, wines, salamis, olive oil), the old palazzo is like a fascinating museum, the walls of your own house are a metre thick, and the style is cool rustic chic – with a dash of theatricality. Walls are white, floors are matt terracotta, there are lovely pieces of driftwood positioned in innovative ways, and a kitchen that's sheer delight, with a great big fireplace and a stainless steel stove. Where the animals once lived, the cook now prepares your breakfast. You get seven bedrooms (two on the ground floor), a piano to play, a pool to splash in and heaps of space – come for a special occasion. The field-like garden is charmingly unkempt, with two donkeys to carry picnics and hammocks slung between trees (one fits six kids). Views reach to the Bay of Policastro – a seven-minute drive.

Rooms	1 house for 14: €5,000–€8,000 per wk. Daily rates available on request. Breakfast & daily cleaning included. Single rooms available on request.
Meals	Breakfast included. Dinner available on request. Restaurants 2km.
Closed	January/February.

Sebastiano Petrilli
Locanda San Fantino,
Via San Fantino 8,
84070 San Giovanni a Piro

Tel	+39 0974 983442
Email	seba@sanfantino.com
Web	www.sanfantino.com

Entry 377   Map 14

Calabria, Basilicata and Puglia

Il Giardino di Iti Agriturismo

The farm, peaceful, remote and five minutes from the Ionian sea, has been in the family for three centuries. Less grand than in former days, a massive arched doorway leads to the courtyard and huge garden, safely enclosed with rabbits for the children, and pigs, goats and cats, too. The large, cool guest bedrooms have been simply, traditionally decorated; ask for one that opens off the courtyard, its brick-paved floor and big old fireplace intact. Each room has a wall painting of one of the farm's former crops and is correspondingly named: Lemon, Peach, Sunflower, Grape. Bathrooms are old-fashioned but charming. Courses are held here on regional cooking and weaving, but if that sounds like hard work, sit back and soak up the atmosphere and the gastronomy and atone for the calories later. On warm nights you eat (deliciously) in the little walled garden, where lemon and orange trees are sprinkled with fairylights. Signora is gentle and charming; nearby Rossano is an atmospheric Calabrian town, all rosy rooftops and crumbling walls, and churches lovingly restored.

Rooms	2 doubles (sharing bathroom);
	10 family rooms for 2-4;
	2 apartments for 3 (1 double, 1 sofabed):
	€45-€65.
	Dinner, B&B €45-€55 p.p.
	Dinner, lunch, B&B €55-€65 p.p.
Meals	Half-board or full-board only.
	Wine from €10.
Closed	Never.

Francesca Cherubini
Il Giardino di Iti Agriturismo,
Contrada Amica, 87068 Rossano
Tel   +39 0983 64508
Email   info@giardinoiti.it
Web   www.giardinoiti.it

Entry 378   Map 15

Praia Art Resort

A private beach, your own loungers, a free mini-bar, fresh fruit while sunbathing… and five types of cake at breakfast, almost always served out by the pool thanks to year-round sunshine. The dress code is simple. Bathing suit by day, then later something arty and colourful for pool-side drinks and a meal in the bamboo-roofed restaurant. Natural foods are on the menu: fresh salads and seafood with herbs from the garden and a hint of Calabrian hot pepper. Wines are local, and so are the wood carvings, abstract artworks and naïve tiles created by master craftsmen and artists. Bedrooms, each with a private terrace, cluster amid pine trees a quick flip-flop from the beach. With their warm peach or green walls and über-modern bathrooms – rain showers, glass sinks, fluffy robes – they make a luxurious retreat for couples. Take a good map because the resort is well hidden in a quiet complex by Capo Rizzuto marine reserve. Tucked in Italy's toe, the province of Crotone is blissfully free of tourism yet filled with attractions from Capo Colonna archaeological park to the wild beauty of Valli Cupe's waterfalls.

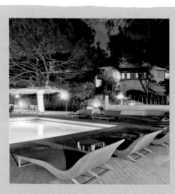

Rooms	5 doubles: €300–€340.
	1 suite for 2 (with rooftop terrace): €400–€440.
	Singles €300–€440.
	Extra bed/sofabed €80.
Meals	Lunch from €25. Dinner from €45.
Closed	4 November to 1 January.

Claudio Felix Gherardini
Praia Art Resort, Loc. Praialonga,
88900 Isola Capo Rizzuto

Tel	+39 0962 1902890
Mobile	+39 320 7592495
Email	info@praiaartresort.com
Web	www.praiaartresort.com

Foresteria Illicini

Come for the views of the tiny islands of Matrella and Sant'Ianni, the caves and rocky coves, the water lapping at the beach. This bewitching place could be a set for *The Tempest*. Guglielmo's father bought the whole spectacular promontory and surrounding land with olive trees, holm oaks and myrtles 50 years ago; they spent every family holiday here. Now Guglielmo, a gentle architect, and his wife Diane have turned it into a deliciously unmanicured resort. Foreigners have barely discovered the area so, apart from two weeks in August, the five-acre park, the two small beaches and the large pool are beautifully peaceful (the restaurant only opens in August). Wrought iron furnishes garden and terrace (a festival of flowers in June) but the view is the thing. The small breakfast room also overlooks the sea. The bedrooms are housed in little cottages just a few yards back from the shoreline, each with a deckchair'd terrace and a view of the sea. Each is neatly and simply furnished, with tiled floors, comfortable beds and a spotless bathroom. The sunsets are exceptional. Good value, great for families.

Rooms	8 doubles; 2 family rooms for 3-4; 1 single: €70-€130. Dinner, B&B for 2 €180-€200 (August only).	
Meals	Lunch €15-€30 (July-August only). Wine from €10. Restaurants 5-minute drive.	
Closed	Mid-October to mid-May.	

Guglielmo & Diane Rivetti
Foresteria Illicini,
Loc. Illicini,
85046 Maratea
Tel   +39 0973 879028
Email   staff@illicini.it
Web   www.illicini.it

Entry 380   Map 15

L'Orto di Lucania

Relish this organic family farm in an unspoilt region of Italy — and the delicious food that Fulvio and his brother grow using time-honoured methods: tomatoes, artichokes, rare red aubergines... Much turns up on your dinner plate, for the restaurant serves farm-fresh meals by the fire in a big old barn, or on the terrace among gnarled olives. Bubbly multilingual Cinzia (Fulvio's wife) takes care of the smattering of smart white bungalows, set among meandering paths on shrubby lawns. Apartments have full kitchens, terrace doors and open fires; B&B guests get a homemade, home-grown feast for breakfast. And you can buy farm produce in the shop: olive oil, fruit jams, honey... Swim up an appetite in the large parasol-ringed pool, borrow a bike or arrange horse riding nearby: this area of Basilicata, on the Puglian border, is an undiscovered delight with heaps to see and do. Visit ancient Matera, famed for Sassi cave dwellings and rock chapels, and sweet Montescaglioso with its Benedictine monastery and 15th-century castle. Or head through Puglia to Ionian beaches. Great value for a special farm stay. *Minimum stay two nights. Pets by arrangement.*

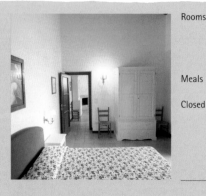

Rooms	2 doubles; 1 suite for 2-4: €95-€100. 6 apartments for 2-4; 1 apartment for 2-5: €110-€200. Dinner, B&B €85-€95 p.p. Extra bed/sofabed available at no charge.
Meals	Breakfast €7. Dinner €25. Wine from €6. Restaurants 10-min drive.
Closed	Rarely.

Fulvio & Cinzia Spada
L'Orto di Lucania,
Contrada Dogana, 75024
Montescaglioso

Mobile	+39 333 9802592 / +39 333 9800730
Email	info@ortodilucania.it
Web	www.ortodilucania.it

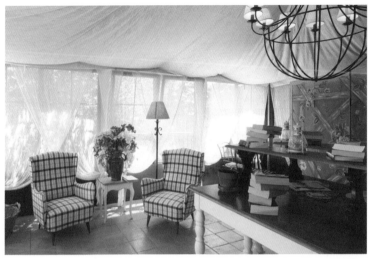

La Chiusa delle More

The Italians flock here in August but foreigners have not yet discovered Peschici, so come out of season when the beaches and fish restaurants are idyllically uncrowded and you can watch the fishermen sort their catch on the front. Francesco and Antonella's 16th-century farmhouse is 500 metres from the sea: park under an ancient olive tree and climb up to the reception terrace to drink in the views. On another terrace, teak loungers flank a sparkling pool and the air is scented with citrus. The bedrooms, some in the main house, some in an attractive separate building, are light, cool and simply furnished, with good little shower rooms. Family rooms have ladders up to childrens' mezzanines. Your hosts, a delightful pair, vibrant and full of fun, have five hectares of olive groves and a big kitchen garden. The olive oil and vegetables supply their restaurant and the food is divine – hard not to love the typically Puglian dishes and the local wines. Breakfast on the terrace is a wonderful start to a day among the splendours of the Gargano National Park. Fabulous for walkers.

Rooms	4 doubles; 4 doubles (in cottage); 2 family rooms for 4 (in cottage): €160–€240.
Meals	Dinner €30. Wine €5–€50.
Closed	October–April.

Francesco & Antonella Martucci
La Chiusa delle More,
Loc. Padula,
71010 Peschici
Mobile   +39 347 0577272
Email   lachiusadellemore@libero.it
Web   www.lachiusadellemore.it

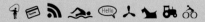

Lama di Luna – Biomasseria Agriturismo

The sister of Pietro's great-grandmother lived here until 1820; Pietro bought the farm in 1990, then discovered the family connection. It was 'meant to be'. Lama di Luna is the most integrated organic farm in Italy: 200 hectares of olives and wines, 40 solar panels for heat and hot water, beds facing north, feng shui-style. Pietro, who lives here with his family, is young, lively, charming, passionate about the environment and this supremely serene place. The farm goes back 300 years and wraps its dazzling white self around a vast courtyard with a central bread oven, its 40 chimney pots 'telling the story'; of the many farm workers that once lived here. Each bedroom, complete with fireplace and small window, once housed an entire family. Pietro searched high and low for the beds, the natural latex mattresses, the reclaimed wood for the doors. There's a library for reading and a veranda for sunsets and stars, and views that reach over flat farmland as far as the eye can see. Breakfast here on homemade cakes and jams, orchard fruits, local cheeses. Remote, relaxing, memorable. *Check in after 4pm. Call owner to give time of arrival.*

Rooms	9 twin/doubles: €160–€180.
	2 suites for 3-4: €230–€300.
	Extra bed/sofabed €50.
Meals	Dinner €30. Restaurants 3km.
Closed	Never.

Pietro Petroni
Lama di Luna – Biomasseria Agriturismo,
Loc. Montegrosso, 70031 Andria

Tel	+39 0883 569505
Mobile	+39 328 0117375
Email	info@lamadiluna.com
Web	www.lamadiluna.com

Masseria Serra dell'Isola

An unadorned 1726 *masseria*, a charming family home – you couldn't find a better place to stay for your discovery of Puglia. The outskirts of Mola di Bari may be unprepossessing but Rita's smile as she ushers you in, brings instant cheer. The great hall with its uneven stone floor was once part of an olive mill (see where the presses used to stand) and is filled with books, portraits and antiques with stories to tell. Lofty whitewashed vaulted rooms and metre-thick walls keep you cool in summer, and the light, gracious bedrooms are named after the women who once occupied them – Aunt Michelina, Grandma Rita, Great Aunt Annina, their mother Angelina, great grandmother Ritella: four generations of women whose precious notebooks inspired the little cookery school here. You're welcome to browse through her impressive library of history books; she'll also happily tell you about less well-known local places. Enjoy the food, the conversation and the atmosphere; dine by candlelight and you'll sample ancient family recipes and liqueurs from the time the Bourbons reigned in southern Italy. Unusual and authentic. *Minimum stay two nights.*

Rooms	4 doubles; 2 twin/doubles: €130.
	Whole house €3,300–€3,900 per week.
Meals	Dinner, 3 courses, €35–€40.
	Wine €12–€18.
Closed	Rarely.

Rita Guastamacchia
Masseria Serra dell'Isola,
S.P 165 Mola, Conversano n.35,
70042 Mola di Bari

Mobile	+39 349 5311256
Email	info@masseriaserradellisola.it
Web	www.masseriaserradellisola.it

Abate Masseria & Resort

Locals in the know flock to the restaurant at Abate Masseria; they'll be treated to some of the finest antipasti around. How satisfying then that you can dine on local ingredients (expertly matched with Puglian wines from the cellar) then retire to elegant rooms in the domed 17th-century trulli or the converted stables. Mino and his family restored the buildings years ago, keeping the sense of history and adding new bathrooms, dark wooden furniture and deeply comfortable beds. Though there's not much to choose between them, you'll be assured of a good night's sleep in all. The finest details are found elsewhere – the quietly grand dining room, the mosaic'd pool and the fabulous grounds full of walnut and fig trees, wisteria and jasmine surrounded by acres of olive groves. You can eat outside or retreat to the guests' private garden for a siesta. The staff are efficient and Mino and his wife are on hand to make each day feel like a new discovery. There's stacks to do: a wine festival in Noci in November, the caves of Grotte di Castellana nearby. In summer you have concerts galore. *Minimum stay three nights in high season.*

Rooms	5 twin/doubles: €99–€159.
	3 suites for 2-4: €139–€199.
	Singles €69–€169.
Meals	Restaurants nearby.
Closed	November–March.

Mino Tinelli
Abate Masseria & Resort,
Zona F, 70015 Noci

Tel	+39 0804 973352
Email	info@abatemasseria.it
Web	www.abatemasseria.it

Masseria Serralta

A gentle wind up through a mosaic of small grazed fields and olive groves bound by dry stone walls (so typical here) delivers you to refreshingly cooler climes… and a higgledy-piggledy collection of old buildings that make up this stunning *masseria* – searingly white against the cobalt sky. Some people just get it when it comes to restoring an old building, and these owners – young, enthusiastic, instantly likeable – do. Beniamino, a talented architect, and Maria who has a profound interest in local tradition, have together restored their 17th-century trulli with the sort of sensitivity that would make the most exacting restorer proud. Four guest suites, housed under four conical roofs, are fresh, cool and stylish with whitewashed walls, pretty blue shutters and an elegant mix of antiques and funky modern pieces; bathrooms, not huge, are well kitted out. Outside, mulberries, olives, prickly pears and lavenders have been newly planted, and a jasmine shaded pergola with a vast stone slab of a table has views over the Murgia plateau to the shimmering sea – *the* spot for a sunset aperitivo! *Minimum stay two nights, five nights in high season. Pets by arrangement.*

Rooms	2 twin/doubles: €90–€135.
	1 triple: €120–€180.
	1 quadruple: €160–€220.
	Singles €60–€95.
Meals	Restaurants 3km.
Closed	January/February &
	November/December.

Marta Gagliardi La Gala
Masseria Serralta, SC 86, Contrada
Serralta 39, 70010 Locorotondo
Tel   +39 0804 431193
Mobile   +39 392 7122660
Email   info@masseria-serralta.it
Web   www.masseria-serralta.it

Trullo Malibran

In a charming part of Italy, distinguished by olive trees, trulli and houses sparsely spread, is this haven, hidden down back lanes yet very close to Cisternino. Your multi-coned trullo is surrounded by a neat farmland landscape of olive groves and drystone walls, with barely a neighbour in sight. Enter to find a white-plastered, stone vaulted, single-storey house, its cosy rooms full of nooks and crannies and enhanced by a comfortable contemporary décor – all feels fresh and new. The corner kitchen is well-equipped (and includes a dishwasher), the bedrooms, refreshingly cool in summer, have crisp linen and decorative iron beds, and the pale stone bathrooms are top-notch. Bathrobes and beach towels are provided, while chunky stone floor tiles, great big wooden shutters and splashes of modern art add character. In summer you'll be spending your days outside, dipping in and out of the sleek pool lined with striped loungers, or dining under the pergola. Once you've finished the generously provided welcome pack, there's Cisternino market to plunder; it opens two mornings a week.

Rooms	1 house for 6: £950–£1,950 per week. Extra bed available in twin room.
Meals	Restaurants 2km.
Closed	Rarely.

Rebecca Russell
Trullo Malibran,
Contrada Chiatante,
70100 Locorotondo
Mobile   +44 (0)7968 194440
Email   rebecca@tidemark.co.uk
Web   www.trullomalibran.com

Valle Rita

Here is a rambling but beautifully maintained organic estate where citrus groves, ubiquitous olives, grapes for the table and swathes of seasonal fruit and veg flourish. Families and couples will flourish too – happily whiling away a week dipping in and out of the prickly pear-fringed pool, playing tennis and ping pong or borrowing bikes and shooting around the tracks of the estate. So much heat-drenched activity will surely warrant a lazy lunch on the terrace of the super restaurant with its seasonal, home-grown delights and wines from the owners' other estate in Basilicata – locals flock in too (always a good sign). There are pleasant enough rooms for B&B while a series of traditional one-storey apartments and houses with little gardens and barbecue areas for DIY-ers dot the estate (note: all prices include breakfast). The owners don't live on site but manager Giorgio is hugely helpful and weekly film nights and occasional jazz evenings in the old stables sound like fun. No need to be nonplussed by the slightly featureless landscape en route: breathe a sigh of relief at your lucky find.

Rooms	6 doubles: €79–€159.
	2 apartments for 2; 5 apartments for 3;
	1 apartment for 5: €59–€179;
	€400–€1,300 per week.
Meals	Breakfast for self-caterers included.
	Lunch/dinner €25. Restaurants 10km.
Closed	Mid-November to mid-March.

Carlo Lunati
Valle Rita,
Contrada Girifalco,
74013 Ginosa
Tel   +39 0998 271824
Email   info@vallerita.it
Web   www.vallerita.it

Masseria Tagliente

Slip back a century when you stay here. Cattle are still housed in the trulli, goats potter and, twice a day, the noble Murgese horses, bred by the owners, pass by – children will be charmed. Built in 1849 by Carlo's ancestors, the neo-classical house has a delightful air of faded elegance – look out for the slits through which brigands could be shot at after the unification of Italy. You enter through huge old wooden doors and up a grand sweeping staircase to living quarters on the first floor. Here are a stately drawing room and guest bedrooms with family heirlooms, oil paintings, gilt mirrors, high bedsteads, vaulted ceilings and original tiled floors – time stands still. Bathrooms are functional not luxurious; one at the front takes up the space between two cupboards – tiny! Beneath the kitchen's copper pans, or out on a terrace with views to Calabria, you breakfast on eggs from the hens and homemade cakes and crostata, ricotta so fresh it's still warm, home fruits and pecorino…Take time to roam this beautiful estate, full of treasures and hidden corners.

Rooms	1 double; 1 twin/double: €110–€130.
	2 triples: €110–€150.
	Singles €90–€110.
	Extra bed/sofabed available, €20.
	Free cot available.
	Reduced rates for weekly stays.
Meals	Restaurants 2km.
Closed	November-April.

Simonetta Pascali Fumarola
Masseria Tagliente,
Contrada San Paolo,
74015 Martina franca

Mobile	+39 347 8293199
Email	info@masseriatagliente.it
Web	www.masseriatagliente.it

Trulli La Macina

Tucked away in a patchwork of olive groves, reached via a maze of stone-walled lanes, are two pretty trulli and one square-shaped lamie, renovated with eco sensitivity and an urbane sense of style. You can rent the lamie for two, the trullo for four or the 'trulleto'… or take the whole lot and sleep eight plus a child. The flexibility is fabulous, your host is warm and loquacious and takes care of it all. Fancy breakfast? He'll provide it, a sunny feast from the summer kitchen of crostata, fresh cakes and just-squeezed juices; there's babysitting on offer, too. Dazzling white, with thick walls to keep out the heat, the 200-year-old trulli have cosy snug bedrooms and diddy new kitchens, natural earth colours and country antiques, and bathrooms with big shower heads and baskets of thick towels. But outside is where you'll mostly be, by the pool, surrounded by lavender and jasmine, bamboo and cacti, lanterns, candles and hammocks in the woods – it couldn't be lovelier! Wine villages and summer food festivals abound; the sand beaches and flowering maquis of the Adriatic coast are an easy drive. *Extra link apartment 'Trulletto' (sleeps two) available, to create apartments for four, six or eight.*

Rooms	1 lamie for 2; 1 trullo for 6;
	1 trulletto for 2: €650-€3,200 per week.
Meals	Breakfast on request.
	Restaurants 1km.
Closed	Rarely.

Vincenzo Porcino
Trulli La Macina,
Contrada Calongo 36,
72014 Cisternino
Mobile   +39 328 4211023 / +39 333 8469747
Email   info@trullilamacina.it
Web   www.trullilamacina.it

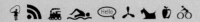

Entry 390   Map 16

Masseria La Rascina

A charming country house – with charming hosts and staff – five minutes from the Adriatic's sandy coast: an elegant base if you enjoy birdsong and beach. Its peachy stone walls rise from immaculate lawns ringed by olives, palms, figs. Inside breathes Leonie's light-touch style: Mediterranean hues, world ornaments, beautiful dried flowers in spacious communal rooms. On the vast chandelier'd veranda, settle on sofas and sweep your gaze across the horizon: a stunning breakfast spot. Or lounge – all day if you wish – by the deep, inviting pool. Bedrooms sprinkle the house, with three off a cool inner court, others across the lawn. All are beautiful: lemon walls, four-posters draped in voile, a terrace for the evening aperitif. Families may prefer more homely self-catering apartments so pick up ingredients in Rosamarina or fine-dine in Ostuni, just minutes away. You can horse ride, hire bikes, hit the beach, snorkel in a nature sanctuary, tour the Valle d'Itria, join in summer festivals… the area teems with activity. Back at the house, with lovely Leonie, Paolo and the dogs, all is peaceful and refined. *Minimum stay two nights, seven nights in apartments.*

Rooms	6 doubles: €100–€140.
	1 apartment for 4;
	3 apartments for 2: €110–€240.
Meals	Breakfast €10 for self-caterers.
	Restaurants 2km.
Closed	November–Easter.

Leonie Jansen Schiroli
Masseria La Rascina,
Strada Provinciale 19, Rosamarina,
72017 Ostuni

Mobile	+39 338 4331573
Email	larascina@inwind.it
Web	www.larascina.it

Villa Cervarolo

A trulli house, marooned in rolling countryside dotted by fruit and olive trees – a beautiful Puglian blend of ancient vernacular and minimalist modern. A surprising find at the end of an unpaved track, this is a designer dream: exquisitely chic, sublimely inviting. The living spaces are open plan. Via the unobtrusively swish kitchen (modish appliances, Smeg fridge) you enter the sitting room, with large TV (for DVDs or local only) and built-in sofa. Beyond, a study with a dusky pink chaise longue. Bedrooms are a serene marriage of gleaming linen, sheepskin rugs, pale velvet cushions, cool polished cement. Bathrooms ooze style, one with a tub with views: gaze on the garden as you soak. A beach-style pool (unheated) is an invitation to laze, with its outdoor 'room' alongside: relax on the cushioned swing seat, recline on Moroccan kilims, cook up a storm in the outdoor kitchen, dine at table hewn out of rock. If you don't feel like cooking you can always employ a chef, and other treats can be arranged, from yoga to massage. Make sure you find time to explore the lovely wine villages of Valle d'Itria. *Minimum stay seven nights. Bookings Saturday to Saturday.*

Rooms	1 house for 6: £2,600–£3,500. Winter heating supplement £100 per week.
Meals	Self-catering.
Closed	1 November 2013 to 12 April 2014.

The Owner	
	Villa Cervarolo,
	Ostuni
Mobile	+44 (0)7771 713070 /
	+44 (0)7941 142054
Email	info@homeinpuglia.com
Web	www.homeinpuglia.com

Masseria Impisi

Hidden but not hard to find, close to hilltop Ostuni, is a 15th-century *masseria* and two inspirational new builds. Artists David and Leonie, garden and nature lovers both, have lived in Italy for years; his sculptures dot the grounds, her mosaics shine like jewels. Find two apartments – one in the 16th-century Gatehouse and the other which featured in TV's *Grand Designs*. Both are quietly stylish with extra bedrooms, cool Trani stone underfoot, bed frames made by David and creamy plaster walls with Leonie's paintings on them. Kitchens are well-equipped, wet rooms are tiled with local stone, towels and gowns are dazzling white; spill out onto colonnaded areas for al fresco dining. There's much to visit, including an underground olive mill that dates from the 10th century, original cisterns that still harvest rain water, open air markets and Michelin starred restaurants in town. The semi-wild grounds are filled with pampas grass, cacti, ancient olive trees and a unique natural pool hewn from limestone rock. Borrow bikes, play boules, picnic on the beach just a mile away… heaven in Puglia! *Short stays available. Minimum stay three nights.*

Rooms	1 apartment for 2; 1 apartment for 4: €670–€1,350 per week.
Meals	Restaurants 2.5km.
Closed	November–February.

Leonie Whitton & David Westby
Masseria Impisi,
Il Collegio, Contrada Impisi,
72017 Ostuni
Mobile   +39 340 3602352
Email   info@ilcollegio.com
Web   www.ilcollegio.com

Masseria Il Frantoio Agriturismo

So many ravishing things! An old, white house clear-cut against a blue sky, mysterious gardens, the scent of jasmine – and private beaches five kilometres away. Armando and Rosalba spent a year restoring this 17th-century house (built over a sixth-century oil press) after abandoning city life. Inside – sheer delight. A series of beautiful rooms, ranging from fairy tale (a froth of lace and toile) to endearingly simple (madras bedcovers and old desks) to formal (antique armoires and doughty gilt frames)… a glorious mix. Dinner is equally marvellous – put your name down. Rosalba specialises in Puglian dishes accompanied by good local wines; Armando rings the courtyard bell at 8.30pm: the feast begins, either in the arched dining room or outside in the candlelit courtyard. It will linger in your memory – as will other details: an exterior white stone stairway climbing to a bedroom, an arched doorway swathed in wisteria. Armando is passionate about his totally organic *masseria*, surrounded by olive groves and with a view of the sea; Silvana is on hand ensuring you bask in comfort. *Minimum two nights in August.*

Rooms	5 doubles; 3 family rooms for 4; 2 triples: €139-€269. 1 apartment for 2-4: €319-€389. Child €39-€69.
Meals	Dinner with wine, €59, by arrangement. Children €34. Supper €44. Restaurant 5km.
Closed	Never.

Silvana Caramia
Masseria Il Frantoio Agriturismo,
SS 16km 874,
72017 Ostuni

Tel   +39 0831 330276
Email   prenota@masseriailfrantoio.it
Web   www.masseriailfrantoio.it

Entry 394   Map 16

Masseria Cervarolo

It will be love at first sight. Serried ranks of immaculate trulli, sunlight bouncing off pristine walls, expansive terraces shaded by billowing fabric, manicured lawns and luxurious sunloungers around the pool... Not only is this 16th-century *masseria* blessed with film star looks, it is run sustainably by incredibly thoughtful and affable owners. Old doors have been crafted into bed heads, mirror frames made out of washboards, driftwood fashioned into art, and hand-knitted blankets come from the lovely old ladies of Bari. It's breathtakingly stylish. Each trullo, once a peasant's workshop, is now a cosseting bedroom: pebble-coloured, calming, embracing; and there are more bedrooms in the farmhouse. Learn to cook, unwind with a yoga session, hike or bike the much-conquered Puglian plains, or take a quiet moment in the private baroque chapel. Beaches are 20km, Ostuni six. Come evening, Teo and Patrizia may join you for a craft beer or a glass of excellent wine before you settle down to superb fresh Puglian produce. Perfection? We think so.

Rooms	10 doubles: €160–€285.
	1 suite for 2; 5 suites for 4: €220–€440.
	1 triple: €220–€385.
	Extra bed €55. Cot €10 per night.
Meals	Dinner €36; €18 for children.
	Restaurants 6km.
Closed	10 November to 28 February.

Teo Avellino
Masseria Cervarolo,
S.P. 14 Contrada Cervarolo,
72017 Ostuni

Tel	+39 0831 303729
Email	info@masseriacervarolo.it
Web	www.masseriacervarolo.it

Trullo Bellissimo

Hidden away in gentle rolling countryside and down a quiet, single track road this renovated 300-year-old trullo is light, airy and frightfully grown-up. Sophisticated souls will appreciate the swish electric gates, the manicured garden with immaculate pool, the marble floors and modern kitchen. Romantics will hone in on the Arab feel created by stone archways, crocheted curtains, tapestries, beads and swags. Light floods in from glass doors; high ceilings and tiled floors keep you cool in summer; a log-burner is cosy in winter and there are plenty of books to browse. Bedrooms lead off from here down stone corridors – one with windows set high up in the stone walls – both have mosquito-proof shutters, built-in wardrobes and shower rooms tiled in vibrant colours. Laze on the outdoor terrace, wander the pretty gardens, enjoy views over olive groves while sipping a sundowner, cook up a storm with a wood-fired BBQ, eat at an impressive marble table. The hill city of Ostuni with its dazzling whitewashed houses and tiny alleyways is close, as is the coast. *Minimum stay seven nights in high season.*

Rooms	1 house for 4: £1,325–£1,975 per week. Two child's beds & cot available.
Meals	Restaurants 4km.
Closed	Rarely.

	Keith Brown
	Trullo Bellissimo,
	133 Contrada Certosa, 72017 Ostuni
Tel	+44 (0)1985 844664
Mobile	+44 (0)7789 501456
Email	info@trullobellissimo.com
Web	www.trullobellissimo.com

B&B Masseria Piccola

It is a simple, unsophisticated village place – and utterly endearing. Who could fail to be enchanted by the round walls, the conical roofs, the charming little rooms? These trulli were built a century ago by Nicola's great-grandfather (he paid the equivalent of one euro for the site); now they have been converted into this delightful, good-value B&B. The 'little farm' is in a quiet side street in Casalini di Cisternino, with a terrace at the front and a patch of garden behind. A wicker sofa and chairs welcome you in the hall. Snug, spotless bedrooms have pale walls and stone arches and are furnished with country antiques; beds are very comfortable, shower rooms are well-equipped and breakfast is at the big table in the kitchen or out under the flowers on the terrace. Nicola, young, busy, charming, looks after his guests well and will point you to a choice of decent restaurants five minutes' walk away – or possibly do an unpretentious supper on his wicker-chaired terrace. The town is nothing special but Cisternino, with its lively twice-weekly market, is well worth the visit. Perfect for the young at heart.

Rooms	3 doubles: €70–€90. 1 single; 1 single (child's room): €30–€60.
Meals	Dinner on request €20. Wine from €8. Restaurant 1km.
Closed	Rarely.

Nicola Fanelli
Via Masseria Piccola 56,
72014 Casalini di Cisternino

Tel   +39 0804 449668
Mobile +39 328 2228827
Email   info@masseriapiccola.it
Web   www.masseriapiccola.it

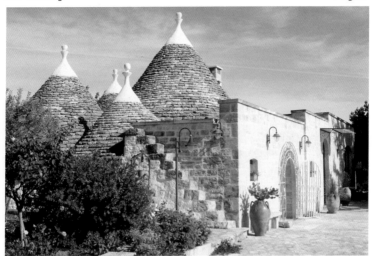

Trullo Giardino

Grapes droop lazily over the terrace, peach and plum trees melt into Apulian countryside, the pool invites a cool dip... this is a glorious Italian getaway, with friendly owners next door to make you feel *in famiglia*. Be greeted at this 19th-century trullo – its chunky walls topped by five conical roofs like magicians' hats – by an aperitif in the beautiful wine cellar, or try delicious local cheeses and meats with wines from Puglia. Inside is doll's house-pretty, a warren of softly lit white walls, local tiles and low arches. Find a log fire, a stencilled dresser, a wooden dining table, a compact kitchen. Quirky antiques – candlesticks, ceramics – peek from nooks and crannies. Duck into two plain bedrooms, with little windows, pictures, a tiny shared shower room. It's cosy, yes, but much of the time you're outside. A lazy barbecue on the terrace, a snooze by the shady cedar, a splash in the shallow pool... why not ask Michele and Mimma to cook breakfast or dinner, or fire up the pizza oven? They know the best local markets, the best joints in Cisternino town, and the best spots on the Adriatic coast – a short drive.

Rooms	1 house for 4: €700–€1,700 per week.
Meals	Self-catering.
Closed	January.

Cosima Vita Semeraro
Trullo Giardino,
Contrada Calongo 25,
72014 Cisternino
Mobile   +39 320 3676037
Email   palumbo.2007@libero.it
Web   www.trullogiardino.com

Trullo Solari

At the end of the lane, three trulli framed by pine, olive and fruit trees: a delightful sight. Inside is just as good, open plan with a dining area and a small but stunning kitchen. But it's the sitting room that dazzles, with its eight-metre wall of glass overlooking the pool… fold the doors back in summer and merge your living space with the elements. This is a spectacular renovation: four big whitewashed bedrooms with sleek bathrooms, simply and beautifully furnished, a rooftop sundeck, a volleyball pitch close by, an outdoors dining area with a barbecue and a pizza oven and now, a large multi-purpose studio space perfect for those who would like to run courses. There are a couple of other trulli in sight, but that won't stop you feeling private and remote. The owners, fun and easy-going, live nearby, leave you a luxurious welcome pack and can lend you a pre-programmed GPS so you don't get lost finding their favourite places! They're keen greenies – the sun heats the underfloor heating and the pool – and will help you plant a tree of your choice to reduce your carbon footprint when you go. *Pets by arrangement.*

Rooms	1 house for 8: £2,000-£3,600 per week.
Meals	Self-catering.
Closed	Never.

Cathy & Keith Upton
Trullo Solari,
Contrada Petrelli,
72013 Ceglie Messapica
Tel +39 0831 342153
Email cathyupton@hotmail.it
Web www.trullosolari.com

Villa Magnolia

Off the road to Brindisi, yet refreshingly peaceful and calm, is a dusky pink 18th-century *villa nobile* fronted by two magnificent palms. Eco aware owners Lesley and Ron welcome you with a bottle of wine; they live in a house to the side. The villa itself has four bedrooms opening to a central *salotto*, beautifully decorated in an apricot finish and furnished with charming antiques; a wonderful tapestry hangs on one wall. Each bedroom is light, luxurious, with polished antiques on old patina'd floors, and stylish bathrooms with big wet rooms and stone walls; one has its own patio behind a sweet jasmine hedge. The large pizza oven is fired up once a week for pizza-making evenings – not to be missed! Breakfast on homemade jams, fresh fruit and pastries under a pergola covered in grape vines. Straight Roman roads whisk you to the beach (5km), or Ostuni – summer festivals aplenty. Then back to gardens: bougainvillea, almond and olive trees and a Romanesque saltwater pool, exquisitely lit for night swims. A massage can be organised in the temple area. Heaven. *Minimum stay three nights, five nights in high season.*

Rooms	4 doubles: €120–€170.
Meals	Once weekly pizza night: 3 courses with wine, €25. Restaurants 2km.
Closed	November–March.

Ron & Lesley Simon
Villa Magnolia,
Contrada Argentieri sn, Serranova,
72012 Carovigno

Tel	+39 0831 989215
Email	info@villamagnoliaitaly.com
Web	www.villamagnoliaitaly.com

Roof Barocco Suite

Lecce is an architectural treasure. White stone on baroque façades against intense blue skies… dazzling. Keep the faith as you follow the directions through narrow alleys to a tiny square in which Italian drivers perform ingenious manoeuvring feats. You'll spot the house immediately – pots of wildly colourful flowers spilling from every sill, succulents trailing from balconies like Rapunzel's hair. No need to climb up: Elisabetta will welcome you like an old friend and take you past her floor to the apartments. Each has its own heavenly terrace – flower-filled oases on which to laze and gaze at the wonders of Lecce (some of her guests have found it hard to go exploring, preferring a shady corner with a good book). Peaceful rooms are traditionally furnished with a few modern touches, bathrooms are spotless, little kitchens have welcome hampers. Breakfast – a treat – is left at the door in a basket: freshly squeezed juice, a tin of warm croissants, a little glass pot of yogurt and fruits and jams from Elisabetta's country house. Just wonderful.

Rooms	1 apartment for 2; 1 apartment for 4: €90–€170. Extra beds available.
Meals	Restaurants nearby.
Closed	Rarely.

Elisabetta Achiardi
Roof Barocco Suite,
Piazzetta Arte della Stampa 13,
73100 Lecce
Mobile   +39 331 7585656
Email   roofbaroccosuite@gmail.com
Web   www.roofbaroccosuite.it

Mantatelurè – Dimora esclusiva

You are in Lecce, 'Florence of the South', filled to the brim with shops, bars and Baroque beauty. Step off the street into a 1550s palazzo built of creamy *pietra Leccese*, with stunning vaulted ceilings and grand doorway mouldings, elegantly and stylishly restored. Marta, vivacious assistant, speaks brilliant English; Marco, designer-owner, is not so fluent but his charm and his passion for Lecce compensate for any missing word. The house's tranquil courtyard, set with small tables, is the highlight of this B&B, and it is here that you are spoilt every morning... with fresh fruits and Marco's cakes and biscotti, an array of Italian hams, and enticing jams from the courtyard's trees (orange, mandarin, medlar), all presented with love and care. To the side is a jacuzzi, lit with candles at night; below is a stylish, vaulted cellar, with tables for tastings and four shabby-chic sofas. Set off for Otranto, Gallipoli or the sea, come home to immaculate bedrooms, airy and serene, with a caramel, cream and white palette, pops of bright colour, accents from India, and bathrooms to linger all day in. *Children over 11 welcome. Ask about parking.*

Rooms	2 suites for 3, 2 suites for 3; 2 suites for 2: €110–€250. Singles €100–€190.
Meals	Restaurants nearby.
Closed	Rarely.

Marco Cimmino
Mantatelurè – Dimora esclusiva,
Dei Prioli Vittorio, 42,
73100 Lecce

Tel	+39 0832 242888
Email	info@mantatelure.it
Web	www.mantatelure.it

Palazzo Bacile di Castiglione

Stay in your own private palazzo – its 16th-century walls dominating Spongano's Piazza Bacile. The charming *barone* and his English wife offer apartments for couples or families full of comforts. On the first floor, a series of large terraces and four bedrooms open off a vaulted baronial hall with beige check sofas and an open fire (fir cones and logs are home-grown). Expect fine fabrics and four-posters, pink, yellow or marble bathrooms, wardrobes dwarfed by lofty ceilings and great kitchens – cookery courses are run here too, in a vast purpose-built kitchen. The outbuildings (*casettes*) at the end of the long garden are similarly swish but cosier: olive wood tables, big lamps, framed engravings, books and CDs; again kitchens emphasise the owners' passion. (They are also keen greens, saving energy, going solar and composting madly.) The garden is lovely, all orange trees and wisteria, secluded walkways and corners, old pillars and impressive pool; at twilight, owls chime like bells. Beyond lie the baroque splendours of Lecce, Gallipoli and Otranto – and the coast. Borrow the bikes!

Rooms	2 apartments for 2; 1 apartments for 4; 1 apartment for 5; 2 apartments for 6; 1 apartment for 8: €720–€2,770 per wk.
Meals	Self-catering.
Closed	Never.

Sarah & Alessandro Bacile di Castiglione
Palazzo Bacile di Castiglione,
73038 Spongano

Tel	+39 0832 351131
Mobile	+39 349 8329308
Email	albadica@hotmail.com
Web	www.palazzobacile.it

La Macchiola

The courtyard walls drip with creepers and geraniums; in front, across a little road, is a verdant citrus grove worth resting in. All this is part of a vibrant working farm. La Macchiola, a 17th-century *azienda agricola*, is devoted to the production of organic olive oil (massages available) and Anna's family make some of Puglia's finest oils. Go through the massive gates and the Moorish-arch portico and you leave the narrow and unremarkable streets of Spongano village for a white-gravelled, white-walled courtyard dotted with elegant wrought-iron tables and chairs. Off the courtyard, ground-floor apartments have been carefully converted into a series of airy, old-style rooms. Walls are colourwashed warm yellow and soft blue, sleeping areas are separated by fabric screens, ceilings are lofty and vaulted. One apartment for two has a dining space squeezed into an ancient fireplace, bathrooms have pretty mosaic mirrors, most of the kitchenettes are tiny. There's a vast roof terrace *marmellata* and cakes for breakfast in an impressive stone-vaulted room. Beaches are a short drive. *Minimum stay three nights.*

Rooms	4 doubles: €80-€110. 1 triple: €90-€120. 4 apartments for 2; 1 apartment for 4: €480-€1,500 per week.
Meals	Breakfast €6 for self-caterers. Restaurants 300m.
Closed	9 January to 16 March & 5 November to 22 December.

Anna Addario-Chieco
La Macchiola, Via Congregazione
53/57, 73038 Spongano

Tel	+39 0836 945023
Mobile	+39 339 5451307
Email	lamacchiola@libero.it
Web	www.lamacchiola.it

Masseria Varano

Wines and olive oils from the estate, local breads, pasta and cheeses – the generous welcome sets the tone for your stay. Victoria and Giuseppe combine the best of English and Italian hospitality – gentle, warm, easy – reflected in their handsome creamy stone and green-shuttered *masseria*. The apartments, each with private entrance and terrace, are in the main house and two cottages. Elegant and airy, with creamy tiled floors, white walls and handsome chestnut fittings, rooms are decorated with modern furniture and old family pieces. Dotted with family photographs, Victoria's paintings, pretty fabrics and objects collected from travels, there's a gentle country-house feel, a home from home; the best wows you with a fleet of French windows and a vast terrace. Kitchens are light and modern, equipped to please the serious cook. Masses to do: beaches, Gallipoli, the harbours of Tricase and Santa Maria di Leuca… or just make the most of the pretty walled gardens and the pool. The owners are happy to leave you alone or have a chat over a glass of wine. *Apartments for four are also suitable for two.*

Rooms	1 apartment for 2; 5 apartments for 2-4: €400-€1,500 per week.
Meals	Self-catering.
Closed	November-Easter.

Giuseppe & Victoria Lopez y Royo di Taurisano
Contrada Varano, 73056 Taurisano

Tel	+39 0833 623216
Mobile	+39 348 5151391
Email	lopezyroyo@hotmail.com
Web	www.masseriainsalento.com

Sicily and Sardina

Hotel Signum

Leave the car and Sicily behind. Salina may not be as famous as some of her glamorous Aeolian neighbours (though *Il Postino* was filmed here) but is all the more peaceful for that. The friendly, unassuming hotel sits so quietly at the end of a narrow lane you'd hardly guess it was there. Dine on a shaded terracotta terrace with chunky tile-topped tables, colourful iron and wicker chairs; gaze out over lemon trees to the glistening sea. Traditional dishes and local ingredients are the norm. Then wind along the labyrinth of paths, where plants flow and tumble, to a simple and striking bedroom: cool pale walls, pretty antiques, a wrought-iron bed, good linen; starched lace flutters at the windows. The island architecture is typically low and unobtrusive and Clara and Michele (Luca's parents) have let the hotel grow organically as they've bought and converted farm buildings. The result is a beautiful, relaxing space where, even at busy times, you feel as if you are one of a handful. Snooze on a shady veranda, take a dip in the infinity pool – that view again – or clamber down the path to a quiet pebbly cove.

Rooms	24 doubles; 2 singles: €130–€400.
Meals	Dinner à la carte, €35–€70.
	Wine from €18.
Closed	Mid-November to mid-March.

Luca Caruso
Hotel Signum,
Via Scalo 15, Malfa,
98050 Salina, Aeolian Islands

Tel	+39 0909 844222
Email	info@hotelsignum.it
Web	www.hotelsignum.it

La Locanda del Postino

No surprise this was the setting for the film *Il Postino*. The tiny settlement of Pollara sits in a natural amphitheatre of a valley, rising steeply on three sides before opening onto the warm blue of the Mediterranean – and mesmerising views of further islands. From the port, you drive up through 14km of Salina's coastal woodland and vineyards, and wash up at the converted stone farmhouse. Once owned by a priest, built into the hillside, it's a perfect place to catch the sunsets, especially from your colourful hammock. There's a friendly informal feel, as you help yourself to Sicilian breakfasts of homemade cakes, croissants and jams, and later, regional dishes, al fresco with a glass of full-bodied house wine. A giant old wine press tells of hard yet good living, while the bedrooms are unpretentious affairs of terracotta tiles, walls pale yellow and white, and decorative wrought-iron beds. Amelia and her husband carefully restored the building and remain hands-on owners; Amelia also writes novels. In the visitor's book one guest writes: 'a special place where the soul is reborn.'

Rooms	6 twin/doubles;
	4 family rooms for 4: €120–€260.
Meals	Dinner with wine, €30.
Closed	November–April.

Mauro Leva
La Locanda del Postino,
Via Leni 10, Pollara, Malfa,
98050 Salina, Aeolian Islands

Tel	+39 0909 843958
Email	info@lalocandadelpostino.it
Web	www.lalocandadelpostino.it

Entry 407   Map 18

Villa L'Aquilone

The road winds like a corkscrew up from the coast, high above Capo d'Orlando, to a yellow-painted villa, old but new, overlooking the bluest of blue seas. What it lacks in rusticity it makes up for in views; among the most breathtaking in Sicily, they take in the Aeolian Islands including Stromboli – watch it erupt on a clear night! Everything is hugely comfortable within. There's a spacious sitting room with two sofas, a log fire and a big satellite TV, family photos on the mantelpiece, pictures of kites (*aquilone*) on the walls, big French windows for a blissful breeze, and ceiling fans throughout the ground floor. The kitchen is thoughtfully, generously equipped (copper-bottom pans, a six-burner cooker), there's a barbecue outside and a tile-topped table for al fresco meals. Below: an infinity pool, not huge but gorgeous, fringed with greenery and palms. You can walk or ride in the Nebrodi Regional Park, bask on white sands, swim in the sea: there's a train to Capo d'Orlando but your own car is a must. Nod off in the hammock, or under an Indian cotton bedspread in an air-conditioned room.

Rooms	1 house for 10: €3,200–€3,900 per week.
Meals	Chef available on request for in-house dinners.
Closed	November–March.

Anna Venturi
Villa L'Aquilone,
Contrada Piano San Cono,
98074 Naso – Capo d'Orlando

| Mobile | +44 (0)7714 759703 |
| Email | Anna@italiansecrets.co.uk |

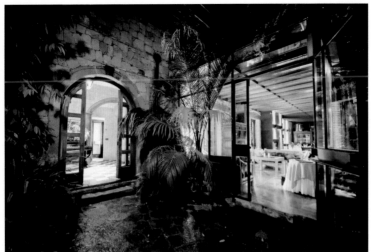

Green Manors

Your hosts spotted the remote 1600s manor house years ago; it has been theatrically, gloriously, revived. Bedrooms, some with terraces, are part baroque, part contemporary: rich colours, tiled floors, Sicilian patchwork, laced linen, family antiques, flowers. Tapestries and paintings are illuminated by chandeliers, tapered candles stand in silver candelabra; bathrooms come with huge baths or showers, delicately scented homemade soaps and waffle towels. Chris, Paolo and Pierangela have also been busy establishing their bio-dynamic orchard and you reap the rewards at breakfast, alongside silver cutlery and antique napkins. The homemade jams are divine – cherry, apricot, ginger; the juices are freshly squeezed. Languid dinners are totally delicious, served outside behind a curtain of shimmering plants, or by the huge fireplace when the weather is cooler. There's a wooden cabin for two in the olive groves (with outside kitchen and bathroom); a lush tropical park with peacocks and ponies; a deep pool. Expect occasional summer concerts beneath the mulberry tree, and the distant chimes of Castroreale's churches. *Minimum stay two nights.*

Rooms	5 doubles; 1 single; 3 suites for 2: €100-€180.
	1 cottage for 4-6: €200-€260.
	1 cabin for 2 (summer only): €80.
Meals	Dinner €35. Wine €10-€60.
	Restaurants 1km.
Closed	Rarely.

Pierangela & Chris Jannelli Christiaens
Green Manors, Borgo Porticato,
98053 Castroreale

Tel	+39 0909 746515
Mobile	+39 338 4340917
Email	info@greenmanors.it
Web	www.greenmanors.it

Entry 409   Map 18

Santa Marina

In the historic centre of hilltop Castroreale – 500 souls, a scattering of restaurants, 26 churches – is a noble palazzo behind whose doors three apartments lie, each steeped in aristocratic character. Cobalt blues and soft ochres, thick walls and arched windows, personal possessions and inherited antiques – no designer could dream up such an atmosphere. Although divided into three, the house has the feeling of a family home, thanks to owner Pierangela, gracious and gregarious, who settles you in (be sure to book a meal at her hotel, the legendary Green Manors). Kitchens and dining rooms vary in size but not in style, bedrooms glory in grand four-posters, a Greek column makes a stunning coffee table and one shower stands in a small square marble pool, originally intended as a bath! The top apartment has a terrace, a small forest of pot plants with views; the bottom apartment stays super-cool in summer. You are a short drive from the beaches and Milazzo, launch pad for the Aeolian Isles, and the surroundings are beautiful: lush valley, wooded mountain, distant sea.

Rooms	1 apartment for 3; 2 apartments for 2: €700–€1,400 per week.
Meals	Breakfast €15. Restaurants within walking distance.
Closed	Rarely.

Pierangela & Chris Jannelli Christiaens
Santa Marina,
98053 Castroreale

Tel	+39 0909 746515
Mobile	+39 338 4340917
Email	info@greenmanors.it
Web	www.greenmanors.it

Entry 410   Map 18

Hotel

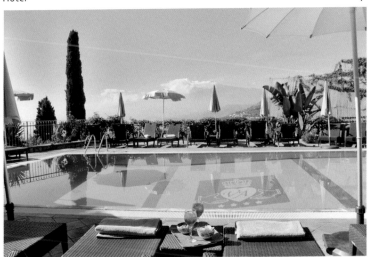

Hotel Villa Angela

Wend your way up Monte Tauro's hairpin bends, past Taormina's historic centre, to arrive at a hotel with the most perfect views out to sea — and Etna's steaming summit. Reception is on the top floor of this golden hillside villa, where you get a warm welcome from bubbly Katharine and the team. Rooms are bright and elegant, with terracotta tiled floors and gorgeous furniture in chestnut and wrought iron. En suites are luxurious, with vast jacuzzi tubs or hydromassage showers. All is charmingly Sicilian, not least the exquisite hand-painted ceramic ornaments from Caltagirone. Take breakfast downstairs in the spacious dining room or on the pool-side terrace: a buffet laden with pastries, breads, jams, yogurts, cereals, you name it. You can tread carefully down the short yet steep steps to the heart of Taormina, or opt for the hotel's shuttle bus. Don't miss the Greco-Roman theatre, the botanic gardens and Corso Umberto, the pedestrianised main street, awash with shops, bars and restaurants. Etna National Park is close by, as is Catania and some of Sicily's most beautiful beaches. *Children under four free.*

Rooms	23 twin/doubles: €120–€240. 1 suite for 2; 1 suite for 3; 2 suites for 4: €190–€360. Singles receive discount on booking. Extra bed/sofabed available in some rooms: €40 adult, €25 child 4–12.
Meals	Dinner available Mondays & Thursdays; lunch & snacks everyday. Restaurants nearby.
Closed	November–March.

Katharine Dix
Hotel Villa Angela,
Via Leonardo Da Vinci 71E,
98039 Taormina

Tel	+39 0942 28513
Email	hotel@hotelvillaangela.com
Web	www.hotelvillaangela.com

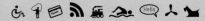

Le Case del Principe

This vast walled estate with an impressive 17th-century palazzo amid an ocean of citrus trees lives up to its name; your host Gabriele is a prince. Overlooking a vineyard, across a labyrinth of pot-holed tracks linking the various parts, are a villa and five converted farm buildings. The villa, with its own garden and gazebo-covered terrace with tiled banquettes, has a 12-seater dining room with lacquered cane ceiling, a living room with an open fire and formal bedrooms with large beds, all quirkily decorated with unusual period pieces. The terraced row of single-storey cottages, backing onto a quiet road, have hedged-off terraces, cotto floors, neat kitchens, mezzanine bedrooms for children (with ladders) and pretty, traditional bathrooms tiled top-to-toe in blues and whites. Tucked away in the formal garden, a rose-smothered, thyme-scented pergola provides shady recess and a discreet pool with sleek recliners has a good view of the smoking volcano. Taormina with all its cultural hot spots, and Etna with all of hers (lava flows are visible during eruptions) are a short drive, as are the beaches. *Pets by arrangement.*

Rooms	Villa for 12: €2,600–€4,800.
	3 apartments for 2; 2 apartments for 4: €300–€1,600. Prices per week.
Meals	Dinner available for groups only.
Closed	Never.

Principe Gabriele Alliata di Villafranca
Le Case del Principe,
Tenuta Alliata,
98039 Taormina
Mobile   +39 349 7880906
Email   gabrielealliata@gmail.com
Web   www.lecasedelprincipe.it

Hotel Villa Schuler

Late in the 19th century, Signor Schuler's great-grandfather travelled by coach from Germany and built his house high above the Ionian Sea. He built on a grand scale and he chose the site well: the views of the Bay of Naxos and Mount Etna are gorgeous. When he died in 1905, Great Grandmama decided to let out some rooms and the villa has been a hotel ever since. Though restored and brought up to date, it still has an old, elegant charm and a relaxed, peaceful atmosphere. Lavish organic breakfasts are served in the chandelier'd breakfast room or out on the terrace. Bedrooms vary, some with beautifully tiled floors, antique furniture and stone balconies; the more modern top-floor suites have beamed ceilings and large terraces. All come with organic bed linen, jacuzzi showers heated by solar panels, heating from biomass – it's all super-eco – and views to gardens or sea. Hidden away behind a stone arch, in subtropical gardens scented with jasmine, is a delightful, very private little apartment; a path from here leads all the way to the town's pedestrianised Corso Umberto. *Minimum stay two nights in mid/high season.*

Rooms	17 doubles; 5 suites for 2; 4 triples: €99-€212. 1 apartment for 2-4: €258-€400.
Meals	Breakfast for self-caterers included. Restaurants 100m (special prices for Hotel Villa Schuler guests).
Closed	Mid-November to February.

Christine Voss & Gerhard Schuler
Hotel Villa Schuler,
Piazzetta Bastione, Via Roma,
98039 Taormina
Tel   +39 0942 23481
Email   info@hotelvillaschuler.com
Web   www.hotelvillaschuler.com

Hotel Villa Ducale

The ebullient Dottor Quartucci and his family have restored their fine old village house with panache. Rosaria has travelled the world for ideas – her style is antique-Sicilian – and cherishes every guest. From the delicious little pastries at tea to the large umbrellas on loan, from the valet parking to the private beach shuttle, every detail has been considered. Now the big roofed terrace high on the hill has clear plastic walls – perfect for the wetter months – and distance lends enchantment to the view, so gaze on the sweep of five bays and looming Mount Etna as you breakfast on Sicilian specialities. This is Taormina, the chicest resort in Sicily, and rich in archaeology and architecture. Flowers are the keynote of this romantic little hotel: bunches in every room, pots placed like punctuation marks on the steps, private terraces romping with bougainvillea. Bedrooms, not large, are full of subtle detail, each with a luxurious shower room, bathrobes and slippers; warm old terracotta tiles carry family antiques and hand-painted wardrobes, and five of the suites are across the road. One of our favourites.

Rooms	11 doubles: €140-€300.
	6 suites for 2-4: €220-€450.
Meals	Lunch/dinner €30-40. Wine €18-€45.
Closed	10 January to 10 February.

Andrea & Rosaria Quartucci
Hotel Villa Ducale,
Via L. da Vinci 60,
98039 Taormina
Tel   +39 0942 28153
Email   info@villaducale.com
Web   www.villaducale.com

Villa Carlotta

There's a pretty, peaceful village above (Castelmola), a private beach below (Lido Stockholm), and a roof terrace that catches the sea breezes. It's a joy to have breakfast up here, looking out to Mount Etna. The setting is perfect, the hotel is comfortable, the staff are attentive and friendly – this must be one of the best-loved hotels in Sicily. It's an aristocratic 19th-century villa with 15th-century pretensions, renovated in modern style with theatrical flourishes. Breakfast chairs are dressed in pleated linen, dove-grey sofas face glassy tables that mirror the sea, bedrooms trumpet generous beds and swagged curtains, a square blue pool sinks into a lush garden and shaded loungers line up on two sides. Here a barman serves stylish drinks on silver platters – magical at night. No indoor sitting space but an exotic bar in the Roman catacombs (there's a perfectly preserved Roman road in the garden, too); a restaurant on the roof, and more in clifftop Taormina (a stroll away, or a hotel shuttle). It's a pretty little town but gets busy when the cruise ships are docked. Better by far to be chez Carlotta.

Rooms	7 doubles: €150–€300.
	16 suites for 2: €250–€600.
Meals	Lunch/dinner €20–€30.
	Wine €18–€40.
Closed	Mid-January to mid-February.

Andrea & Rosaria Quartucci
Villa Carlotta,
Via Pirandello 81,
98039 Taormina
Tel   +39 0942 28153
Email   info@villaducale.com
Web   www.hotelvillacarlottataormina.com

Casa Turchetti

Turn back the clock a hundred or so years and you would have heard Puccini or Vivaldi resounding from deep within this 19th-century townhouse. The music academy is no more, but Casa Turchetti has not let go of its musical past: you'll spot the little lyre, the B&B's motif, dotted all over the place. Cheerful hosts Pino and Francesca are understandably proud of their restoration and will be as hands on or off as you want. Big bedrooms are elegant and supremely comfortable: soft yellow walls, generous red swags at balconied windows, marble floors that sparkle, embroidered white linen on antique beds. Bathrooms are designed for serious grooming; you'll want to spend far longer than necessary in here, wrapped in a fluffy towel or relaxed under a rain shower. Breakfasts are a talking point – the guest book is heaped with praise. Catch your breath on the rooftop terrace: the Greek amphitheatre to your left, smouldering Etna to your right, the uninterrupted sweep of blue straight ahead, the hum of Taormina just below. All without having to step foot outside the door. *Minimum stay four nights.*

Rooms	3 doubles; 1 twin: €200–€250.
	1 suite for 4; 1 suite for 2: €350–€450.
Meals	Restaurants within walking distance.
Closed	November to 20 March.

Pino & Francesca Lombardo
Casa Turchetti,
Salita dei Gracchi 18/20,
98039 Taormina

Tel	+39 0942 625013
Email	info@casaturchetti.com
Web	www.casaturchetti.com

La Casa di Pippinitto

The farm is small, delightful and organic, the coast is a short drive, and you can walk to simple cafés, restaurant and museum. But the star is Mount Etna, the largest active volcano in Europe. Come for organised treks to the crater, skiing in winter, walking the rest of the year. Back at the farm, delightfully hands on, is Cesare. His wife is a teacher; the family is multi-lingual and well-travelled. This is a lovely set up for a family stay, with gardens to run around in, hammocks slung between walnut trees, a guest kitchen in which to rustle up a meal, and two friendly labs to chase. You can also self-cater, in the characterful old *casita* dedicated to Pippinitto, the farmer who once lived here with his family and donkey. Expect new mattresses and good linen, en suite showers, wood-burning stoves; the décor, complimented by wonderful country beams and old terracotta, is simple, modern and comfortable throughout. As you'd expect, Cesare's breakfasts are plentiful and delicious – warm rolls, yogurts, home fruits, cakes and jams – served at wooden tables in a lovely airy room. *Minimum stay two nights.*

Rooms	4 doubles: €75–€85.
	1 cottage for 4-5: €75–€100.
Meals	Guest kitchen. Restaurants in village.
Closed	Rarely.

Cesare Gulisano
La Casa di Pippinitto,
Via Pennisi 44,
95010 Santa Venerina
Tel   +39 0959 53314
Email   info@lacasadipippinitto.it
Web   www.lacasadipippinitto.it

Monaci delle Terre Nere

Wend your way up the volcanic slope of Mount Etna to this noble retreat: a dusky pink 1800s palazzo overlooking the Med. First impressions don't get more arresting than this. When not tending to their apiary, olives and vines, Guido and Ada run their baroque boutique hotel with warmth, humour and generosity. Relax beneath towering pines or on sunny terraces, or lend Guido a hand on the land. Balconies are traditionally tiled, with terracotta pots in cloistered stone archways; the terrace's deep well has a resident green eel to purify its water. Inside, the textures linger. Stunning black lava rock walls and gargantuan timbers frame suspended staircases and glass-panelled bathrooms, with striking paintings and objets d'art adorning the simply sumptuous suites. The imaginatively restored winemaking cantina has chestnut beams, a wood-burner and bar... perfect for secret, Sicilian soirées. Feast on house honey, olive oil and wine, fresh croissants, meats and cheeses – with spoiling treats from the organic vegetable and herb gardens – or visit the seriously good restaurant in the next village.

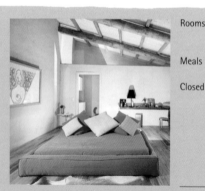

Rooms	8 doubles: €125–€320. Singles €125. Extra bed/sofabed €35–€50.
Meals	Breakfast included. Lunch and dinner on request. Restaurants nearby.
Closed	Rarely.

Guido Alessandro Coffa
Monaci delle Terre Nere,
Via Monaci, 95019 Zafferana Etnea
Tel   +39 0957 083638
Mobile   +39 331 1365016
Email   info@monacidelleterrenere.it
Web   www.monacidelleterrenere.com

Palmento La Rosa Agriturismo

A chunky ten-metre beam dominates the lofty living area, a reminder that Palmento La Rosa once housed a wine press. Now it is a sophisticated estate – Franz loves his wines and has an excellent cellar – and a charming place to stay. Your stylish, lively, delightful hosts have swapped Paris for this green haven at the foot of Europe's most celebrated volcano, 700 metres above sea level (never too hot) and surrounded by acres of Etna vines, sharing their passion for life, culture, sunshine and good food with guests. Served at one big granite table on the terrace in summer, meals are fresh colourful Sicilian and desserts are magnificently baroque; wines are from Biondi and Benanti. There's a generosity of spirit here; high ceilings and sweeping chestnut floors, sprawling sofas, two fireplaces, original art and bedrooms flooded with light. Those on the ground floor open to palm trees and roses, those on the first have sea views. Trek in the National Park or climb the lower craters of Etna – cable cars can replace legs if need be – or dine simply at La Tana del Lupo in Pedara. *Minimum stay two nights.*

Rooms	3 doubles; 1 twin: €130–€170. Extra bed €30.
Meals	Dinner €35–€45. Wine from €15. Restaurants 3km.
Closed	6 January to 28 February & 2 November to 20 December 2014.

Toni & Valeria La Rosa
Palmento La Rosa Agriturismo,
Via Lorenzo Bolano 55,
75030 Pedara

Tel   +39 0957 896206
Email   info@palmentolarosa.com
Web   www.palmentolarosa.com

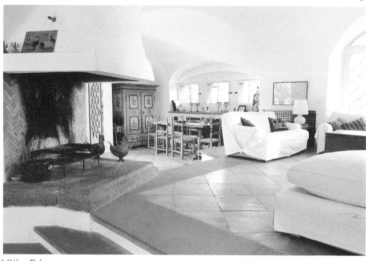

Villa Edera

Views reach to Mount Etna from this graceful, grown-up, French-designed family house, half an hour from Catania airport. Once vineyards grew here; now a gated group of modern villas includes this one, its privacy maintained by a large walled garden with mature chestnut, lemon, orange, fig, palm and pine trees. You can dine on the terrace, lunch in the shade, swim in the big inviting pool. Inside: high vaulted ceilings, arched doors, dark lava pillars, muted colours and beautifully chosen antique and contemporary pieces. The split-level sitting room has a central open fireplace; the generously equipped kitchen has coloured tiles and lovely blue and white crockery. Bedrooms are light, fresh, airy and uncluttered, with snowy linen and towels; from the master bedroom you can step into the garden. Local architect and owner Paul lives nearby and arranges a welcome snack of breads, cheeses, olives etc. Talk to him about shopping, hiring more bikes, and guided activities 'off piste' – skiing on Mount Etna with sea views is seriously special! You're 20 minutes from beaches, and the same from Taormina.

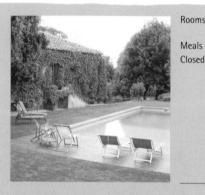

Rooms	1 house for 10: €1,500-€3,500 per wk. Extra bed available in single room.
Meals	Self-catering.
Closed	Never.

Paul Barthelemy
Villa Edera,
Via Giacomo Leopardi 4,
95029 Viagrande
Mobile   +39 347 0058174
Email   pl.barthelemy@gmail.com

Borgopetra

In the historic centre of Mascalucia, an exquisite revival of a 400-year-old manor house surrounded by orchards and gardens. Journalist Cristina left the high life in Milan to join Toto in the restoration of his family *borgo*. On the southern slopes of Mount Etna, self-contained yet unremote and ten kilometres from the sea, the luxurious apartments wrap themselves around a square courtyard brimful of cacti and jasmine. The attention to detail is exceptional, from the ergonomic beds to the soaps hand-made in Catania, from the Mascalucian olive oil in the kitchens to the thyme-infused honeys at breakfast. Stunning antique rubs shoulders with stylish modern: perhaps a chic red basin on an ancient terracotta floor, an old country wardrobe, a sleek chaise longue. Among apricot and orange trees and the pergola of an ancient vine is a cool pool; in the old marionette theatre, a massage room, gym, bar, and shelves crammed with Cristina's crime mysteries and board games. Cristina and Toto are the warmest pair you're ever likely to meet, in this oasis of beauty and peace. *Minimum stay two nights.*

Rooms	1 suite for 2: €135–€160.
	2 apartments for 6;
	1 apartment for 2-3: €170–€400.
	Singles €120–€145.
Meals	Restaurant 300m.
Closed	4 November – 1 April.

Cristina Pauly
Borgopetra,
Via Teatro 9, 95030 Mascalucia

Tel	+39 0957 277184
Mobile	+39 333 8284930
Email	info@borgopetra.it
Web	www.borgopetra.it

Piano Alto

Delicate, ethereal Noto is one of Sicily's baroque gems; it may be smaller than Ragusa but it still attracts a crowd. Above the more touristy centre, flanked by discreet offices and atmospheric shops, is a traditional house beautifully renovated by Angelica. A modest front opens to a charming maze of light airy rooms on varying levels, with tall 1900s windows and decorative floor tiles delightfully intact. You can rent the ground floor apartment (with garden) or the floor above (with balcony and terrace) – each has an entrance off the street – or you can take them together: they interconnect. The décor throughout is creative and stylish, an imaginative mix of muted 1930s pieces and bright patterned modern: an old-fashioned cast-iron radiator, a contemporary basin, a chair upholstered back to life. Jasmine and roses ramble in the garden at the most peaceful back; peaches and pomegranates, lemons and figs flourish. Stock up at the Monday market, pick a café for a creamy cassata or an iced coffee with whipped cream, cool off on the beautiful beaches and crystal-clear coves of Vendicari. *Minimum stay three nights.*

Rooms	1 apartment for 5; 1 apartment for 7: €750–€1,500 per week. Special rates for small groups.
Meals	Self-catering.
Closed	Never.

Angelica Grizi
Piano Alto,
Via Principe Umberto,
96017 Noto

Mobile   +39 333 2927231
Email   angelicagrizi@gmail.com
Web   www.pianoaltonoto.com

Bed & Breakfast Villa Aurea

Once the family's summer house, Villa Aurea is now a gentle, friendly place to stay, thanks to the owner's son, Enrico, who used to manage city hotels. His father shaped these surroundings, his architect's eye and his attention to detail ensuring the place feels calm, spacious and uncluttered; his mother bakes fabulous cakes and tarts and delivers a divine breakfast, enjoyed in the garden in summer. Cupboards blend discreetly into the walls, stylish shutters soften the Sicilian light and low round windows are designed to allow moonlight to play in the corridor. Bedrooms are minimalist with bright white walls and bold bedcovers. Upstairs rooms share a long terrace shaded by a huge carob tree; two rooms interconnect for families. Tiled bathrooms – some huge, with sea views – sparkle and use solar-heated water. A tree was planted to mark the birth of each of the three children and the garden is now luscious and filled with all kinds of tree: banana, orange, lemon, almond... you can idle in their shade, work up a steam on the tennis court, or cool off in the striped pool.

Rooms	7 doubles: €60–€110.
Meals	Restaurants 2km.
Closed	Rarely.

Francesco Caruso
Bed & Breakfast Villa Aurea,
Contrada Senna,
97014 Ispica

Tel	+39 0932 956575
Email	villa.aurea@gmail.com
Web	www.marenostrumpozzallo.it/villaaurea

Entry 423   Map 18

Torre Marabino

Arrow slits for sea views remain – but with the bandits gone by 1868, Baron di Belmonte turned the thick walls of this coastal watchtower into a holiday retreat. Today it feels almost English, as oak, ash and poplar mix with figs, lemons and prickly pears. Manicured lawns are punctuated by palm and magnificent olive trees, while the pool and children's play area are discreetly tucked away. There's plenty of space to wander, picking tomatoes, exploring polytunnels of organic produce, and touring the olive groves and vineyards of this working farm. Inside, divergent living and dining rooms are elegant and comfortable beneath their high ceilings: deep pink furnishings here, the carved side of an old Sicilian cart there – a lovely authentic touch. Three of the bedrooms divide onto mezzanine floors reached by staircases with wrought-iron railings. All have kitchenettes perfect for picnic-making. Food matters here: even the locals come for homemade pasta, local sausage, fish of the day... For anything else, delightful Francesco and Simona are at hand. Heart-warming.

Rooms	7 doubles: €110–€190. Singles from €110 to €150.
Meals	Breakfast & dinner €30–€60. Wine €14–€30.
Closed	End January to early February.

Francesco Pluchinotta
Torre Marabino,
C. da Marabino C.P. 18,
97014 Ispica

Tel   +39 0932 795060
Email info@torremarabino.com
Web   www.torremarabino.com

Nacalino Agriturismo

Concetta and Filippo have bags of enthusiasm for their agriturismo, their food (it's exceptional), their children, and their eventful lives. They've been doing B&B in this pretty area of southern Sicily for over a decade now but there's no sign of their slowing down; everything is done with Sicilian energy, humour and flair. Simple bedrooms in the old stables border a grassy square with tables and chairs so you can sit out in the sun, while the rooms above the restaurant are more elegant, with high ceilings and polished chests at the foot of handsome beds. Dinner is a fabulous regional experience and everything is home-produced, from the olive oils to the wines. It's a great spot for families too – children will enjoy getting to know the friendly donkeys, and there's a communal sitting room stuffed with books and games for dreary days. The sea isn't far; Modica is a half-hour drive. Little English is spoken here but you'll leave with new friendships made – even if you haven't managed to exchange a single word in the same language! *Minimum stay five nights in high season. Pets by arrangement.*

Rooms	3 twin/doubles: €80–€130.
	3 family rooms for 4; 4 family rooms
	for 3: €100–€160.
	2 triples: €100–€140.
	Singles €50–€70.
	Dinner, B&B €70–€85 p.p.
Meals	Dinner with wine, €30.
Closed	Rarely.

Filippo & Concetta Colombo
Nacalino Agriturismo,
Contrada Nacalino sn, 97015 Modica

Tel	+39 0932 779022
Mobile	+39 338 1611135
Email	info@nacalinoagriturismo.it
Web	www.nacalinoagriturismo.it

Casa Talia

A surprise awaits as you wend your way through the narrow streets of Modica's Jewish quarter. Marco and Viviana's *albergo diffuso* combines past and present exquisitely; what was once a scattering of simple dwellings is now an array of thoughtfully remodelled rooms that blend Arabic influences with modern comforts. Architects from Milan, the owners have cleverly used natural materials and juxtaposed strong colours with paler tones; dark tiles contrast with whitewashed stone walls. Rooms are connected by wooden walkways in a labyrinth of private terraces and small gardens set out over the different levels of the land. From here you look across the valley to the wealthy baroque churches and elegant palazzi; steps lead down to the centre of town where you can marvel at the ancient architecture. The sea is not far if you feel like a swim – sandy beaches and rocky coves characterise the coastline. Feast on homemade jams, pastries and fresh fruit for breakfast amongst olive and walnut trees; on cooler mornings, eat in the glass-fronted dining room. Either way, the view is incredible. *Minimum stay two nights.*

Rooms	6 doubles: €140–€220.
	3 triples: €230–€280.
	2 quadruples: €300–€320.
	Singles €110. Extra bed €50.
	No charge for children under 3.
Meals	Restaurants within walking distance.
Closed	Mid-January to March &
	mid-November to March.

Marco Giunta
Casa Talia,
Exaudinos 1,
97015 Modica
Tel   +39 0932 752075
Email Info@casatalia.it
Web   www.casatalia.it

Le Lumie

Views from the leafy garden terrace spill over the city's baroque buildings and narrow, winding lanes – a glorious sight at breakfast and at night, when atmospheric lights glow amid the exotic plants, ceramic tiles and lawn. Inside the house, rooms are anything but baroque: cool, contemporary spaces with natural purple and chocolate colours, polished oak floors, and crisp white sheets on modern beds. Bathrooms, decked in local stone and colour-themed mosaics, have drenching showers and scented lotions, and high ceilings give a light, airy feel. Breakfast is a chance to chat with kind owners Anna and Carmelo and to sample some *dolci di Modica*: pastries made with local chocolate, honey, sweet ricotta, cinnamon, almonds, citrus... Afterwards, wander three minutes down to town, where you'll find enough restaurants and museums to keep you busy for days. Or strike out to the coast or other towns in Val di Noto. It's a steep walk back up to the house, but if you have luggage Anna can meet you at San Giorgio church in her Smart car – the only vehicle tiny enough to tackle these ancient streets.

Rooms	3 doubles: €100–€110. Singles €70-€80. Extra bed/sofabed €30. No charge for children under 3.
Meals	Restaurants nearby.
Closed	Rarely.

Anna Labichino
Le Lumie,
Via Raccomandata 13, 97015 Modica

Tel	+39 0932 751439
Mobile	+39 389 1179059
Email	info@lelumie.com
Web	www.lelumie.com

Palazzo Failla Hotel

Straddling a busy corner in spire-embellished Modica (there are dozens of churches on your doorstep) is this grand old hotel. Hemmed in by a lively café bar on one side, and its own Michelin-starred restaurant on the other, the place buzzes with locals and tourists. The very smart exterior, with red-carpeted stone steps and handsome red awnings, belies the atmosphere inside: informal, relaxed and friendly. Cheerful staff welcome you through sparkling glass doors and whisk you up wide stairs, through a beautiful old room with original floor-to-ceiling wood panelling, and into opulent bedrooms. Polished marble floors are decorated in exquisite geometric patterns; cherubs dance across high frescoed ceilings; and beautiful antiques from all corners of Italy pose against sumptuously papered walls. Chandeliers, gilt-framed paintings, rich embroidered bed linen: it's fabulous. Further rooms are found off a lovely sunlit courtyard a minute's walk from the main hotel. Have breakfast in the café, supper in the restaurant, and spend every hour in between exploring this beautiful town.

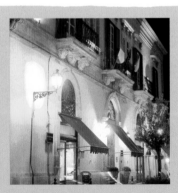

Rooms	6 twin/doubles: €69–€149.
	2 singles: €59–€79.
	1 triple: €99–€169.
	1 quadruple: €119–€189.
Meals	Restaurant next door. Wine €3–€12.
Closed	Rarely.

Paolo Failla
Palazzo Failla Hotel,
Via Blandini 5,
97015 Modica
Tel   +39 0932 941059
Email   info@palazzofailla.it
Web   www.palazzofailla.it

Anime a Sud

In Modica's baroque heart is a small 19th-century townhouse in which history and modernity magically combine. It has been remodelled by artist and eco engineer Luca – zero-impact energy applies and feng shui principles shine. Off a narrow, broad-stepped alley to a solid wood front door, and a friendly housekeeper invites you in and shows you the ropes. Find a cool, calm, unexpectedly spacious interior, bright with natural colours and bold canvases, polished cement floors and wrought-iron banisters... and stylish candle lanterns for bedrooms, balcony and terrace. The double is off the open-plan living room while the family room is up some steps and opens to a big dining terrace, replete with lemon trees in pots and a roofscape that twinkles at night. White and chocolate brown linen enfolds simple wrought-iron bedsteads, there are antique floor tiles and painted wooden shutters, and bathrooms small but perfectly formed. Modica has endless fiestas and a jazz festival in July; lovely beaches are 20 minutes away. The serenity nourishes the soul.

Rooms	1 house for 5: €910–€1,260 per week.
Meals	Self-catering.
Closed	Never.

Luca Giannini
Anime a Sud,
Via S. Lucia 9,
97015 Modica Alta

Mobile	+39 338 9275393
Email	info@animeasud.it
Web	www.animeasud.it

Tenuta Cammarana

Deep in Sicilian countryside, wrought-iron gates lead to a rare delight: a rich green lawn framed by rambling roses and scented plants. This gorgeous country house, built in 1778, remains in the family; so does impeccable taste. Arrive to vaulted stone ceilings that create elegant cocoons in which to unpack and unwind. Classic, understated furnishings have charming touches (old lace tablecloths, warm rugs, fine china) while bedrooms are modest but modern, with small spotless bathrooms and delicious local soaps. One room opens to its own shaded piece of garden. At the heart of the baroque golden triangle, Roman mosaics, beautiful towns and stunning woodlands are yours to unravel; you could also hire horses from next door's farm and ride to the coast. If asked, Giuseppe will make you exquisite dinner using recipes from his aristocratic roots, focusing on ricotta, milk, vegetables and herbs from the farm, matched by excellent wines. Stroll along flagstones, admire the views, relax beneath star-dusted skies. A stunningly lovely place – one for the grown-ups! *Minimum stay two nights, three nights in high season. Children over 14 welcome. Only 35km from Comiso airport.*

Rooms	3 doubles: €165–€180. Singles €125–€150.
Meals	Dinner on request.
Closed	Rarely.

Giuseppe Pulvirenti
Tenuta Cammarana,
Contrada Cammarana sn, 97100 Ragusa
Tel   +39 0932 616158
Mobile +39 339 8196562
Email info@tenutacammarana.it
Web   www.tenutacammarana.it

Fattoria Mosè Agriturismo

The town creeps ever up towards the Agnello olive groves but the imposing house still stands proudly on the hill, protecting its private chapel and a blissfully informal family interior. High, cool rooms have superb original floor tiles, antiques and family mementos; the B&B room is plainer, has an old-fashioned idiosyncratic bathroom and olive-grove views. Breakfast is in a huge, shutter-shaded dining room or on the terrace, the dumb-waiter laden with homemade jams served on silver. Three generations still work this farm where Chiara's family used to come to escape Palermo's summer heat; today she runs cookery courses and all ages are invited to join in the olive harvest. The stables, now six airy modern apartments, have high, pine-clad ceilings, contemporary fabrics and good little kitchens, plain white walls, no pretensions. Most have their own terrace, all spill onto the lovely plant-packed courtyard (with barbecue), and there are Chiara's olive oils, almonds and fruits and vegetables to buy. The 'Valley of the Temples' is a short and hugely worthwhile drive. You may never want to leave. *Minimum stay two nights.*

Rooms	1 double: €100.
	1 apartment for 6; 3 apartments for 4;
	2 apartments for 2: €500–€1,100 per wk.
Meals	Dinner with wine €25, by arrangement.
	Restaurants 2km.
Closed	7 Jan to March & November to 22 December.

Chiara Agnello
Fattoria Mosè Agriturismo,
Via M. Pascal 4,
92100 Villaggio Mosè
Tel   +39 0922 606115
Email   info@fattoriamose.it
Web   www.fattoriamose.it

Agriturismo Sillitti

Drive through rolling farmland, up past the almond and olive groves, until you can climb no further. This is it: stunning 360 degree views over the island and, on a clear day, Mount Etna in the distance. Silvia's family have farmed for generations. She's passionately organic – grows olives, almonds, wheat, vegetables – and loves to share both recipes and kitchen garden. The farmhouse is new, its apartments bright and simple, furnished in unfussy style with cream floor tiles, modern pine and colourful fabrics. Open-plan living areas include tiny kitchens for rustling up simple meals. Rooms won't win design prizes but are spotless and airy and have superlative views. Silvia and Bruno (a doctor in nearby Caltanissetta) are open and welcoming; you'll be won over by their warmth and her cooking. Breakfast on homemade bread, cakes and jams; dinner is a feast of Sicilian dishes. A great spot from which to explore the island – castles, temples, Palermo, Taormina – or enjoy the views from the lovely large garden, with pool, terrace and shady pavilion. Space, peace, delightful people. *Minimum stay two nights.*

Rooms	5 doubles: €80–€90. 2 apartments for 4; 1 apartment for 2: €500–€1,000 per week.
Meals	Dinner with wine, €25. Restaurants 5km.
Closed	Rarely.

Silvia Sillitti
Agriturismo Sillitti, Contrada Grotta d'Acqua, 93100 Caltanissetta
Tel   +39 0934 930733
Mobile   +39 338 7634601
Email   info@sillitti.it
Web   www.sillitti.it

Regaleali Winery Estate

Rosemarie continues her family's 180-year legacy in tending the vines, olives, almonds and orchards of this secluded estate on top of a long vineyard valley, and guests – including Prince Charles! – wax lyrical about her warmth and generosity. If you fancy eating in, they praise the dinners too, homemade, home-grown and served with prize-winning wines in a conservatory overlooking vine-clothed hills and olive groves. After dinner: a nightcap on the terrace, then deep sleep induced by country peace. Decorated with much-loved artworks and ornaments, and toasty warm in winter, the two cosy bedrooms have colourful bedspreads and wooden furniture, and children will love sleeping under the rafters on the double's mezzanine. Back in that wonderful conservatory, breakfast is another homemade feast (fruit tarts, ricotta cheese), and if Rosemarie is not working in Palermo you can chat to her about the farmers' markets, and the temples of Agrigento. Her staff are equally warm, helpful and make you feel at home. Blissfully remote – just be sure to arrive in daylight.

Rooms	1 family room for 2-4 (1 double, 2 child beds); 1 twin/double: €100. Singles €80. Children 4-14 €5-€20. Cot available. Rates vary according to length of stay.
Meals	Dinner on request €40; €20 for children over 3 years. Kitchen sometimes available for use. Restaurants 10-minute drive.
Closed	Never.

Rosemarie Tasca d'Almerita
Regaleali Winery Estate, Azienda
Regaleali, 93010 Vallelunga Pratameno

Tel	+39 0921 544032
Mobile	+39 334 7880152
Email	rosemarie@tascadalmerita.it
Web	www.sicilyathome.it

Villa Mimosa

Fifteen minutes from the jolly resort of Selinunte is Villa Mimosa, surrounded by orange trees, olive groves and umbrella pines. The great thing is you can self-cater here and do B&B: lovely Jackie delivers local breads and pastries each morning. Three of her apartments stretch along the back and open onto a long pergola-shaded terrace and a garden bright with poppies in spring. The fourth apartment is on the first floor, with a balcony. Each is open plan, with a simple shower room and a kitchenette, homely spaces furnished with carved Sicilian armchairs, high antique beds, good linen. If you dine with Jackie, it's outside on the terrace on her side of the house, or in her *salotto* on cool evenings. She's lived in Sicily for years (having managed to collect a fair few cats and dogs along the way!) and is a great enthusiast about food and wine. The main road that passes close by (some traffic hum) whisks you to medieval towns, nature reserves, great sand beaches... and the most beautiful temple site in Sicily, at Selinunte. A favourite with our readers.

Rooms	4 apartments for 2-3: €70–€100; €400–€600 per week. €10 per extra night.
Meals	Dinner, 3 courses with wine, €35–€40. Restaurants 2km.
Closed	Rarely.

Jackie Sirimanne
Villa Mimosa, La Rocchetta,
Selinunte, 91022 Castelvetrano
Tel   +39 0924 44583
Mobile   +39 338 1387388
Email   sirimannej@gmail.com
Web   www.villamimosasicily.com

La Casa di Argo

A delight to find B&B in the fishermen's quarter, bright with bobbing boats, still unposh, still unspoiled. Nice and peaceful too: there are no through roads and the sea is on three sides. Slip into the hall of this 1900s block – past Enzo's bike and canoe – then up a narrow stone stair to the flat on the first floor. Warm generous Enzo, ex lecturer in tourism, lives with his much-loved dog – Argo! To the right are the two guest bedrooms; to the left, a small living area and a strikingly colourful terrace; find a couple of sunloungers, bright flowers, a potted olive, objets trouvés. This is where Enzo brings you a breakfast of fresh breads, great coffee, exotic jams. Steps continue to a larger terrace bright with Tunisian tiles, and up to a small secluded patio from which you can gaze on the Egadi Islands: a pretty spot for a glass of wine and a snooze. The two bedrooms, not large but interesting and original, have firm beds, decorative antique floor tiles and domed ceilings. Trapani's once neglected baroque centre is rich with churches, museums, restaurants and shops; the beaches are sandy and gorgeous. *Minimum stay three nights.*

Rooms	2 doubles: €60–€70.
Meals	Restaurants within walking distance.
Closed	1 December to 28 February.

Vincenzo Lo Coco
La Casa di Argo,
Via Baracche 17, 91100 Trapani

Tel	+39 0923 360323
Mobile	+39 333 9500424
Email	enzolococo@libero.it
Web	www.bandblacasadiargo.it

Zarbo di Mare

A simple stone-built house, slap on the sea, on a beautiful stretch of coast to the north-west tip of the island. Sun worshippers can follow the progress of the rays by moving from terrace to terrace through the day; those who prefer the shade will be just as happy. A vine-clad courtyard behind is a lovely place to take breakfast; for lunch, move to the large shady terrace with a barbecue; take dinner on the front terrace looking out to sea. Inside: two bedrooms, which can be used as either doubles or twins, an open-plan living area with a pine-and-white kitchen and a sitting room with an open fire; heating and aircon in every room. Below the house are steps down to a private swimming platform, perfect for confident swimmers; the sea is deep and great for snorkelling. Families with small children should swim from the beach at San Vito, where the water is shallow. There are some lovely things to see in the area, above all, the Greek temple at Segesta. You're just a few minutes from San Vito, for shops, festivals, bars. *Short stays available in low season. Minimum stay four nights.*

Rooms	1 house for 4: €750–€950 per week.
Meals	Self-catering.
Closed	Rarely

Barbara Yates
Zarbo di Mare,
Contrada Zarbo di Mare 37,
91010 San Vito Lo Capo

Mobile	+32 474 98 48 99 / +39 348 8537250
Email	barbara.yates@belgacom.net

Palazzo Cannata

The stone escutcheon over the door justifies the palatial name, the tenderly scruffy yard inside tells today's humbler tale. One of the most exuberantly, generously hospitable men you could hope to meet, Carmelo inhabits the top of the former bishop's palace and from the big plant-packed terrace your gaze plunges into the grand Palazzo dei Normanni. Palermo's domes are beyond, all the treasures are within walking distance (and quite a bit of the traffic). The flat is as full of eclectic interest as Carmelo's captivating mixed-lingo conversation. He teaches mechanics, with deep commitment, and breathes a passion for dance and music. Everywhere are paintings and photographs, bits of furniture and cabinets of mementos, yet there's space for everything to make sense. One could explore the details for hours, the madonnas in the high-bedded double room, the painted beds in the triple... A fount of insight into his home town, eco-conscious Carmelo will tell you all about it, and his eco-shop recycling project, too. After the pastry breakfast he has prepared before going to work, set out to discover his fascinating city.

Rooms	1 double sharing bathroom; 1 triple: €80-€90.
Meals	Restaurants nearby.
Closed	Rarely.

Carmelo Sardegna
Palazzo Cannata,
Vicolo Cannata 5, 90134 Palermo

Tel	+39 0916 519269
Mobile	+39 333 7200529
Email	sardegnacarmelo@hotmail.com

Le Terrazze

Don't tell! This is one of Palermo's sweetest secrets. Down one of the few quiet streets of this vibrant city, Le Terraze is hard to find (harder still to book into: advance bookings only). But as you climb its five plant-filled terraces, each level revealing yet more fine rooftop views, you know it's been worth it. Set in a 16th-century palazzo, this calm and gracious apartment B&B opens up into lofty sunlit rooms bedecked in antiques, ceramics and paintings, all of which tell of a wealthy family history. During the renovation, Sicilian-born Giovanni and Magda made two remarkable discoveries: a stunning painted wooden ceiling in the sitting room, and fragments of frescoes in the grand, traditional bedrooms. Elegance is de rigueur here, even when sitting down to breakfast. Whether on the shaded terrace or in the dining room, lace table cloths, heirloom silver and fine china add distinction to pastries, fruits and jams. What better way to begin a day of cultural exploration? Then end it with a gentle *passeggiata* towards dinner in one of the many local restaurants.

Rooms	1 double: €110. 1 quadruple: €160. Singles €80.
Meals	Restaurants nearby.
Closed	Rarely.

Giovanni & Magda Rizzo
Le Terrazze,
Via Pietro Novelli 14,
90134 Palermo

Tel	+39 0916 520866
Email	leterrazze_palermo@yahoo.it
Web	www.leterrazzebb.it

Chez Jasmine

Such a pretty, peaceful little place, reached through a private courtyard and up steps splashed with flowers. Jasmine stands away from tourist bustle in a 10th-century courtyard in the old Arab quarter; you are enveloped in the history of handsome Palermo yet all you hear are the birds. Irish-turned-Sicilian, the delightful Mary lives round the corner, leaves breakfast supplies in your kitchen, is involved in conservation, and can keep you entertained for hours with her insights into local mores. Her vertical, newly renovated 'doll's house' is adorable and the layout's fun. You step up to the bedroom on the first floor, then up to the little living area, then up again to the rooftop terrace. The bathroom is cute, the bedroom has its own wicker sofa and the living room has a lovely lived-in feel – plenty of books and well-chosen fabrics and furniture. Finally, an iron spiral leads to that leafy terrace, an oasis shaded by bamboo blinds, bliss for breakfast or a pre-dinner drink. From spring to late autumn, evenings in La Kalsa are a feast of fun and street theatre. Winter has its own charms. *Minimum stay three nights.*

Rooms	1 house for 2-4: €700–€770 per week. Extra bed €30.
Meals	Self-catering.
Closed	Rarely.

Mary Goggin
Chez Jasmine, Vicolo dei Nassaiuoli
15, 90133 Palermo

Tel	+39 0916 164268
Mobile	+39 338 6325192
Email	margoggin@hotmail.com
Web	www.chezjasmine.biz

Entry 439   Map 18

Palazzo Prestipino

A two-minute walk from the station but a world away from hustle and bustle, welcome to a cool elegant refuge. Duck down a side street and into a courtyard sandwiched between a delicatessen and a restaurant that serves beautiful Sicilian food – both are charming. Then it's up the wide marble stair to a stunning restoration of two chic, minimalist apartments. Tangible evidence of the splendour of the 18th-century building remains: vaulted ceilings, once covered in ornate and colourful frescos, have been restored and sit alongside the muted hues of designer furniture and state-of-the-art fittings. Walls dazzle in white, sweeping wooden floors gleam, windows are double-glazed. In the apartment for two, a cupboard at the end of the sunlit sitting room opens to reveal an Italian kitchen, simple but lovely, white units, high beams, limed floor. So live like a local and gather supplies from the wonderful Ballarò market: it's a short walk. Charming young caretaker Lycia, justifiably proud of the apartments in her charge, lives on site should you need help and advice.

Rooms	1 apartment for 3; 1 apartment for 2: €700–€1,000 per week. Sofabeds available.
Meals	Restaurants on doorstep.
Closed	Rarely.

Federica Sapuppo
Palazzo Prestipino,
Via San Nicolò all'Albergheria 4,
90134 Palermo
Mobile   +39 338 6994011
Email   info@palazzoprestipino.it
Web   www.palazzoprestipino.it

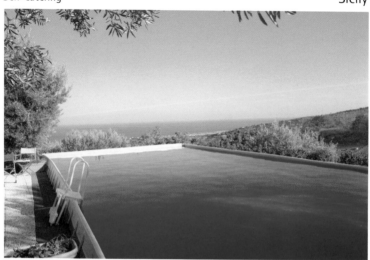

Casa Margaret

Stay in one of three freshly converted stone houses perched thrillingly on top of a hill. Reached by a rough wiggling track (be warned!), surrounded by ancient gnarled olive groves, each is filled with gorgeous bits and pieces from the owners' travels. 'Margherita', the highest, feels relaxed and laid back: a large covered terrace, wooden ceilings, terracotta floors, colourful objets old and new, sofas by the open fire. There's a glass-topped dining table and a mod-conned kitchen, and comfy bedrooms with hand-painted details. 'Rosita', above a main road, is the largest house, stylish yet cosy, with lots of bare stone and tiles, an iron candelabra in a snazzy dining room, and a children's bedroom under the rafters. 'Bianca', dinky and cute, has a peek-over wrought-iron mezzanine to the living room below, lined with lovely pottery and characterful tomes. All have barbecue terraces for the views: a glorious panorama of snow-capped mountains and sea. Far enough apart for privacy they are close enough for friends to enjoy. There's a swimming pool on site — a bit of a hike — and acres of ancient olive estate to roam wild in.

Rooms	1 apartment for 2: €700–€1,300.
	2 cottages for 4: €900–€2,100.
	Prices per week.
Meals	Self-catering.
Closed	Rarely.

Margherita Carducci Artenisio
Casa Margaret,
Km 4 della strada provinciale 9,
Pizzillo, 90016 Collesano

Tel	+39 0916 199221
Email	info@casamargaret.it
Web	www.casamargaret.it

Casa Serena

Deep in hazelnut country is a white minimalist house with sliding glass doors and stupendous views. The mountain soars above, the valley plunges below, the peace is profound and walkers are in heaven: you have the beech woods of the Madonie National Park to explore. Walker or sybarite, you will be supremely comfortable in this perfectly insulated home. Downstairs is fully open-plan, all sweeping polished concrete floors and lofty white walls, with urban-sleek living areas and super-duper kitchen wrapped around a central sculptural stair. Expect cutting-edge LED lighting and abstract paintings on the walls, top-notch furnishings and fittings, and a white and grey palette with accents of fuchsia, violet and red – a strong stark personal style. For your entertainment are music, TV, board games and a wood-burning stove – no need to worry if you get snowed in! For summer: a four-acre garden, generous terraces on two sides, a sloping orchard behind, a barbecue and a plunge pool. As for civilisation, it's no distance at all: the unspoilt hilltop town of Polizzi Generosa is under three miles. *Minimum stay one week April-October, Christmas & New Year.*

Rooms	1 house for 6: €1,080–€1,750 per wk.
Meals	Self-catering.
Closed	Rarely.

Carl Gardner & Sylvie Pierce
Casa Serena,
90028 Polizzi Generosa

Tel	+44 (0)20 7724 8543
Mobile	+44 (0)7967 158206
Email	carl@csglightingdesign.com

Ca' La Somara Agriturismo

A short drive to stunning bays, a far cry from the fleshpots of Costa Smeralda, Ca' La Somara's white buildings stand out against the wooded hills and crags of Gallùra. As you'd expect from the name, donkeys feature here – one of Laura's passions. A vivacious ex architect, she has converted the stables with charm and flair. Welcome to a serene, Moroccan oasis around a lovely central courtyard smothered in bougainvillea, hibiscus, plumbago, guarding a Turkish bath, a hay bath, a sauna, a yoga room, a massage room and a gym. Bedrooms, small and rustic-stylish, have floors of coloured cement or painted boards, Sardinian bedcovers, zingy hand-painted tiles, and lamps, rugs, objects from their travels. Visit the pretty village of San Pantaleo, an artists' community just up the hill, return to cushioned benches in the garden or hessian hammocks in the paddock, and views of the valley and its windswept cork oaks. Dinner is fresh Mediterranean, served with Sardinian wines and enjoyed at the convivial table. It's all deliciously restful and undemanding – and there's a fabulous pool.

Rooms	9 doubles: €60–€134.
Meals	Dinner €20. Guest kitchen.
Closed	Rarely.

Alberto & Laura Lagattolla
Ca' La Somara Agriturismo,
Loc. Sarra Balestra, 07021 Arzachena

Tel	+39 0789 98969
Email	info@calasomara.it
Web	www.calasomara.it

Sardinia

Self-catering

La Vignaredda – Residenza d'Epoca

Twenty minutes from northern Sardinia's sandy beaches, in a mountain village famed for weaving, an 18th-century family house to make you feel at home. It's set in a tree-filled garden near the village museum, bright geraniums spilling from cast-iron balconies against a tall stone façade. Inside has a country feel with big fires, terracotta tiles and local rugs, and walls of chunky granite hewn from nearby hills. But there's period elegance in the antique chests, ornate lamps, carved mirrors and white walls of the apartments; these come with kitchenettes and terraces balconies. Views tumble over cork oaks and rocky outcrops, and a maze of boulders in 'Moon Valley' below. Milan-based owner Maria Cristina may greet you in summer; otherwise a friendly housekeeper looks after the property. The village's high position gives cool relief from Sardinian summers, but there are terraces for soaking up sun. Aggius is an intriguing village with tapestry, carpets, gold filigree, hot springs, horse riding and quiet, star-filled nights. *Short stay rates available.*

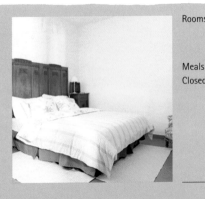

Rooms	3 apartments for 2; 1 apartment for 4: €519-€989. Singles €291-€395. Prices per week. Extra bed/sofabed €15-€25.
Meals	Brunch €20. Restaurant 100m.
Closed	Rarely.

Maria Cristina Zara
La Vignaredda – Residenza d'Epoca,
Via Gallura 14, 07020 Aggius Olbia-Tempio

Tel	+39 0796 20818
Mobile	+39 335 8018240
Email	info@lavignaredda.com
Web	www.lavignaredda.com

Entry 444   Map 19

Li Licci

Not so long ago, this tranquil place was inaccessible among immense rocks and cork oaks. Deserted after the death of Gianmichele's grandfather, it was rescued by Jane and Gianmichele in 1985. Then they began entertaining friends. English-born Jane is an inspired cook of Sardinian food and they eventually created a delightful restaurant, now under a Moroccan chef who uses home-grown, organic produce – pecorino, ricotta, salamis, hams, preserves, liqueurs – to prepare well-reputed traditional and local food. And they have added four immaculate, simple, white-painted bedrooms, each with a shower. Jane looks after guests as she would like to be looked after herself, so staying here is like being in the home of a relaxed and hospitable friend. Li Licci has its own wells, producing the most delicious clear water, and a 2,000-year-old olive tree. Breakfast is outside in summer, overlooking the oak woods and hills of Gallùra, or by the fire in the converted stables in winter: either way, a superb start to a day's walking, climbing or sailing... or lazing on the north coast beaches. *Minimum stay two nights.*

Rooms	2 doubles; 1 twin; 1 family room for 4: €100. Dinner, B&B €65–€75 p.p.
Meals	Dinner with wine, €30–€40.
Closed	October–March.

Agri Mar
Li Licci,
Via Capo d'Orso 35,
07020 Palau

Tel	+39 0796 651149
Email	info@lilicci.com
Web	www.lilicci.com

Entry 445   Map 19

Stazzo Chivoni

Cordiality, tranquillity, simplicity, at the end of a long winding road. Built in 1850, modernised in 2003, the plain granite *stazzu gallurese* still keeps its reed-woven ceiling, its corner fireplace, its little windows: there's no artifice here. This charming Milanese couple swapped the city for nature and beaches (eight miles away), lone cattle grazing, peasant foods and homemade wines: life in the slow lane. He is a garden designer and has created an ornamental and a vegetable garden in harmony with the landscape; she is a translator. They give you your own bright sitting room with a rustic bohemian décor – vine branches and sea shells, a comfortable sofa, a simple table and chairs – off which is a sweet bedroom with soothing colours and polished cement floor. The bathroom has a bath with a curtain and a washing machine; all is spotless, frill-free. Breakfasts, in contrast, are sumptuous: yogurts, fruits, pastries, cakes, quiches, cheeses, eggs and cold cuts, brought to the pergola in summer. Discover a hinterland of cork oaks and wild olives, return to a hammock slung between the trees. *Minimum stay two nights.*

Rooms	1 double: €60-€70.
Meals	Restaurant 5km.
Closed	Rarely.

Leo Rescigno
Stazzo Chivoni,
07020 Luogosanto

Mobile	+39 328 6914505
Email	bbsardinia@gmail.com
Web	www.bbsardinia.it

Hotel Su Gologone

The white buildings of Hotel Su Gologone stand among ancient vineyards and olive groves at the foot of towering Supramonte. Lavender and rosemary scent the valley. The hotel began life in the 1960s as a simple restaurant serving simple Sardinian dishes — roast suckling pig, wild boar sausages, ice cream with thyme honey; it is now known throughout Europe. Run by the founders' daughter, committed Sardinian Giovanna, it employs only local chefs and has a brilliant mountain-view terrace. In this remote wilderness region of the island this is an elegant and magical place, super-friendly despite its size, and only 30 minutes from the coast and wonderful beaches. Juniper-beamed bedrooms have intriguing arches and alcoves and lots of local crafts and art: embroidered cushions, Sardinian fabrics, original paintings, ceramics and sculpture. There's a new group of local crafts shops, too. Browse through a book about the island from the library, curl up in one of many cosy corners. Hiking can be arranged; the pool is fed by cold spring water, there's a spa, a hot tub outside… A real treat.

Rooms	54 twin/doubles; 15 suites for 2: €210–€320. Prices are for dinner, B&B.	
Meals	Half-board only. Wine from €10. Restaurant 8km.	
Closed	Rarely.	

Luigi Crisponi
Hotel Su Gologone,
Loc. Su Gologone, 08025 Oliena
Tel   +39 0784 287512
Email   gologone@tin.it
Web   www.sugologone.it

Entry 447   Map 19

Sardinia

B&B

Su Dandaru

A totter down a cobbled alley in Bosa's impossibly quaint old town brings you to a prettily painted 1700s house with a red and yellow exterior. In contrast to the lovely old arches, the wooden beams, the stone floors is a fresh and imaginative décor. Four bedrooms are spread over three floors. The first, earth themed, is warmly hued and cosy with a big wrought-iron bed. The second, inspired by the river, is in greens and yellows, with linen curtains and a basket-weave bed; off the room, just before the bathroom, is a small room with a single bed. The third room, the suite, is all sea blues and greens, with a French armoire and antique lace curtains. Charming and inviting are one and all, with small but perfectly formed bathrooms. Above is a sitting room with a comfy sofa, and a big roof terrace with views up to the medieval castle, down to the rooftops of Sa Costa; lovely for an evening under the stars. Or a chilled chianti after a day's boating on the river or lazing on the beach. You breakfast in an Italian café and can dine anywhere in town, perhaps at the owner's own little place, by the river under the palms. *Minimum stay two nights in high season.*

Rooms	1 double; 1 double (sharing bath with 1 single); 1 family room for 4: €50–€125. 1 single (sharing bath with 1 double): €35.
Meals	Restaurants within walking distance.
Closed	Rarely.

Giacomo Forte
Su Dandaru,
Via del Pozzo 25, Bosa
Mobile +39 347 9680120
Email info@sardiniabandb.com
Web www.sardiniabandb.com

Entry 448   Map 19

Hotel Lucrezia

A fabulous find, a gorgeous old house on the edge of town within striking distance of 20 beaches. Its courtyard garden steals the show and will have you sneaking back early. You'll find tables and chairs at the foot of ancient trees, pots of colour, sofas and armchairs on a shaded terrace. The house has been in the family for over a hundred years and is run with great affection. When it became a hotel ten years ago, the idea was to preserve its history while adding contemporary comforts, a trick pulled off in spades. You find Roman amphora and 18th-century gaslights dotted about, then seven beautiful bedrooms that come in crisp country-house style. Expect pressed white linen, antique furniture, lovely bathrooms. There's a sitting-room fire for cooler nights, billiards for optimists, a snug dining room for delicious breakfasts. West coast beaches are on your doorstep, as are the ruins of Phoenician Tharros. You can nip down to Cagliari in less than an hour, then check out the World Heritage site of Su Nuraxi on your way home – it's the best preserved Nuragic site on the island. *Minimum stay three nights in August.*

Rooms	5 doubles; 1 twin: €129–€169.
	1 suite for 2: €219–€259.
	Singles 25% discount.
	Extra bed in double or twin €35–€45.
Meals	Restaurants 6km.
	Dinner available on request.
Closed	5 November to 30 March.

David Loy
Hotel Lucrezia,
Via Roma 14a, 09070 Riola Sardo

Tel	+39 0783 412078
Email	info@hotellucrezia.it
Web	www.hotellucrezia.it

Alastair Sawday has been publishing books for over 20 years, finding Special Places to Stay in Britain and abroad. All our properties are inspected by us and are chosen for their charm and individuality, and now with 17 titles to choose from there are plenty of places to explore. You can buy any of our books at a reader discount of 25%* on the RRP.

www.sawdays.co.uk/bookshop

List of titles:	RRP	Discount price
British Bed & Breakfast	£15.99	£11.99
Special Places to Stay in Britain for Garden Lovers	£19.99	£14.99
British Hotels and Inns	£15.99	£11.99
Pubs & Inns of England & Wales	£15.99	£11.99
Venues	£11.99	£8.99
Cotswolds	£9.99	£7.49
Wales	£9.99	£7.49
Dog-friendly Breaks in Britain	£14.99	£11.24
French Bed & Breakfast	£15.99	£11.99
French Self-Catering	£14.99	£9.74
French Châteaux & Hotels	£15.99	£11.99
Italy	£15.99	£11.99
Portugal	£12.99	£9.74
Spain	£15.99	£11.99
India	£11.99	£8.99
Go Slow England & Wales	£19.99	£14.99
Go Slow France	£19.99	£14.99

*postage and packaging is added to each order

How to order:
You can order online at: www.sawdays.co.uk/bookshop/
or call: **+44 (0)117 204 7810**

Alastair
Sawday's

'More than a bed
for the night...'

Britain
France
Ireland
Italy
Portugal
Spain

www.sawdays.co.uk

Self-Catering | B&B | Hotel | Pub | Treehouses, Cabins, Yurts & More

① Lombardy B&B ②

③ **Alberghetto La Marianna**

④ On the banks of Lake Como, a very charming family-run hotel, housed in a villa simply modernised and redecorated with a nicely laid-back feel. Bedrooms are humble, functional, with cheery shower rooms and (mostly) lakeside views. Some have balconies, one has its own little terrace. A road runs between you and the busy lake, so if you're a light sleeper, it may be worth giving up those shimmering views for a room at the back – at least in summer. No need to tip-toe round the owners: Paola is a delight, very generous and treats guests as friends. Breakfasts include homemade bread, cakes, savoury offerings and jams, husband Ty prepares a different menu of wholesome food every day, while Paola is a "mistress of desserts". You can eat inside and admire the ever-changing local art work lining the walls or outside where you can embrace the lake views on the terrace that juts onto the water. You won't be short of advice here on things to do: visits to gardens and villas, boat tours to Isola Comacina, day trips to St Moritz and the Engadine. The ferries are a step away.

Rooms	7 doubles: €85–€95. ⑤
	1 single: €60–€65.
Meals	Dinner with wine, €30. ⑥
Closed	Mid-November to mid-March ⑦
	(open 26 December to 6 January).

Paola Cioccarelli
Via Regina 57,
22011 Cadenabbia di Griante

Tel   +39 0344 43095
Mobile   +39 333 9812649
Email   inn@la-marianna.com
Web   www.la-marianna.com

⑧ Entry 28   Map 2   ⑨